THE SCOTTISH
ANTIQUARIAN
TRADITION

11th Earl of Buchan, by John Brown.

THE SCOTTISH ANTIQUARIAN TRADITION

*Essays to mark the bicentenary of the
Society of Antiquaries of Scotland
and its Museum,
1780-1980*

Edited by
A. S. BELL
Rhodes House Library, Oxford

JOHN DONALD PUBLISHERS LTD
EDINBURGH

ISBN 0 85976 080 4

Phototypesetting by Burns & Harris Limited, Dundee
Printed in Great Britain by Bell & Bain Ltd, Glasgow

Preface

The eight essays in this volume were commissioned by the Society of Antiquaries of Scotland for publication in the Society's bicentenary year. The book forms part of a series of celebrations organised by the Society throughout its anniversary year, which have included special meetings and ceremonies, and a group of exhibitions at the National Museum of Antiquities of Scotland, the Scottish Record Office, and the National Library of Scotland. The National Library's exhibition was accompanied by an illustrated general essay by its organiser, Dr Iain Gordon Brown, *The Hobby-Horsical Antiquary: A Scottish Character 1640-1830*, which helps further to depict the learned world of seventeenth and eighteenth-century Scotland in which the Society of Antiquaries was conceived.

The editor is grateful to the Society's bicentenary sub-committee for their invitation to take charge of this volume. He acknowledges much helpful advice from his contributors, including the current president of the Society, Dr Ronald G. Cant, and also thanks Dr Iain Brown for much practical encouragement throughout his task, and Mr David Bogie, advocate, for timely assistance on matters of heraldry and Scots law.

Edinburgh   A. S. Bell

The Contributors

Ronald G. Cant, D.Litt., Reader Emeritus in Scottish History, University of St Andrews, President of the Society of Antiquaries of Scotland

R. B. K. Stevenson, C.B.E., D.Litt., formerly Keeper of the National Museum of Antiquities of Scotland, Past President of the Society of Antiquaries of Scotland

Marinell Ash, Ph.D., Radio Producer, Educational Broadcasting Department, BBC Scotland

D. V. Clarke, Ph.D., National Museum of Antiquities of Scotland, Co-editor of *From the Stone Age to the 'Forty-Five: Studies in Scottish Material Culture Presented to R. B. K. Stevenson, Former Keeper, National Museum of Antiquities of Scotland* (forthcoming)

Angus Graham, sometime Secretary, Royal Commission on Ancient Monuments (Scotland)

Ian Stewart, Litt.D., F.B.A., M.P., author of *The Scottish Coinage* (1955; 2nd edition 1967), and other numismatic works

Charles J. Burnett, D.A., National Museum of Antiquities of Scotland, Secretary of the Scottish Heraldry Society

Contents

Illustrations

Acknowledgement is made to the Trustees of the National Galleries of Scotland for permission to reproduce portraits in their custody; and to the Trustees of the National Museum of Antiquities of Scotland for items in their collections and library (marked † above), and for portraits deposited in the Scottish National Portrait Gallery (marked *). We are also indebted to the owner for permission to reproduce the portrait of Sir George Mackenzie, in private hands.

On page 220

'The Urrn'. Pencil drawing by James S. Richardson of Sir George Macdonald and Dr Graham Callander at a Council meeting, *ca* 1930. From the Society's library.

David Steuart Erskine, 11th Earl of Buchan:
Founder of the Society of Antiquaries of Scotland

Ronald G. Cant

Ancestry and upbringing

David Steuart Erskine, founder of the Society of Antiquaries of Scotland, was born in Edinburgh on 12 June 1742, the second son of Henry David Erskine, 10th Earl of Buchan, and Agnes Steuart, younger daughter of Sir James Steuart of Goodtrees, sometime Lord Advocate of Scotland.[1]

The title to which David Erskine became heir, as Lord Cardross, on the death of his elder brother (another David) in 1747, and to which he succeeded as 11th Earl in 1767, was among the most venerable in Scotland.[2] It was, in origin, one of the ancient mormaerdoms or earldoms that can be identified in the early twelfth century but which corresponded to very much older divisions of the kingdom. In the early thirteenth century it passed, by the marriage of its heiress, to the great family of Comyn, but the hostility that developed between this and the house of Bruce during the Wars of Independence led to the forfeiture of the title and its annexation to the crown. After two relatively short-lived grants to members of the royal family, first the notorious Alexander Stewart, 'Wolf of Badenoch', son of King Robert III, then the rather more admirable John Stewart, Constable of France, son of the elder Regent Albany, it was revived in 1469 for James Stewart, son of Joanna, queen dowager of King James I by her second marriage to Sir James Stewart, 'the Black Knight of Lorne'.

From this time the title had an uninterrupted history, but on two occasions, through the succession of a female heir, it passed to families with different surnames. The first of these changes occurred when the Countess Christian, who had succeeded her grandfather the 3rd Earl in

1551, married Robert Douglas, second son of the laird of Loch Leven, who was thereafter, in 1579, recognised as Earl *jure uxoris.* On their deaths in 1580 their son James succeeded as 5th Earl but he was to die in 1601, leaving a daughter Mary as his heir. It was when she, in 1617, married James Erskine, second son (but eldest of his second marriage) of John, 7th Earl of Mar, that the title passed to the family which has held it ever since, although on two further occasions, on the failure of the direct line, it proved necessary to seek out somewhat remotely related descendants of cadet branches to maintain the succession.

The first occasion on which this happened was in 1698 when William the 8th Earl died unmarried and was succeeded, in accordance with the arrangements made in 1617 and 1625, by his second cousin once removed, David Erskine, 4th Lord Cardross. This particular title, now to be associated with the Earldom of Buchan and customarily assigned 'by courtesy' to the heir apparent, had been created for John, 7th Earl of Mar, in 1610, but on the understanding that it should pass to some member of his second family otherwise unprovided. Thus on his death in 1634 the Earldom of Mar was inherited by the sole son of his first marriage, John, and the Earldom of Buchan having been acquired, as we have seen, by the eldest son of the second marriage, James, the lord-ship of Cardross descended to David, son of his younger brother Henry. On the extinction of the line of descent from Earl James in 1698 the Buchan title passed to the grandson of this, 2nd, Lord Cardross of whom, in turn, Henry David the 10th Earl was the son.

There can be little doubt that the long and complex history of the Buchan earldom and its association with so many of the most famous families of Scotland exercised a powerful influence on the mind of the young Lord Cardross. In 1781, when it seemed possible that he might have to bear most of the expense involved in securing a home for the newly founded Society of Antiquaries, he professed himself prepared for the 'sacrifice of my domestick convenience to the honour of my country and the promotion of usefull learning', adding: 'To aspire after Fame founded on the performance of noble and disinterested actions is no less than habitual to the family from which I have the honour to derive my descent.'[3]

Insofar as any hereditary characteristics can be attributed to his own more immediate ancestors, they might be described as an insatiable curiosity and an independence of thought and action, both quite often carried to lengths that more conventional persons considered in-judicious or even eccentric. David Erskine, 2nd Lord Cardross (1616-

'71), like many of his age and rank a prominent Covenanter, was one of the few to oppose the surrender of King Charles I to the English puritans in 1646. His son Henry, the 3rd Lord, suffered severely in the 1670s through his involvement in conventicles. And at a less significant level, in 1745 the newly succeeded 10th Earl of Buchan, although far from Jacobite in his sympathies, was so anxious to see Prince Charles Edward at Holyroodhouse that he narrowly escaped imprisonment and forfeiture of his estates.

It is perhaps typical of this amiable but slightly feckless man that this is almost the only episode in his life for which he is remembered. By contrast his countess, Agnes Steuart, was a woman of strong personality and high intelligence. Prior to her marriage in 1739 she is believed to have studied mathematics under the great Colin MacLaurin at Edinburgh University, like her brother, and indeed her future husband. But even if she received no formal instruction MacLaurin and such other members of the Edinburgh intelligentsia as Allan Ramsay and David Hume were frequent visitors at Goodtrees (the later Moredun), situated as it was within four miles of the capital. It was also undoubtedly from the legal expertise of her family that her two younger sons Henry and Thomas inherited the abilities that made them in later life among the most distinguished advocates of their age.

Although characterised by a profound evangelical piety, Lady Buchan was at the same time perfectly capable of employing her own and her husband's political connections, all of an impeccably Whig complexion, to assist her family fortunes. There was much need of this, for the blunt fact was that Lord Buchan, despite his possession of considerable properties, especially at Kirkhill in West Lothian which had become the principal family seat, derived an income from them that was perpetually inadequate. For a prolonged period following his succession he lived in a modest apartment in Gray's Close off the High Street of Edinburgh and then, in pursuit of an even more economical mode of life, in a rented house at St Andrews.

In these circumstances Lord Cardross received much of his early education from his parents, who encouraged him in habits of intellectual self-reliance and responsibility towards his younger brothers.[4] He also derived much benefit from the presence in the household as 'pedagogue' or private tutor of James Buchanan, later Professor of Oriental Languages at Glasgow. From this period he emerged with a good command of English and Latin, and if his subsequent style of speech and writing was somewhat orotund, this was the fashion of the day and it was in general very adequate for its purpose. Thereafter, between 1755 and 1763, he attended classes at three of the Scottish universities — St Andrews (1755-59), Edinburgh (1760-62), and Glasgow (1762-63), and if Aberdeen was not included in this process it nevertheless featured, like the others, among his later benefactions.[5] At St Andrews, to which his father is said to have been attracted by 'the virtuous habits of the people and diligence of the professors', his teachers included Walter Wilson in classics, David Gregory in mathematics, Robert Watson in philosophy, and at Edinburgh his kinsman John Erskine of Carnock in civil law and William Cullen in chemistry.

It was at Glasgow, however, that the young nobleman seems to have found the most congenial milieu for his intellectual interests, now at a more mature stage of development. Not only did he take courses in jurisprudence and politics under Adam Smith, chemistry under Joseph Black, civil law under John Millar, and theology under William Leechman. He was also able to meet them socially and to enlarge his understanding of their subjects by personal discussion. But what appealed to him as much as anything were the opportunities afforded by the 'Academy of Art' established within the college precincts by the university printers Robert and Andrew Foulis.[6] Here he studied drawing, etching, and engraving, an example of his skill being the 'view of the ruins of the abbey of Icolmkill' (Iona) attached to his account of the same in the first volume of the *Transactions* of the Society of Antiquaries of Scotland.[7]

In the intervals of these academic activities Cardross found time, in 1758, to visit London where he was presented to King George II and met several of the leading politicians of the day. In 1761 he made an extensive tour of the northern Highlands, much of it on foot. Here he was particularly interested in the structure of the landscape and in the distinctive culture of its inhabitants, an interest that continued thereafter, as in his gift of a library to the Synod of Glenelg, in his plan for 'a topographical and etymological dictionary of the Celtic language', and in part at least in his proposal for the recording of notable Scottish landscapes. The tour concluded with an examination of the antiquities of Old Aberdeen, the first strong indication of what was to become the main preoccupation of his later years.

In 1764 Cardross was in London once again and it was during this visit, at the age of 22, that he was painted by Sir Joshua Reynolds. The portrait, the first of a whole series, depicts him in 'Van Dyck dress' and in a markedly theatrical posture, but it conveys the fine appearance and eager manner of the young lord, who was so pleased with it that he had copies made (with suitable Latin inscriptions composed by himself) for presentation to the Scottish universities, Glasgow having already awarded him its LL.D. in 1763, as St Andrews and Aberdeen (Marischal College) would do in 1766. Nineteen years after this first portrait he was attractively commemorated for the Society of Antiquaries in a pencil drawing by John Brown, and in the same year (1783) his friend James Tassie executed a handsome medallion. The portrait by Alexander Runciman presented to the Perth Antiquaries in 1785 is less happy and the extraordinary set-piece by W. H. Lizars in 1808 merely absurd. On the other hand the more formal portraits by George Watson and Henry Raeburn from the same period have a warmth and dignity that do justice to the Earl's appearance in his later years.[8]

When the Reynolds portrait was painted the question of its subject's career was under active consideration. In 1762, while at Glasgow, he obtained a commission in the 32nd Regiment of Foot, his military and academic commitments being adjusted accordingly. But his father's desire was that he should obtain a diplomatic appointment, and through his friendship with the Earl of Chatham he was able, in 1766, to secure the offer of a post as secretary in the British embassy at Madrid. Cardross himself, who was anxious to extend his knowledge of Europe but was prevented from making 'the grand tour' through the straitened circumstances of his family, seems to have been attracted by the offer but is said to have declined it in the end on the grounds that the ambassador, Sir James Gray, was of inferior rank to himself. With his strong sense of the importance of his family, this is at least conceivable, and Samuel Johnson — who may have had the story from Cardross's youngest brother Thomas — not only accepted it but gave it his august approval.[9]

Yet the primary motive for the rejection of the embassy appointment given by Cardross himself is that when it was made the Earl of Buchan was mortally ill and he felt that as the eldest son and heir it was his duty to support his father and mother in this family crisis. The Earl, who had been moved south to Walcot near Bath on medical advice, there came under the influence of Methodists of the Countess of Huntingdon's Connexion, and on his death in 1767 his widow persuaded her son, now the 11th Earl, to make public profession of the same beliefs, thereby incurring considerable ridicule which he bore with characteristic fortitude. Although he did not maintain his

Methodist principles after his return to Scotland, he had a profound respect for his mother's standpoint, being bound to her by the most exemplary filial affection until her death in 1778, and himself remained, as he consistently maintained, a devout Christian throughout his life.

Early public activities

On his succession to his inheritance the new earl was concerned to restore the fortunes of his house.[10] He honourably assumed full responsibility for the burden of debt left behind by his father and did all in his power to increase the profitability of his estates, of which he had already made an intensive study from 1764 onwards. Here he proved to be not only an enlightened but a particularly successful 'agricultural improver'. To his tenant farmers he granted leases of nineteen and quite often of thirty-eight years, while on the land retained under his own management he introduced new methods of production, better breeds of livestock, 'enclosure', and tree-planting, these being combined with a general replacement of estate buildings. Having achieved solvency, he went on to acquire considerable affluence by means of which, among other things, he was enabled to embellish the grounds of Kirkhill in 1777 with a large-scale orrery, its scientific basis being obtained through his friendship with Alexander Wilson, Professor of Astronomy at Glasgow.[11] But although of a naturally generous disposition, in financial matters he never lost the penurious habits developed, of sheer necessity, in these early days.

An important consideration in this rehabilitation of the Buchan family fortunes by its young head was being able to promote the careers of his two brothers Henry and Thomas, four years and eight years his juniors respectively. Like himself they had received much of their early education at home, but both had in addition some formal instruction at the grammar school of St Andrews under Richard Dick, later Professor of Civil History in the university. To the university Henry himself proceeded, in 1759, to a full four years' course in Arts and thence to legal studies at the universities of Glasgow and Edinburgh. With the help of his elder brother he was enabled, in 1768, to become a member of the Faculty of Advocates and to embark on his long and distinguished career at the Scottish bar. Thomas, by contrast, did no more than attend certain classes at St Andrews University (without formal matriculation) as a preliminary to a military career, but

1. The Society's Charter, 29 March 1783.

2. Interior of the Museum, The Mound, *ca* 1890.

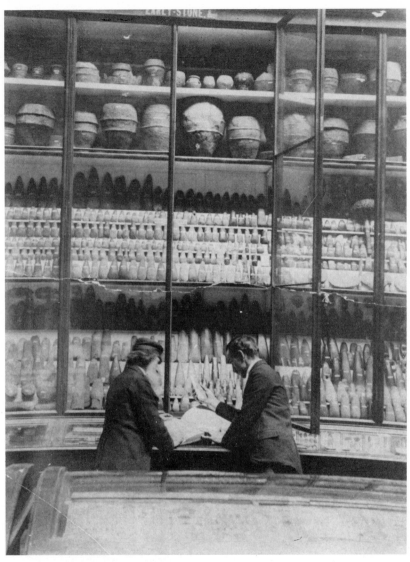

3. Museum showcase, *ca* 1890, with Joseph Anderson
and G. F. Black at work.

4. Sir George Steuart Mackenzie, 7th Bt, of Coul,
attributed to Sir John Watson Gordon.

5. William Smellie, by George Watson.

6. David Laing, by Sir William Fettes Douglas.

7. Sir Daniel Wilson, by Sir George Reid.

8.   Joseph Anderson, by Henry Wright Kerr.

9.   R. W. Cochran-Patrick,
by W. Graham Boss.

10.   Adam Black Richardson,
by W. Graham Boss.

unfortunately his father could not afford to purchase a commission for him, so that he entered the navy instead as a midshipman. In 1767, however, his eldest brother was able to obtain a commission for him in the army, in which he served for no less than eight years (1767-75) before proceeding to Cambridge University and Lincoln's Inn to begin a career at the English bar which was to culminate in his appointment as Lord Chancellor in 1806.[12]

Having discharged his initial obligations to his brothers — to whom he continued to be deeply attached throughout the whole prolonged period of their common lives — the Earl, now in his thirtieth year, made the marriage expected of all holders of hereditary titles. If it seems ungenerous to speak of his betrothal to Margaret Fraser of Fraserfield in 1771 in such terms, it would appear to have been motivated more by a sense of dynastic responsibility and family association — the bride being his own second cousin — than by the kind of intense emotional attachment that generally characterised Buchan's personal relationships. Although the marriage was quite amicable in its way, and the Earl was profoundly distressed when it ended with his wife's death in 1819, it failed to produce the desired heir. Indeed, one of the first duties that fell to the new countess was to provide a home for an illegitimate son of her husband born in this very same year. Who the mother may have been is not known, but David Erskine was brought up as a member of the family and provided with a commission in the army, in which he eventually achieved a professorship at the Royal Military Academy and a knighthood. Finally, when his father died, being succeeded in the title and entailed estates by his brother Henry's eldest son, he arranged for Sir David to inherit all his other properties including his principal residence of Dryburgh Abbey.[13]

After his succession to the Earldom Buchan assumed the natural authority and responsibilities that pertained to a member of the great nobility in the eighteenth century. He had a strong sense of duty and wished to play his due part in public life but, although a vigorous upholder of the integrity of Hanoverian Great Britain, it was within that part of it embracing the ancient Scottish kingdom that he wished to exert his influence, and in as comprehensive a range of activities as possible. In his political standpoint he adhered to the Whig principles traditionally supported by his family, but while his two brothers were active in party affairs and came to hold government office, he himself preferred to concentrate on broader issues.

B

Typical of such was his criticism of the method of electing the Scottish representative peers in the British House of Lords. On the first occasion after his own succession, in 1768, Buchan found that it had long been the practice for the government of the day to send down a list of the candidates expected to be returned. By a most vigorous protest, repeated in the parliamentary elections of 1774 and 1780 and in a by-election in 1781, he eventually established the principle of free and un-restricted choice.[14] While this issue was at its climax, it led to his being approached by the 'Yorkshire Committee' formed in 1779 to secure shorter parliaments and more equal representation between Commons constituencies. Similar committees were in course of formation in various parts of Scotland but Buchan, while assuring the promoters of his 'most strenuous efforts . . . to meet the virtuous wishes of the Con-stitutional Friends of Liberty', pointed out the limitations of activity open to 'one of those wretched anomalous beings called Peers of Scotland'. This concern for 'constitutional liberty' was one of his most enduring passions, sometimes leading him into what might be regarded as dubious and dangerous associations, as in his early enthusiastic support for 'Wilkes and Liberty' in the 1760s and his membership of the Society of the Friends of the People in the 1790s.[15]

Another issue in which the young lord became involved in his earlier life concerned the status of the British colonies in North America. His interest in it seems to have derived initially from his friendship with Benjamin Franklin, originating perhaps in the course of the latter's visit to Scotland in 1759.[16] What is certain is that in 1764 Cardross had several conversations with Franklin in London on the question of Britain's 'foolish and oppressive conduct towards the colonies'. This conduct he held to be 'radically fixt in the complexion of a mercantile nation and an ambitious and grasping system of monarchical adminis-tration', so that it came as no surprise when, in due course, it led to open revolt and a declaration of independence.

No doubt Buchan was here inclined, as so often, to simplify the issues, but he showed considerable shrewdness in his estimates of the British politicians involved, as well as commendable courage and con-sistency in his support of the American cause. He was very conscious of the fact that his own great grandfather the 3rd Lord Cardross had settled for a time in South Carolina, and as the War of Independence drew to a close in 1782 he himself seriously considered emigrating to the United States and involving himself in the public affairs of this new sanctuary of 'truth and freedom'. As it was, he remained in Scotland, but he conducted a prolonged and notably cordial correspondence with George Washington, for whom he had a particular admiration and whose birthday he publicly commemorated for many years.[17] At a more practical level his recommendations of Scottish academics for appointments in American colleges were marked by good sense and a concern for the educational wellbeing of this country which came second only to Scotland in his affections and interests.

Foundation of the Society of Antiquaries

It was in 1780 that the Earl effected what he at the time held to be and many have since regarded as his most memorable contribution to the cultural identity of Scotland, the foundation of its Society of Antiquaries.[18] The considerations that prompted his initiative are explained in the printed *Discourse* read by him at the initial meeting held in his house at No. 21 St Andrew Square in the New Town of Edinburgh on 14 November of that year: 'It has long been a subject of regret that no regular society for promoting antiquarian researches has subsisted in this part of Great Britain.' In his letter calling the meeting he said that he had 'for some years past meditated' the formation of such an organisation, but with a modesty with which he was not often credited he insisted that there were many persons better qualified than himself for 'suggesting a plan' and hoped that those present would 'prepare their opinion on this subject' for a subsequent meeting. In the meantime he set out his own thoughts 'concerning what has already been done, and yet remains to be explored, in the line of our Scottish History and Antiquities'.[19]

These 'loose thoughts', as he termed them, show the speaker as possessing a remarkable grasp, for the period in question, alike of the historical development of Scotland and of the earlier scholars involved in its elucidation back to the time of Hector Boece, John Major, and George Buchanan. What is particularly interesting is his identification of a group of historians and antiquaries of the early eighteenth century who persuaded Sir James Dalrymple to publish his *Collections* in 1705. Dalrymple himself detailed some of these, headed by Sir Robert Sibbald, in his own preface, but Buchan's list is more comprehensive, including such personalities as Alexander Gordon, pioneer in the study of Roman antiquities, James Anderson, compiler of the *Diplomata Scotiae*, David Crawford, Historiographer Royal for Scotland, Alexander Nisbet, the heraldic expert, and the great Latinist, editor and librarian, Thomas Ruddiman.

Buchan states further that these and others of like interests 'formed themselves into a society which had regular meetings'.[20] If so, the Scottish society of 1780 might have had a precursor in the same general period as the Society of Antiquaries of London initiated in 1707. But the latter had itself a precursor of yet more venerable origins. According to the 'Historical Account' introducing the first volume of its *Archaeologia*, 'there was a society of antiquaries so early as the reign of Elizabeth'. Said to have originated in 1572 and acquiring as its acknowledged leader the great William Camden, whose *Britannia* was published in 1586, in that same year it 'resolved to apply to the Queen for a charter of incorporation', but what became of this or the society is not known. The later tradition was that it was dissolved by King James or at least 'ceased to exist publickly for fear of being prosecuted as a treasonable cabal'.[21]

If the second explanation seems rather extraordinary, the apparently innocent and recondite study of history and antiquities might well have political implications, and it is interesting to note that William Smellie, in his parallel account of the origins of the Scottish society, gives as a reason for the delay in bringing it into being the consideration that 'till we were cordially united to England, not in government only, but in loyalty and affection to a common Sovereign, it was not perhaps altogether consistent with political wisdom to call the attention of the Scots to the ancient honours and constitution of their independent monarchy'.[22]

Such talk of 'ancient honours and constitution' indicates the wide area still thought to be embraced by 'antiquarian studies' in the later eighteenth century, an area given more precise definition in the stated objectives of the Society of Antiquaries of Scotland when it came into being towards the end of 1780 but even so of considerable extent. The fact is that 'antiquities', when the term began to be used in the sixteenth century, were regarded as a branch of history, the visible evidence in documentary or structural form of an older way of life. This meant that they might include the reconstruction of ancient codes of laws, political and ecclesiastical constitutions, economic activities, and social customs, these being studied, very commonly, on a strongly topographical basis. Indeed, the first recognisable 'antiquaries' tended to be topographers, like John Leland and William Camden in England, Élie Vinet (the friend of Buchanan) in France, Johan Bure and Ole Worm in Scandinavia.[23]

In Scotland the development of antiquarian studies owed most to three personalities, as remarkable for their longevity as for the range of their interests — Sir John Scot of Scotstarvit (1585-1670), Sir Robert Sibbald (1641-1722), and Sir John Clerk of Penicuik (1676-1755). There were, of course, many others, as Lord Buchan emphasised in his *Discourse*, but it was Scot who did most to preserve the cartographic and topographical work of Timothy Pont, as later of Robert and James Gordon, and secured its eventual publication in the Blaeus' great atlas of 1655, so providing a comprehensive and reliable base on which further studies could be made. It was Sibbald's role alike to extend the scope of these investigations, as in his *Scotia Illustrata* of 1684, and also to deepen it by his detailed study of his own homeland of Fife and Kinross. And it was under Clerk's patronage that there took place what might well be termed the first archaeological investigation of Roman remains in Scotland, undertaken by Alexander Gordon and published in his *Itinerarium Septentrionale* in 1726.

At the same time, Clerk's interest in antiquities had something of a dilettante quality, and he must take part at least of the blame for the situation from which Lord Buchan hoped his new society might rescue the 'name of antiquary' as 'the butt of fashionable and humorous stricture'.[24] On the other hand he himself developed somewhat fanciful notions on the kind of enterprises that the society should promote. But such occasional vagaries where perhaps unavoidable in an age when cultural developments depended as much as they did on the noble patron, and it can be conceded that the variety of well-considered schemes far outweighed ventures that were either quixotic or merely absurd.

Apart from the benevolent support of individual aristocrats for particular projects, the relatively small size of their order and the close ties that existed within it on the basis of intermarriage or personal friendships meant that new ideas circulated with comparative speed and a fair assurance of positive support. While no Scotsmen seem to have been involved in the early informal meetings of the Society of Antiquaries of London from 1707 onwards, or in its more regular constitution in 1717-18, from the 1720s quite a few were to be found among its fellows, including Sir John Clerk, elected in 1724, while his protégé Alexander Gordon (also a fellow from 1724) served as its Secretary between 1736 and 1741. Buchan himself became a fellow, as Lord Cardross, in 1764 and regularly attended its meetings — with those of the Royal Society, of which both he and his father were likewise fellows — when he was in residence in London.

It is clear from these links, and from direct references in Buchan's own *Discourse*, that the London society provided much of the inspiration of the Scottish society inaugurated in 1780. But there were other considerations to which the founder also referred, in particular an acute awareness on his part of the dangers inherent in a reliance on the enterprise of individual scholars whose collections, laboriously assembled during their lives, might be dispersed thereafter and lost to posterity.[25] It was in any event apparent that the inspiration which had produced the remarkable group of Scottish antiquaries of the early eighteenth century already mentioned had long since faded or, with some notable individual exceptions like Sir David Dalrymple, Lord Hailes (1726-92), had moved into areas less directly concerned with history and antiquities.[26] Hence the establishment of a society expressly committed to this area, holding regular meetings, and having a building of its own for these and for housing a museum, was particularly timely. And yet, according to William Smellie, in his *Account* of the foundation of the society, 'though these and many other advantages were to be derived from an institution of this nature, it continued to be the subject of speculation only' until the Earl of Buchan arranged for the crucial meeting of 14 November 1780.[27]

Buchan's general proposition was that the society should concern itself with 'the antient, compared with the modern state of the Kingdom and people of Scotland', and this in the most comprehensive manner. The primary objective would be to compile what would now be termed an ethnographic survey resting on an accurate topographical basis and including particulars of natural resources and their use, population, language, and social customs. But beyond these there was to be an examination of constitutional, military, and ecclesiastical organisation. Admittedly this was to include the recording of such tangible survivals as castles, mansions, and mote-hills, churches and religious houses, coins, seals, and weapons, though equally of portraits and other more miscellaneous particulars, 'and, in general, every thing that may tend to compare our antient with our modern attainments, and to show us how happy we are in the midst of all our losses'.[28]

As regards organisation, it was envisaged that the 'Society of the Antiquaries of Scotland' should comprise no more than fifty members who should meet on each St Andrew's Day to elect (by ballot) a President, four Vice-Presidents, a Treasurer, and a Secretary, and on eight or nine other occasions during the winter to receive 'communications' on topics within the wide range of its interests. Remarkably, there was to be no annual subscription, the original notion being that the published *Transactions* should be financed by *ad hoc* 'associations' among the members of the society and its 'house' — including residential quarters for the Secretary as well as a hall for meetings and adequate accommodation for 'books, records, and antiquities' — by individual benefactors acting through a trustee.[29]

Of the thirty-seven persons invited to the meeting on 14 November fourteen actually attended, including such prominent Edinburgh figures as Alexander Tytler (later Lord Woodhouselee), Hugo Arnot, historian of the city, William Creech, bookseller, and William Smellie, printer and principal creator of the *Encyclopaedia Britannica* (1771). The others, headed by the impressive judicial triumvirate of Lord President Hope, Lord Kames, and Lord Hailes, and comprising celebrities as varied as Sir William Forbes, Dr Hugh Blair, and Dr Gilbert Stuart, mostly 'sent letters highly approving of the scheme',[30] although James Boswell, for his part, having heard 'a ridiculous account of the meeting, wrote next day a card evading the Society'.[31] Despite this discordant note, it was agreed by the majority that there should be a further meeting in Lord Buchan's house on 28 November, at which those present 'unanimously resolved to meet on the 18th day of December in order to form themselves into a regular and permanent body under the designation of THE SOCIETY OF THE AN-TIQUARIES OF SCOTLAND'.[32]

It was, then, at this third meeting, held in the rooms of the Society for Propagating Christian Knowledge in Wariston's Close off the High Street, that the Society of Antiquaries was officially constituted. The founder, who had kept a record of all the earlier proceedings entered into what came to be the first minute-book of the Society, had also prepared a list of potential members and obviously had the main influence in the choice of the initial officers. These were: President — The Earl of Bute; Vice-Presidents — The Earl of Buchan, Sir John Dalrymple Hamilton M'Gill, John Swinton of Swinton, Alexander Wight, and William Tytler of Woodhouselee; Treasurer — Sir William Forbes of Pitsligo; Secretary — James Cummyng. In addition to the fifty ordinary or 'constituent' members, who were now to pay a subscription of one guinea *per annum*, there were to be corresponding and honorary members, the first of whom were elected at the inaugural meeting.[33]

The founder and the Society, 1780-1790

Since Buchan was the unquestioned founder of the Society and had acted as *praeses* of all the meetings that brought it into being, it must seem strange that he was not its first President, all the more so in view of the charges of personal vanity that were directed against him throughout his life. But the fact is that if he sometimes appeared agressively self-assertive it was because of an overwhelming sense of public responsibility and quite often with little concern for his own position. In the case of the Society of Antiquaries he wished to provide Scotland with the most effective means of safeguarding its national heritage and felt that this demanded the presence at its head, even if only nominally, of the most influential Scotsman in the public life of the day.

That John Stuart, 3rd Earl of Bute, should be viewed in this light may seem almost more curious than Buchan's own self-effacement in his favour, all the more so in view of the latter's earlier criticism of his political conduct, but despite the hostility and contempt which Bute aroused among the London politicians of his time, his elevation to the premiership in 1762 had been due as much to his parliamentary status and skill as to his influence with King George III. By 1780, at the age of 67, he was something of an elder statesman. He was also a known friend of cultural enterprises, being largely responsible for the formation of the Royal Botanic Garden at Kew, as later in finding a new site for its more venerable Edinburgh counterpart, and in securing government pensions for Samuel Johnson and the Scottish playwright John Home. Beyond this, he was the controller of immense personal wealth through his marriage to the heiress of one of the greatest fortunes of eighteenth-century England.[34]

Bute did in fact attempt to decline the presidency of the Society on the grounds that he would be unable to take much, if any, part in its work, but was persuaded by Buchan to accept and indeed continued in office until his death in 1792. In his absence the direction of the Society's affairs fell to Buchan himself as senior Vice-President. As such he had perhaps as much influence as if he had been President but seems to have been far more concerned with his responsibilities than with his status. His supreme desire was that the Society should develop a vigorous identity of its own, that it should be financially viable, and generally in a position to embark on a wide range of activities to conserve and record everything that contributed to the distinctive identity of Scotland.

The first meeting of the Society after its formal inauguration was held on 16 January 1781 with Buchan in the chair, when it was agreed that in addition to the officers already elected there should be a committee of seven to deal with routine matters or to give preliminary consideration to questions of major importance, the two groups together constituting what came to be known as the Council. A communication on 'The Antient State of Agriculture in Scotland' was read by Mr Roger Robertson and the first donations to the museum were received.[35] Since the development of the collections is the subject of a separate study, this account of the early history of the Society will be concerned with other aspects of its work in which its founder was involved. Most urgent at the outset was the securing of the 'house' to which Buchan had referred in his inaugural *Discourse*. The building in question was located towards the west end of the Cowgate and belonged to a Colonel Charles Campbell of Barbreck, although for some time in use by the Post Office. While it was originally thought that it could be acquired for £800, in the outcome it cost £1,000, most of the sum involved coming from Buchan himself.[36]

Once the Society had consolidated itself and settled in its new home it was considered 'that in order to secure and perpetuate the valuable and multifarious property so early acquired a Royal Charter was the only effectual measure'.[37] On 21 May 1782 accordingly a petition to this effect was signed by Buchan as *praeses* of the special meeting of the Society and James Cummyng as Secretary. The petition set out the objects for which the Society had been founded, namely, 'for investigating antiquities, as well as natural and civil history in general'. It was on the second of the interests specified, natural history, that the Society now ran into difficulties that might well have been foreseen.

At the centre of the controversy was the complex personality of William Smellie, already noted as one of the leading members of the group involved in the inauguration of the Society of Antiquaries. Five years before, in 1775, he had been an unsuccessful candidate for the Chair of Natural History at Edinburgh University. It was accordingly not surprising that the University should have been deeply offended when in 1781 Smellie was not only appointed Keeper of the natural history collections which it was planned to add to the more strictly 'antiquarian cabinet' of the new Society but, with Buchan's encouragement, proceeded to give a course of lectures on natural history in its hall. The upshot was that when the Society presented its petition for a royal charter the University objected. In these objections it was joined by the Faculty of Advocates on the grounds that if the Society proceeded with its plan to collect documents relating to the history and antiquities of Scotland, they would be lost to the Advocates' Library in which they had tended to be deposited, in large measure, during the previous hundred years.[38]

If it is difficult to be certain about the sincerity of these objections, the arguments advanced undoubtedly carried some weight. Both groups of objectors emphasised that Scotland was too small a country to divide its cultural resources between competing institutions, and there was much sense in the University's proposal that instead of granting a charter to the Antiquaries the King should be persuaded to incorporate a single 'Royal Society' embracing all concerned to promote scholarly research. As it was, the Society of Antiquaries received its charter on 6 May 1783 with monarch as its Patron, but on the same date the members of the Philosophical Society, predominantly though not exclusively of scientific interests, were incorporated as the Royal Society of Edinburgh. At the height of the controversy Buchan, who was extremely upset by the whole affair, resigned his membership of the Philosophical Society, but Smellie found no difficulty in transferring from the old organisation to the new while continuing as an active member of the Antiquaries.[39]

In his handling of this situation the Earl undoubtedly showed a certain lack of judgment. The simple truth is that once he had brought the Society of Antiquaries into being he saw it as the instrument for the realisation of all his plans for Scotland, often with insufficient regard for the interests of other organisations and even for its own primary function. His energy in the direction of its affairs was equalled by the variety of the enterprises which flowed from his fertile and ingenious imagination and in which he sought to involve the Society. In the first three years of its existence over ninety meetings were held, at all but a handful of which Buchan himself presided. He made a particular point of delivering a special address at what he himself termed 'the anniversary meeting', held on 14 November, the date of the first meeting in his own house in 1780 and conveniently about two weeks before the annual election of officers on St Andrew's Day.[40]

In practice, relatively little progress was made on any of these projects during the period of Buchan's involvement in the Society of Antiquaries, one of the reasons being the ambitious character of so many of them and the fact that while their promoter was splendidly equipped to invent and expound them, he was very much less effective in creating the necessary organisation to put them into operation. To be fair, he was usually prepared to set an example by himself contributing to the ventures in question but, as he was to find, this was not enough.

In the case of one of the earliest and most interesting of the projects Buchan seems to have appreciated that this difficulty might be surmounted by means of an existing organisation, or at least of its individual members, the ministers of the Established Church. This was the plan for a 'general parochial survey' which Buchan had apparently thought of as early as 1761 and which was the subject of a notice inserted in the press on behalf of the Society of Antiquaries early in 1781. For the form of this notice William Smellie was later given the credit by his biographer Robert Kerr, but when in July of this same year Buchan presented his own account of Uphall to the Society it was said to have been 'drawn up in conformity to the plan prepared by his lordship for a History of the Parishes of Scotland'.[41]

In the actual publication of this account in the first *Transactions* of the Society, delayed until 1792, it was accompanied by others of Liberton, Aberlady, and Haddington by the ministers of these parishes, by now involved in the scheme for a *Statistical Account of Scotland* inaugurated by Sir John Sinclair of Ulbster two years previously. But it is evident that these accounts, together with the articles on the antiquities of Lewis by Colin Mackenzie and of Orkney by Principal Gordon of the Scots College in Paris, derived from Buchan's earlier initiative. As he and Sir John were reasonably good friends, no conflict was involved, and the use of the parochial ministry for this kind of work had precedents extending back to Sir Robert Sibbald's time. But Sinclair's success in producing a complete survey in no more than a few years (1791-9) with the backing of the General Assembly contrasts with Buchan's failure to achieve his comparable objective through the Society of Antiquaries. In fact, the two schemes were somewhat different in character, for whereas history and antiquities formed a relatively small part of the *Statistical Account*, they were to be a major concern of the other project which might thus have produced something more akin to the *Origines Parochiales* of Cosmo Innes (far more extensive but likewise incomplete) a full two generations before that great venture.[42]

In addition to this 'topographical survey', Buchan also wished to compile a *Biographica Scotica* in the form of a series of volumes containing accounts of the lives of eminent Scots. Towards this he himself provided a study of John Napier of Merchiston, the inventor of logarithms, enlisting the help of a brilliant young scientist Walter Minto to deal with the mathematical problems involved. The work was published in 1787,[43] Minto in the meantime having emigrated to America where he secured a professorship at Princeton on Buchan's personal recommendation. The study reflected considerable credit on both its authors but no further volumes were published in the projected series, although Buchan himself returned to the scheme in later years, as he did to the parallel concept of an *Iconographia Scotica* to reproduce the best portraits of Scottish celebrities. This latter plan was a more practical version of the quaintly titled 'Temple of Caledonian Fame', originally envisaged as a room within the Antiquaries 'house' containing portraits and busts of persons adjudged worthy of this special recognition. More pleasing altogether was a set of drawings by John Brown of the first members of the Society headed by the founder and executed at his expense.[44]

Another of Buchan's projects was his plan for building up, under the auspices of the Society of Antiquaries, as comprehensive an assemblage as possible of 'old Scottish documents'. He was anxious that this should include such previous collections as that gathered together earlier in the century by James Anderson for his *Diplomata* and transcripts of documents in repositories outside Scotland like the Vatican, the Scots College in Paris, and other continental archives. Arguably, however, it would have been better for all this to be added to existing Scottish collections such as those in the Advocates' Library or the official Record Office for which at this very time a splendid new building was being provided in Robert Adam's General Register House (1772-89).

After his own acquisition of Dryburgh Abbey in 1786 Buchan made a special plea at the ensuing 'anniversary meeting' of the Antiquaries for the compilation of a *Monasticon Scoticanum* embracing collections of documents with historical accounts and illustrations of the fabrics.[45] The proposal was in fact a revival and enlargement of one made in the first days of the Society by Lord Hailes, the most distinguished Scottish historian and antiquary of his time, and was appropriate to its interests. But whereas Hailes, with his special knowledge of the difficulties involved, planned to proceed one step at a time, Buchan wished to advance on as broad a front as possible. It can at least be said that he was firmly, and most sensibly, opposed to the use of the Antiquaries' own *Transactions* for the printing of papers delivered at its meetings when these might be of no more than ephemeral or minor importance. In 1783, when urging William Smellie to produce his promised account of the foundation and early history of the Society, he referred to 'the pompous circulation of the papers . . . among the censors' and suggested 'that it would be much better to publish on a smaller scale and to give only select papers such as may tend to augment the reputation of the society'.[46]

But if he wished in this way to concentrate on matters of major and lasting significance, his plans were unduly ambitious and far beyond the resources of the Society as it existed in the 1780s. When it was being formed, Lord Hailes had warned its enthusiastic founder of the inherent apathy of most Scotsmen for cultural enterprises of this kind, and by 1786 Buchan was himself beginning to feel that his fellow-countrymen would only support projects which offered some financial or other advantage to themselves.[47] Yet the ideas which he propounded were eventually taken up by others, some within his own lifetime, though even the combined resources of a whole succession of government commissions, learned societies, and individual scholars have not attained more than a proportion of his objectives after two centuries of almost continuous endeavour.

In January 1787, during one of the founder's now fairly frequent absences from meetings of the Society of Antiquaries, it was decided to sell its house — at a loss of £235 on the fabric and certainly very much more in total cost. Despite this, and his increasing depression regarding the prospects of the Society, Buchan did what he could to obtain alternative accommodation, first, without success, in the Palace of Holyroodhouse, and then, for a time at least, in rented rooms in Milne's Square off the High Street. While his attendance at ordinary meetings was now only spasmodic, he gave his accustomed 'anniversary address' in November of this year, as also in 1788, and 1789, but when the time for it approached in 1790, on 14 November, he sent a letter to say that not only would he be making no address but would be submitting his resignation from the Society.[48]

This was a decision apparently taken after much thought, but one might even so have expected some attempt on the part of the Society which he had founded and in which he had been the principal moving force thereafter, to dissuade him from this course. A letter to this effect was in fact prepared but, for whatever reason, it was never sent, and on 14 December, almost ten years to the day from the institution of the Society, it was agreed to accept his resignation. Insofar as any explanation can be offered for this apparently ungenerous decision, it would seem that there were quite a few members of the Society who found Buchan's domination of its affairs oppressive and his management of its finances both arbitrary and questionable. In addition, he for his part had made clear his feeling, which even his supporters did not feel able to dispute, that he could accomplish nothing further for or through the Society of Antiquaries of Scotland. Undeniably, his plans for it had been unduly ambitious and advanced over-much on his own initiative and without enlisting sufficient support from those who might have co-operated in their implementation. And yet his intentions were, for the most part, to be admired. Without him the Society might never have been founded, or at least not at this particular time, and its endurance after his withdrawal — if sometimes by the narrowest of margins — confirmed the relevance of its primary declared purpose of investi-gating and preserving the antiquities of Scotland.

When the first volume of the Society's *Transactions (Archaeologia Scotica)* was at long last published in 1792, two years after the Earl's withdrawal but nevertheless with his assistance, it had included since its inception 107 Ordinary Members drawn mainly from Edinburgh and its vicinity, 181 Corresponding Members from elsewhere in Great Britain, 81 Honorary Members, including quite a few foreigners, and 23 'Artists Associated', embracing not only painters and engravers but architects, surveyors, and booksellers, and in all categories men not only of intellectual distinction but sufficiently devoted to its interests to ensure its survival into more propitious times.[49]

Later life and associations

In the course of the 1780s Buchan came under increasing strain and perplexity regarding his place in public life. As we have seen, he had always viewed his responsibilities with unusual seriousness and the fertility of his imagination led to his promoting schemes of such number and variety that it was inevitable that only a few would reach fruition. But beyond this circumstance — which explains his eventual discouragement with the Society of Antiquaries, with which most of them tended to be connected — it is clear that he was never entirely at his ease within the social and other conventions that applied to men of his rank at this time. His low opinion of contemporary political activity is well attested, and the alternative group of activities in which he became involved reached a climax in the decade which also witnessed his own transition from early manhood to middle age.

This unsettlement and frustration provided the context of his notion, already mentioned, of leaving Scotland for America in 1782. In the end, however, and as his disillusionment with corporate antiquarian activity increased, he found a solution for his predicament by a withdrawal from public affairs for a life of seclusion at Dryburgh Abbey. This ancient Premonstratensian foundation had earlier associations with his family which had held it as commendators from 1541 and then from 1604 as part of the secular lordship of Cardross, raised in 1610 to the dignity of a peerage. In 1682, however, the third holder of the title, having been accused of organising, or at least of tolerating, conventicles within its bounds, had disposed of it on emigrating to South Carolina. Having himself rejected the notion of a second family migration to the New World, his great-grandson took the opportunity to re-purchase Dryburgh in 1786. During the next two years he enlarged and remodelled the mansion house adjoining the abbey ruins in an appropriately romantic style and entered on what was to prove to be a forty years' residence in 1788.[50]

In withdrawing to Dryburgh Buchan certainly seems to have had thoughts of a retirement from the world of 'publick affairs' in which he had been so much involved, *more suo*, during the previous twenty years. But it was impossible for a man of his physical and intellectual vigour to cut himself off altogether from the kind of activities in which he had hitherto been engaged. As we have seen, his interest in politics was limited to general issues, and he had no greater opinion of the parliamentarians of this next period, such as the younger Pitt, than he had held of their predecessors. He still participated regularly and conscientiously in the election of Scottish representative peers but otherwise limited himself to correspondence, writing directly to King George III and members of his family to express his views on current issues.[51] As with his correspondence with George Washington,[52] continued throughout the 1790s, he entertained notions that it rested on some distant kinship, but the fact is that Buchan had never been inhibited from speaking his mind on any matter to any person if the occasion seemed to demand it, his motivation in most cases being his acute sense of public responsibility rather than presumption or mere eccentricity.

His main interest in these years, however, was still with the antiquities of Scotland. Although he never resumed actual membership of the Society of Antiquaries after his resignation, he maintained his interest in its wellbeing, and no fewer than four papers by him — his accounts of Iona Abbey and Uphall and memoirs of his kinsman Sir James Steuart Denham and of the accomplished instrument-maker James Short — were included in the long-delayed initial volume of its *Transactions*.[53] His 'Remarks on the progress of the Roman Army in Scotland during the sixth campaign of Agricola', like so many of his writings originally put out as a pseudonymous article in a periodical, had by now been published in a more definitive form in John Nichols' *Bibliotheca Topographica Britannica*,[54] while his account of Dryburgh Abbey, with appropriate illustrations from his hand, was included in Francis Grose's *Antiquities of Scotland*.[55]

Beyond this involvement in the Antiquaries' *Transactions*, when William Smellie became Secretary in 1793, after a short period of inactivity and confusion, Buchan made a point of writing to him to enquire how matters stood with the Society. In his reply Smellie paid tribute to the Earl's role in bringing it into being and assured him of its revival, as a symbol of which it had been able to rent 'a noble house' belonging to the Hume Riggs of Morton in Gosford's Close off the Lawnmarket.[56]

Buchan also continued to assist, in a private capacity, in the promotion of various enterprises with which he had been associated when Vice-President of the Antiquaries. One was the scheme for the publication of reproductions of portraits of famous Scots which had engaged the interest of the ingenious but unreliable John Pinkerton, as well as of the Antiquaries, in the 1780s. It was eventually brought to a conclusion by Pinkerton in 1797 under the title *Iconographia Scotica*, yet much of the biographical detail, together with several of the illustrations, and perhaps the actual title, were the contribution — but scantily acknowledged — of his collaborator.[57]

Another of the Earl's notions was to continue the biographical series inaugurated by his *Napier*, publishing a pair of essays on Andrew Fletcher of Saltoun and the poet James Thomson[58] and contributing short studies of George Heriot, William Drummond of Hawthornden, and of his own progenitor John 7th Earl of Mar to his favourite periodical *The Bee* in the same general period.[59] Beyond these he had thoughts, in 1794, of including such more recent figures as Francis Hutcheson, Lord Kames, and the brothers Robert and Andrew Foulis for whom, as we know, he had an early and enduring admiration. He also considered extending the scope of the enterprise to embrace such 'inventors and benefactors of mankind' as Copernicus, towards a biography of whom he invoked the assistance of John Robison, Professor of Natural Philosophy at Edinburgh. But of all this there was nothing in the end, partly because, with the passage of time, the ingenious promoter of these enterprises — too numerous and varied in any event — lost the sheer physical energy which had sustained him in their earlier phase.

So far as Buchan allowed himself to be involved with any actual antiquarian organisation in Scotland after 1790, it was with the Literary and Antiquarian Society of Perth founded in 1784. In 1785 he accepted an invitation to become one of its honorary presidents, took part in some of its early meetings, and made several donations to its collections. He was much concerned that it should, like the Society of Antiquaries of Scotland, embark on a systematic programme of publication and was full of admiration for the initiative of the Morison family in publishing historical works relating to the locality.[60] In the outcome, however, the Perth society's *Transactions* were even longer in appearing than those of its precursor, the one solitary volume being published only in 1827 at the very end of Buchan's own life.[61]

In his eager and far-ranging circle of interests the Earl was aware of the great progress made in 'northern antiquities' in the later eighteenth century and their relevance to much of early Scottish history. As we have seen, Denmark and Sweden had been in the forefront of antiquarian studies in the early seventeenth century, and in 1745 and 1753 respectively new organisations were brought into being in both countries to assist their further development. In Norway and Iceland, too, contained for so long within the Danish cultural orbit, the creation of comparable bodies in 1760 and 1791 symbolised a revival of interest in their own distinctive identities.[62]

Buchan was elected to honorary membership of the Royal Danish Society in 1785 and of its Icelandic counterpart in 1791, these developments being of special interest since they were the product of a close and enduring friendship with the great Icelandic scholar Grímur Jonsson Thorkelin that had begun, through correspondence, in 1783. As Assistant Keeper of the Royal Archives in Copenhagen Thorkelin was anxious to locate documents relating to Danish, Norwegian, and Icelandic 'antiquities' in British repositories. Buchan, for his part, wished to secure copies of Scottish source-material from abroad, especially from countries having strong historic ties with his own. There thus began an amiable interchange of letters, books, and transcripts, and between 1786 and 1791 Thorkelin took up residence in London in pursuit of his researches. There he formed a close friendship

C

with George Dempster of Dunnichen who arranged for him to visit Scotland in 1787. Buchan and Sir John Sinclair — who had met Thorkelin in Denmark — helped by providing introductions, and in Buchan's case the encounter of the two men was followed by a more intense and cordial correspondence that was to continue for a further twenty years.[63]

As the eighteenth century drew to a close and he himself approached his sixtieth year Buchan became convinced that his life's work was done and that he owed it to posterity to explain what he had been attempting to achieve in his various public activities. To this end, as early as 1794 he began to assemble his papers in a 'depot' or depository and gradually enlisted Dr Robert Anderson, editor of *The Poets of Great Britain* and author of several major literary biographies, as his collaborator in a projected publication. If, however, this was to be a single work, it would seem to have been envisaged less as a conventional biography or autobiography than as a series of 'literary memoirs' containing copious reproductions of the correspondence of 'antiquaries, typographers, and bibliographists' with whom the Earl had been associated during his life.[64]

In the outcome, although both parties to the arrangement were to live for many years after the project was first broached, Buchan until 1829 and Anderson until 1830, no real progress was made towards its completion, mainly because of its promoter's imprecise and ambivalent attitude towards it. At no time, indeed, does Anderson seem to have been specifically commissioned to undertake the work, while its subject alternated between thoughts of his own impending dissolution and a round of activities that were to continue, albeit with decreasing intensity, for a further thirty years.

Many of these activities were concerned with the embellishment of Dryburgh where he liked to entertain distinguished visitors, as well as old friends and neighbours, in the manner of a cultured patrician landowner. In 1791 he began to adapt the abbey chapter-house as a setting for his still persisting notion of a Temple of Caledonian Fame but, perhaps fortunately, carried it no more than a short distance. In 1791, however, he erected a memorial *stele* nearby 'in honour of his ancestors' whom he envisaged as including Hugh de Moreville, founder of the abbey, King James I, and King James II. He also built on an eminence above the Tweed a classical temple in honour of John Thomson as well as an obelisk on Ednam Hill above his birthplace. It was characteristic of the Earl's intense enthusiasms that he should have become obsessed to this extent with one literary figure. As early as 1791, indeed, he had instituted an annual festival in his honour, but after the death in 1796 of Robert Burns, who had visited Dryburgh in 1787 and provided a special poem for the inaugural commemoration, he added a tribute to his memory in succeeding ceremonies. A more ancient Scottish hero who came to form the subject of a landscape feature of the locality was William Wallace, of whom an enormous statue by the self-taught sculptor John Smith — who had also designed 'the temple of the muses' — was inaugurated in 1814.[65]

By this time Buchan was a man of advanced years and impaired vitality. In 1801, during a visit to London, an accident had deprived him of the sight of one eye, and he now spent rather more time in his town house in Castle Street in Edinburgh, reserving Dryburgh for his summer residence. But despite his disabilities he managed, in 1811, to complete a vast epic poem on the *Irish Chiefs*, a strange mixture of ancient mythology and contemporary political philosophising, yet not devoid of literary merit. In the following year, having attained the alloted biblical span of 70, he decided to publish the first of what was intended to be a series, or at least a pair, of volumes containing his *Anonymous and Fugitive Essays collected from various periodical works* duly acknowledged and authenticated by himself.[66]

He was now growing undeniably eccentric, a tendency that became more pronounced after the deaths of his brother Henry in 1817 and of his wife in 1819. It was in the latter year that there occurred the extra-ordinary episode involving Walter Scott and cited by his son-in-law and biographer Lockhart as typical of Earl David's vanity and general absurdity. Buchan had in fact known Scott since he had examined him as a schoolboy in 1783 for a prize which he awarded to pupils of the High School of Edinburgh for proficiency in translation of Latin verse.[67] In 1791, shortly after the Earl had settled at Dryburgh, he made over the ancient burial-place of the Haliburtons in the abbey to Scott's father and uncles as heirs of this family through their mother. There-after, as Scott grew to fame, Buchan became increasingly concerned that he should be buried here, and when Scott became gravely ill in a house not far from the Earl's in Castle Street in Edinburgh the old man tried to force his way into the sickroom, as he said,'to embrace him before he died' and to assure him that he would personally supervise all the funeral arrangements and pronounce an appropriate oration.[68]

As it so happened, Scott outlived Buchan, if only by some three years, and having attended his funeral at Dryburgh on 20 April 1829 entered in his diary the oft-quoted observation: 'Lord Buchan is dead, a person whose immense vanity, bordering on insanity, obscured, or rather eclipsed, very considerable talents'.[69] The biographical memoir in *The Gentleman's Magazine* was rather more sympathetic and that in the *New Scots Magazine* — used by Robert Chambers for his *Biographical Dictionary* — paid due tribute to his many excellent qualities.[70] The fact is that the exaggerations and undoubted absurdities of conduct that characterised Buchan's life must be seen in proportion and as part of his entire personality. Only at the very end of his immensely long career did they eclipse, as Scott said, his 'very considerable talents'. Next, it may be said that these failings were due less to vanity or an exaggerated sense of his own importance than to an ebullience of temperament inclined to advance proposals in such abundance and with so little concern for the difficulties involved that they were too often destined to failure. And yet in themselves these proposals were the product of an unusually alert, imaginative, and well-informed intelligence motivated by a strong sense of patriotism and public service and allied to an admirable magnanimity of temperament.

To many of his contemporaries Buchan was altogether too 'enthusiastical', he and Sir John Sinclair — in their very different ways — being often regarded by Scott and others as the supreme bores of their age.[71] But when set in a more extended context, their enthusiasms appear most timely and meritorious. If Buchan had done no more than found the Society of Antiquaries of Scotland it would still entitle him to the gratitude of his countrymen, but this achievement can be seen as part of a general and truly commendable concern to preserve and enhance every aspect of the historic identity of his native land.

NOTES

1. This paper, while offering a fresh assessment of its subject, does not claim any particular originality of research. Written at relatively short notice, its preparation has been considerably assisted by the kindness of Dr J. G. Lamb in permitting use to be made of his thesis, 'David Steuart Erskine, 11th Earl of Buchan: A Study of his Life and Correspondence', submitted for the degree of Doctor of Philosophy of the University of St Andrews in 1963. It has also benefited greatly from the encouragement and advice of Mr R. B. K. Stevenson and Mr A. S. Bell.

2. Particulars of the Buchan peerage and Erskine family have been obtained from Sir James Balfour Paul (ed.), *The Scots Peerage* (9 vols, Edinburgh 1904), ii.250-80, and G.

E. Cokayne (rev. V. Gibbs and others), *The Complete Peerage* (13 vols, London 1910-40), ii.373-84.

3. S[ociety of] A[ntiquaries of] S[cotland], minutes.

4. Details of Cardross's education and early life, with the quotations cited, are drawn in great measure from his own diary and letter-books collected by Dr David Murray and presented by him to Glasgow University Library.

5. In particular the institution in Marischal College in 1769 of the Greek prize competition for what came to be known as 'The Earl of Buchan's Silver Pen' (R. S. Rait, *The Universities of Aberdeen*, Aberdeen 1895, 317-18).

6. D. Murray, *Robert and Andrew Foulis and the Glasgow Press, with some account of the Glasgow Academy of Fine Arts* (Glasgow 1913).

7. D. S. Erskine, Earl of Buchan (hereafter 'Buchan'), 'Account of the Island of Icolmkill', *Arch[aeologia] Scot[ica]*, [*or Transactions of the Society of Antiquaries of Scotland*] i(1792), 234-41.

8. Scottish National Portrait Gallery catalogue, with additional information through the kindness of the Keeper, Mr R. E. Hutchison. The original of the Reynolds portrait is now thought to be in the South African National Gallery, Cape Town. Among the copies is one by James Wales, presented by him to the Society of Antiquaries of Scotland in 1781.

9. *Boswell's Life of Johnson*, ed. G. B. Hill and L. F. Powell (6 vols, Oxford 1934-50), ii.177 and n.

10. For this section the Buchan papers in Glasgow U.L. (Murray MSS) continue to be of importance; also the MS collections of the National Library of Scotland.

11. Buchan, 'Account of the Parish of Uphall', *Arch. Scot.* i(1792), 139-55.

12. A. Fergusson, *Henry Erskine, his kinsfolk and his times* (Edinburgh and London 1882).

13. Sir David Erskine, *Annals and Antiquities of Dryburgh* (2 ed., Kelso 1836).

14. *Speech of the Earl of Buchan, intended to have been delivered at a meeting of the Peers of Scotland October 17th, 1780* (Edinburgh 1780).

15. Buchan papers, Glasgow U.L. The reply to the Yorkshire Committee is printed, with other details, in C. Wyvill, *Political Papers* (6 vols, York 1794-1802), iv.523. Buchan also published, anonymously, *Letters* 'on the partiality and injustice of the charges . . . against Warren Hastings' (London 1786) and 'on the impolicy of a standing army in time of peace' (London 1793).

16. 'Letter from Benjamin Franklin to the Earl of Buchan, 1783', *Gentleman's Magazine* lxiv (1794), 587.

17. *The Earl of Buchan's address to the Americans at Edinburgh on Washington's birthday, February 28th 1811* (Edinburgh 1811).

18. A difficulty of timing is created by the fact that the title-page of Buchan's inaugural *Discourse* in N.L.S. is dated 1778. It may well be that he intended to deliver it then and had copies printed for circulation among prospective members. But there can be no doubt that the first meeting to form the Society, and the delivery of the 'discourse', actually took place two years later, in 1780, albeit on 14 November, a date to which the Earl seems to have attached particular significance. This interpretation, which owes much to discussions with Dr I. G. Brown, is supported by a ms. alteration of '1778' to '1780' on the title-page of the New York Public Library copy.

19. Buchan, *Discourse delivered at a meeting for the purpose of promoting the*

institution of a·Society for the investigation of the History of Scotland and its Antiquities, November 14, 1778 (Edinburgh 1778); R. Kerr, *Memoirs of the life, writings, and correspondence of William Smellie* (2 vols, Edinburgh 1811), ii.32-4.

20. Buchan, *Discourse* (1778), 18-19.

21. 'Introduction, containing an Account of the Origin and Establishment of the Society', *Archaeologia, or miscellaneous tracts relating to Antiquity published by the Society of Antiquaries of London* i (1770), iii, xv.

22. W. Smellie, 'An historical account of the Society of Antiquaries of Scotland' (incorporating earlier accounts, separately printed: part I, Edinburgh 1782; part II, Edinburgh 1784), with a list of members since the inception of the Society, *Arch. Scot.* i (1792), iv.

23. The treatment of early antiquarian activities here has benefited from the studies by I. G. Brown, 'Critick in Antiquity: Sir John Clerk of Penicuik', *Antiquity* li (1977), 201-10; A. Graham, 'Records and Opinions, 1780-1830', *P[roceedings of the] S[ociety of] A[ntiquaries of] S[cotland]* cii (1970), 241-84 (especially 241-6); A. Graham, 'The development of Scottish antiquarian records: 1600-1800', *PSAS* cvi (1975), 183-90; Ole Klindt-Jensen, *A History of Scandinavian Archaeology* (London 1975), especially chs. 2 and 3; S. Piggott, *Ruins in a Landscape: Essays in Antiquarianism* (Edinburgh 1976), especially chs. 1, 3, 6 and 7; S. Piggott and M. Robertson, *Three Centuries of Scottish Archaeology* [exhibition catalogue] (Edinburgh 1977).

24. Buchan, *Discourse* (1778), 23.

25. *Ibid.*, 20.

26. R. H. Carnie, 'Life and Writings of Sir David Dalrymple, Lord Hailes', St Andrews University Ph.D. thesis, 1954, St Andrews University Library.

27. Smellie, 'Historical Account', *Arch. Scot.* i (1792), v.

28. Buchan, *Discourse* (1778), especially pp. 28, 31.

29. *Ibid.*, 24-8.

30. Smellie, *op. cit.*, vi.

31. J. W. Reed and F. A. Pottle, eds., *Boswell, Laird of Auchinleck, 1778-1782* (New York 1977), 271.

32. Smellie, *op. cit.*, vi.

33. SAS minutes.

34. J. S. Watson, *The Reign of George III* (Oxford 1960), 69-70.

35. SAS minutes.

36. *Ibid.*, and C. B. Boog Watson, 'Notes on the Names of the Closes and Wynds of Old Edinburgh', *Book of the Old Edinburgh Club* xii (1923), especially 131-2.

37. Smellie, 'Historical Account', vii.

38. For details of this controversy from the point of view of Smellie and the Society of Antiquaries, see R. Kerr, *Memoirs of . . . Smellie* (1811), ii.33-44; and from the point of view of other parties, including the Royal Society of Edinburgh, S. Shapin, 'Property, patronage, and the politics of science: the founding of the Royal Society of Edinburgh', *British Journal for the History of Science* vii (1974), 1-41, especially 15-36. It is typical of Buchan that having been involved at the height of the controversy in a violent personal confrontation with Principal Robertson (Shapin, 27-9; Piggott and Robertson, *Three Centuries of Scottish Archaeology* 1977, no. 51), he should then have instructed Smellie, in preparing his annual report for the Society of Antiquaries, to omit 'any remarks whatever . . . on the business of the opposition to the charter',

adding, with regained dignity and restraint, 'The memorials and answers speak for themselves' (Kerr, *Memoirs of Smellie*, ii.62).

39. Kerr, *Memoirs of Smellie*, ii.41-4.

40. SAS minutes.

41. Kerr, *Memoirs of Smellie*, ii, 83-4; SAS minutes.

42. Sir John Sinclair (ed.), *The Statistical Account of Scotland* (21 vols, Edinburgh 1791-9). The early accounts prepared by Buchan were, understandably, curtailed for publication in Sinclair's compilation. C. Innes, *Origines Parochiales Scotiae* (2 vols, Bannatyne Club, Edinburgh 1851-5). It is interesting to note that the Society of Antiquaries later returned to Buchan's plan in its circular letter requesting information on 'monuments of antiquity' from 'the parochial ministry of Scotland' in *Arch. Scot.* ii (1822), xvii-xviii.

43. Buchan, and W. Minto, *A account of the life, writings, and inventions of John Napier of Merchiston* (Perth 1787).

44. They are listed in Kerr, *Memoirs of Smellie* (1811), ii.85-6, and are now in the Scottish National Portrait Gallery, Edinburgh, on loan from the Society of Antiquaries of Scotland.

45. SAS minutes.

46. Kerr, *Memoirs of Smellie*, ii.61-2.

47. E.U.L., Laing MSS; J. Nichols, *Illustrations of the Literary History of the Eighteenth Century* (8 vols, London 1817-33), vi.514.

48. SAS minutes.

49. Smellie, 'Historical Account', xxi-xxxiii.

50. The Buchan papers in Baillie's Library, Glasgow, Edinburgh U.L. (Laing and other MSS), Glasgow U.L. (Murray MSS) and N.L.S. are of great importance for this section which also depends, even more than the others, on the pioneer work of Dr J. G. Lamb (see note 1 above). See also Nichols, *Illustrations* (1817-33) and, for Dryburgh, Sir David Erskine's *Annals* (see note 13 above).

51. A. Fergusson, *Henry Erskine* (1882), 492 ff.

52. *The Writings of George Washington*, ed. J. C. Fitzpatrick (39 vols, Washington, D.C., 1931-44), especially vols 29-36.

53. Buchan, 'Memoirs of the life of Sir James Steuart Denholm', *Arch. Scot.* i (1792), 129-39; 'Account of the Parish of Uphall', *ibid.* 139-55; 'Account of the Island of Icolmkill', *ibid.* 234-41; 'Life of Mr James Short, optician', *ibid.* 251-6.

54. Buchan, 'Remarks on the progress of the Roman army in Scotland during the sixth campaign of Agricola' [by 'Albanicus'], in J. Nichols, *Bibliotheca Topographica Britannica*, vi. no. 6 (London 1786).

55. Buchan, 'Dryburgh Abbey'; description and two plates in F. Grose, *The Antiquities of Scotland* (2 vols, London 1789-91), i.101-9.

56. Kerr, *Memoirs of Smellie*, ii.63-5.

57. J. Pinkerton, *Iconographia Scotica, or Portraits of illustrious persons of Scotland, engraved from the most authentic paintings, &c., with short biographical notes* (Edinburgh 1797).

58. Buchan, *Essays on the lives and writings of Fletcher of Saltoun and the poet Thomson* (London 1792).

59. A complete list of Buchan's multifarious contributions to this periodical, almost all anonymous or pseudonymous (though the identity of 'Albanicus' must have been

generally known) is provided in a special appendix to Dr Lamb's thesis (see note 1 above). Most of those of major significance were however published in a more definitive form, and it was their writer's intention to include all such in successive volumes of his collected *Essays* (see *The Anonymous and Fugitive Essays of the Earl of Buchan collected from various periodical works*, i, Edinburgh 1812).

60. R. H. Carnie, *Publishing in Perth before 1807*, Abertay Historical Society Publication no. 6 (Dundee 1960).

61. *Transactions of the Literary and Antiquarian Society of Perth* i (1827).

62. O. Klindt-Jensen, *History of Scandinavian Archaeology* (1975), ch. 3.

63. Many of Thorkelin's letters to Buchan and other Scottish correspondents are among the Laing MSS in Edinburgh U.L.; others are in the Murray MSS (Glasgow U.L.) and the MSS collections of N.L.S.

64. Biographical notice of the Earl of Buchan, *New Scots Magazine* ii (1829), 494.

65. This statue, still extant, is said to have been based, somewhat improbably, on a contemporary French water-colour ('Note on the Wallace statue at Dryburgh', *Gentleman's Magazine* lxxvii (1817), 621). In the memorial *stele* the figure of James I is clearly derived from the sketch of James II by Jörg von Ehingen, used as the basis of a painting at Kielberg in Swabia. In consequence, the figure of James II on the Dryburgh *stele* seems to be largely conjectural (see Pinkerton, *Iconographia Scotica* 1797; *The Diary of Jörg von Ehingen*, ed. and tr. M. Letts, London 1929; also Sir David Erskine, *Annals of Dryburgh* 1836).

66. Buchan, *Irish Chiefs or the Harp of Erin* [by 'an Irish gentleman'] (Edinburgh 1811); *Anonymous and Fugitive Essays* (1812) (see note 59 above).

67. *Letter from the Earl of Buchan to his brother, the Hon. Thomas Erskine, on the subject of education, accompanying a Latin address to the Rector of the High School of Edinburgh and one in English to the boys in the highest class of the school* (Edinburgh 1782); *The Journal of Sir Walter Scott*, ed. W. E. K. Anderson (Oxford 1972), 552n.

68. J. G. Lockhart, *The Life of Sir Walter Scott* [1839] (10 vols, Edinburgh 1902-3) vi.83-5.

69. Scott, *Journal* (1972), 550.

70. *Gentleman's Magazine* xcix (1829), 75-8; *New Scots Magazine* ii(1829), 494; R. Chambers, 'David Steuart Erskine, Earl of Buchan', *Biographical Dictionary of Eminent Scotsmen* (4 vols, Edinburgh 1835) ii.217-19.

71. Scott, *Journal* (1972), 198.

The Museum, its Beginnings and its Development

Part I: to 1858: the Society's own Museum

R. B. K. Stevenson

I suspect that that Society [a bright constellation of Caledonian Naturalists and Antiquaries in the late seventeenth century], as well as all others which are instituted for the study and collection of Antiquities and the objects of Natural History, failed on account of their having no house in property, nor any private interests to care for their books, museum, and other necessary appurtanences; and that having met in taverns, their meetings degenerated into convivial and anomalous conversations. All these hazards I mean, with your approbation, to guard against, and ever to exclude.

Lord Buchan, 14 November 1780.*

For much of the two centuries following Lord Buchan's Introductory Address, the Museum, and the need to care for it, was indeed central to the varying fortunes of the Society. For much of the first century his belief, that looking after a museum and having to house it would be what held his society together, proved to be true, as in successive generations a few men rose to the challenge. To show the converse, that collections needed a society, he went on to cite 'the Balfourian and Sibbaldian museums', given as his hearers knew to Edinburgh University, which had been dispersed through, as we might say, the lack of a home of their own and of the personal involvement of an interested membership. Another factor in survival is quality, which he did not mention. Perhaps those vanished university collections were less

---

* This chapter draws very largely on the minute-books and other records retained by the Society, and the printing of detailed references would be impracticable. An annotated copy giving specific references will be deposited in the library of the Museum and Society. For a general bibliographical note to both parts of this chapter, see p. 210.

remarkable than those that were more fortunate, the Ashmolean then a century old at Oxford, and Dr William Hunter's which was to be bequeathed to Glasgow in 1783.

The Earliest Years, to 1787

Curiously, perhaps, the Founder did not elaborate on the value of collections for study, except to say that it was impossible to proceed further with historical annals and disquisitions than the material already collected would permit. However, in editing and printing Buchan's Address in his *Account* of the Society a year or so later, the encyclopaedic William Smellie explained that the labours of some individuals, 'unassisted by powerful patronage', had excited a taste for antiquarian enquiries 'which for some years past has continued to diffuse itself over the nation':

> An Association accordingly, similar to the Antiquarian Society of London, was projected by several gentlemen of eminence and learning, some of whom had made private collections, and were anxious that these, and others which they knew to be scattered through the country, should be preserved in a secure and permanent repository . . . They considered that some useful materials, which had been amassed by interested Antiquaries, were now perishing in the possession of persons who knew not their values; that others still existing, in public libraries, depended upon the fate of single copies, and were subject to obliteration, to fire, and other causes of destruction; and that it was an object of national importance to bring all these, either in their original form, or by an accurate transcript, into one great repository, which should be rendered accessible to the republic of letters.
>
> In Lord Buchan's interesting discourse [Smellie continued], it was hinted, that the objects of the Society were not limited to Antiquities alone, but that they were to extend to the Natural productions of the country. This conjunction requires explanation. The penury of Scottish Antiquities, it was thought, would neither afford sufficient scope to the researches, nor gratify the tastes of such a number of men as were necessary to carry the views of the Society into execution . . . Besides, though this branch of the institution has not yet been fully unfolded, the donations received during the last twelve months show that Natural productions of every kind will form the most numerous, as well as the most ornamental part of our collections.

In this development the Society could be said to be following the wide scope of the British Museum, nationally owned from the start, which had opened some twenty years earlier. It comprised the historical and literary books and manuscripts of the Royal, Cottonian and Harleian libraries, and those of Sir Hans Sloane including his natural history collections and curiosities, to which the classical antiquities of

Sir William Hamilton had been added in 1772. The London Antiquaries, chartered in 1753 though active since 1707, accumulated
miscellaneous antiquities and works of art, as adjuncts to their library
and rooms rather than as a museum. The Scottish Antiquaries, like
those of London but in contrast to the British Museum and those
university museums of Oxford and Glasgow, formed their collections
without having any major nucleus from individual collectors who had
had the concentrated interest, the money, and perhaps the time, which
societies — and in later days museum staffs — cannot devote to systematic acquisition. We shall see how far they succeeded over the years
in overcoming this disadvantage by collecting collections, valuable if
more modest.

By concentrating, though not exclusively, on things Scottish, little
more than thirty years after the last of the Jacobite risings which had
strained the relations of even loyalist Scots with England, they were
running a conscious risk. Again it was Smellie rather than Buchan who
was explicit on this point:

> Till we were happily united with England, not in government only, but in loyalty
> and affection to a common Sovereign, it was not, perhaps, altogether consistent
> with political wisdom, to call attention of the Scots to the ancient honours and
> constitution of their independent monarchy. Not many years have elapsed since
> the jealousies of the two nations were succeeded by a warm and mutual attach-
> ment to the same family and constitution. During this short period, however, it
> will be allowed, that the progress of the Scots, in every species of art and science,
> has been rapid.

Looking back we can see that the romantic and unpolitical enthusiasm
for things Scottish, originally fired through western Europe by Macpherson's Ossianic poetry of the 1760s, to which Buchan referred
devoutly in his Address, matched by the self-confidence and success of
the Scots themselves, kept national pride clear of the suspicions of
nationalism for a very long time afterwards. Recently it has again
become a practical problem, how far it would be actually counter-
productive to stress the Museum's Scottishness strongly.

'Soon after the institution of the Society,' Smellie tells us, 'the number
and value of the donations, daily received, rendered the purchase of a repository necessary at a more early period than was
expected. The funds of the Society were by no means adequate to such
an expense.' The expectations of the Founder had in fact been more
sanguine, and well before the donations could have justified it he had in
January 1781 inspected a house with the Secretary. The reference to a

self-contained house shows indeed that he had selected it before the
initial Address. The purchase price estimated on that occasion (£800)
was offered in February, but not accepted. In March entry was successfully negotiated, the price of £1,000 to be paid up in full by Martinmas
1782 (guaranteed by Lord Buchan, from whom the first £100 also
came); in the meantime 5% p.a. was to be paid regularly on whatever
was outstanding.

This 'large and commodious' house, with some open ground on
every side, was a rarity in the Old Town of closely packed tenements
up to fifteen storeys high, or even in the growing New Town of long
terraces. It was 'not liable to the communication of fire from neighbouring edifices', and was to survive a conflagration in 1829. It lay
almost straight down from the east end of St Giles' and a short way up
from the Cowgate, immediately west of the fish-market. The coach-
house and stables, with the main gate between them, were on the Cowgate. As Buchan said in February, the property would 'admit all the
additions the Society may require for centuries to come'. Extending to
about 60 feet by 150, it may be compared with the 65 by 110 of the
Museum's building of 1890 in Queen Street, which was not seriously
supplemented until 1953. Seventy years ago C. B. Boog Watson eluci-
dated its history — built about 1742 by Alexander Lockhart, advocate
(later a judge, Lord Covington), it was square with a central cupola;
sold in 1766 to Colonel Campbell of Barbreck, in the service of the East
India Company, it was rented as the Post Office for two or three years
before the Antiquaries' occupation. It was then in fair condition, for
only £10 was spent at the time of moving in, while later repairs to
chimney heads cost £14 18s 2d. Three years later £1 17s 8d was paid for
painting the principal staircase 'straw colour in Syze' to do away with
the gloomy appearance.

By November 1782 only part of the purchase price had been paid,
and a loan of £600 was needed, to be obtained by Lord Buchan on the
Society's behalf from the Royal Bank. In reporting this debt to the
Anniversary Meeting he hoped that there might be an increase of fees
or voluntary contributions to extinguish it. But there was little
response to his plea that the Society, 'consisting of between two and
three hundred persons' (though only eighty were on the roll of ordinary
members), should not 'permit themselves to be accused of sordid in-
attention to [its] pecuniary interest'. Even the loan was delayed for a
year, partly because the Earl hoped that it would be obtained by the
Society itself once it was a chartered body, and it was not until 13

November 1783 that £575 then outstanding was paid, and he held the title deeds.

The Society did not occupy all the premises on its own. The two out-buildings, or 'pavilions', were let out at £4 each. For the 'great gate' between them the magistrates were asked to provide a lamp. The main building was referred to as the Museum, but part of it was lived in by the Secretary and his family, rent-free. He was James Cummyng, who worked in the office of Lyon King of Arms as keeper of records, for which he received no salary though he had once held for a short time the paid post of herald painter. His work for the Society was also unpaid. One honorarium of £50 was voted him by the Council in 1782, but 'out of arrears due to the Funds', which then mounted instead of de-creasing; payment was finally made early in 1784. A letter from Lord Buchan to the Home Secretary for government support for Cummyng, in the form of 'some small office in the Scottish civil list', got no reply. The Society provided a 'proper stove' and a bookcase for his study.

The Hall for meetings, and in which at first the museum or repository was to be set up (only from the fireplace to the south-east corner), measured 36¾ feet by 16½ and 10½ high. Iron bars were ordered when an acquisition of coins was being considered. Dirt was guarded against by making the windows fit better, and 'as open fires occasion dirt' the hall was to be fitted with stoves in the form of urns, a large vase at one end and a smaller at the other. The expense of coals, candles and other incidentals (£9) was incurred by Mrs Cummyng and repaid, and it was estimated that an additional servant for her might cost the Society £10 or more a year. Several additional rooms came to be occupied by museum objects, so in winter 1784 arrangements were made 'for heating and drying the different rooms of the Museum in rotation'. Further details are lost because normal current expenses early ceased to be included in the Council's minutes, and no financial books remain though correspondence and communications were kept, and later bound. A students' room, for which five chairs were presented, subsequently reported as being little used, was probably the same as the reading room to be open twice a week, mentioned as being on the Parlour floor of the building.

The payment of window light and house duties, amounting to £6 19s 0d for the first year, was deferred by agreement with the Town's Assessor, until it could be discovered what was done in London. Pay-ment of £19 15s 4d had to be made in June 1784, six months after a court action against the Society. Later still it was ascertained that taxes were paid by the British Museum and by the Royal and Antiquarian Societies. A further attempt at exemption was made by an appeal to the Barons of Exchequer in Edinburgh, at least one of whom was a member, but this was simply referred to their officials. After 'nuisances and encroachments on the Society's property' were mentioned, evergreens to cover the walls of the area were received from Sir Alexander Dick of Prestonfield. This was perhaps as much in psychological warfare as for amenity, as it appears that the encroachments were some sort of boundary dispute, since an unspecified decision by the Dean of Guild Court on the Society's complaints was reported next year.

Smellie's *Account*, published in May 1782, traced progress up to April of that year. An excellent feature of it, repeated in its second part ending in June 1784, is the descriptive list of donors and donations to the museum and library which was laid before each meeting of the Society and minuted. Purchases seem to have been exceptional, but unfortunately they were only referred to in general terms in the minutes and not published. Donation lists in substantially the same form were continued (though long after the events) in later volumes of *Transactions*, and in annually issued *Proceedings* from 1852 up to 1939. There can be few museums or libraries of such age with so full a serial publication of their earlier accessions. This record would be prouder if it did not contain uncomfortable evidence of what (from a variety of causes over the years) had disappeared or lost its identity, even if most of the missing items were of very minor consequence. Yet a check on certain classes of accessions, using 1781 as a random example, shows a respectably high survival rate for what was not readily perishable (thus out of 41 prehistoric and later complete museum objects from Britain, other than flints, 37 survive), so that the first half century can be absolved from later imputations of serious carelessness. There have been transfers and disposals, particularly in the second century, almost all long after the items had become irrelevant to the main interests of the Society (with some sad exceptions), or when they could clearly be better looked after elsewhere. The basic facilities for preservation — space and people's time — have never been adequate to the size of the task, as much because of reasonable hopes disappointed as of an overoptimistic biting off of more than could be chewed.

The earliest mix can be indicated by the number of donations in 1781 and 1782 that contained one or more items from twelve arbitrary categories: books, broadsheets, maps and transcripts 34 and 42; drawings, prints etc. 14 and 21; manuscripts 10 and 25; objects —

Roman and prehistoric 11 and 18, Viking and medieval 7 and 3, later 13 and 22, plus specifically foreign and ethnographical 11 and 14; coins and medals 44 (1729 items) and 91; natural history — animal 20 and 24, vegetable 6 and 2, mineral 14 and 14; money, for the building (not listed later) 8 and 2.

Two items from those years that have, perhaps fortunately, dis-appeared silently, are 'the scalp of a French soldier . . . the queue tied with pink ribbon', and a 'hand-grenade, charged' found near Hawick. On the other hand, of the very first objects minuted, on 16 January 1781, fifty-one of the fifty-three pieces of late bronze age weapons and cauldron are still present (several then inevitably destructive analyses were made in 1850 for Daniel Wilson), but not the lump of fused metal or the 'sculls and other human bones together with the horns of animals of the deer and elk species' dredged up with them from Duddingston Loch, Edinburgh. This entry in the *Account* is more detailed than the Secretary's early minute, but in line with his full listing of manuscripts in March. It seems possible that we owe to William Smellie not only the description of the bones but of the artefacts, and the good standard of more than the natural history in the entries that followed. As he used to spend weekends at Prestonfield, the gift of the hoard by Sir Alexander Dick was probably also due to him.

The Duddingston weapons, and various bronze axes that have come down to us from small hoards at Nairn and Dingwall, as well as a decorated cauldron of later date from Stirlingshire — the spread from the start was national as intended — were all described as Roman. This was not, of course, through ignorance of the absence of iron in Homeric times, but because it was known from classical literature that the Romans still used bronze for armour. A long paper by the reverend donor of the Nairn find was read to the Society in 1783, on Roman weapons of copper and iron, specifically arguing this case. Nearer the mark was the ascription to the Romans of the extremely fine and rare heavy bronze collar of the second century AD, ornamented with Celtic spirals, from Stichill in Roxburghshire, which the landowners had pre-served for thirty-five years. It was listed as a *cestus* (knuckle-duster or girdle). Roman glass from forts in Perthshire and Dumfriesshire was correctly identified, and kept even in small fragments. On the other hand a more than life-sized marble head of a Roman, found in the wilds of the upper Tweed, was for well over a century supposed to represent a medieval priest.

A good descriptive paper on the earthworks at Birrenswark in

Dumfriesshire, identifying the Roman camps as besieging the native fort, may be credited to Dr Robert Clapperton, though the later editor omitted his name; he donated an enamelled bridle-bit from the back of the hill, and tiles and bricks from the baths at Birrens. The first excavation report, a rarity in the volumes of *Transactions* and very detailed, was contributed by Adam Cardonnel in 1783, on Roman military baths found at Inveresk near Edinburgh, illustrated by a view of the hypocaust. He praised a local resident, James Wedderburn, for 'endeavouring to preserve for the inspection of the curious, under the unskilled hands of the workmen, such of the buildings as are most worthy of preservation, and collecting together specimens of the different things found'. Some mortar and tiles were given to the Museum; three of the hypocaust's stone pillars were added eighty years later. Besides accounts of the finding of prehistoric objects that were donated, descriptive field surveys were presented with early papers, on the 'druidical' stones and 'Norwegian' brochs of the island of Lewis, and on iron age forts as on Hill o' Noth in Aberdeenshire. John Williams, a mineral surveyor, and author of the first monograph on such vitrified forts (a subject liable to excite controversy to this day) was an early active member of the Society, as an Associated Artist, but his papers were on current not antiquarian subjects.

The first paper to use the Museum's collections for typological study, 'On the warlike and domestic instruments used by the Scots before the discovery of metals', was delivered in 1782 by W. C. Little of Liberton, an advocate much concerned with the business side of the Council. He discussed stone axes and jet ornaments, placed for functional reasons what are now called leaf-shaped flint arrowheads earlier than those with barbs, and illustrated examples with their museum-numbers. Two of the arrowheads and one of the ornaments came from the Rev. Donald McQueen of Skye, along with two Viking silver bracelets — 'fibulae of white metal with which the sagum was fastened'; described as very learned, McQueen figures prominently in Johnson's and Boswell's accounts of their tour to the Hebrides a few years earlier.

More recent objects received in these first six years are even more varied and no less interesting. Medieval antiquities include an inscribed fragment of West Highland stone cross from Eilean Mor, to which another piece was added in 1936; two seal matrices and an octagonal latten flagon, separate finds; not to speak of several common three-legged pots, 'Roman camp-kettles', that have now lost their provenances. An openwork ivory representing two mailed knights among interlace foliage, given by Lord Macdonald as the 'handle of a durk', may be a chessman, of still uncertain date.

Among the weapons are a two-handed sword almost six feet long, and a unique sporran-top given by MacNab of MacNab — the four little pistols concealed in it inspired Sir Walter Scott to give Rob Roy one in his novel. More sinister, because more practical, are thumbkins as used to torture seventeenth-century Covenanters, and a lockable brass collar found in the Firth of Forth, inscribed with the sentence on a man reprieved from the death penalty but given as perpetual servant to Erskine of Alva, an exhibit supported by the entry in the judicial records. One of the many and varied donations from Lord Buchan was the guidon of the dragoons raised in 1688 by his ancestor Lord Cardross, one of the oldest flags of a British cavalry regiment. In contrast to all these was what should have been the beginning of the present country life collections, a light wooden plough from Orkney, which has not survived.

Even at this early stage the Museum attracted information that was not only valuable in itself but also led to material additions, notably a letter along with a drawing sent in 1785 by an otherwise unknown Oxford scholar William Thomson. He recorded his visit to a man in Killin, who although only a day labourer was there the envied possessor of a Relic, the head of St Fillan's crozier. The letter with a later note pencilled on, both published in 1831, led directly to a search in Canada by Daniel Wilson, after which the last Scottish-born Dewar (Keeper) returned the relic in 1877 — to the Museum, 'there to remain in all time to come, for the use, benefit and enjoyment of the Scottish nation'. When the fourteenth-century silver reliquary was opened, the much older bronze head was found inside.

Many of the objects in the early donations were not, and often could not be, sufficiently described to be distinguishable from others of the same kind. The old markings for this purpose, alleged to have been changed in 1818 without cross-referencing, could have been paper numbers stuck on. For in the minutes each donation was given a number, perhaps when the first *Account* was being prepared in 1782 but starting from the beginning, and reaching 700 by June 1784. The system was continued till 1821, though omitted by the 1831 editor.

Soon after the first *Account* had been published an audit was made. A sub-committee of two was appointed to check what the Secretary had been doing. They were described as Curators, and this soon became a

D

regular office on the Council. They reported that 'Having made an exact and careful survey of every book, manuscript, medal, seal or other curiosity in the custody of Mr Cummyng, Secretary' they found all corresponded to the inventories, and 'the most minute article may be come at in a very short time'. They recommended that a more complete arrangement should be made, starting with the manuscripts and books, then coins by country beginning with Greek and Roman. There should be a separate printed inventory of 'other Effects', but this does not seem to have been done. They ended by advising that things should be shown to visitors 'on only one day a week, as the labour of the Secretary is daily increasing'.

An early gift of manuscripts, announced in Lord Buchan's annual Anniversary address but omitted from the donation list in the *Account*, consisted of 'thirteen volumes' of papers of the seventeenth century poet and writer William Drummond of Hawthornden and of his uncle William Fowler, secretary to James VI's queen, given by Dr Abernethy-Drummond. These have been deposited on loan in the National Library since 1934, along with many others of the Antiquaries' manuscripts; those from 1781-84 form in all 49 numbered lots, some quite bulky. There is an Antiphoner taken from Cadiz in the English raid of 1596, and two or three other religious works, one said by Buchan possibly to have come from Iona. A seventeenth-century Gaelic translation of Gordon's *Lilium Medicinae* (1574) was given by the Rev. Donald McQueen, who contributed a paper on it, never printed; apparently he thought the manuscript much older than it was. Henry Erskine, one of Buchan's advocate brothers, gave two volumes of MacFarlan of MacFarlan's collection of Scottish Airs, c. 1740. Volume I, recorded as given separately, has long been lost (p. 57). Lord Buchan tried to buy MacFarlan's 'collections on Scottish antiquities and natural history' (now the Geographical Collections) to keep them in Scotland, but found the price too high, and expressed satisfaction at their being bought by the Advocates. Less happy was the failure to obtain the mass of papers left by the author of *Diplomatum et Numismatum Scotiae Thesaurus*, James Anderson, which were stored in the attics of George Heriot's school, and which it seems have not been heard of since.

The number of early gifts among the very many charters, writs and other miscellaneous and formal documents deposited in 1935 in the Scottish Record Office has not been ascertained, partly because re-arrangement and binding in the early nineteenth century has altered the composition of lots not fully described on receipt: already in 1785 they were to be re-arranged by date and subject. One 'large collection of old Scots law deeds' went missing before 1820, when the Council inquired whether the executors of Alexander Jeffrey knew its whereabouts.

The selection of manuscripts retained as exhibits by the Museum also includes early donations. Such are a letter signed by Mary Queen of Scots, the large decorated copy of the National Covenant, 1638 and a plainer copy, a bound copy of the printed Solemn League and Covenant signed in Newbattle parish, 1643 (another copy seems to have long vanished), a Quartermaster's commission superscribed by Cromwell, Dr Pitcairn's elaborately illuminated diploma from the College of Aberdeen, 1699, and the Loyal Address of 102 heads of Highland clans and chief heritors to George I on his accession, which the Secretary of State for Scottish Affairs, the Earl of Mar, was prevented from presenting (given, along with a communication on the subject, by Lord Buchan). In short the initial manuscript donations to the Society go far to explain why members of the Faculty of Advocates, jealous for their much older library, joined in the protest against the Antiquaries' petition for a Royal Charter.

Source and date of donation are generally of rather less consequence for library volumes than for museum exhibits, for which pedigree is often a major part of their significance, and there are as yet no convenient lists to show the history of the older books now on the shelves of the joint library of the Society and the National Museum. There was no original marking system. Prints and drawings for which a magazine portfolio was to be bought in 1781, mainly of people and with a few portraits in oils, were a part of the library much encouraged by Lord Buchan. Having kept alive his advocacy of a national collection, the survivors now form part of the history of the National Portrait Gallery.

On the whole books were not collected for their own sake. Yet there were exceptions, as in later generations too. Most of these, together with books and pamphlets more strictly historical in the political sense than directly relevant to antiquities, were transferred outright to the other libraries about 1950 (see p. 204). From 1781-4 the National Library received three fifteenth-century items, nine sixteenth, and a first folio Shakespeare. A large part of the early gifts were naturally current or relatively recent works, often given by the authors. Those that were then relevant as being on natural history shaded off into purely medical, in line with the interests of some of the members. Thus Dr John Aitken gave five of his volumes, such as *Elements of the*

Theory and Practice of Surgery, and *Outlines of the Theory and Cure of Fever,* as well as a *Description of Double-shot Firearms,* the only one kept for the Museum. Fifty-five volumes, unspecified but probably in part to do with coins and medals, were bought in 1784 from the Society's bookseller, William Creech. He also donated volumes, among them Lord Kames's *Sketches of the History of Man,* handsomely bound in red Turkey (not traced), and Linnaeus' *Systema Naturae* and *Amoenitates Academicae.* By November 1783 there were said to be 292 volumes on the shelves.

Before coming to the natural history collection we must look at the beginnings of the other most numerous, but in the long run sadly maltreated collection, that of coins and historical medals. By 1783 it numbered 2,200, of which the majority had been listed, sometimes in detail. 'Proper caskets' were soon got for 'one of the largest drawers . . . for the reception of the more valuable coins'. Later the drawers were to be subdivided for coins by country and reign. The proposal that the President (the meeting chairman, not the titular nobleman) should keep the key, and that opening required the presence of two Vice-presidents, is unlikely ever to have been implemented — there was a distinct tendency to pass resolutions and not act on them.

Besides the quantity of miscellaneous coins, many of them foreign, given a few or one at a time, some groups of recently found hoards were received, notably two Roman (Fife and Linlithgow) and one Anglo-Saxon (Tiree), besides single coins from other Anglo-Saxon hoards (Orkney and N. Uist). More came from a William the Lion hoard at Dyke in Moray, James V and Mary from Corstorphine near Edinburgh, while unspecified and unlocalised hoards were doubtless represented by a hundred and twenty-three 'pennies Scots' of Charles I, and forty-nine of 'Edward I', listed by mint, with six of Alexander III and one Robert.

If any coins from these hoard groups retained their donation number, this was lost sooner or later. Neither the potential importance of such association, nor the detail of varieties and individual dies into which later numismatists would want to go, was even suspected. The ninety-six coins from Dyke were said to represent twenty-four varieties, and the bulk were considered to be useful for exchange — Buchan thought that in this way they might make the Society's series of Scottish coins complete — but there is no evidence that any were discarded till much later. The discrepancy between ninety coins from Tiree and sixty-four listed Anglo-Saxons present in 1831 has been thought simply due to loss. (After late nineteenth-century duplicate sales, and possibly some exchanges in 1831, fifty-three can more or less certainly be recognised.)

Another explanation might be provided by a minute of March 1783, when the Council decided to let Dr William Hunter (who however died that month) have duplicates from this series, no doubt in part return for the fine representation of Scottish coins he had given in 1781, one hundred and nine coins from William the Lion to Anne, twenty-four of them gold, with two dies of seventeenth-century royal privy seals. These formed in effect the nucleus of the Antiquaries' contribution to the present national collection. The Council then agreed in principle that other duplicates might be exchanged with the concurrence of the donors. They had also been considering buying from James Cummyng another collection of Scottish coins more than twice as large, proposing to give him a bond with yearly interest on it for them. This did not go through, as a posthumous auction catalogue shows. Cummyng read seven papers to the Society, one on prices of provisions in sixteenth-century Glasgow. Another, on the silver coins of the first four Jameses, dealt in particular with the groats that have an arched or imperial crown, a feature that interested him more than their remarkable Renaissance portrait, which he assigned to James IV rather than James II; only recently has James III at the end of his reign been wholly accepted as correct. Though Adam Cardonnel did not write on coins for the Society, Buchan claimed that his *Numismata Scotica* (1786) owed a great deal to their collection.

Ethnography was perhaps considered, as in some American museums today, as linked to natural history, for it is not easy to see what it had originally to do with the Society's concern with Scotland. Later the worldwide arts of mankind were retained for comparison with Scottish archaeology, with emphasis on stone and bone artefacts. Little other than the least perishable has indeed survived from the eighteenth century, so that only a fine Tahitian warrior's gorget, and reed pan-pipes from Tonga, remain with half a dozen imperishables out of the feathered finery, textiles and implements given in July 1781. The long descriptive entry in the *Account* records that they came from Captain Cook's last expedition (which had returned only nine months earlier) and had been given by his widow to the donor, Sir John Pringle, Bart., MD. Pringle (1707-82), who had recently returned to Edinburgh, was an important figure in the history of military medicine and had presented to Cook the gold medal of the Royal Society of

London (of which he was President) for his paper on anti-scurvy measures. He and Cook may have been linked by more than this shared interest; for James Cook senior, a farm labourer, came from Ednam in Roxburghshire, where he was a contemporary of Pringle's elder brothers at Stichill House nearby.

That the Society at first appreciated what they had been given appears from the Curators' report in July 1782: 'It is absolutely necessary that a Repository be fitted up without delay for the reception of a variety of articles lying in the Otaheite Room, which are gradually spoiling by being exposed to the air.' In addition to the Cook collection there would have been there a couple of bows from the Caribbean, three Chinese ladies' shoes, and 'several pieces of (American) Indian dress', shoes, garters, hose and a pouch, all decorated with coloured porcupine quills. A dozen gifts in the following four years were not notable, though there were three other Tahitian items from separate donors, and a Canadian 'iceboat' five feet long, which had to be painted before being left outside in winter — one hopes not with 'all its furnishings and tacklings . . . furnished with bells', yet sooner or later it all vanished like much of the rest.

The 'west room on the principal floor of the Museum' was to be fitted up with shelves and a glass case, sufficently commodious for 'the articles in natural history' which needed protection from dust. Lord Buchan added that the Secretary should provide proper phials for the better preservation of the animals in spirits. The jaws of a whale, 16 feet long, were set up as an arch on the slope beyond the house, forerunners of quite a number still to be seen around Scotland. By 1783 the Society had been given, as well as many lesser items, the jaws of a shark, five alligators up to $7\frac{1}{2}$ feet long, exotic birds, several recent monstrosities, and more significantly also six ancient stag and *bos primigenius* heads from different parts of Scotland which are still in the Museum. There were mineral and pebble collections, and a *hortus siccus* of six hundred Jamaican plants from Lord Buchan (passed on in 1870 to the Regius Professor of Botany). He also gave one of two smaller collections of 'Scots plants'.

So Smellie was quite justified in emphasising the size and visual impact of that part of the Antiquaries' Museum, even though the initial impetus was not kept up. He himself was, with Lord Buchan, the key figure in this development, and in its immediate important consequences. He was, further, much the most regular attender of Council meetings, along with the Secretary whom he later succeeded. Now in his early forties, Smellie was a man of remarkable diligence and attainments. As an apprentice printer in Edinburgh he had been given generous day-release, three hours daily, for university classes, and had attended all the medical classes, also chemistry and botany. Before setting up on his own in 1765 he edited the *Scots Magazine* for five or six years. He planned, compiled, and wrote much of the Dictionary of Arts and Sciences that was published in parts from 1771 — the three-volume first edition of the *Encyclopaedia Britannica*. Not a good business man, he lost the benefit of later editions by declining to produce the second, in 1776, because the proprietors insisted on introducing a system of general biography. His venture of publishing, and contributing to, the *Edinburgh Magazine and Review* was short-lived (1773-6), and ended in some acrimony. Shortly before that Smellie had unsuccessfully applied for the Regius Chair of Natural History at Edinburgh. He edited and printed various medical books, and as part of his regular business had for long a virtual monopoly of printing medical and legal theses, in Latin. Finally in 1782 there was published his adaptation and translation of Comte de Buffon's *Natural History of the Earth, and of Man and of Quadrupeds*, in eight volumes with engravings by Andrew Bell, who was also a regular attender of the Society's meetings and principal proprietor of the *Britannica*.

Lord Buchan had said little about natural history in his opening address, but he had sent Smellie a special invitation, primarily because of this interest:

> Although . . . the investigation of [Antiquities] appears at first to be a little out of your *beat*; yet as it is meant to widen the field of enquiry to the pursuits connected with it, whether natural, moral, or political; I beg leave, as a mark of the very high and well founded opinion I have of your literary talents, to invite you to make one of us on the 14th.

The early appointment to be Superintendent or Keeper of Natural History alongside the Secretary's responsibilities for all the collections may have been an afterthought, but it was an important part of Buchan's plan to have him publicise the Society's activities and edit its publications. In Smellie's view, 'to excite a taste for natural history' was a main reason for the plan for accounts of the parishes of Scotland which he edited in August 1781, and then printed and circulated for the Society; it was also published in the *Caledonian Mercury* (see p. 17). At the same time he read a paper to the Society 'on methods to be employed for the preservation of quadrupeds, birds, fishes, insects and plants'. Some of this, published by his biographer, makes clear that he had the practical aim of getting fresh specimens to the Museum in a suitable state for more complete conservation, and of showing the range of detailed observations that might come with them. However, this advice does not seem to have been published at the time, and did not result in any flow of material.

The Charter and natural history

Opposition to the granting of a Royal Charter to the new Society, and the consequent foundation of the Royal Society of Edinburgh in rivalry to it, stemmed largely from the natural history collection, and from the personal involvement with it of both Buchan and Smellie. This opposition, as documented in the 1784 *Account*, was most fully stated by Principal Robertson for Edinburgh University. He claimed that they had a Museum which contained those objects of natural history which were exhibited by the professor of the subject to his students; and that the Society's Museum would not only divert many specimens from it, but enable a lectureship in natural history to be instituted in opposition to the university's professorship. The University proposed instead a comprehensive Royal Society of Scotland, with a final proposition 'that whatever collection of antiquities, records, manuscripts shall be acquired by the Royal Society shall be deposited in the library of the Faculty of Advocates, and all the objects of natural history acquired by it, shall be deposited in the Museum of the University of Edinburgh'. Written support for these proposals came from 'some of the Curators of the Advocates' Library', confirmed by a large majority at a Faculty meeting. They rightly pointed out that their Library had 'for a century past been the general repository of ancient manuscripts and monuments illustrating the history and antiquities of Scotland'. They urged delay in the matter of the Antiquaries' charter, so as to ensure a Society which 'will promote inquiries regularly on history and antiquities, [but] may at the same time be conducted as not to interfere, in any degree, with the Advocates' Library'. The Philosophical Society of Edinburgh, which was planning to become the new Royal Society (which it did, bringing with it Smellie, but not Buchan, who resigned), also wrote a protest to the Lord Advocate. A further personal antagonism may have partly motivated the vice-president who signed it, William Cullen, one of the leading medical professors of his time, for he was known to have been extremely angered by an article by Smellie in the original *Britannica*.

From the Antiquaries' long reply it emerges that one root of this quarrel went back to when 'a spirited young nobleman' (identified elsewhere as Lord Buchan, then Lord Cardross, in 1766) gave a collection of natural objects to Edinburgh University. For this was afterwards sold by the late professor's executors, when 'most of the articles were purchased by a Russian and are irrecoverably lost to this country'. To make matters worse, it was declared that 'the College Museum is a very ominous repository', because earlier still it had been given the Museums of Sir Andrew Balfour and Sir Robert Sibbald, and 'neither of these two collections have now the vestige of existence'. The lectures to which the University objected were a series which Smellie hoped to deliver, preferably in the Society's Hall but on his own account, on lines said to be quite different from the University's course. (They were later written, and published in 1790-99 as the *Philosophy of Natural History*.) The Society claimed that its own Museum was open to the public, unlike the immensely valuable library of the Advocates, generous as the Faculty were to the public at all times. It also rejected the University's argument that in a 'narrow' country like Scotland, as already in others that were larger, a single Society was fully sufficient for all branches of science, erudition and taste. (Yet the same argument had been published by Smellie in his first *Account* to justify the Antiquaries' combination of natural history with antiquities.)

Faced with these conflicting proposals and personalities (with political undertones to which Dr Shapin has drawn attention), the Lord Advocate, Henry Dundas, recommended to the King that the Charter should be granted. It was signed on 29 March 1783 — and a charter instituting the Royal Society of Edinburgh on the same day. The objects of the Society of Antiquaries of Scotland were very briefly stated as the investigation of ancient things, and of natural and civil history in general, and the powers granted were almost equally wide; and in so far as the Monarch is perpetually Patron, the Society was, as it continues to be, a Royal one (Appendix, p. 275). There were, however, no provisions for any financial support from the Crown or Government. The Society as a chartered body was now entitled to buy its own house and borrow for the purpose, but its credit was in reality no greater than before. The idea of a petition to the Treasury for a grant, suggested by a Baron of Exchequer, does not seem to have been supported by other influential members. So Lord Buchan had to continue to be responsible in his own name.

Recession, 1787-93

It was natural that the initial flood of donations should peak in the second and third years of the Museum. The number of donors halved in the next two years, to still over one hundred in each and nearly 1,000 items, even if of lesser quality. This might have been a welcome period of consolidation, despite a further drop in number and interest in 1786. But the whole scene was to change dramatically for the worse in the course of a few years, leaving new men to hold on to the Museum while the ideas and ideals of the Founder were ultimately more often developed elsewhere.

The immediate cause was finance. Appeals and threats in Buchan's Anniversary Addresses, and circulars issued by the Council, failed to get half the necessary capital donations, or even to stimulate more members to pay their subscriptions. Already at the beginning of 1785 the Council had minuted that as 'funds would not allow the house to be cared for properly, it was expedient to ask Lord Buchan to sell it and rent a temporary house in the new town, until convenient and proper to purchase or build one in a situation safer and better than the present'. Alternatively some of the area in front of the Museum might be feued for building. It would get more difficult later to move out the collected 'effects'. Security as well as finance was seriously on their minds about then, without a specific reason being recorded. They noted that there was 'no defensive weapon in the Museum, to be used in case of an attempt on it by Housebreakers', and wished to recommend to the members that a blunderbuss and large pistols should be purchased; but they must have quickly had second thoughts, as the question was not put to the next meeting. Their other proposal was accepted, to pay half-a-crown annually to the fund for prosecution of housebreakers, 'the Rogue fund in this county'.

The Council, despairingly it would seem, almost gave up meeting in 1786, and left the Founder to shed as best he could the £600 outstanding bank loan and the mounting costs. Intimation came in January 1787 that the house and grounds had been sold at a considerable loss, for £765, with entry at Whitsun. (The purchaser was Patrick Heron of Heron, who had given several Roman coins to the Museum five years earlier, and owned an inn in Glasgow. He transformed the place into the 'British Inn', which after some ten years gave way to a printing house before being demolished about 1830.) Several members of Council quickly went to inspect an empty house near the head of the

Cowgate. They reported that it was commodious and could be bought or rented. Buchan optimistically told the meeting that he had applied to the Duke of Hamilton for apartments in the Palace of Holyroodhouse to accommodate the Society, but nothing more was heard of this. Next month, after it had been agreed to rent a house on the west side of Milne's Square, several other houses were visited. A house on the front Land of Chessel's Buildings — a flat looking on to the upper part of the Canongate from the south — was considered to be 'as proper as any that was to let in the old Town at present', and the decision was left to Buchan, Little, and Smellie. In May its lease was fixed, for three years at 30 guineas. Living space required for the Secretary may have been less than before, as Mrs Cummyng had died in 1785 and one son at least was grown up. (He had run a 'minor society of antiquaries' at the Museum in 1783-85, of which the minute book is in the Bodleian Library.) In June the removal of the Museum was advertised in the newspapers; and the Council discussed what was to be a recurrent theme, of prosecuting members 'residing in Town who are in arrears to the funds'.

Just when they learned that they had to move, the Council were embarrassed by the arrival from Sweden of a granite boulder 5½ feet high, an eleventh-century tombstone incised with runes on a shackled serpent surrounding a large cross. It was a gift from A. B. (later Sir Alexander) Seton, the heir of a Stockholm merchant. They sought the advice of a marble cutter on the practicability of having the face sliced off. Evidently this was not feasible, for it is still complete (p. 57). In the following month two large gilt brooches from Caithness came with other ornaments, found in a Viking woman's grave, recorded as intruded into the ruins of a Pictish house (in fact a broch). Two years later another pair came from Islay.

Altogether 1787 was a year notable for those links with Scandinavian archaeology and archaeologists which were to be strengthened in later generations. For there was also a visit from Professor Thorkelin, who had 'explored this country for many months at the desire of the Antiquarian Society of Copenhagen in order to collect accounts of all the Norwegian and Danish remains to be found here', and who had discovered several hitherto undescribed Danish [iron age?] forts while on a tour of the northern coasts and western isles with George Dempster of Dunnichen. Stimulated by a communication from Dempster on the present state of Gaelic poetry in the western Highlands, a forerunner of a literary phase in the Society, the Council wrote to the ministers of the Synod of Glenelg asking them 'to write down from the recital of the old Bards these songs in the Gaelic language'. They asked for them to be transmitted to the Society, addressed to George Dempster MP. It does not appear than any came, in spite of his right of free postage.

Lord Buchan in his annual address in 1787 referred to these matters, and to the relief from heavy public taxes and bank interest as a result of the move. A lessened commitment to natural history is shown by the suggestion to 'learned correspondents proposing to send valuable specimens' that they should 'in so far as they do not come within our plan' present them to the University of Edinburgh in the Society's name, for the instruction of students. He spoke too of a 'prospect of combining with other public bodies to erect a new building for their permanent and proper accommodation'. More positively, past papers selected for publication were now being prepared for the press.

The first volume of *Transactions* when it finally appeared was dated 1792, but unrecorded in the minute book. The agreement with William Creech was that he should be publisher, but that the Society retain the copyright. A handsome volume of 570 pages, it contained a very short version of the *Accounts*, two long accounts of parishes (see p. 17), and forty-six papers, a dozen relevant to the Museum. More than a quarter of the papers had been delivered in the new premises despite the cancellation of a number of meetings from 1788 onwards, and attendances as low as half a dozen. There were no lists of donations or of communications. Silent intimation was given, to anyone who read the lists of members and office-bearers attentively, that Lord Buchan was no longer first Vice-President.

The evidence of what exactly led to the Founder's resignation from the Society in November 1790 is lost with the several letters exchanged that summer. One may infer that there had been a growing uneasiness among members that the Society was financially no less dependent upon Buchan than it had been before the house was sold. While many stayed away, those who remained most involved came, it seems, to feel that his very individual methods of sponsorship were no longer worth the disadvantages, both within the Society and in the impression they made on outsiders. The correspondence in 1790 began in February with a request that the Earl should account for the sums in his keeping belonging to the Society, starting with the £500 believed present in 1783. In March Buchan came and presented a general accompt of the state of the funds, without vouchers which were 'in the country'. What they covered is not stated, but presumably at least the house sale in 1787 and his expenditure out of the balance left following the repayment of the £600 loan from the £750 received; he had been paying, under pressure, rent on the premises in Chessel's Buildings, now due again. Of Buchan's letters that followed the reference of this account to the auditors, it is only known that in the last one he advised that members in arrears with their subscriptions should indeed be sued for them. The active members of Council who received this were highly responsible people, who had been office-bearers for ten years, including Smellie and William Tytler of Woodhouselee, WS. With the few other members able or willing to attend a subsequent business meeting, they were clearly in varying degrees fed up with the way the Earl was dealing with the finances. They had thought, apparently, to put further pressure on him to have things straightened out, by taking his advice so literally as to have Buchan himself sent the lawyer's letter for all in arrears.

When Samuel Hibbert and David Laing in 1831 published their sequel to the 1784 *Account*, they stated in a footnote that Buchan 'was treated unquestionably with anything but the consideration to which as the Founder, and principal benefactor of the Society, he was in common courtesy entitled'. Unfortunately they not only failed to take into consideration the immediate background, but in trying to find instead of 'petty jealousies' a serious enough case for the rift, they assumed that there must have been a real demand not just for one guinea but for a special £20 per annum which Buchan had, on unfulfilled conditions, offered and allowed to be minuted eight years before, and which was certainly still remembered. It seems more consistent with the strong feelings roused on both sides to suggest that the rift was over the proper accounting and management of the balance of the Society's capital, and because some of it was believed still due. Buchan indeed paid two further instalments of rent after his resignation was accepted. There is no sign in the minutes of the 'trifling or factious spirit' alleged in 1831, when the persistent efforts to keep the Museum together were underestimated.

Unsatisfactory premises away from the growing New Town were one major hindrance to attendance at the meetings, and to attracting new members, or donations of any consequence for the Museum and library. In the next two and a half years the most notable gift was from Sir John Sinclair, 'a specimen' of the *Statistical Account*, which, in a way, the Society had inspired. Sir John, now a Vice-President, also came himself to propose that application should be made to the King for a moderate annuity. A delegation was planned, to write and speak about it to the Duke of Montrose, who had newly agreed to become titular President. But at this point, in the summer of 1792, all activities ceaséd owing to the Secretary's illness, followed by his death in January.

A letter by Smellie in April, replying to an enquiry from Buchan, relates the next moves:

> After the decease of our late Secretary, Mr Fergusson of Craigdarroch and Mr John Dundas were the only Antiquarians who appeared to look after the interests of the Society. Along with Mr Robert Bell WS, who was Mr Cummyng's agent, we sealed every repository that contained any of the effects belonging to the Society. Immediately after the interment, we procured a meeting of the Council, who ordered me in case of accident, to carry the cabinet of coins etc to my own house, where they now lie under lock and key; and, what is a better security, they are four stories high, and the stair is at least an angle of 60 degrees; so much the worse for my poor limbs.
>
> At a subsequent meeting of the Council I was elected Secretary to the Society; and was empowered to hire the house, and a noble one for the purpose, built by Mr Home Rigg, at the foot of Gossfords close, Lawn-market, behind which is an excellent little area, for receiving the *runic* stones, and such heavy articles. That house is now hired, or taken, as we say, and the entry is to be at Whitsunday next.
>
> I have now given, my Lord, a concise and, I hope, a satisfactory account of the Society of Antiquaries of Scotland. I shall only remark upon the whole, that the present is the crisis of the *fever*. I shall exert all my powers; and I am happy to find that many of our most respectable members exhibit an unusual keenness. Your Lordship's exertions, I am confident, will not be withdrawn.

Holding on, 1793-1813

Sadly, however, Smellie's powers were failing, and the basic struggles to keep the Society alive and its collections housed were to be very long drawn out. While these were unresolved, meetings sometimes ceased, and collecting was even more inhibited. The extreme span of the interests which it had been trying to foster meant that there was insufficient support and follow-through for the few intellectual tasks occasionally put forward. It should not be forgotten, too, that the times were unpropitious. Already in 1782 Lord Buchan in his Address had stressed that they were 'cultivating the Arts of Peace and Tranquillity in the midst of a dangerous and expensive War', and looking back the writers of the 1831 *Account* noted the growing inconvenience of the Old Town situation, and suggested that 'The volunteering system and the agitated state of the country in general in regard to the threatened French Invasion, had the effect of withdrawing people's minds in a great degree from scientific pursuits of every description'. They might have added 'in regard to politics': Thomas Muir, advocate, elected member in 1787 and Curator for the next year, was transported for sedition in 1793.

William Smellie's biographer recorded that he 'was much indisposed for a considerable time before his death, and bore his illness with the utmost patience'. By 1793 he was 'suffering from a feebleness in my limbs and want of an appetite', so he 'took a room at the Citadel of Leith and bathed my limbs in sea water a very little heated'; but his digestion grew worse and in May 1794 he wrote, 'my former debilitated limbs are hardly able to support my small tabernacle. My drink is port, or rather port and water'. He died in June 1795.

His son Alexander, formally associated for a few weeks as Assistant Secretary, then began what was to be nearly thirty years continuously as Secretary of the Society, with a reappearance much later. He succeeded to the printing business, and to the 'use of the Society's house'; the 'key of the Museum', temporarily removed, was returned. He was voted ten pounds a year, which his father had had, 'for coal and candles'. 'The small room adjoining the Museum' was to be fitted up with shelves, a carpet, table and two chairs, 'for the reception of the Society's books', which sounds as if William had kept them beside his own.

This house was the fourth to be occupied by the Society. It will be clearer if at this point the tales of accommodation and finance are mainly told separately, before we scan the collection of things and information. After Cummyng's death at Chessel's Buildings a move had been made to another flat, at the bottom of Gosford's Close off the Lawnmarket; the upper part of Victoria Street now runs across the site, opposite the National Library. It was 'more convenient' though still in the Old Town and at nearly twice the rent — £50, plus £5 for 'damage to walls by hanging up the Society's Effects'. Just over a year later in March 1794, with rent outstanding for two houses, it was decided 'that a house be bought for the accommodation of their curiosities etc, as this would save them from being destroyed in moving them from place to place'. A house 'in the Castle Hill lately possessed by Mr Rae, surgeon, would be very convenient' and 'the money might be got on the subject'. Built about 1740 uphill from his manse by the Rev. Dr Alexander Webster (famous for his census of

Scotland in 1755) for occupation as a banking house by William Hogg, it was on the south side of the present approach to the Esplanade just above the Tolbooth Kirk. After twice raising their bid over the 'upset price of £550' in the traditional — and continuing — Scots practice, the agreed price was £630, 'to include income from an insurance' (£4 p.a.). There was some open ground at the back of the property, approached through the 'outer gate' which had later to be repaired. Immediate repairs to window frames were required, as well as some wright work and white washing of the passages. passages.

Remarkably, perhaps, the Society stayed at Castle Hill for twenty years, with periods of suspended animation, to be roused again by financial pressure. Due credit must be given to those who did not give up in 1793-5, and then held on. Soon after Cummyng died the landlord at Chessel's Buildings got a sequestration order on the collections, 'the Effects'. An urgent Council meeting gathered guarantees from four of those present, which allowed money to be borrowed to pay off arrears of rent, and move. Some months later a vexatious prosecution was raised against the Society on behalf of Cummyng's heirs, groundlessly claiming £1,200 as twelve years' salary unpaid. Sir John Sinclair was asked to revive the approach to the Government, for an annual £100, but it is not clear how far this went; and William Smellie, having reported as Secretary that most of the members had 'refused' to pay their subscriptions, tried in a circular letter to stem desertions with a patriotic call and to 'inlist fresh troops'. Whether or not his tone was right for the times, one might have thought it better to wait till the further move to Castle Hill, already being negotiated, could be mentioned and used as a stimulus.

The Council, including John Dundas WS and Gilbert Innes of Stow, who were mainstays throughout many years, met in May with the outgoing and incoming Lord Provosts of Edinburgh, both members from early days — Thomas Elder, wine merchant and sometime Postmaster General of Scotland, and Sir John Stirling, banker. They discussed finance, underwrote a credit of £100, and adjourned for six months for the accounts to be investigated and the removal completed. At the Museum in November 1794 those four and four others agreed to raise funds on their personal security to pay off over £800, but the 'bill of £100' was to be kept unexpended. For their repayment the Society would pledge its 'whole moveable effects and property'. The next regular meeting was held (uniquely) in a tavern, the Douglas in Anchor

Close, presumably with a dinner — there is rarely evidence for the Society's convivial side, initiated by Lord Buchan. It was agreed that members should be visited personally by Council, and the election of fresh troops began. At forty-seven in the next five years, those elected were more numerous than in the previous eleven, or in the following fifteen: no fewer than five Dundases including the Lord Advocate, Robert Dundas of Arniston, a high proportion of other lawyers, among them Walter Scott, and several other young men who were to be key figures of the later truer revival. By the end of 1795, £800 had been borrowed from the Edinburgh Friendly Insurance Society and presumably spent; the process in the Court of Session against unpaying members was in doubt and would be dropped; reinstatement without payment of arrears would be allowed.

It is not known how well the annual guineas came in (life membership twelve guineas, entrance two), and though in 1800 'the cash book was being kept very correctly by the Secretary', by 1805 the £40 interest on the loan was two years in arrears, the disposition of the house had not yet been registered, and £45 was still owing to Innes and Dundas for payments in 1796 and 1803. So they and four others advanced £100. (This may have been an episode in the life of the 1794 bill of credit, stated in 1812 to have been 'repeatedly renewed and lies at present in the Royal Bank'.) It was soon overspent, while Alexander Smellie agreed to give up (for the present) the ten guineas p.a. for heat etc. Two years later annual income was reported as £50 or £60, including the £4 from the Friendly Society insurance (share), subscription arrears £172, debt £114 additional to the whole principal of the house-loan. When in 1810 a demand for over £30 for taxes was considered, the Council decided that (until the Society was flourishing again) the Secretary would have to pay a proportion. A letter to the Duke of Montrose, the titular president, about procuring an annual sum from His Majesty, was considered in draft but probably not sent. Soon the Secretary was asked for a rent of £25 plus tenant's taxes, to begin at Whitsun 1811, but this was balanced later by £25 for salary, coals, candles and cleaning. The annual deficits were now small, yet the total debt was large and the taxes heavy.

The impetus provided by the 1794 crisis did not last long — in the years 1808-13 only two papers were read and 31 donations of any kind received. Yet the whole period had not been quite fruitless. After the standstill of two and a half years during which William Smellie had moved the collections twice, a trickle of books and coins had started to

E

come in before his death. Alexander succeeded to the responsibilities for the collections and, 'once the Museum was properly arranged', was to open it for three hours one day a week, when any friends might be brought. He seems to have been more of a caretaker than a keeper. A succession of supervising Curators was appointed, but the office of Superintendent of Natural History was left vacant for several years till John Graham Dalyell was elected at the age of thirty. Though a lifelong naturalist in addition to historical writer, he apparently continued a policy of not seriously adding to that side of things, yet retained the office for most of the thirteen years that he was a Vice-President, from 1805.

Two notable antiquities were early received. One is the Covenanters' flag carried at Bothwell Brig and then, refurbished, briefly in Edinburgh in 1745. The second indicates that the Museum was not cramped, and was now thought viable enough for the Lord Provost and Magistrates of Edinburgh to pass on what Lord Buchan had written asking for in 1781 and probably again in 1789 — The Maiden, Scotland's beheading machine of 1564, unused since 1697, so that in 1797 its move to the Museum was perhaps a symbolic contrast to recent Terror elsewhere. Scott's first, and for many years only, attendance was for the donation. In line with the original, and present, policy of the Museum a series of newly struck specimens and a pair of dies of 'provincial halfpennies' and other tokens, with a communication on them, were accepted from James Wright junior. He had himself designed and had them made, when what one might call the medallic souvenir craze coincided with the shortage of small change at the end of the eighteenth century. Thereafter donations became fewer and of less interest, except the Gown of Repentance from West Calder. 'About 108' base-metal coins of Queen Mary, with no location, was the first gift from the Barons of Exchequer, exercising in 1808 the Scottish Crown's claim to ownerless things, rather than only treasure in the strictest sense as in England.

There is not much evidence of the activity of the successive pairs of Curators over these years, other than their being provided with keys when Sir George Steuart Mackenzie of Coull was one in 1800 (the time when, only twenty years old, he discovered the chemical identity of diamond and carbon). A suggestion that at each meeting 'part of the curiosities' should be examined 'in the order of the catalogue', with the original description read, was only once followed. Dr James Miller, already probably preparing the 4th edition of the *Encyclopaedia*

Britannica, tried to get the books catalogued, but whether the special committee of nine, including Constable and Scott, ever met is not evident. A catalogue, however, was to be compared with the books eighteen months later, in 1808, before the Secretary was given the key. Earlier it was agreed that a regular catalogue of manuscripts should be made, and the policy that they should not be borrowed was restated. Yet in 1806 a member of Council was granted extension of the loan of one volume of MacFarlan's musical collection; by 1819 it was being pursued in vain.

A paper unusual in being relevant to the Museum was passed on from the Literary and Antiquarian Society of Perth in 1798 — an observant typological discussion by the Rev. John Dow of stone and 'brass' *celts* in which they are, as we know, correctly arranged, and the functions of the thin butt of the bronze axe and its stop-ridge are deduced. It is interesting that he mentions examples of varied kinds of find-association and refers to other countries of northern and western Europe. Most communications in the decade to 1807 were historical or, predominantly, literary and linguistic. It was a time when a few members, with an extreme episcopalian the Rev. Donald Macintosh as prime mover, discussed Gaelic poetry and the authenticity of Ossian in a dozen papers, and co-operated with the Highland Society of London under Sir John Sinclair in publishing Macpherson's 'originals'; and when the pioneer linguist Professor Alexander Murray spread his account of the history and language of the Picts over five meetings, Macintosh had earlier written about some 'druidical' stone circles in the Highlands, and presented a wooden pot-hook, already a rarity.

A committee optimistically set up 'to survey the antiquities of the city of Edinburgh' had its single report presented by Dalyell in 1802. This may have stimulated a new member, the Board of Ordnance's Store-keeper at the Castle, to take 'the very great trouble' to move the Runic Stone, after seventeen years at Chessel's Buildings, to the 'area behind the Society's house'.

Revival with the Geologists, 1813-26

Early in 1813 the future pattern of sharing a building with a kindred body was set. The Society moved to the New Town following an offer from the Royal Society of two south rooms on the bedroom storey of 42 George Street for Library and 'Cabinet', and the use of its hall for meetings. Laing commented in 1831 that, as he remembered it, with Urquhart the perfumer on the ground floor and a common stair, neither Society can have been very flourishing. In fact the Royal Society was itself making a new start. It had acquired the property in 1810, when compelled to leave its rooms in the College because of a fundamental quarrel with the University. This was over the use of the Hutton geological collection, lost to it at a time when geological theory was central to its activity and to its new scientific reputation; a revised charter to allow it to hold its own collections was obtained in 1811.

The catalyst for change at the Antiquaries was evidently Sir George S. Mackenzie, though this is not brought out in the 1831 *Account.* At the end of 1812 he rejoined the Society after an absence of five years, during which he had travelled and published on Iceland and Faroe. He then appears as the Royal Society's representative in the negotiations, along with Thomas Allan, banker, and a notable mineralogist like himself. With John Dundas and Gilbert Innes for the Antiquaries was Henry Jardine, King's Remembrancer at the Exchequer. It was agreed that the Antiquaries should pay £42 rent for a minimum of five years, to include fire, the services of the porter, and cleaning and painting the rooms. Moving and fitting up was paid for by the Antiquaries. Though the Secretary quickly moved out his own furniture, shifting the collections may have taken much longer, for there was an unexplained six month's delay in considering an offer of £600 for the old house, which was then accepted with immediate entry.

In December, in 'the Museum', Mackenzie was elected senior Vice-President and took the Chair. He also became a Curator along with Andrew Coventry, professor of agriculture in the university, with Dalyell still in charge of natural history. Smellie ceased to be acting Treasurer, and was joined as Secretary by John Jamieson DD, author of the Scottish Dictionary, who seems later to have been given chief credit for the Society's revival; this may well have been justified in the matter of stimulating and editing communications. The revival flagged somewhat after a few years, at least as far as the Museum was concerned, but soon got its second wind, as we shall see.

The sale of the house and its insurance had netted nearly £750. Debts, including what was by then an overdraft in the Royal Bank, amounted to £1,048. All were to be paid off except £350, part of the loan from the Friendly Insurance still retained on the security of the 'Obligants in the Bond' of 1794, to whom the pledge of moveable effects and property was renewed; five years later the accounts in the hands of one of them, Gilbert Innes, had still not been cleared up.

In December 1815 new statutes and bye-laws were adopted, which are in essence still in force. Apart from a general tightening of the formulation, the most substantial changes were to reduce the number of vice-presidents and secretaries, abolish censors and the class of associated artists, restrict honorary members to twenty-five, and provide for failure to pay fees. The number of ordinary members was unlimited and of corresponding members unspecified. Instead of two Curators and a Superintendent, a committee of the Council was to have custody of the 'property of the Society'; in practice this was a weakness, and a single Curator was appointed from 1822. The Secretary's primary responsibility for the Museum had evidently faded.

While the statutes were being rewritten, various moves were made toward bringing the Society to wider notice. A letter to the clergy was prepared for printing, asking them to communicate even short notices on remains of antiquity, ancient writings capable of throwing light on the general and local history of Scotland, etymology of names illustrating parochial antiquity, manners and customs. Further, Mackenzie stressed the importance of establishing a connection with learned societies abroad, particularly with Denmark from which there had come a volume of the Royal Commission for Antiquities. Count Bedemar was then elected an honorary member; by 1815 this had been reciprocated by Mackenzie's being made an honorary member of the Copenhagen Antiquaries, who sent nine stone and bronze artefacts for the Museum. Another contact was established by the receipt of the first Report of the Newcastle Antiquaries. Arrangements were started too for publishing a first part of the second volume of *Transactions*, but apparently an agreement with Constable fell through.

Although Laing in 1861 withdrew the suggestion, made in the 1831 *Account*, that neglect by Cummyng had caused the loss of no inconsiderable part of the Museum (and in 1843 overcame his doubts over the care of the Hawthornden manuscripts), he did not modify the strictures that at the removal in 1813 the Museum continued to receive no degree of attention whatever, that no means of finding accommodation for it had been resorted to, and that it might soon have been forgotten but for some later efforts. While doubtless things were stowed away *en masse* on arrival at George Street, and the problems were underestimated, the rooms which had been rented (other than the share of the hall) were specifically for the collections, and these had been reviewed beforehand. For the minutes of the Council that authorised the final negotiations go on: 'a number of articles which were in a perishing state to be given away gratis, viz. a number of bottles containing objects of natural history, alligators, horns, an old gown, velvet bag etc etc'. (These sound like the Lord Treasurer's robe and purse given in 1783.) A year later Mackenzie asked for a committee to help him 'to complete the arrangement of the Books and Museum', because he could not do this by himself as he intended to leave town soon; Dalyell, Innes, Allan (now an Antiquary), Jardine and the Treasurer were appointed, to meet weekly, two to be a quorum. After nine months Mackenzie and the first three of the committee were appointed along with three others — one being Dr Brunton, minister of the Tron Kirk and professor of oriental languages — to 'examine such articles in the Museum which might appear useless and which of course ought to be removed'. There is no further report or evidence of what was discarded in those years, and while most was probably trivial natural history specimens, some may have been deteriorated ethnographical material, always very vulnerable in museum purges.

Mackenzie did not hand in his key of the Museum until October 1815, when he wrote to the Society's solicitor about minor matters, and told him of his 'determination not to hold any office in the Society, tho' I shall be ready to give any assistance in my power'. He does not explain why but adds that this 'will I hope ultimately be for the good of the Society, tho' I am still of the opinion that it ought to break up'. He became a Vice-President again three years later, having continued to be a regular attender, councillor and selector of papers for publication, and the significance of his last phrase is not known.

It can hardly refer simply to the component parts of the collections, but conceivably to a merger with the Royal Society, once mooted tentatively many years earlier. As in London, there were quite a number of members common to both bodies — some two dozen in the early 1820s, when the Royal numbered just under 200 and the Antiquaries' ordinary members probably many fewer. All through this period it seems that the Royal's Literary Class as such was dormant compared with the Physical Class, though still continuing to have office-bearers of its own,.including some leading Antiquaries, and that members of both classes used the Antiquaries as an outlet for the less scientific side of their interests, some already before the Societies shared a house. Such in the Physical Class were David Brewster, even before his researches into light were at their height in his early thirties or his subsequent guiding Secretaryship of the Royal from 1819, Patrick Neill the printer and, rather later, Robert Stevenson of the lighthouses, while Dr

Andrew Duncan senior, professor of the theory of physic, an original Antiquary, was a fairly frequent attender for two decades from 1807. Prominent Antiquaries in the Literary Class were Henry Jardine, John Jamieson and Alexander Brunton. Another way of judging the membership of the Antiquaries at this time is to note that although there might have been twenty or fewer at a meeting, between a quarter to a third of these appear in the *Dictionary of National Biography.*

Rather few donations were recorded from 1813 to 1818. Among them were a coin of Henry VIII forwarded officially by Jardine from the Exchequer, two prehistoric urns given by Lord Buchan from separate finds, the Danish prehistoric specimens already mentioned, and the popular but perhaps apocryphal Jenny Geddes' stool. Good drawings of inscribed Roman altars at Birrens, Dumfriesshire, were received, and also an illustrated account of the Ruthwell Cross and its runes. John Stuart, professor of Greek in Aberdeen and a corresponding member, reported briefly on the subterraneous habitations — now known as souterrains — near Kildrummy. Worried by the need 'to prevent the total loss and destruction of our remaining monuments of antiquity', he suggested that a small sum of money 'might be collected sufficient to defray the expenses of two or three well qualified persons' or even two or three active young men, 'who might perambulate the whole of Scotland in the course of one or two summers, and make out correct drawings and descriptions of them, to be afterwards either published or deposited in their archives'.

One of the urns given by Buchan, a 'food-vessel' in modern terms, was the starting point of a paper in 1815 by Dr Jamieson on Ancient Sepulture, which ranged over classical and other literary references but also recorded finds from various places in Scotland, and considered, on the basis of the material evidence, whether there were two *ages* in Britain (his italics), characterised by inhumation and cremation, perhaps respectively Pictish and Celtic. Jamieson also wrote about sites of castles in Forfarshire, and on the vitrified fort at Finavon. These papers were among those published in 1818 along with older ones, including the 1783 Inveresk excavation report and the typological discussion of 'celts' of 1797. This was *Transactions* II, 1, of 288 pages, edited by Jamieson, sold to members for a guinea and a half.

The second stage of the revival was already under way. It began soon after James Skene of Rubislaw, advocate and geologist, joined the Society, and it coincided with the return to office of Sir George Mackenzie. In 1817 several of the periodic Council meetings failed to get a quorum, but a new committee for arranging the Museum may have met, consisting of Mackenzie, Brewster, and James Haig, a merchant. Late in 1818 another committee was appointed, with no minuted explanation, 'to look out for a house to the Society'. The reason is unlikely to have been financial, as the cash balance at the time was £60, with subscription arrears of £51 9s 0d. On Dalyell's then retiring from his long vice-presidency, warmly thanked for his un-remitting zeal and attention to the Society's affairs, Mackenzie became third Vice-President. The next ordinary meeting next month, with Mackenzie in the chair, decided that though a house in Frederick Street was available at £50 p.a. it was not expedient to move. A committee of five, quite new except for Allan, was also appointed to arrange the Museum and make a catalogue under Skene as convener; thanks were voted it two months later. The 1831 Account says that Skene spent about six months of nearly daily attendance, but that he was perplexed by 'the old markings of a great proportion of the collection having been removed for the purpose of substituting new ones; to which a table of reference had either not been prepared, or, if it had been prepared, had soon disappeared'. However, the accession numbers in the Minute Book continue uninterrupted till 1820, when they jump from 1336 to 3337, presumably on the introduction of a new system. Late next year they stop entirely, at 3356. Purchases had never been included, and at this period it was the rule that there should be none.

At the end of 1819 Skene's committee was reappointed. The use of a third room was soon granted by the Royal Society; their Museum too was curated by Allan, succeeded by Skene. A long report by Skene to the Antiquaries was minuted in full, though without its lists. He explained that:

> As inconveniences arising from the disorder into which the Society's collections had fallen are likely to be most experienced from the inaccessible nature of the library, I was induced to make the books the first subject of arrangement . . . and [now] present a complete catalogue of all the books actually in possession in alphabetical order both of authors and subject, and shelf references; also donors as far as ascertained from the minute book.

Skene's catalogue does not survive. Manuscripts that were bound, and as many of the loose papers as could be arranged in volumes were to be added by John Dillon, soon to succeed Jamieson as Secretary; later Brewster helped him. Books had not been protected by any distinctive mark, and there had been an unaccountable relaxation of rules in recent years. Another list, 'very long, a sort of obituary of books that are not', included 'some of the most valuable'; Skene proposed that it should be circulated in order to recover them. He also proposed that 'books foreign to our researches should be exchanged . . . we might at least establish a respectable nucleus instead of the meagre and hetero-geneous assemblage that now cumber our shelves of Law, Medicine, Midwifery and all sorts of rubbish'. The usefulness of the library was soon being increased by publications of other societies, to whom Trans-actions were being sent — from the Society of Antiquaries of Copen-hagen (1822), from the Society of Antiquaries of London all their 'ex-pensive and splendid works' (1824) — in addition to the series already begun from the Newcastle Antiquaries and, much earlier, from the American Philosophical Society, Philadelphia (1802) and the Asiatic Society (exchange stopped 1825).

Skene next turned to the collection of coins and medals, 'which con-sists of Scottish and English Coins pretty complete, Roman, Greek, a mass of foreign coins of most of the European nations, and a few Oriental, with a collection of Medals commemorating particular events. Considerable progress has been made in the general arrange-ment of the whole [the coins numbering about 4,500], but the only series which is completed, with a descriptive catalogue, is the Scottish'. Skene listed the Scottish denominations not represented, balanced by a summary of 492 which were 'duplicates' according to the elementary standards of the time, which 'may be used as a fund of barter for those coins wanted to complete the collection, or [preferably] sold for the same purpose'. This disaster did not take place till fifty years later, though three sixteenth-century 'dollars' were exchanged in 1823 for a 'half-guinea' of Charles I.

The coin report, catalogue and lists were printed in *Transactions* II.2 (1822), in which there was reprinted from the *Edinburgh Philosophical Journal* (edited by Brewster) a full account of the Society's 1821-22 session, containing extracts from the report 'in the hopes that it may be the means of obtaining some of those deficiencies'. Brewster's account added a sort of manifesto on the aims of the Society and its Museum: '. . . subjects of antiquity . . . when collected together supply a very valuable record of ancient manners and history, offering facilities to antiquarian research . . . The importance of ancient coins, *and the par-ticular circumstances under which they may be found* [my italics], are only valuable when collected into a series, as evidences of ancient history'.

This second half of the *Transactions* vol. II has many more illustrations than the first, fifteen compared to four, most of them engraved by W. H. Lizars, who was a member. One is of the Swedish stone and its runes (p. 49 above), at last provenanced as from Lilla Ramsjø i Vittinge, in Uppland; by then it was at or near its present position north of the Esplanade. Others illustrate Jardine's report as Remembrancer on the opening of Robert the Bruce's tomb at Dunfermline, including prominently the inscribed coffin-plate, which was a hoax, but not a small carved head or several fragments of alabaster also given to the Museum. Further papers and illustrations show the Society attracting records of fieldwork: sculptured stones in the North East with a discussion of their 'so often repeated symbols', a plan (only) of the entrenchment — a henge — at Contin, Ross-shire, a map of Largs as the site of the battle, in a long historical paper, and a range of medieval tomb sculpture. A useful comparative study dealt with cross-slabs and runes in the Isle of Man. Less satisfactory is an account of howking in the theatre at Milo, from which a half-ton Parian marble cornice is stated to have been presented to the Edinburgh Museum, as the University's Museum was then sometimes called. (Lord Elgin, elected President a couple of years later, had nothing to do with it.)

The 1822 *Transactions* were prefaced by a copy of a revised circular for the Parochial Ministers of Scotland: the Society was 'desirous of obtaining information regarding the National Antiquities . . . If drawings could be obtained of such objects as may be particularly interesting, it would make the Memoirs more acceptable'. Ancient writings and place-names were also asked about. The last sentence brings in a notable addition: 'I take the opportunity to mention that the Barons of Exchequer, for the purpose of preserving the remains of Antiquity, have signified their intention of allowing the value of such Coins, and other articles of Gold and Silver, as may be discovered, and transmitted to their Lordships.' Sadly this major concession in Treasure Trove administration seems in practice to have been withdrawn, and did not have any significant result until revived later (see also p. 72). A 'golden rod' found near Inverness was exhibited to the Society in 1824 by the Remembrancer, but not seen again.

Such exhibitions of antiquities, ethnographical objects and documents, in addition to what was being donated, were becoming a useful custom. Notes on some of them and their associations, and on other prehistoric and later discoveries and sites, with or without donations of finds, were indeed a feature of the following years — some came from parish ministers, presumably due to the circulated letter, some resulted from the growth of Edinburgh's New Town. (Between 1823 and 1827 one of the Secretaries was specifically responsible for obtaining communications for the meetings, and preparing them for publication; he was Samuel Hibbert, another geologist-antiquary, with a medical degree.) Temporary exhibition was not infrequently a first step to acquisition for the Museum, possibly long afterwards, and in the interval helped to ensure inclusion in Wilson's *Prehistoric Annals* (1851). Similarly, the Anglo-Saxon drinking-horn mount from Burghead, Moray, was given in 1861 after a drawing was shown in 1826. *Transactions* III.1 (1828), in which it was illustrated, was exchanged more widely than the previous part, to Norway and France, Dublin and Inverness. Notices of archaeological donations then included jet ornaments (parts of an early bronze-age set of spacer-plate necklace and bracelet) from a grave at Assynt in Ross-shire, and 'apparently plates of copper armour' (three later bronze-age razors) from near Dunbar.

These were discoveries made during agricultural improvements. In contrast, two notices (from the same writers) mark the beginning of more scientific archaeological digging in Scotland where, despite Sir John Clerk of Penicuik's exploration of cairns before 1726, 'barrow-opening' never developed as a landowner's pursuit as in England. In the first, Sir George S. Mackenzie illustrated in 1825 a section he got cut through the rampart of a vitrified fort at Dun Fionn near Inverness (not published till *Transactions* IV.1, in 1831, in a sort of symposium on such sites). Earlier the same year our first careful account of an excavated barrow — a stratified sand and cairn structure, containing a cist without identifiable grave-goods — at Machrihanish in Kintyre was communicated by Alexander Seton, son of the donor of the Swedish runic stone and nephew of Henry Jardine. Though the report, published in 1828, was listed in 1831 as 'drawn up' by the landowner, this is not stated in it, and the author and excavator-in-charge was no doubt Seton. For not only did he submit various other notices, give the Museum a papier maché cast of the early Christian inscription of the Catstane near Edinburgh, and become a corresponding member, but he carried out in the next three years before his death in 1828 serious pioneer excavation in the cemetery of what is now turning out to be a most important Viking period trading-site, Birka near Stockholm. A monograph on his finds there, and on Seton himself, was published in 1945.

In short, during this decade or so of revival there was growing in

Edinburgh, in a geological atmosphere, an intellectual awareness of the value of antiquities as material evidence, able to supplement literary evidence, rather than as instinctively collected curiosities. This was fostered by the Antiquaries' intimate association with the Royal Society. That there was still lacking a framework in which to systematise observations on early times, other than vaguely Ancient British, Pictish, Roman, and even more speculatively Danish, was in part due to the shortage of material, and of recurrent associations. The same decade also saw of course the strengthening of a national romantic consciousness, developed from the earlier literary preoccupations, fanned by Scott's poetry and novels, and expressed in George IV's visit to Edinburgh in 1822, when seven of the Society's Council presented the loyal address to their Patron at Holyroodhouse.

In the Royal Institution Building, 1826-44

At this time of new-found confidence a major development was being prepared. Already in January 1822 formal discussions had been started by a letter from the Institution for the Encouragement of the Fine Arts (founded in 1819), 'as to the propriety of adopting a general plan for having a suitable building for the accommodation of the various societies in this place'. Space for the Antiquaries, annual rent (£100 p.a. plus interior repairs etc), and the intention to take up a 19-year lease were soon agreed, though the much better-off London societies were rent-free in Somerset House. The architect, W. H. Playfair, joined the Society, as did his rival William Burn. Besides the two royal societies, the Institution had interested the Government's century-old Board of Trustees for Fisheries, Manufactures and Improvements. This was in course of losing its regulation of the linen industry, and for some time had been only nominally concerned with fisheries, so that its Drawing Academy was a chief function. For this, and because of its affinity with the Institution's exhibitions of paintings, the Board had quickly taken over the project, which would also provide space for its own offices and for a gallery of sculpture casts for its drawing pupils.

Several of the most faithful of the Antiquaries were on the Board — Gilbert Innes, Henry Jardine, Sir Robert Dundas the Society's Agent — and Lord Meadowbank, one of the judges, was a leading member of all the bodies concerned. However, to make the move the Antiquaries had to borrow; they increased their bond to the Friendly Insurance to £600, after having brought it down to £200 in 1824. So the Board was taking no chances, and required as security 'an assignation to the Board's Cashier of their whole effects and Museum, and of the Annual Sub- scriptions of their Members' — which were providently raised to two guineas for new entrants in 1825.

The classical building at the foot of The Mound in the centre of Princes Street, since then much enlarged, and much altered inside to house the Royal Scottish Academy, was given the Institution's name (Royal in 1827). The Society moved in during 1826, to two or three of the smaller rooms of the first floor on the west side. A considerable number of glass cases were needed for 'the various interesting and highly valuable articles of the Museum'. The cost of the cases and of fitting up the rooms was estimated at £200. The hall measured about 20 by 24 feet. Entered from it was a Museum room 32 by 12 feet, beyond which was the Royal Society's museum of the same size. The Royal's library and hall were on the ground floor below. James Skene was still (honorary) Curator in both Societies; for the Antiquaries he had an Assistant, Alexander Macdonald of the Register House staff, who would succeed him in 1836. A gallery alongside the two museum rooms may have been shared. These first floor rooms all had rooflights, and there may have been no artificial light for exhibitions, though there was for the picture galleries. A sub-let by the Antiquaries to the Society of Arts for Scotland of some use of their hall and cupboard-space (granted free to the Bannatyne Club's annual meeting) marks the step forward from candles, for at £21 p.a. it was to include 'coal and gass'. Stoves instead of grates were installed in 1828 in the Museum and Library 'because of smoke'.

The Anniverary meeting on 30 November 1826 inaugurated the New Rooms. In December Skene gave a report, primarily as Curator, with reflections also on the state of the Society and on the state .of antiquarian studies in general — to be considered with a paper by Hibbert which unfortunately has not survived, 'a general view of the leading objects of Inquiry in the subject of Scottish Antiquities and the importance, in a national point of view, of that study'. Skene wrote with some confidence that 'at a period which is likely to prove con- spicuous as an era in the history of this Society we conceive that some advantage in promoting its views might thence arise'. After looking back on the Society's 'state of hopeless decay' from which it had gradually emerged to a period of plentiful communications and new accommodation, Skene looked south and then overseas:

> On the Continent, indeed, there is scarcely a town of any note that cannot boast

of an establishment in full activity, where local Antiquities are accurately investigated with a view to the elucidation of history, and where a common repository is formed, to which everyone feels the propriety of contributing. With us, on the contrary, objects of curiosity and interest are not infrequently assigned to dusty garrets, where they are as little useful to their owners as satisfactory to the public. When we consider that the relics of our common ancestors . . . are objects of general interest, to the means of consultation or inspection of which the public have a peculiar claim, we ought not to forget that it is a gratification which is only attainable from the arrangements of such an establishment as this; and that, while the accumulation of these relics into one general repository affords the most likely means of eliciting light upon their general origin, it becomes, at the same time, the means of converting what is otherwise useless lumber into valuable records of ancient history.

He went on to ask for some occasional donation from each member of the Society or their friends, to give a character of respectability to the Museum and Library, without which the

elegant apartment for the arrangement and display of the collections will only tend the more to expose their poverty. Nor can I suppose any person . . . so indifferent to the creditable appearance of a *national collection* [my italics], as to contemplate these bare walls without experiencing a desire to contribute . . . Monuments obviously intended by some former race of inhabitants as historical memorials to their posterity are to be found in every quarter of the country, and many more have been destroyed under our eyes, . . . upon the elucidation of which the Antiquary might profitably be employed. Of the historical periods of a later day, which still remain the subject of controversy, the field is unbounded.

He ended by emphasising the importance of prompt publication of communications in the *Transactions*.

Upon completion of the arrangement of the Museum, 'in which some few of the Office-bearers took an active share', it was

freely opened to the inspection of the Public. A considerable advantage was the result. As a greater extent was obtained for the display of the various articles of the Museum, and much care was exercised in their exposure and arrangement, the Public soon perceived that their donations were duly appreciated, and valuable additions began rapidly to flow in.

Either to encourage or control admission, tickets were printed in 1827 (as already some years earlier), 'to be signed and dated by any Fellow of the Society, to be delivered to his friends for their visiting the Museum at the times and days to be determined'. The assistant curator, the assistant secretary, and a member of Council 'undertook to give attendance of one of them on each public day, for the better security of the Museum and to show attention to strangers'.

One of the first donations received in the new building was the small twelfth-century bronze shrine with an exquisite crucifix on the front, found at Kilmichael Glassary, Argyll, with the little iron bell inside. Then there was the highly decorated gold 'ornament' from Shaw Hill (Cairnmuir), Peeblesshire, which remained enigmatic till a complete massive torc of the first century BC was found in Norfolk in 1950. A small bronze cannon, the only Scottish cast cannon now known from its period, by James Monteath, Edinburgh, 1642, was given (with permssion from the Governor General and Council of India) by Captain L. Carmichael who had found it in the Rajput fortress of Bhurtpore when stormed in 1828. The now fine collection of Scottish charms was started conspicuously by a calf-heart full of pins, brought in by Sir Walter Scott, and a slab of ivory from Argyll, Barbreck's Bone, which cured all degrees of madness.

A donation list was left out in December 1826 and there is evidence of later omissions; however, in the four years beginning 1827, 304 donations are recorded, of which 140 contained books, 104 antiquities (including classical Mediterranean), 42 ethnographical material (with some Egyptian — two mummies were on loan for some years), 25 manuscripts and 16 drawings. The classical antiquities were becoming prominent. Thirty-two Roman pots from Colchester were given by E. W. A. Drummond Hay, who succeeded Hibbert as Secretary in 1827. (His bequest in 1846 of 2,600 Roman coins probably provided much of the unprovenanced part of the existing collection. He may too have influenced the Colonial Office's gift of a collection of antiquities from Cyrene in 1830, which included a four-foot statue of Æsculapius; these were described and some illustrated in a long-delayed part of the *Transactions* (IV.3) in 1857.)

Among the books was a Book of Common Order with full Metrical Psalms, in Gothic type and lacking its title-page, given through David Laing. Still unique and inadequately published, it appears to be the very first edition ordered by the General Assembly in 1562, and if so is evidence that the Scots spelling into which it was transposed was deliberately rejected by the Reformed Kirk in favour of the English of England.

Items of Natural History (with skeletal evidence for animal species in early Scotland among the exceptions) were relinquished in 1828 when 'the Antiquarian and Royal Societies in this place' transferred 'to the Museum of each whatever articles might be in their possession but more particularly adapted to the Enquiries of the other'. Burmese idols in marble and other articles came to the Antiquaries, but the full list then made has not been traced. From another source came a Malay dugout canoe which was suspended from the roof of the staircase.

At the meeting at which the exchange was announced Robert Bald (a mining engineer and a pillar of the Society), described the Museum of northern antiquities in Copenhagen, where 15,000 articles 'had been collected in less than 16 years under the supervision of Professor Thomsen' (whom Seton too had visited on his way to Sweden three years earlier). The seminal arrangement of weapons and tools by Stone, Bronze, and Iron Ages is not mentioned in the brief minutes. It was being defended by Thomsen against criticism from Austria already in 1824, and is unlikely to have escaped Bald's comment to his audience of 83 people. A couple of years later several leading Danish antiquaries were elected honorary fellows or corresponding members, though Thomsen himself was not until 1846. A larger number of scholars in different parts of France were also elected, though connections with that country were less obviously close.

The size of Bald's audience was minuted because exceptional, but there was an even fuller meeting next month to hear about the Society's first official involvement in fieldwork, when the Secretary reported on his visit to Alloa with Bald, 'for the purpose of prosecuting their enquiries into the discovery of an ancient British cemetery'. He produced 'two bracelets weighing about six ounces of the finest gold, [found] with the remains of a human body in one of several stone cists' — an extremely rare late bronze-age find. The Council were unhappy at paying the finders 'full value about £20', and rather more than half was subscribed by Fellows at a maximum of 10s each. The Exchequer does not seem to have been directly concerned.

A more complex outside activity involved the Society being granted by the King temporary possession of the great gun Mons (as she should strictly be called). Though her return from exile in the Tower of London is generally credited to Sir Walter Scott, this was not really the case. Other members of the Society, particularly the indefatigable Drummond Hay, on the initiative of Graham Dalyell, together with the Duke of Gordon, Governor of Edinburgh Castle, serving Officers, and the Edinburgh and Leith Steam Packet Company, achieved the difficult task over a period of twelve months in 1828-29. (The full story has recently been published elsewhere.)*

* In David Caldwell (ed): *Scottish Weapons and Fortifications* (Edinburgh 1981).

Peripeteia with the Historians

Sadly this Silver Age was to last only a few more years. Drummond Hay's expected posting, to be Consul in Tangier, came through. He was given a great send-off dinner in May 1829, and it was said that 'the numerous additions of distinguished individuals both in this country and on the Continent to the lists of the Society's members, and the walls of their Museum which had been enriched by many valuable donations, bore testimony to Mr Hay's zealous discharge of the duties of his office'. He was succeeded as Secretary by the much younger Donald Gregory, historian of the Highlands and founder of the Iona publishing club, one of quite a number of record historians of a generation later than Dalyell who were more or less active members of the Society. So that at the time of Lord Buchan's death the Society was closely linked through them with the surge of archive publications which he had wished it to undertake; besides Laing with the Bannatyne, they included Pitcairn, Fraser Tytler, Maidment and Thomas Thomson. But the Society was only one channel for all the money and energy needed, and somehow became a backwater. On Gregory's premature death in 1836, W. F. Skene, James's son, became Secretary. Unfortunately he had to give this up — and history too for a long while — for professional reasons in 1838.

Though in his 1861 *Account* Laing blamed the serious decline on Alexander Smellie's return to the Secretaryship after Skene, that was a symptom and aggravating factor rather than a cause, for the decline can be traced further back. The actual proposal of Smellie came from Dalyell, who himself was a Vice-President again from 1835 to 1841 with a statutory year's gap, and it may indicate a final reaction by the old guard after the scientific group had moved away. The other active Vice-President then was Jardine, now Sir Henry, more or less continuously in office from 1817 to 1845. Brunton, who was among other things university librarian, lasted longer still, as Secretary for Foreign Correspondence from 1813 to 1854.

Up to 1834 all seems to have been well. Prehistoric finds, some important, kept coming to the Museum: gold rings and bracelets from Banffshire, rare bronze-age archers' wristguards from Skye, what is still the largest bronze spearhead from Scotland, found in Fife, pieces of tripartite-disc wooden wheels (probably bronze-age) from moss-reclamation near Stirling. Other times were not neglected, for example an old-fashioned wooden lock from Orkney, engravings of the Nigg and

F

Hilton of Cadboll sculptured stones, Anglo-Saxon copper coins from the Hexham hoard. Eight tenth-century silver coins, selected by Jamieson, were acquired from a find on Inchkenneth, and several fragments, together with drawings of the silver bracelets, from another in Shetland. Though the Sheriff-Substitute investigated the latter, neither seems to have been subject to a treasure trove claim; yet in the same year coins from three sixteenth-century hoards and a single Roman gold coin found near Arbroath were given by the Barons of Exchequer. Also in 1831 the magnificent Hunterston Brooch 'lately found' was exhibited, as were some of the ivory chessmen discovered that year in Lewis, again without overt interest from the Exchequer. (The Society did attempt to raise some money for the chessmen, by a scheme for individual members to buy most for themselves, but they left Scotland and almost all — ninety-eight pieces, not solely chessmen — were promptly bought by the British Museum for £84.) In contrast, after a small medieval bronze seal had been dug up in Parliament Square in 1833, the Remembrancer reclaimed it from the Society, 'in order to vindicate the right of the Crown to articles found in the above manner', and the Barons then directed it to be placed in the Museum.

The Museum was temporarily closed from October 'because of works going on'. Following proposals considered the year before, a third or more was added to its accommodation as a result of an extra third being added to the whole building at the southern end. The Royal Society moved its Museum southward, allowing that of the Antiquaries to have the space vacated.

Up to 1834 quite regularly, and a couple of times in 1837, the series of important exhibits from landowners continued, located perhaps during the search for archives as well as by social contacts — notably the mazer and gold brooch inherited from the Bannatynes of Kames in Bute, the Brooch of Lorne and the Glenlyon Brooch, the Burnett of Leys ivory horn, a Viking sword and shield-boss from Rousay, and Prince Charles Edward's silver-hilted sword.

Reports of field-work as well as notes on antiquities came in, and were often published along with historical papers, but after 1832 the balance of communications was shifting in favour of the latter, and foreign archaeology. *Transactions* III.2 was published in 1831 — free to Fellows — and with it the Appendix containing the *Account* from 1784 by the editors Hibbert and Laing, and lists of donations and communications to date. For these the title was changed to *Archaeologia Scotica* (with new title-pages for the earlier volumes), positively inviting comparison at last with the London Antiquaries. Volume IV.1 and a revised II.2 came from the same editors, still in 1831. The former with 216 pages had 'illustrations superior and less expensive than anything before . . . seven engraved copper plates, numerous wood cuts and two litho engravings' — coloured maps showing the string of real and supposed Roman sites north of the Forth, in the search for Mons Graupius. There was much on vitrified forts, as communicated five or more years before, by Hibbert drawing particularly on Mackenzie. A vigorous full-size multiview engraving by W. Penny of the Museum's bell-shrine and bell, and a facsimile page of its Drummond of Hawthornden manuscripts (accompanying many extracts) certainly set a new standard for the Society. A temporarily exhibited bronze-age hoard from Yorkshire and pull-out plates of wood-panels at Speke Hall, in Lancashire, illustrate wider enquiries.

Part 2, issued only two years later, started with good engravings of the Shaw Hill gold, had the Banffshire gold and its pot drawn by James Skene, a sketch of the pre-Norman sculptured arch then still at Forteviot with notes on earthworks nearby by W. F. Skene, and at the end the Ruthwell Cross, with all sides and inscriptions drawn and described by Dr Henry Duncan — the runes were still baffling. Between these papers Laing's notes and extracts of the Drummond manuscripts were continued. So were the descriptions and discussions of vitrified and other forts, and for good measure vitrified cairns (burnt mounds) in Orkney. Hibbert recommended 'that Members of this Society be encouraged to continue the investigation', but the difficulty of extracting information from such sites short of thorough excavation, the scarcity of datable artefacts to be found (and the great range of date now revealed by carbon 14), more than excuse the fading out of this first in any way concerted archaeological campaign and listing in Scotland. Yet nearly a generation was to go by before another subject — brochs — was attempted as broadly.

A printed address-list of 1831 survives, issued with the billet for the Annual Meeting on St Andrew's Day at Three o'clock afternoon, and dinner at the British Hotel, Queen Street, at half-past Five *precisely*, from the Museum of the Antiquaries of Scotland. It lists 194 Fellows including four MPs, overwhelmingly in Edinburgh. Cash in hand had recently been over £140, with income estimated at £350 excluding arrears and sale of publications, and rent, taxes, wages etc at £150. The Treasurer, Thomas Allan, died in 1833, and next May the Council were told that arrears had been accumulating seriously; in October, that his firm had failed. The actual loss to the Society was small, if any, but it became clear that subscriptions and arrears were in disorder; the increase to two guineas had been unpopular, and some thought that Fellows who had paid the lower rate for upwards of eighteen years should pay nothing more. In an attempt at useful activity in 1835, a committee was appointed to inspect graves discovered a few miles from Edinburgh, but only one member went. Next year two meetings failed to get a quorum, and Gregory the Secretary died.

Before the Anniversary meeting W. F. Skene as joint acting Treasurer reported arrears of £235, and three resignations, with more expected, of supporters of the eighteen years' principle — unnamed but noted as Sir G. S. Mackenzie, Robert Scott-Moncrieff (Treasurer 1815-25), and James Skene, who despite this was re-elected Curator. W. F. Skene, aged twenty-seven, was made Secretary, and David Laing Treasurer. Thomas Thomson, Depute Clerk Register, and W. B. D. D. Turnbull, founder of the Abbotsford Club, joined the Council. Alexander Macdonald, by then a Principal Keeper of Records, became formally Curator next year; Robert Frazer, jeweller, later succeeded him as Assistant. Though with resignations (Brewster claimed to have intimated his in 1830) and strikings-off, no more than 30 names appear to have been removed, the reality was much worse, for a slightly later estimate of income was 'not much above £150'. All that sum was needed, with nothing left for publication, since the Board of Manufactures were pressing for a year's arrears of rent, and there were old accounts unpaid.

As the Friendly Insurance declined to increase its loan (by then only £200), a cash credit was obtained from the Commercial Bank — an encouragement while the Council was preparing an Address to the Queen on her accession. The subscription was settled at two guineas for the first twelve years, reducing then to one, with provisions for compounding. There was even hope of printing a catalogue of the Museum for sale to strangers. A major consignment of treasure trove came early in 1838, though Jardine was no longer Remembrancer. It included coins from fourteen sources, notably twenty-three gold coins of James I and II found in 1815, and two English nobles from the recent find in Glasgow Cathedral. Best of all was the first and largest of the Pictish silver chains, dug up in 1808 from the Caledonian Canal. About then W. F. Skene pointed out that on silver in the Norrie's Law Hoard in Fife there were the same symbols as on the Sculptured Stones of Scotland. John Stuart, who was to use that as the title of his volumes twenty years later, gave a stone vessel and described the Druidical Circle near where it was found. Dalyell presented, besides other things, a bust of himself.

After Smellie's return to office the Treasurer wished to reduce the subscription to one guinea for all; once lowered, and the entrance fee reduced to two guineas (1843), dues remained unchanged for over a century. The trouble was that new members were not joining, and old were not paying. Ordinary meetings were down to four, or in 1840 even two. Donations correspondingly dropped, with more that were unsuitable, such as three separate gifts of fragments from the wreck of the *Royal George*. The Clerks of the Justiciary Court also cleared their cupboards of old evidence, giving in 1841 two spring-guns declared murderous in 1826, coining implements from 1814, and Deacon Brodie's dark lantern and skeleton keys of 1788 — curiosities perhaps, but of perennial interest. These came soon after Frazer had re-arranged the Museum, and had been thanked for the great labour bestowed and the taste displayed. Kemp, the architect of the Scott Monument, was also thanked for displaying drawings of a Norman Hall he wished erected alongside it, 'suitable for the Museum of the Society' with rooms for meetings.

Retreat to 24 George Street and new efforts, 1844-50

The position was already serious when in 1841 the Edinburgh Friendly Insurance Society, then being wound up, pressed harder for repayment of the £200 bond. Two representatives of the original Obligants of 1794 offered to pay £25 each; Innes's heir had already made a gift of £50. The rent of the Royal Society of Arts, previously reduced, was raised to £25; the Botanical Society was paying £10. It was now decided to insure the Museum and Library, for £500 (premium not stated), a wise precaution — that year 'upwards of 4,000 persons had visited the Museum, admission to which is entirely gratuitous and open to everyone who presents an order from a Fellow'. (In addition, at least in 1843, 'very many strangers [were] admitted during Her Majesty's visit [to Edinburgh]'. Prince Albert, to whom a special diploma of Honorary Fellowship had been sent in 1840, also came.)

As income was 'quite inadequate to meet costs', particularly the £100 rent to the Government's Board, successive efforts were made which it is easy to criticise as tactically unsound or even back to front. A deputation sent in 1844 to ask the advice of the Lord Advocate, as head

of Scottish administration, was too late, since early the previous year
the Treasury had turned down a direct written appeal. That Memorial
(which had not been sent before the President, the new Lord Elgin, had
gone as governor to Jamaica) explained that the rent was mainly for the
rooms of the well-attended Museum, but it failed to explain its
character or purpose. The Treasury had not been asked for free accommodation with the Society of Antiquaries of London as precedent, but
for cash in the form of an annual grant of £100.

Meanwhile the chance of future accommodation in a building which
was being reconstructed was rightly seized. The Board agreed that their
lease might be cancelled in just over a year (Whitsun 1844), but refused
to reduce the rent in the interval. As total debts had mounted to near
£500, the Treasury were then asked to remit arrears (£150), and also
refused. Rather frantically prestige was sought by electing foreign
royalty as Honorary Fellows, including the Crown Prince of Denmark
who did visit the Museum and made a gift of 'various objects of
antiquity', and the King of Saxony who does not seem to have fitted in
a visit while in Edinburgh. When in June 1844 it became unlikely that
the Board would allow the collections to be moved without payment, a
petition for help in getting an annual £300 was sent to the Queen; and
so was a fuller letter to the Prime Minister Sir Robert Peel, in which it
was stated that the Society's subscriptions were not sufficient

> to preserve, exhibit and add to the Museum. They consider themselves in some
> measure representing their countrymen, for whom they wish to preserve a
> Museum so closely connected with their past history and most patriotic feelings.
> . . . [They] consider the refusal of their application by their Lordships [of the
> Treasury] a slight offered to Scotland, and they cannot help comparing as others
> have done before, the very stinted measure of support which the Scientific Institu-
> tions of Scotland receive from the Government, with the munificent grants of
> public money annually made to those in England, and all the more to those in
> Ireland . . .

Following rebuffs, a letter came from the Board explaining that
'because of their pecuniary engagements' the Trustees needed to have
the arrears paid, or sufficient security; and that it was their 'intention
to proceed immediately to convert the Society's present apartments
into a continuation of the Statue Gallery, so as to provide more extensive accommodation for the School of Design, which is an object of the
Board's most anxious solicitude'. Neither selling off part of the Museum
nor complete refusal to allow sub-lets to continue was mentioned in
writing, but Laing records them in his 1861 *Account*.

One can now see that space, not money, was what the Board had wanted all along. It seems that pressure to move was also put on the Royal Society even though it had by then a £300 Government grant, but it stayed. The Royal Institution itself had been declining at the same time as the Antiquaries, but the Royal Scottish Academy was developing, using rooms in the building. The Board then wanted these, because it had been enlarging its Drawing Academy to include a school of painting and a life class. The Trustees also had their eye on the University's collection, the Torrie Bequest, as a step towards forming a National Gallery of Scotland; transfer on loan was agreed, and Playfair began to design new buildings, in 1845.

It was the Edinburgh Life Assurance Company which was rebuilding its premises at 22-24 George Street. In January 1843 Turnbull, who became interim Joint Secretary, found that the Company would alter its upper apartments at No. 24, with a large hall lighted from the roof, to suit the Museum. The lease was agreed for twenty years starting Whitsunday 1844, £60 for the first five years and £65 for the next fifteen, the Society to be responsible for the expense of all the interior fittings needed for the Museum. On 31st May the rooms at The Mound were closed, to prepare for removal. A committee of seven, appointed to assist the office-bearers (not just the Curators) in this and in preparing a printed catalogue for sale to visitors, included Hibbert (by then Hibbert-Ware) and J. M. Mitchell, a Leith merchant. A publication committee for *Archaeologia Scotica* was also named, optimistically. The impasse over moving until arrears of rent were paid was resolved in December by a loan of £400 from the new landlords. The Secretary, Treasurer and Curators were personally responsible as Obligants, and the collections (notably coins) were assigned to them 'in security and relief of the Obligation'.

Seven months later a special meeting of the Society inspected the newly installed Museum and library, which would be open to the public on Tuesdays and Fridays from 10 till 4, and on public holidays. Robert Frazer, by then effectively the only Curator, was thanked for his trouble over the arrangement. He had just retired from his jeweller's and seal-engraver's business, selling his private museum, from which the mysterious early nineteenth-century miniature coffins found on Arthur's Seat were many years later to reach the Museum. He could devote much time to the collections over some fourteen years, preparing for their next move. The opening meeting also agreed that the Secretary, W. B. D. Turnbull, should take several unspecified articles to the meeting in Winchester of the new British Archaeological Institute; though he could not go, this way of making the Museum more widely known was approved next year for the York meeting.

A further sign that a fresh leaf was being turned was that the new President, the Marquess of Breadalbane, came to take the chair in person in February 1846. He heard the first draft of an address to the Government, and Mitchell read the second instalment of his paper on the state of archaeology in Scandinavia. Two members proposed at that same meeting were to have major roles in the development of archaeology in Scotland, Professor J. Y. Simpson (shortly to publish his experiments with chloroform) and Daniel Wilson, described as artist.

A successful drive for new members, some of them influential, had started in 1844 after a decade of stagnation. Around the time of its climax in 1848 (though it was long maintained), a striking number of artists of one kind or another joined the Society. This partly reflected and reinforced the Society's concern with the ancient buildings of Edinburgh, shown already before Wilson joined. Even more it can be seen as a consequence of the popularity of historical painting with its new stress on historical accuracy in period details, and the rise of the artist antiquaries and collectors. The social success of such painting, and of the Royal Scottish Academy, was a feature of the mid-nineteenth century. The older antiquaries who were themselves collectors, such as Laing and J. T. Gibson Craig, were able to bring the Society and its Museum into Edinburgh's lively cultural scene. Special evening exhibitions for members and their friends, following a scheme submitted by Daniel Wilson as acting Secretary, stimulated interest by setting out in the Museum new accessions along with loans — topographical illustrations, portraits, manuscripts and objets d'art. At the initial conversazione in 1848, attended by thirty or forty people, the portions of painted ceiling newly rescued from Mary of Guise's house on Castle Hill and mounted on the ceiling of the Museum, could be compared with the more varied scenes on the seventeenth-century panels from Dean House lent by Charles Kirkpatrick Sharpe. These, and the naive Samson and lion carved on a door from Amisfield Castle shown at one of the four conversaziones next session, were to be acquired for the Museum before long. On another occasion finds from bishops' tombs in Kirkwall cathedral were exhibited (fifteen years before being given by the Exchequer), while James Ballantine, one of the recent Fellows, showed his series of Scottish kings and queens in stained glass, made for the House of Lords.

There is no information on how much the Museum's arrangement was altered during its time at 24 George Street. From the beginning there the Copenhagen arrangement by stone and bronze periods was familiar to members, and it must have been discussed during the visit of young J. J. A. Worsaae. His published lectures in 1846 to the Royal Irish Academy, an 'Account of the Formation of the Museum of Antiquities at Copenhagen and the Classification of the Antiquities found in the North and West of Europe', contained a reference to the Danish treasure trove law which the Society promptly brought to the attention of the Lord Advocate. Another exceptional consequence of his visit was an exchange of 'duplicate' bronze objects with the Royal Museum of Antiquities, the Society sending to Copenhagen a particularly fine Viking brooch and four minor items.

So it is probable that the rather mechanical arrangement of the contents of the nine cases, some quite large, according to material as shown in Wilson's *Synopsis,* the catalogue published in 1849, was set out by Frazer and the committee before Wilson became Secretary at the end of 1847: I-IV stone (with bone and ivory), V-VII bronze, VIII ornaments of gold, silver and bronze, with some beads, IX pottery. This would help to explain the occasional discrepancies that result from Wilson's decision to make the broader ideas explicit by using the Periods as headings, under the rubric Celtic; for example the bronze brooches known to be Viking are catalogued under Bronze Period, and the bone pin and jet armlet found with them are placed under Stone Period, cross-referenced. Foreign and ethnographic stone implements were given prominence for comparison. Roman finds, again arranged by material, mainly from abroad along with 'Etruscan' and Greek, occupied five cases; medieval bronze cooking pots found in Scotland were still considered Roman, supported by a note that a coin of Hadrian had been found near one of them. In this and other sections there was much that was freestanding or fastened on the walls. Five more cases contained medieval and later objects, mainly from Scotland, but armour, of which Scotland is notably short, and pole-weapons were soon added from the Tower of London. An Egyptian case, and one India and Mexico, completed the hall. Some portraits and documents were shown in the Council Room, though the Library and its listed manuscripts were restricted. In the lobby were the insignia of the Edinburgh convivial Cape Club (1793-1843). The coin collection, not mentioned, was up till 1849 being arranged by William Ferguson

WS, who had provided John Lindsay in Cork, an honorary member, with much information for his *Coinage of Scotland* (1845). The idea of selling some duplicates to finance a show case for the rest was discussed, and apparently negatived.

Fifteen hundred copies of the catalogue, the *Synopsis*, were printed, having over 150 pages, fifteen small illustrations and the Kilmichael Glassary bell-shrine as frontispiece. Paper-covered copies were sold at the Museum for one shilling. One hundred and fifty copies were to be bound for Fellows not in arrears, and for presentation to other Societies. It was decided to send two special copies to Balmoral for the Queen and Prince Albert, with an address.

After five years of careful preparation, involving the Lord Advocate and two MPs, William Gibson Craig (City of Edinburgh) and Joseph Hume (Montrose Burghs), the Society's submission to the Government about accommodation for the Museum reached its final form in 1849 and was signed by the Marquess of Breadalbane and three other principal office-bearers, Robert Chambers, Laing and Wilson. Prospects were brighter than ever before, and the annual dinner was this time held in the Archers' Hall at 6 pm with the President in the chair. The old order was passing: the oldest member and last of the original Obligants, Sir William Miller of Glenlee, had died during the year, as had Alexander Smellie and Sir George Steuart Mackenzie.

The Conveyance and the Proceedings, Excavators and Artists, 1851-58

Over a year later the Government's agreement in principle was notified to the Board of Manufactures, who wrote in April 1851, after conferring with the Society's representatives, that the Board were prepared to offer to the Society certain accommodation in the Royal Institution free of rent, but not until the new National Gallery had been completed and opened for the reception of pictures. This was conditional on the Society making over the collections for ever to the free use and admission of the public. The arrangements would be made by the Board, but were to be free of all expense to them; a grant from public funds would be sought for alterations and fittings. In reply the Society specified the terms on which they would make over their collections as National Property, adding the need for staff. The conditional sanction of the Treasury, where Sir William Gibson Craig by then looked after Scottish affairs, was given in a detailed Minute dated 1 July 1851, after which the Board's law-agents drafted a Conveyance embodying the various terms. Two adjustments requested by the Society were made, and the Council did not finally insist on a third, intended to guarantee free access to the collections for members, which indeed might merely have been troublesome to interpret.

The Conveyance was signed on behalf of the Society in November 1851, by Breadalbane, Laing and Wilson. It was to take effect only when Parliament had voted funds to adapt apartments in the Royal Institution, or another public building in Edinburgh, to receive the collections. Then it would give and make over to the Board, for behoof of the public, and subject to the general direction and control of the Lords of the Treasury, 'the entire collection of antiquities, coins, medals, portraits, manuscripts and books belonging to the said Society of Antiquaries, *with all such additions as may be hereafter made thereto,* together with the cabinets . . . in which they were contained'. (The phrase in italics here continues to be in force; the one following it was to be important on a later occasion (p. 160).) Fit and proper accommodation was to be provided at all times, after the completion of the National Gallery, for the preservation and exhibition of the collection, and also for the Society's meetings, free of all expense to them.

On administration it was expressly 'declared that the charge and management of the said Collection of Antiquities and others above transferred shall remain with the said Society of Antiquaries subject to such regulation and direction as may from time to time be prescribed' by the Board with the consent and approval of the Treasury; and that the Society shall 'annually elect two Members of the Board . . . being Members of the Society of Antiquaries to be Members of the Council of the said Society'. The Treasury's Minute had not provided for this valuable representation of the Board on the Council.

Although several years, over seven in fact, were to go by before the Society could give up George Street and move the collections at its own expense, the financial worry was lifted. Publication was immediately put in hand, starting with the current session and Daniel Wilson's address at the anniversary meeting, on the past, present and future of the Museum, and on attitudes to antiquities in Scotland and other countries. *Proceedings* I.1, in a more modest and practical format than that of *Archaeologia Scotica*, was distributed to members before the end of 1852. In this first annual part, as on to 1939, lists of additions to the Museum and other exhibits at the meeting of the month, with good illustrations, preceded the communications, many of which were notes or discussion about finds or donations. They included a retrospective account of finds at the later famous Roman site on the Tweed at New-stead, where the new railway cutting had discovered pottery and animal remains in pits. (Details of these were held over for the larger pages of *Archaeologia Scotica* IV.3 (1857), so that the Samian pottery could be illustrated full-size, in colour; most of the other papers there were far less recent.) The author, J. A. Smith MD, was to join Laing as editor for the Society after Wilson left, and became a prolific contributor.

Other contributions to the earliest *Proceedings* show how archae-ology was developing, as well as what was coming to the Museum. A revised date for 'Roman camp kettles' was implied in a note, probably by Wilson, on a ewer found with several of them in Banchory Loch in Aberdeenshire. He compared it to those in medieval illuminated manu-scripts, while the landowner pointed to Roman camps in the area. Some samples from coin hoards, given by the Lords of the Treasury through the Queen's Remembrancer, gave rise to a good catalogue by a young doctor, W. H. Scott, of the Anglo-Saxon coins from Machrie in Islay. If he had lived, Scott would perhaps have brought about a more archaeological appreciation of the Museum's coin collection, of which he was briefly curator. Fragmentary coins and details of unintelligible inscriptions were important to him, and might have led to association and provenance being safeguarded in the numismatic section as they were in the rest of the Museum, and would have ensured that the samples from the Greek coins found anomalously near Shotts in Lanarkshire, and the seventeenth-century dollars from Selkirkshire, were not disposed of later as simply foreign. Wilson recorded a grave in East Lothian which he considered to be Anglo-Saxon because it had grave-goods (a jar, dagger, comb and bodkin), but which surprisingly proves to be sixteenth or seventeenth-century. He also catalogued a hundred Roman coins which had been found at Portmoak in Fife with five hundred or so others, an iron sword and a 'beautiful silver orna-ment' only tantalisingly mentioned — a good example of the failures of the treasure trove law on which he kept insisting. Much in the *Pro-ceedings*, then as later, was of course less directly relevant to the Museum, such as a Shetland folk-tale ('ballad'), cromlechs in India, the physical ethnography of Scotland, a Clanranald manuscript (given a century later), or historical documents on the burial of the Regent Moray, whose monument in St Giles was restored by the city on the Society's prompting.

Altogether the first volume was a landmark in the history of the

Society, the start of modern times, and the beginning of an orderly accumulation, and constant review, of information on and related to the collections, which the physical organisation of the objects would only slowly emulate. Angus Graham has traced and systematically sampled the variety in subject matter and changes in emphasis to be found in the *Proceedings* over their first eighty years, and in the *Archaeologia*, in a most valuable paper, 'Records and Opinions 1780-1930' (*Proceedings* 1969-70), which complements the present essays. He explained in it that he had made 'no attempt to deal with the sheaves of reports on relics, bones and curios that regularly reached the Museum, as they outrun any hope of analysis'. Major trends which he noted, however, generally produced corresponding intakes into the collections; other less obvious trends and abortive interests can also be recognised in the Museum's growth. The influence of the Danish Three Ages (which he missed) was evident, as we have seen, in the *Synopsis*, and in accessions of stone and bronze artefacts from Denmark.

Graham particularly stressed that by 1852-53 the importance of excavation was being recognised, biased towards the recovery of relics. Most of these excavations were in the far North. In Orkney two chambered cairns were opened in 1849, followed by other burial mounds, with few or no relics, and from 1853 there was a long drawn out campaign of partial excavation of brochs by James Farrer, an English MP, reported on by George Petrie the local sheriff-clerk, a corresponding member of the Society. In Caithness a similar series of monuments was investigated somewhat more satisfactorily. The exceptionally thorough investigation of a broch at Kettleburn, where a young local landowner, A. H. Rhind, employed a number of men for nearly three months, exposed the whole plan of the massive structure surrounded by slighter buildings within a circular wall. There was recovered a quantity of the things we should now expect — a wide range of faunal remains, pottery, objects of stone, bronze and iron, none very exciting. Yet thirty years later Joseph Anderson described the gift of these finds as having given 'a new character to the [Museum's] collection of Scottish antiquities, and a new direction to Scottish archaeology': they were at last an assemblage of evidence from a single site of a particular kind, and sufficient for 'the condition and culture of the occupants of the structure [to be] truly disclosed by [their] study, in so far as the objects are capable of affording such indications'. Part of Rhind's report appeared in the *Proceedings* and part was published by the Archaeological Institute of Great Britain. It was already being realised, and by the time Anderson wrote was being taken for granted, that the relics supplied the necessary key to assigning the different kinds of monument to a Period, the only sort of date then possible. To gather such evidence into the Museum and preserve it for study became a major aim of the Society.

To compare and contrast the remains of Scotland's distant past with those of early and primitive cultures elsewhere was seen to be a way of learning more about both, particularly when there was as yet so relatively little from Scotland to study. For a long time it stayed less clear that things from historical periods could similarly be evidence yielding new information, rather than be simply illustrations of what was known from books. Art and the artists, whose arrival has already been mentioned, formed a bridge between the two attitudes and two parts of the collections, particularly significant in the 1850s. Beside Wilson as Secretary, now turned writer and historian, were Sir John Watson Gordon PRSA and W. B. Johnston, first Curator of the National Gallery, both on the Council; Alexander Christie of the School of Art held various offices in the Society including that of librarian, and read a paper on the Bayeux Tapestry; James Drummond was a Curator or councillor for many years. Accessions, as well as exhibits at meetings and conversaziones, reflected their interests. Renaissance carved panels, dated stylistically, were acquired from various parts of Scotland, and a set of photographs of those at Edzell. (Panels among other things were bought at C. K. Sharpe's sale, for which nearly £60 was raised following a circular, while other members bought and donated items from the auction.) Tomb effigies, seals and heraldic sculpture were discussed, and illustrated in the *Proceedings*, and casts of some were naturally added to the Museum, as study and drawing of casts was a normal part of art training. The Board of Manufactures had indeed been anxious to secure special access to the collections for their students.

Another important factor in the artistic studies of that time was the publication of monographs on pre-twelfth-century sculptured stones. This was not undertaken by the Society, but first for Angus by Patrick Chalmers in 1846 (when he also became a Fellow), and for Scotland as a whole by the Spalding Club in Aberdeen, in two volumes in 1856 and 1867; their editor was John Stuart, advocate, who came south to the Register House in Edinburgh and was Secretary of the Society from 1855 to 1877, also remaining Secretary to the Club. Early in the 1850s the Museum was given part of an Anglian cross-shaft from Dumfriesshire boldly carved with saints in architectural niches, and a finely incised symbol stone from Orkney, and purchased a set of casts of the (Pictish) sculptures at St Vigeans in Angus.

Readier access for the general public to see all this was implicit in the Conveyance, even while transfer and public finance hung fire. The opening days were therefore changed in 1854 to Wednesday, for which an order signed by a member was still needed, and Saturday completely free, like public holidays. In consequence attendance jumped that year to over 22,000, nearly double the 1851 figure, steadying then to 17,000 and upwards.

Part II of this chapter, covering the history of the National Museum to 1954, begins on page 142.

'A fine, genial, hearty band': David Laing, Daniel Wilson and Scottish Archaeology

Marinell Ash

On 18 October 1878 David Laing died in his eighty-sixth year. During his fifty-four year membership of the Society of Antiquaries of Scotland he had become not only the Society's oldest serving member, but also one of the most influential and important figures in its history. He was active until within a few days of his death and, according to an obituary notice in the *Athenaeum* of 26 October 1878, one of his last social engagements harked back to a period thirty years before when Laing and his friend, Daniel Wilson, had saved the Society from extinction and in so doing set Scottish archaeology on its modern path:

> It was only the other day that he [Laing] gave a dinner to a number of his brethren of the Society of Antiquaries on the occasion of the visit of his old friend Professor Daniel Wilson of Toronto to Edinburgh, and it was curious to see the old man sipping his Madeira with as much relish, and enjoying the old world talk as keenly as Lockhart in his *Peter's Letters* records his doing some sixty or more years ago.* [1]

The 'old world' David Laing had known in his youth was Edinburgh in the early years of the nineteenth century. He had been born in 1793, the son of William Laing, a successful bookseller. Laing's bookshop

---

*References for this chapter begin on p. 112. The text includes bracketed references to *Arch[aeologia] Scot[ica]*, vols 3 (1831), 4 (1857) and 5 (1890); to the Comm[unications] to the Society, vols 3 (1800-22), 4 (1823-7), 5 (1828-9), 6 (1829-32) and 7 (1842-52); to the Corr[espondence] books, vols 3 (1785-1825), 4 (1826-28), 5 (1829-31), 6 (1831-4) and 7 (1835-43); and to the M[inute] B[ook], vols 3 (9 May 1805-28 May 1827), 4 (30 November 1827-4 May 1840) and 5 (30 November 1840-6 July 1853). The three last groups of MSS are preserved in the Society's Library, National Museum of Antiquities, Edinburgh.

was a gathering place for such luminaries as Walter Scott, Thomas Thomson (first Deputy Clerk Register), the antiquary George Chalmers and John Jamieson the lexicographer, to whom William Laing had once offered a position in his business.[2] It was probably through Jamieson that the Laings met the Icelandic scholar, Grímur Thorkelin: a link with Scandinavian scholarship which was to play an important role in David Laing's life. The Laings were representative of a number of Scottish antiquaries and historians of this period who took a deep and informed interest in the common history and culture of Scotland and Scandinavia. In the Laings' case, such an interest was also good business. For example, William Laing travelled to Denmark in 1799 to buy duplicate volumes from the Royal Library in Copenhagen.[3]

David Laing entered his father's business at the age of fifteen, after a brief period at Edinburgh University. In 1809 he attended his first London book sale. Three years later, while attending the great Roxburghe sale, he formed a close friendship with his father's friend, George Chalmers. The octogenarian Chalmers was testy, conceited and self-opinionated. It was a test of young Laing's self-effacing yet diplomatic character that they became firm friends and remained so until Chalmers' death in 1825. The letters between Chalmers and his young protégé trace the antiquarian development of David Laing. The correspondence begins with Chalmers very much the patronising superior, offering help with Laing's early projects, such as his first published work, a list of Drummond of Hawthornden's books in Edinburgh University Library (1815). By 1820 a reversal of roles had taken place. Chalmers increasingly depended on Laing for literary and historical advice, especially in the preparation of his great work, *Caledonia*. Laing was not blind to the faults of his mentor. He particularly deprecated Chalmers' violent historical likes and dislikes. In 1821 he wrote to reprove Chalmers for his frenzied attacks on those who did not share his belief in the total innocence of Mary Queen of Scots. The letter marks David Laing's antiquarian coming of age:

You wished to know what alterations I meant to suggest when I wished you to republish the Life of Queen Mary. You may not remember—but I do, many conversations we have had on the disputed point of her innocence — and whatever my sentiments may be, I have no wish, or rather have no hope to be able to influence you. What I object to therefore is expressions more than sentiments — and in particular I dislike the epithet *cats-paw* which occurs so often. I wish you press some other substitute into service for it — and to say the truth, though it be expressive, it is too vulgar to make its appearance in such a work. Another thing I regret to see, is your getting angry and abusing your antagonists. Now, as I said before, I wish not to enter into the merits of the case — but certainly it does not strengthen an argument in the doing so. A good cause does not stand in need of it — as it serves to throw a suspicious air over the pleadings. You will therefore easily perceive the drift of my thoughts — and what I should like would be for you carefully to revise the whole, in a dispassionate mood, and to remove such terms of reproach, or hasty expressions either respecting Mary's persecutors, or the accusers which since her own days have been endeavouring to gain the public mind.[4]

The key to Laing the antiquary was the 'dispassionate mood' he urged upon his aged mentor. In this he was the inheritor of all that was best in two centuries of Scottish antiquarian scholarship. In the past historical studies in Scotland had too often been subject to violent religious or political partisanship, but the greatest of Scotland's antiquaries shunned these extremes. They brought to their studies the disengaged mind necessary to understand the past on its own terms: in a sense their attitude was essentially scientific. For Laing, this detached attitude towards the past was not achieved without personal cost. Laing was the most self-effacing of men who never revealed the inner details of his character or feelings, but there are hints of a number of early disappointments which helped to reinforce his own retiring nature. Laing certainly aspired to success in his chosen field: 'energy and vigour will ever be preferred to sober dulness'.[5] In this instance Laing was referring to the spirit informing the early issues of *Blackwood's Magazine*, but the attitude applied as much to himself as the new journal. Many of Laing's youthful disappointments stemmed from his connections with William Blackwood. The two had been friends as early as 1815 when they applied unsuccessfully to the Society of Antiquaries of Scotland for permission to consult the Hawthornden MSS in their care (MB 3, 96). This was Laing's first contact with the Society in which he was later to play such an important role. In 1816 Laing journeyed to the Low Countries with James Wilson, the brother of John Wilson soon to attain notoriety as 'Christopher North' in *Blackwood's*. In Holland Laing met J. G. Lockhart, who versified Laing's attainments in an early issue of the magazine:

> David, the sagacious and the best
>> As all Old Reekie's erudites opine,
> Of Scottish Bibliophiles, who knows the zest
>> And cream of every title-page *Aldine*;
> A famous Bibliomaniac, and a shrewd,
> Who turns his madness to no little good.

On the return journey from London to Edinburgh following this continental trip, Laing accompanied William Blackwood, now full of ideas
for his new magazine.

These friendships brought Laing into a circle of men whose literary
high spirits, especially the notorious 'Chaldee MS.', caused something
of a scandal in Edinburgh circles. Laing seems to have been tainted by
this association in the eyes of some of the Edinburgh establishment.
Chalmers mentions a threat of prosecution against Laing in a letter of
22 November 1817, and in a reply on 9 December Laing made his
position clear:

> . . . in your former letter you refer to prosecutions — do you mean any against
> me? or have such rumours reached so far as London? I make it a rule never to do
> what I would be ashamed to stand up boldly and affirm.[6]

Clearly Laing had a strong appreciation of his own gifts and wished to
find a role in life in which they could find practical expression and use,
for example in the organisation of one of Edinburgh's great libraries. In
1819 he had applied for the vacant position of librarian of the Advocates' Library. Despite support from such figures as Walter Scott, he
failed to gain the appointment because of 'party spirit'.[7]

Following his failure to gain the Advocates' appointment, other disappointments followed. He was blackballed when he was proposed for
membership of the Society of Antiquaries of Scotland in 1820.[8] By this
time Laing was taking active steps to end his close association with the
Blackwood's circle. In 1819 he had asked William Blackwood that he
should no longer receive the magazine *gratis*, but was also at some
pains to assure his old friend that this request should not be 'any
grounds of offence'.[9]

In 1821 Laing became a partner in his father's business, and his care-
free youth was over. His abilities as a literary scholar and biblio-
grapher were by now widely recognised. Early in 1823 Walter Scott
asked Laing to be the secretary of the newly founded Bannatyne Club.
By this time Laing had edited and published six volumes of literary
texts, mostly poetry. The Bannatyne Club was founded to publish
Scottish literary and historical texts in beautiful and accurate editions.
The volumes were not just collector's items for the club's select
membership; they were also intended to be accurate texts for the use of
historical and literary scholars.

The first publishing club, the Roxburghe, had been founded in the
wake of the sale of the Duke of Roxburghe's library in 1812 to create

new, rare volumes. The Bannatyne was conceived on different terms, for it existed not just to produce rare books but useful ones as well. To be useful the books had to attain high critical and editorial standards. This was where David Laing was to play a crucial part in the club's success. Scott had chosen his man well. In early July 1824 he wrote to Laing of his hopes for the Bannatyne:

> I am . . . of decided opinion that to do the club credit and be useful to History the works undertaken by the association should be of a substantial and useful kind . . . In a word let us have the most curious of Scottish authors illustrated by the most curious of Scottish Antiquaries.[10]

Laing's attitude towards the literary and written historical records of his country *was* essentially antiquarian: he valued such survivals for their age and uniqueness as well as their intrinsic qualities. But these feelings were overlaid and disciplined by a more systematic attitude towards the texts than had characterised many literary antiquaries of the previous centuries. In order to make texts accessible to the modern reader it was necessary that they be edited with a full scholarly apparatus. This was manifest in the first volume published by the Bannatyne Club, *The buke of the howlat* (1823). Laing had been working on the text as early as 1821.[11] In the Bannatyne Club edition the text of the fifteenth-century poem was printed in full (in type beautiful enough to delight the bibliomaniacal membership) and was accompanied by full notes, an introduction (including a note by Scott), a discussion by Laing of the poem's origins and probable authorship, along with an appendix giving variant readings of the text and notes on the poem's relationship to contemporary events.

Laing's editorial and administrative abilities set the seal on the Bannatyne Club's success and made his rejection by the Society of Antiquaries of Scotland something of a scandal. He was again proposed for membership (without his knowledge) and was elected on 9 February 1824 (MB 3, 287). An anonymous letter (perhaps sent to Laing in London by his father) indicates that there had been a good deal of feeling over his election:

> I do not know whether you were officially informed of your being unanimously elected a member of the Antiquarian Society — but such was the case a few days after your departure. Dr Hibbert [the secretary] is very proud of it and says that if it had been opposed he and Mr Kinnear were to have left them.[12]

By this election Laing's gifts as a scholar — and perhaps even more important, as an administrator — were brought to the service of the

Society and were to be fully employed during one of the most crucial periods in the history of the Scottish Antiquaries.

Within six weeks of his election Laing had made the first of over one hundred communications to the Society: a letter to Dr Hibbert recommending the publication by the Society of a *Numismata Scotiae* (MB 3, 290). By 1825 Laing was active in Society business, especially in the proposed recommencement of publication of the Society's *Transactions*. He was appointed a member of the publications subcommittee in November 1825 (MB 3, 315).

In the 1820s and early 1830s the Society was passing through a period of relative prosperity under a succession of energetic and able secretaries: Dr Hibbert (later Hibbert-Ware), E. W. A. Drummond Hay and Donald Gregory. Moreover in 1819 a regular curator of the Society's collections had been appointed: James Skene of Rubislaw. He spent six months arranging the Society's collection of artefacts, coins and books (*Arch Scot* 3, xvii). In 1822 a subcommittee was appointed to consider how to revive the Society's 'usefulness and efficiency' (*Arch Scot* 3, xix-xxiii). The Society was already concerned that its collections, of interest to a growing number of their fellow-countrymen, should be displayed in a more fitting manner. It was necessary, therefore, to find a suitable house for the collection, which could not be fully displayed in their current accommodation at 42 George Street.

The apartments in George Street were shared with the Royal Society of Edinburgh. During this period the Antiquaries functioned very much as the literary and historical wing of the Royal Society: a relationship reinforced by a large shared membership and a common curator for their respective collections. Both societies were anxious to enlarge their public roles. The means to this end was better accommodation than they presently occupied in flats over a perfumer's shop. Consequently both societies entered into an agreement with the Board of Trustees for Manufactures to take apartments in the new 'Building for the Societies' being constructed at the foot of The Mound (now the Royal Scottish Academy). The Royal Society took out a twenty-five year lease. The Antiquaries rented their apartments: a distinction which was to have consequences in the future.[13]

The two societies removed to their new contiguous apartments in 1826. It might have seemed that such a change would reinforce the common interests and identity of the two associations, but it appears to have had the opposite effect. A symptom of this growing divorce of interest can be seen in the story of David Laing's blackballing by the

Royal Society in 1827. His friend, fellow antiquary, and member of the
Royal Society, Sir David Brewster, wrote to him on 26 March 1827
about his failure to be elected:

> I think you have just reason to take offence on this occasion — not that five black
> balls were put in against you, for nothing is more common than to see many black
> balls at our elections, and every person is entitled to exercise his privilege — but at
> the absence of so many of your friends on that occasion, as the presence of even
> one more would have carried your election.[14]

Laing later refused election to the Royal Society when it was offered to
him, not so much due to pique at his initial rejection as because of his
recognition of the changing nature of the two societies. Years later he
said of his refusal to stand again: 'At the time there was a general
feeling for reviving its Literary Department — and I was desirous of
some stimulus to make me exert myself'.[15] If the Royal Society was
attempting to create its own 'domestic' literary wing, then the function
of the Antiquaries as its *de facto* literary adjunct was bound to decline.
The failure to elect Laing a member of the Royal Society at this juncture
meant that Laing would continue 'to exert' himself in the literary
societies to which he already belonged: the Bannatyne Club and the
Antiquaries. Laing's literary efforts in the Antiquaries led in 1831 to the
appearance of another volume of the Society's transactions,
Archaeologia Scotica, which he edited as a second to Dr Hibbert.
Laing's role was central in the revived programme of publications
undertaken by the Antiquaries in the early 1830s: a prelude to nearly
forty years' involvement in Society publications.

Another way in which the Antiquaries hoped to reinforce their
identity as an archaeological and historical body was by expanding
their museum. It was hoped that the new rooms for the museum would
encourage further bequests and make the collection more accessible to
the public. At a Council meeting of 27 November 1827 the acting
secretary, Mr Drummond Hay, 'reported on the great advantages that
had resulted to the Society's collections, from the liberal measure of
admitting the public to the museum' (MB 3, 371). In this aim of making
the museum a more public institution the Society was clearly
influenced by the work going on in Scandinavia, particularly Denmark
where, beginning in 1816, the national collections had been re-
organised, catalogued and rehoused under the direction of C. J.
Thomsen.[16] In April 1829 the Society heard a paper by Robert Bald on
the collections in the Copenhagen museum (MB 4, 32).

Connections between Scottish antiquaries and their Scandinavian brethren had long been close, allowing for the disruption of war. In 1783 Grímur Thorkelin became the first Scandinavian to be elected to the Society of Antiquaries of Scotland. Since then there had been a growing number of Scandinavian corresponding and honorary members of the Society. The revival of historical and archaeological studies in early nineteenth-century Scandinavia meant that a growing number of scholars came to Scotland in search of historical manuscripts or the visible remains of Viking settlement. There were similar — if less official — visits by Scots to Scandinavia. In 1819 David Laing had followed in his father's footsteps to Copenhagen to buy the library of Thorkelin. In the course of his visit he made the acquaintance, through the agency of his Danish friend Andreas Andersen Feldborg, of a number of scholars, including Finn Magnussen.[17] From this time onwards Laing remained in close touch with a number of Scandinavian scholars and was a regular point of contact in Scotland for such visitors as Sven Grundtvig, J. J. A. Worsaae and P. A. Munch. The growth of these personal contacts was complemented by the opening of formal relations between the Society of Antiquaries of Scotland and the Royal Society of Northern Antiquaries in 1829 (Corr 5, 15 June 1829). Although the Danish body had been founded only four years previously, the Scottish Antiquaries were aware even before then that they had much to learn from Denmark. Especially important was the way the collection and preservation of antiquities was the concern of the state and not left to private bodies. The Scots were particularly struck by the enlightened laws governing compensation paid to those finding valuable archaeological material. In Scotland by contrast, the law of treasure trove was ill defined. When objects did fall to the crown there was no legal requirement to give compensation to the original finder. This meant that finders either attempted to hide their discoveries, sold them quickly for ready cash or even allowed them to be melted down for their metal value. By contrast Denmark had since 1752 had a law which promised 'full reimbursement' for the value of any coins or valuables of antiquarian interest.[18] From the 1820s onwards some objects which fell to the crown were handed over to the Antiquaries' Museum by sympathetic Kings' and Lord Treasurers' Remembrancers — but the basic problem of a lack of defined treasure trove law remained.[19]

Even before the move to their new apartments on The Mound there were signs of financial strain in the Society. The original rent of £75 per annum had been raised to £100. Attempts were made to collect the large amount of arrears and, after the move, further money was made by subletting the Antiquaries' apartments to such bodies as the Bannatyne Club and the Society of Arts (Corr 4, letters dated 17 November 1826, 25 January 1827). Despite these problems, however, the move to The Mound was a justified success. The Society's collection was growing and being seen by an increasing number of people. Tickets allowing access (which had to be signed by members) were printed and arrangements made for members to be in attendance on public days 'for the better security of the Museum and for the convenient opportunity of shewing attention to strangers' (MB 3, 371). In 1828 the Society entered into a arrangement with the Royal Society for exchanges between their respective museums (MB 4, 31). This meant the Society of Antiquaries could turn over its natural history exhibits to the Royal Society and confine its collection to purely historical material.

With its elegant new home the Society ventured to assume a more public role in the study, collection and discovery of historical material. On a number of occasions members were asked to contribute to special appeals for funds to buy important pieces for the Museum, an example being the two gold bracelets found in a burial site at Alloa in 1828 (MB 4, 34). In 1829 members were invited to contribute to proposed excavations at Absembal [sic] by Robert Hay of Linplum (MB 4, 103-5). Circulars were sent by the Antiquaries to local authorities asking that archaeological finds made in their areas be reported to the Society. In 1828 the Society played a leading role in the campaign to have Mons Meg returned from London to Edinburgh (MB 4, 33 and 58-9).

The Mons Meg campaign was an early example of the Antiquaries engaging in a project which had a wider application than merely to add to the Society's collections. It was becoming clear, even in the 1820s, that the accelerating changes taking place in Scotland would have a profound effect on Scottish antiquities. The opening chapters of Daniel Wilson's The archaeology and prehistoric annals of Scotland (1851) are full of prehistoric finds turned up in the course of field drainage works, and the excavation of canal and railway cuttings. With the growth of railways, especially during the period of 'railway mania' in the 1840s, these problems would reach something like crisis proportions, forcing the Society to continue its role as a public spokesman for the preservation of antiquities. At the annual general meeting of 1845, for example, the Society addressed itself to the problems posed by railway development:

The society expressed a hope that the Directors of the several Railways now in progress would give orders for the transmission to the Society of any Antiquities discovered in the course of excavation (MB 5, 127).

In some cases the railway companies did co-operate, but in others they did not. A major archaeological disaster struck when the Trinity College Chapel in Edinburgh was demolished (despite petitions and protests by the Society and others) to make way for the Waverley Station shunting yard. The Antiquaries were successful in organising the reinterment of the supposed bones of Mary of Gueldres at Holyrood. Having obtained their shunting yard, the North British Railway Company could afford to be magnanimous: the Society were allowed to take casts of a number of important stone carvings from the Chapel into their collection and they also purchased two gargoyles (MB 5, 224, dated 5 May 1848).

Other campaigns of the Society included one for the return of the Trinity College altarpiece to Edinburgh and the restoration of Queen Margaret's Chapel (rediscovered by Daniel Wilson who recognised it in the guise of a powder magazine in the mid-1840s). But this growing public role for the Antiquaries was played out in the 1830s and 40s against a background of crisis in the affairs of the Society: a crisis which David Laing was later to claim brought the Society of Antiquaries of Scotland to the verge of extinction in the early 1840s.

Financial weakness was a recurring problem. As early as October 1828 a permanent committee of three members was appointed to audit the Society's accounts and recover arrears. One of the three members was David Laing (MB 4, 59 *passim*). The committee found that after all the expenses of the Society had been met, including the printing of the third volume of transactions, there remained a balance of £7 6s 3d. They began to try to collect arrears and to send regular notices to defaulters (MB 4, 72-4). Despite these attempts, however, the financial state of the Society became even more precarious. The situation was exacerbated by the withdrawal of many of the more scientifically orientated members, due to the growing split of interests between the Royal Society and the Antiquaries. A further problem was the death, in 1833, of the Antiquaries' treasurer, the banker-mineralogist, Thomas Allan. The decline of his business affairs (which led to the failure of the family bank within a few years of his death) may have been paralleled in his work as the Society's treasurer. What was more important, however, was the fact that he had no successor for over a year until, in what he called 'an evil hour for myself', Laing was appointed treasurer in the winter of 1836 (*Arch Scot* 5, 20). By the following year he was receiving threatening letters from the Board of Manufactures about delays in paying the Society's rent. Laing himself was to spend the decade following his appointment as treasurer trying first to avert the threatened termination of the Society of Antiquaries and then to re-organise the Society so that it could become the useful national body he felt it should be.

Laing's first action as treasurer was to print a circular asking all members to pay any arrears owing to the Society. Because of dis-organisation in the Society's records his circulars offended many fully paid-up members, and Laing was inundated with a number of irate letters and resignations. The financial records of the Society were of little help in bringing the membership records up to date. Furthermore the secretary's minutes were incomplete due to the death of Donald Gregory in 1835 and the resignation of his successor as secretary, William Forbes Skene, in 1837. Skene was replaced in the following year by the aged Alexander Smellie, who had first acted as secretary to the Society in 1795. From 1839 to 1841, therefore, in addition to his other duties Laing also acted as assistant secretary until a replacement could be found.

By 1840 the Society's debts amounted to £400. These consisted mainly of £150 rent due for their apartments, £200 outstanding on a bond entered into by various members of the Society in 1794 for the purchase of the Castle Hill house, and a loss of revenue due to the failure of the Society's claim for exemption as a learned body from assessment for the newly created Edinburgh police burgh. A further blow fell in 1840 when the Board of Manufactures refused to allow the Society to continue to sublet its rooms (Corr 7, dated 3 December 1840; *Arch Scot* 5, 27). In order to meet immediate expenses Laing and Alexander Smellie opened up a cash credit account for £100 on their personal security.

Laing's circular letter of 1837 had brought in some much needed funds and allowed the membership lists to be brought up to date. Out of this crisis a new Society was emerging.

Whatever its financial fortunes, the Society's Museum was becoming increasingly popular with the general public. The Museum had been seen by 4,000 people in 1841, and by even more in the following year, especially in the week Prince Albert visited the collection (MB 5, 50). In this the collection complemented the archaeological popularisation being done by such new middle-class journals as that edited by Robert

Chambers, who became a Fellow of the Society in 1844. Besides Robert Chambers, other new members included the pioneer anaesthetist J. Y. Simpson (who was also a gifted archaeologist), the photographer D. O. Hill, and the Leith merchant John Mitchell. In addition to his commercial activities, Mitchell acted as Belgian consul and had a wide range of scholarly interests including archaeology, natural history, mineralogy and Scandinavian languages. These men were bound together by their common devotion to Scottish antiquities, but they also brought new attitudes to the Society, not least of which was a strong desire that the Society should be useful to society at large. They were men of experience in many walks of life, endowed with ability and common sense, and it seemed to them that the Society was in an anomalous position; a private association engaged on what should be public business. Such a role might have been acceptable for the Bannatyne Club in its heyday under Sir Walter Scott, but it would not do for the Society of Antiquaries of Scotland in the mid-nineteenth century.

The problem was to convince the government of this truth. By the early 1840s the Society had decided to appeal to the government for a grant to pay for the running of their Museum. Their case seemed a strong one, for in addition to the Scandinavian examples many of the members had seen for themselves, grants were made by the British government to historical collections in London and Dublin. Nevertheless the Society's petition for a grant to cover their arrears of rent was refused. It seems that the Antiquaries had much to learn about the proper way to ask for government money, and not least how to phrase their requests: a petition for a remission of rent might have stood a better chance of success than a request for an outright grant. It is clear from the terms of the Society's reply to the government's initial refusal that Scottish antiquarian tempers were running very high; a further indication perhaps that the Society had yet to acquire the tact and diplomacy necessary to see such a campaign through to a successful conclusion. The Antiquaries claimed to be acting on behalf of their fellow-countrymen:

> . . . to whom they wish to preserve a museum so closely connected with their past history and most patriotic feelings. In this view of the case, the Council and Fellows of the Society consider the refusal of their application . . . as a slight offered to Scotland; and they cannot help comparing . . . the very stinted measure of support which Scientific Institutions in Scotland receive from the government, with the munificent grants of public money annually made to those in England, and still more so, to those in Ireland, a country which, while it contributes much

less than its due proportion to the public revenue, receives incontestably more
than its due proportion of the public money (MB 5, 91-2).

The Society continued to ask for support from the early 1840s, but it
became clear that if their attempts were to be met with success they
must be more tactfully presented and that the Society must give an
indication that they were indeed the national and responsible body
they claimed to be. In order to put their house in order the Antiquaries
turned increasingly to the model of Scandinavia, and in this the visit of
the Danish archaeologist J. J. A. Worsaae in 1846 was of crucial
importance. In his letter to the Society's secretary after his arrival in
Edinburgh Worsaae announced that '. . . part of my mission is to unite
the efforts of the British and Scandinavian antiquaries more than
hitherto has been the case' (Comm 8, 3 November 1846). Following his
visit, the Dane was elected a corresponding fellow of the Society, and
an exchange of objects between the Copenhagen Museum and the
Society's collection was arranged (MB 5, 156-7). It seems significant
that shortly after Worsaae's visit the Society became very much
concerned with the reform of treasure trove laws along Danish lines.
Worsaae is directly quoted to this effect in the foreword of Daniel
Wilson's *Prehistoric annals*.[20]

In 1846 John Mitchell had journeyed to Scandinavia and upon his
return had presented two papers to the Society on the state of
archaeology in Copenhagen and Uppsala (MB 5, 131 and 134). A few
years later Robert Chambers made a similar journey and returned with
a collection of Swedish stone-age artefacts for the Antiquaries'
Museum (MB 5, 298). In 1850 he read a two-part paper to the Society,
'On the collection of objects for antiquarian museums, with special
reference to the practice in Denmark by a Gentleman connected with
the Museum of Northern Antiquities' (MB 5, 330).

Another major Scandinavian influence on the Scottish antiquaries of
this period was the Norwegian historian P. A. Munch who arrived in
Scotland late in 1849. Munch was introduced to David Laing by John
Mitchell, and it was in the Signet Library (where Laing had been
librarian since 1837) that Munch saw the Panmure manuscript, containing the earliest history of Norway. Munch formed a number of
lasting friendships amongst the Society's members, including Mitchell,
Laing and Daniel Wilson, and was elected a corresponding member
(along with three other Norwegian historians) in 1850. He contributed
a number of papers to the Society after his Scottish visit.

By the time of Munch's visit the Antiquaries were well on their way to proving their claim to be a national body, worthy of government support. The first priority was housing. In 1840 George Meikle Kemp, the architect of the Scott monument, had proposed the construction of a 'Norman Hall' beside his monument to house the Society's collection. Nothing came of this intriguing but expensive suggestion (MB 5, 11). Instead the affairs of the Society became increasingly precarious, so that in 1843 Laing was constrained to write to the Board of Manufactures:

> The Society of Antiquaries having recently made an unsuccessful attempt to obtain from the Lords of the Treasury some aid to enable them to pay the rent of their apartments . . . a proposal is about to be made as to the propriety of removing to less expensive premises (Corr 7, 21 February 1843).

Laing ended his letter with a request that the Society's lease be terminated at Whitsuntide the following year. The Board replied that they were agreeable to this, provided arrears were first paid. In fact the Board were most anxious for the Antiquaries to move, since they wished to expand the accommodation for their School of Design. In July 1843 the second appeal for government aid was turned down and Laing informed the Board that the Society were unable to pay the £150 rent still outstanding, but that the Antiquaries still wished to remove in the following year. In the meantime the Council of the Society decided to launch another appeal to the government. In fact, the genesis of the Society's salvation came from a closer and less elevated quarter, the Antiquaries' energetic new assistant secretary, W. B. D. D. Turnbull. Turnbull was an advocate who had had a somewhat erratic career as founder and secretary of the Abbotsford Club, a publishing club founded in 1833. This was due to the enthusiasms and instabilities of Turnbull himself who in the 1830s and 40s was passing through a series of religious conversions, punctuated by printed outbursts, which alienated many people in the highly charged atmosphere preceding the Disruption of 1843. Nevertheless, unlike some other projects in which he concerned himself, Turnbull's work for the Society was to bring lasting benefit.

Early in 1843 he had opened negotiations with the Edinburgh Life Association, suggesting that the Society might take up rooms in their proposed new building at 24 George Street. The rent was to be £65 per annum for three rooms: a large hall for the Museum, a library and a committee room (Corr 7, 15 February 1843). There the matter rested until the government once again refused the Society's petition for aid.

In March 1844 a special Council meeting was convened following this refusal, and the notification by the Board of Manufactures that unless outstanding rent was paid 'the Library, Museum, and other chattels pertaining to the Society would inevitably be distrained for payment' (MB 5, 74). Years later Laing claimed that the Society had been 'told, most distinctly, if not in such precise words, that the property of the Society would be arrested and sold off, if necessary, in order to pay the accumulating arrears' (*Arch Scot* 5, 28). That the Board was within its rights to threaten this is borne out in the clause in the original lease that the Society was to 'grant an assignation to the Board's cashier of their whole effects and Museum . . .' (MB 3, 333).

The Society and its collection were rescued from this threatened impasse by Turnbull's agreement with the Edinburgh Life Association, which made a loan for the amount owing to the Board and other outstanding debts, using the Society's apartments in their building as security. All the Society's financial liabilities were thus put into one basket, where they could be settled in a more regular manner.

Just as the affairs of the Society had to be put on a sound and regular footing, so had the basis of Scottish archaeology. The man who was to make the first attempt to do this was Daniel Wilson, elected to the Society in 1846, and elected secretary in 1847 when the aged Alexander Smellie was finally persuaded to retire.

Wilson had been born in Edinburgh in 1816, the son of a wine merchant. He had six brothers and sisters, one of whom was the chemist, George Wilson, later professor of technology at Edinburgh University and first curator of the Royal Scottish Museum. Wilson's childhood homes on the Calton Hill and later in James Square were bases for exploring and sketching trips in the Old Town of Edinburgh. The drawings done on these excursions were the sketches for the engravings in Wilson's first published work, *Memorials of Edinburgh in the olden time* (1847). In the course of his sketching trips Wilson discovered the remains of many early buildings, one of which was later the subject of his first paper to the Society of Antiquaries: St Margaret's Chapel in Edinburgh Castle (MB 5, 152). Wilson attended classes at Edinburgh University but left without taking a degree to go to London to train as an engraver. There he met the artist J. M. W. Turner and in 1837 was given permission to engrave one of his paintings. Half a century later Wilson still recalled the experience of translating the light and colour of a Turner painting into the hard steel lines of an engraver's plate as 'a lesson to me for life'.[21] The problems he faced as an engraver were to reconcile the detail necessary for cutting the plate with the 'atmospheric effect' of a Turner painting. This necessary attention to minute detail in order to understand and render an overall effect was to spill over into his work as an archaeologist and ethnologist. His artist's eye provided a useful tool for his archaeological studies, particularly his concern for the human and social context of artefacts which is central to Wilson's importance as an archaeological pioneer and thinker.

When he had gone to London, Wilson had thought that art was 'to be in some form, my life pursuit',[22] but by the early 1840s his attention was turning towards literature. In addition to writing several books, he undertook reviewing work for such journals as *Chambers*. By the time he returned to Scotland in 1842 he was becoming increasingly interested in Scottish history and antiquities. When he was elected to the Society of Antiquaries of Scotland he had already begun to contemplate the writing of his great work, *The archaeology and prehistoric annals of Scotland* (1851). His work for the Society during a testing time had a direct bearing on the book.

With Daniel Wilson's election to office a new and more purposeful spirit enters the affairs of the Society. If David Laing was the last of the great traditional antiquaries, then Daniel Wilson was the first of a new archaeological breed, determined to put the Society and its collections on a more public and scientific footing. To do this he had not only to help save the Society financially, but to reorganise the study of Scottish archaeology in a systematic way. To Wilson, archaeological studies had hitherto been 'laborious trifling' but now they were to be organised so that they could take their rightful place as 'an indispensable link in the circle of the sciences'.[23] An important part of the reformation Wilson wished to bring about was to create a wider popular interest in archaeology and to generate patriotism: the social context in which the revived study of the past was to take place was of crucial importance to Wilson.

The example Wilson had before his eye was not just the popularising work of C. J. Thomsen in Copenhagen, but even more his work as a systematiser of prehistory, which was completed and popularised by Worsaae. In his *Primeval antiquities of Denmark* (1843) Worsaae had established Thomsen's tripartite division of prehistory on the basis of the materials used for artefacts: stone, bronze and iron. Wilson was certainly familiar with the work before it appeared in English translation in 1849, for on his journey to Scotland in 1846 Worsaae had left a copy of the work (inscribed in his own hand) in the Society's Library.

The vast difference between the treatment of archaeological and historical studies in Scandinavia and their own country was a constant preoccupation of the leaders of the Scottish Antiquaries in the later 1840s. Further petitions for state aid were contemplated but no government aid was likely to be forthcoming at a time when the Irish potato famine (and the famine closer to home in the Scottish Highlands) was taking up so much government time and resources. Gradually a feeling grew up within the Society that the answer was not government help, but rather a transfer of their collection to the care of the state. It was recognised, however, that if this end was to be achieved the Society must (literally) put their house in order. By early 1848 the Society had begun to campaign for a return to The Mound, where a new building was being planned for the Royal Society of Edinburgh and the Royal Scottish Academy (MB 5, 190, 214-16). As part of this campaign Daniel Wilson undertook the 'pure labour of Love'[24] of compiling a synopsis of the Museum's collection along the lines of the tripartite division (MB 5, 290). Wilson was not, however, a slave to this system any more than Worsaae had been. The tripartite division of prehistory had to be modified to fit local conditions. After his visit to Scotland Worsaae had gone to Ireland, where he addressed the Royal Irish Academy on the subject of his system and its local application. Shortly after it was delivered, a copy of his paper arrived in the Library of the Scottish antiquaries, where Wilson must have seen it.

Worsaae saw Ireland as the closest non-Scandinavian parallel to the archaeological history of Denmark. Ireland had not been conquered by the Romans and its prehistoric development before the iron period was largely indigenous. This meant that there were striking parallels — but not exact identities — between the artefacts and structures produced in the stone (and even more in the bronze) period in Ireland and Denmark. Like the best Enlightenment social philosophers, Worsaae argued that cultural development was conditioned by the state of Society: roughly similar societies produced roughly similar artefacts and structures.[25] Wilson took this concept and gave it practical expression in his *Synopsis*. The tripartite system was used, therefore, in its 'freest signification'. The stone and bronze periods, for example, were 'classed under the general head Celtic'.[26] Already Daniel Wilson was concerned with what might be called the 'atmospheric effect' of archaeological periodisation: the cultural, social and linguistic context of artefacts. The key to understanding context was Man himself.

Wilson recognised the social basis of his thought in his claim that Sir Walter Scott was the source of the 'zeal for Archaeological investigation which has recently manifested itself' because the past he created in his novels was peopled by real men and women.[27] The budding ethnologist in Wilson was also apparent in the *Synopsis*, for in the foreword he makes comparison between Scotland and the stone and bronze age periods in Assyria, Egypt and Mexico. These were some of the earliest steps Wilson took towards the study of comparative ethnology which was to occupy so much of his time in his later years in Canada.

The idea that societies at similar stages of development display similar characteristics was a legacy from the Enlightenment social thinkers of Scotland. This belief, transferred to archaeological theory, meant that societies at similar stages of development produce similar artefacts. The new arrangement of the Antiquaries' Museum reinforced this general theme of similarities (but not total identity) between different peoples in roughly similar stages of development. For example, the first case in the Museum contained British and Irish stone arrowheads and axes, labelled with their provenance (where known), donor and date. The next case contained Danish stone age artefacts, part of a gift from the Royal Society of Northern Antiquaries and the Danish Crown Prince who had visited the Society's Museum in 1844. The comparisons afforded in the Museum did not end with Europe, however, for the same case also contained American Indian and South Seas exhibits. Cases three and four contained stone vessels, earthenware and personal ornaments from Britain, along with bone and ivory amulets from Africa 'for the purposes of comparison'. The concern with comparative exhibits is stressed by a letter to Wilson (probably from Robert Chambers) in which the writer tells him to locate Scandinavian objects in the Museum 'so that they may be contrasted as well as compared with the analogous or rather similar objects drawn from Scotland' (Corr 8, 21 October 1849).

The *Synopsis* of the Society's Museum appeared in 1849 and was a sketch for Wilson's great work of systematisation of Scottish prehistory which would appear two years later. In both the *Synopsis* and *Prehistoric annals*, Wilson went beyond the strictly prehistoric (or preliterate) periods to deal with the relics of medieval and more modern times. Aside from the 'Celtic' and iron age exhibits, the Museum contained Egyptian, Roman and Greek material, medieval items, Jacobite relics, mementoes of Sir Walter Scott, 'Jenny Geddes' stool', and the Edinburgh guillotine, 'The Maiden'.

The range of the Society's collection revealed in the *Synopsis* strengthened the Antiquaries' claims for the national character of the Museum. As soon as the possibility of being again housed on The Mound had arisen, Daniel Wilson had gone to London to pursue the matter. There his main contact was William Gibson Craig, the politician brother of a leading Scottish antiquary, James Gibson Craig. At the time Gibson Craig (a Lord of the Treasury) was involved in the enquiry into the state of the arts in Scotland that led to the proposal to build a National Gallery on The Mound. In a letter of 23 June 1848 Wilson made a progress report to David Laing:

> I have been very courteously and kindly received. Government officials say, what was to be expected — that there is no money at present to spare. But Mr Gibson Craig heartily acknowledges the reasonableness of our claims and holds out fair though indefinite promises for the future.[28]

By the following year the Society had gained some more allies. Early in 1848 Charles Cowan MP promised help in presenting the Society's claims for accommodation in the new building on The Mound. Another Parliamentary ally was the radical MP Joseph Hume. For him the campaign for the Society to be given government support had an added ideological significance: the Museum was to be 'considered as a training school for the mass of the working population' (Comm 8, memorial to Lord John Russell, 28 March 1850). It was at Hume's suggestion that Wilson drew up a memorial, which the MP undertook to present to Lord John Russell. After explaining that a large proportion of their funds had always been devoted to the exhibition of a National Museum of Archaeology in the Scottish capital, and that the extent of their success rendered their private income insufficient, the memorial concluded:

> Should her Majesty's Government be pleased to provide them with suitable accommodation such as has long been enjoyed by the Society of Antiquaries of London in Somerset House, they will be pleased to place their valuable Archaeological Museum on the same liberal footing for the gratification and instruction of the People as other National Collections (Comm 7, 6 December 1849).

Hume delayed presentation of this memorial until he could discuss the matter with the Prime Minister, and accompanied it with a letter of his own, making additional points informally:

> If your Lordship . . . therefore will enable the Society to get suitable rooms, they intend to *present the Collection of 70 years formation* to the government for the use of the public forever . . . (Comm 8, 28 March 1850).

Hume went on to suggest that the collection should again be housed on The Mound and enclosed a copy of the Society's rules and accounts, now happily on a sound footing. In April 1851 B. F. Primrose, secretary of the Board of Manufactures, wrote to David Laing:

> . . . by certain mutual arrangements and exchange of apartments, accommodation in the Royal Institution Building could be provided for the Society after the completion and opening of the new National Gallery [EUL MS.]

Laing met with the Board on the following day and final arrangements were made. At a meeting of the Antiquaries' Council on 5 May these arrangements were agreed. In return for accommodation in the Royal Institution Building for their Museum and meeting hall, the Society made over their collection and all subsequent additions to form the basis of a national archaeological museum, reserving the 'charge and management' of the collection to the Society, subject to the Board regulations and directions, as approved by the Treasury. There was a last-minute hitch when the Treasury attempted to demur at the Society's request for free accommodation and free access for all Fellows to the Library and collections (MB 5, 407). An agreement with Gibson Craig was finally reached, leaving the question of access unspecified. At an extraordinary general meeting (with Robert Chambers in the chair) held on 5 May 1851 the Society agreed to these terms (MB 5, 382-3). A copy of the deed of conveyance was laid on the table at the annual general meeting in November and agreed to (MB 5, 420). The Board was to be responsible for all new display cabinets and the employment of staff. The Society was to look after arranging the collection and appointing the curator, and it also retained the power to exchange duplicates for new materials. (MB 5, 277 *passim*). The transfer was finally effected in 1858.

The campaign to transfer the Society's collection to government control had brought other changes in its wake. Once again Daniel Wilson was the main innovator. He began a series of popular evening conversaziones during which Fellows and their guests heard short talks or had the chance to view interesting finds and exhibits. At the first conversazione held under Wilson's direction in 1848 D. O. Hill exhibited calotypes of 'Scottish topographical antiquities and portraits', perhaps the earliest instance of the use of photography in archaeological studies (MB 5, 205).

The growth of railways in the 1840s meant that the Society for the first time was able to hold meetings and undertake archaeological excursions outside Edinburgh, thus increasing the 'national' scope of its activities. Amongst the earliest such excursions was one to Inchcolm in 1848 (MB 5, 182, 239 and 248). A less admirable railway excursion was a day trip to excavate a tumulus at Duntocher in the same year. (MB 5, 183, 285; Corr 8, 18 January 1848). In June 1849 an excursions committee was appointed, consisting of Robert Chambers, David Laing and Daniel Wilson, charged with arranging summer trips for the Fellows (MB 5, 290).

There was also a new scientific spirit abroad amongst the Society's membership, reflecting the interests of many of the new members. In 1850, for example, David Laing requested that several bronze objects found at Duddingston and presented to the Society in the year following its foundation should be subject to chemical analysis (MB 5, 331).

Meanwhile the Society's Museum continued to attract a growing number of visitors. On New Year's Day 1851 the Museum (still in its inconvenient upstairs premises in George Street) was opened to the public and was '. . . inspected by 1330 visitors, almost entirely of the working classes without the slightest injury to the Collections' (MB 5, 360). In the previous year over nine thousand people had visited the Museum.

All these changes were pointers towards the future role of the Society and its Museum, once it had been taken into state ownership. At the anniversary meeting in the November following the agreement to transfer the Museum, Daniel Wilson took the opportunity not only to look at the changes that had already come about but also to consider the changes necessary for the future. Although he was clearly pleased and relieved by the transfer, he recognised that there was still a long way to go before the Museum could be full and comprehensive enough to bear comparison with the great continental collections. The creation of the National Museum was 'only the first instalment of an act of tardy justice'.[29] Amongst the problems which would have to be dealt with urgently was the reform of the treasure trove law. The question of treasure trove had been an intermittent or implicit concern of the Society since the reorganisation of its Museum in the 1820s. Not only did the Society's leaders wish to have the law clarified and strengthened as part of the transfer of their Museum to the state, they were also concerned by the destruction of archaeological material in the wake of such changes as railway development. Daniel Wilson deplored the practical effects of the ill-defined legal situation which, as he said, '. . .

frequently compels the students of a liberal science to pursue their researches with the stealth and secrecy of the lawless spoiler or resetter
. . .'[30] A major reason for the transfer of the Museum to state control
was the hope that the collection would thereafter be endowed with
objects falling to the Crown, but given the ill-defined nature of the law
of treasure trove there was no guarantee that this would happen. Until
finders of valuable historical material were given compensation for
their finds, as was done in Scandinavia, many chance discoveries
would not be reported or would be lost or destroyed. In the wake of
Worsaae's visit Wilson had raised the matter at a meeting of the Society
on 8 February 1847 and was delegated to raise the question with
the Lord Advocate (*Arch. Scot.* 4, App. 38). Following the reading
of a paper on the archaeological Museum in Copenhagen on 11
March 1850, Wilson read a paper on treasure trove to the Society
(*Arch. Scot.* 4, App. 45). Eventually, besides writing to the railway
companies asking them to report any chance finds, the Society asked
the Queen's Remembrancer to write to Procurators Fiscal asking them
to claim finds so that they could be deposited in the Museum. The
Society also planned to place advertisements in Scottish newspapers.
The success of all these plans is somewhat doubtful: certainly there are
no railway finds listed amongst the Society's accessions in this period.
The reform of the treasure trove law was never fully carried out as
Daniel Wilson would have wished it to be, although the national status
of the Museum after 1851 did ensure that more material was deposited
there both by private donors and the government.

In his 1851 talk Daniel Wilson proposed another innovation which
was more successful: the commencement of a regular series of printed
proceedings of the Society dealing not only with the activities of the
Antiquaries but with Scottish archaeological matters in general. This
series, to be called *Proceedings of the Society of Antiquaries of
Scotland*, would appear regularly (unlike the irregular transactions,
Archaeologia Scotica) and would be funded by the money which had
hitherto been taken up with running the Museum (MB 5, 366). The
editors of the *Proceedings* were to be Wilson and David Laing (MB 5,
453). According to a plan laid down by Wilson, the new journal was to
include an abstract of the year's proceedings, along with illustrations of objects of particular interest. Papers of a general interest were
to be printed from time to time (at the behest of the Council) in
Archaeologia Scotica (MB 5, 425).

All of these innovations were part of the process of transferring the

Society's collections to government care and were intended to consolidate the Society's position as the national archaeological body. But Daniel Wilson had one further service to render to Scottish archaeology. He recognised that the study of Scottish archaeology could not proceed further until it was given some sort of order. It is no coincidence that Daniel Wilson's *The archaeology and prehistoric annals of Scotland* appeared in the same year as the future of the Society's Museum was assured. The work was revolutionary in many respects, not least for its introduction of the word 'prehistoric' into the English language.[31]

A major influence on Wilson while writing the *Prehistoric annals* had been the visit of P. A. Munch to Scotland. The Norwegian quickly joined in the convivial antiquarian circle of Edinburgh. He seems to have been an especially welcome visitor in the Wilson household. A good deal of the discussion between Munch and Wilson concerned the projected book on Scottish archaeology.[32] The text and notes of Wilson's book make it clear that Munch was consulted by letter on a number of points in the course of the writing of *Prehistoric annals.* Later Wilson confessed in a letter to Munch that he had thought of dedicating the work to him:

> . . . but I have made so many attacks in it, not only on our own native theories of Danish origin for our Antiquities, but also some directly traceable to Copenhagen that I thought it would be a questionable compliment.[33]

Munch's sceptical and rather distrustful attitude towards his Danish colleagues is not the least of his legacies to Wilson. On the whole, however, his influence in *Prehistoric annals* is much more positive and beneficial. His hand can be detected in the wide-ranging evidence Wilson brought to bear in his survey of early Scotland. For Munch the past could only be reconstructed by a thorough knowledge not only of the literary sources, but also of other evidence such as place-names, inscriptions and field monuments. An example of this technique occurs in his notes in *Prehistoric annals* on the standing stones at Stennis in Orkney (after leaving Edinburgh Munch had gone to Orkney where he was shown local sites by the antiquary George Petrie). It was a commonplace to attribute these standing stones to a Viking origin. Wilson dismissed this claim and as part of his evidence used place-name and literary evidence produced by Munch during his visit to Orkney: the name *Steinsnes* (promontory of the stones) was given to the place by the Viking settlers, for it occurred in the account of the death of Earl Havard in 970 according to the saga of Olaf Trygvesson:

. . . in other words . . . the standing stones belonged to the population previous to the Scandinavian settlement'.[34]

Munch was also decisive in shaping Wilson's concern for exact terminology. Like modern Scots who resent being called English, Munch abhorred the general use of the term 'Danish' to describe any field monument of the Viking period. The term might be exact in an English context, but it was misleading in Scotland. As a patriotic Norwegian Munch deprecated its general use by his Copenhagen colleagues and others, but even more he disliked it because it was inaccurate. Wilson followed his Norwegian friend in deprecating the use of this adjective (in the face of archaeological and literary evidence to the contrary) to describe anything showing 'any remarkable traces of skill distinct from the well-defined Roman art'.[35] There was also an element of patriotism in Wilson's dislike, since the use of the term for any non-Roman art implied that native Scottish craftsmen were incapable of producing anything of distinctive quality without outside help or influence. Wilson's final objection to 'Danish' was simply that it was wrong and was one of those 'convenient words which so often take the place of ideas and save the trouble and inconvenience of reasoning'.[36] If there is a key to understanding Wilson's method in the writing of *Prehistoric annals* it was this desire to do away with convenient (and misleading) words and begin to look directly at the past, and try to understand it on its own terms.

To this work Wilson brought all of his considerable gifts as a writer, artist and ethnologist. He refused to be bound by any preconceptions, not even the neat and beguiling simplicity of the Scandinavian tripartite system. For Wilson the tripartite system was a useful concept but it was not holy writ, as it often seemed to be to Scandinavian archaeologists. Wilson recognised the usefulness of the system as a tool for getting beyond the classical and literary bias of so much Scottish antiquarian and archaeological thought, but his first priority was understanding the past on its own terms rather than imposing an ill-fitting or extraneous system upon it. To do this he had to recognise that there were major differences between the archaeologies of Scotland and Scandinavia.

A major feature of Scandinavian archaeological thought had been the 'purity' of Scandinavian prehistory, untouched as it was by Roman penetration or settlement. In the early nineteenth century, with the disastrous effects of the Napoleonic Wars on Denmark, this 'purity' was seen as a great and patriotic virtue. In Scotland the reverse was true. Although Scotland had not been settled by Roman civilians, she had been garrisoned by Roman soldiers. This 'imperfect' Roman period seemed to many Scottish antiquaries, most notably Sir John Clerk of Penicuik, a kind of national disgrace. A corollary to this attitude was that any native artefacts or structures untouched by Roman influence were *ipso facto* inferior. Wilson dismissed this kind of value judgement in history and attempted merely to present the past as it was.

Another question Wilson had to deal with was change. He recognised (just as Worsaae had done) that, though change in early societies might follow broadly similar lines, the rate and nature of change could vary very widely, not only between different areas but within homogeneous cultures as well. His account of the results of the chemical analysis David Laing had asked to be carried out on the Duddingston finds showed this:

> The results will be found to differ very markedly from that ideal uniformity which had been supposed to establish the conclusion of some single common origin for the metal, if not indeed for the manufactured weapons and implements. The experiments have been made in the laboratory and under the directions of my brother, Dr George Wilson, whose acknowledged experience as an analyst is sufficient guarantee for the accuracy of the results.[37]

The archaeology and prehistoric annals of Scotland is a pioneering work in many ways, not least in its attempt to deal with the relativities of the past: to show that change was merely change and not imbued with moral or philosophical qualities.

But if the working out of the structure of prehistory must be done without preconception and bias, Wilson was less disengaged when he came to consider the feelings he wished to be engendered by reading his work or visiting the new national Museum. Wilson saw both as means for creating patriotic feelings:

> In Dublin . . . as in Copenhagen, a keen spirit of nationality and patriotic sympathy has been enlisted in the cause of Archaeological science [but in Scotland] our native nobility have stood aloof from us . . . [and] we mourn the decay of the old generous spirit of nationality, which is evinced by the array of names of our nobility, members of Parliament, and Scottish gentry, figuring in the lists of the more fashionable Societies of London.[38]

The Museum was to be a focus of patriotic sentiment, but already in 1852 Wilson was feeling that in this goal he had failed:

> . . . I grieve to say it, our Scottish nationality, which was once so fervid and healthful an element of action, has degenerated into a species of empty vanity and conceit, little less ridiculous than that of the 'slickest nation in all creation'. I have

tried to enlist it on behalf of an object I had much at heart, the establishing of a Museum of National Antiquities here. In Copenhagen a genuine nationality has been awakened on this; and it is wonderful what has been effected in Dublin. But Scotsmen seem to me beginning to be ashamed of Scotland — surely a woeful symptom.[39]

Despite this disappointment, Wilson did succeed in most of his other aims for the Society and its collections. It is interesting to speculate what the future of Scottish archaeology and the Society of Antiquaries of Scotland might have been if Wilson had remained in Scotland. In 1853, however, he was offered the chair of history and English literature at the University College of Toronto (MB 5, 477, 480).

Wilson was to have a long and distinguished career in Canada, both as a pioneer ethnologist of Canadian Indians and as a university administrator, but he never lost his interest in the Society nor abandoned hope that one day he might return to live in his beloved Edinburgh. In 1858 he wrote to David Laing after receiving the news that the Society was about to move to its long-promised apartments on The Mound:

> I learn, both from the newspaper, and from private sources, that the long pending negotiations for the proper accommodation of the Museum of Antiquities have at length been happily brought to a close; and that they will be speedily transferred to the rooms of the Royal Institution. Mr Stuart [the secretary] also tells me of your probably acquiring the Pennyciuck [*sic*] Collections; and I doubt not than many more will follow. I wish I was amongst you once more to catalogue and arrange them anew.[40]

He went on to list the places where new exhibits for the Museum might be found:

> Backed by the plea of your collection now being national property, your secretary ought to play the beggar to good purpose. I presume also that you will now be able to expend a larger portion of the Society's income on printing; though if what I learn is correct, I suspect you have been too modest in your demands on government for an annual allowance. But that can be amended hereafter . . . Altogether I imagine the Antiquaries and Antiquities of Scotland are in such a flourishing condition as at one time you little hoped to see them.[41]

Early in 1878 Wilson looked back again to those exciting days for himself and the Society, when he and David Laing and other friends had fought the good (but losing) fight to save Trinity College Chapel. Of all his associates from those days only one remained:

> . . . David Laing, who was an author before I was born . . . He is a wonderful man; an old bachelor, still busy with his pen and among his books. But he cannot survive long; and if I still remain, it will be [as] the sole representative of what was

once a fine, genial, hearty band of fellow-workers in the by no means barren field of antiquarian research.[42]

The two friends had one more meeting at the antiquarian dinner Laing gave for Wilson during his visit to Scotland in 1878. Shortly after his return to Toronto Wilson had to write in his diary: 'News of the death of my old friend David Laing, to whom I dedicated my "Reminiscences of Old Edinburgh".'[43]

The circle was broken, but Scottish archaeologists ever since have been deeply in the debt of this 'band of fellow-workers' who brought their gifts as antiquaries and archaeologists to the reformation of mid-nineteenth-century Scottish archaeology and the Society of Antiquaries of Scotland.

NOTES

1. D. Murray, *David Laing, Antiquary and Publisher* (Glasgow 1915), 23.

2. Edinburgh U.L., MS.La II 453/1.

3. G. Goudie, *David Laing, LL.D., A Memoir of his Life and Literary Works* (Edinburgh 1913), 8.

4. E.U.L., MS.La II 453/1, Laing to Chalmers, 12 March 1821.

5. *Ibid.*, dated 9 December 1817.

6. *Ibid.*

7. Goudie, *David Laing*, 26.

8. *Ibid.*, 25. Goudie, reprinting Laing's own memoir, puts the date of Laing's blackballing by the Antiquaries in '181—'. The Society's Minute Books show that Laing was proposed at a meeting on 10 January 1820, but failed to gain election at the meeting of 14 February.

9. National Library of Scotland, MS.4004, ff.167-8.

10. E.U.L., MS.La IV 1, Scott no. 13.

11. E.U.L., MS.La II 453/1, dated 8 January 1822.

12. E.U.L., MS.La II 453/1.

13. E. Gordon, *The Royal Scottish Academy* (Edinburgh 1976), 70.

14. Goudie, *David Laing*, 253.

15. *Ibid.*, 25-6.

16. O. Klindt-Jensen, *A History of Scandinavian Archaeology* (London 1975), 50 and *passim*.

17. E.U.L., MS.La IV 18, no. 2 and Feldborg, 1 October 1819.

18. Klindt-Jensen, *Archaeology*, 34 and *passim*.

19. P[roceedings of the] S[ociety of] A[ntiquaries of] S[cotland] i (1855, for 1851-4 sessions), 4-5.

20. D. Wilson, *The Archaeology and Prehistoric Annals of Scotland* (Edinburgh 1851), xix.

21. Sir Daniel Wilson's diary, University of Toronto Library, Department of MSS. (typescript of extracts made by H. H. Langton for his *Sir Daniel Wilson*, 1929), 153.

22. *Ibid.*

23. Wilson, *Prehistoric Annals*, xii.

24. Wilson Diary, 173.

25. *Proceedings of the Royal Irish Academy* 1847, 328-30.

26. *Synopsis of the Museum of the Society of Antiquaries of Scotland* (Edinburgh 1849), 1.

27. Wilson, *Prehistoric Annals*, xi.

28. E.U.L., MS.La 17, Daniel Wilson no. 2.

29. *PSAS*, i.3.

30. *PSAS*, i.4-5.

31. This point has been discussed by Glyn Daniel in *The Origin and Growth of Archaeology* (London 1967), where it is shown that the term first appeared in French in 1833. There is, however, no evidence that Wilson knew of this French precedent. Indeed in a letter of 1865 to Sir Charles Lyell (Edinburgh U.L., Lyell MSS. no. 1) he claims to have coined the word 'prehistoric'.

32. *Laerde brev fra og til P. A. Munch* (3 vols, Oslo 1934-71), nos. 217, 234.

33. *Ibid.*, ii, no. 256.

34. Wilson, *Prehistoric Annals*, 112n.

35. *Ibid.*, xiv.

36. *Ibid.*, xv.

37. *Ibid.*, 245.

38. *PSAS*, i.4.

39. National Library of Scotland, MS.2623, f.135.

40. E.U.L., MS.La 17, Wilson no. 6.

41. *Ibid.*

42. H. H. Langton, *Sir Daniel Wilson, A Memoir* (Edinburgh 1929), 193-4.

43. Wilson Diary, entry for 5 November 1878.

Scottish Archaeology in the Second Half of the Nineteenth Century

D. V. Clarke

This contribution is not concerned to chart the history of the Society of Antiquaries of Scotland in the period under review. Rather it seeks to examine some of the broader trends which underpinned the activities so liberally documented in the Society's *Proceedings*. Archaeological writings, then as now, have never contained a large number of essays which were intended to provide a theoretical basis for the subject; theory and methodology are, of course, implicit in the numerous available pieces of description and analysis but they seldom receive any treatment in their own right. In trying to tease out these underlying beliefs and the approaches to which they gave rise, I have perhaps been unduly reliant on the few explicit statements which are available to us. Nevertheless, such statements do provide a yardstick by which to measure the achievements of those not given to theorising on their own account, as well as indicating the overall goals which no single person could by himself hope to achieve. We cannot, however, totally ignore the organisational basis and the changes that were taking place if we wish to understand the theoretical developments.

Throughout the second half of the nineteenth century the Society dominated Scottish archaeology through its *Proceedings*, its management of the National Museum and its other activities, most notably the Rhind Lectures. This may seem so self-evident as to be unworthy of comment, but to adopt such a view is to ignore the fact that this represents a situation which made Scottish archaeology significantly different from its English counterpart in organisational terms. Prior to the 1840s there were only three societies in Britain with the principal aim of furthering the study of antiquities, namely the Society of

Antiquaries of London (founded 1717), the Society of Antiquaries of Scotland (founded 1780) and the Society of Antiquaries of Newcastle upon Tyne (founded 1813), which maintained some semblance of activity. There were of course other groups, in particular the literary and philosophical societies, which included antiquities within their ambit, but their contribution was at best spasmodic. This pattern changed quite dramatically in the 1840s with the foundation of the first of the county societies. The first sign of challenge to the dominance of the established societies was the formation in 1843 of the British Archaeological Association. It grew out of the belief among its leading members that the practices and procedures of the Society of Antiquaries of London were both inadequate and outmoded for the proper development of archaeology, and it took as its model the newly established and highly successful British Association for the Advancement of Science.[1] Internal dissensions among the leadership of the British Archaeological Association led within a few years to the formation of a second society, the Archaeological Institute of Great Britain and Ireland,[2] but both organisations were firmly committed to breaking with the metropolitan-based nature of the London Antiquaries. This split probably ensured that neither society could successfully challenge the primacy of the Society of Antiquaries of London. The intention was plain enough, however, and was to be realised by harnessing the provincial enthusiasm being shown by the formation of county archaeological societies. Such societies began to appear in the late 1840s and new foundations continued throughout the nineteenth century.

Some of the more important factors behind this growth in local archaeological societies have been reviewed by Piggott,[3] who particularly emphasises the role of the Cambridge Camden Society, developments in geology, and the influence of Sir Walter Scott's historical novels. There can be no doubt that by the 1840s a sympathetic climate of opinion existed for the study of the past and more particularly for the material remains of the past. This new attitude developed, thought Haverfield, 'along lines characteristic of the early Victorian age through the formation of societies'.[4] Not everyone shared the optimism shown by the founders of these societies: Lord Lincoln, then first Commissioner of Woods and Works, informed Peel in February 1844 that he believed that the antiquarian societies 'which exist have done, and I believe can do, very little good'.[5] However, most were more positive in their attitudes and sensed a real change in feeling:

'I am quite sure,' wrote Hibbert Ware to an unknown correspondent, 'that even with moderate exertion the Society [of Antiquaries of Scotland] can be revived, for there is now a growing taste for the subject of Antiquities.'[6] Hibbert Ware's view is particularly interesting in that he clearly felt that 'the growing taste for the subject of Antiquities' was to be found in Scotland as well as in England. Yet there was not the same upsurge in local societies in Scotland; indeed they are conspicuous by their absence. This is not a point which Piggott discusses in any detail but he clearly believes that county societies were the product of areas with a strong attachment to the Anglican church and 'an argicultural and squirearchical background'.[7] Nonconformists apparently did not have the same urge to study the past, and in Scotland the lack of a strong Anglican presence, combined with the previous wholesale destruction of medieval church fabric, rendered it wholly unsuitable ground for the formation of local archaeological societies. It is difficult to accept this interpretation when one attempts to reconcile the dates of foundation of local archaeological societies with the only reliable guide which we have to religious affiliation, the so-called Religious Census of 1851. The value of the information collected during the census was hotly disputed at the time but more recent assessments suggest that it was a conscientious compilation with substantial reliability within its own limits.[8] Certainly it offers little support for Piggott's view, which at best provides only a half-truth in explaining the Scottish situation. An important factor must have been the size of population relative to the very considerable area of the country, something which even today still retards the development of local archaeological societies. Of the societies which did get established, all were in southern Scotland, either in areas where there was a sizeable concentration of population, for example Glasgow, or where events in northern England were easily known and consequently more influential, for example Dumfries and Galloway. Yet these isolated examples serve only to emphasise the essential fact that county societies did not become effectively established in Scotland. The situation was such a continuing source of weakness that Joseph Anderson, in cataloguing the shortcomings of local museums late in the century, felt that they could all benefit from 'the energetic co-operation of a local Society'.[9]

It might perhaps be tempting to regard the Society of Antiquaries of Scotland as the equivalent in effect of the large English county societies in much the same way as the Cambrian Archaeological Association with its annual meetings at various localities throughout Wales can be so interpreted. But to do so would be, I think, a grave mistake. The Society did not seriously alter its manner of operation except in one important instance discussed below, and it certainly regarded itself as the society for Scotland, with pretensions and status wholly comparable to that of the Society of Antiquaries of London. This was moreover a view shared in some part by others: in 1844 David Findlay wrote to Alexander Smellie announcing the intention to form an antiquarian society in Glasgow and he continued, 'we will therefore feel much obliged by your favouring us with any suggestions or information which in your experience you may deem useful to us in the formation of such a society'.[10] The fact that the Society had been in existence, however precariously, since 1780 was clearly an important factor in providing this sense of status. Certainly, the Society's past history seems to have given it greater stability than was achieved by the newly founded societies. If we compare the membership figures for the Society of Antiquaries of Scotland and the Surrey Archaeological Society in the second half of the nineteenth century, the contrast is particularly marked (fig.). The slow but steady growth enjoyed by the Society throughout the period has little in common, other than the maximum number of members, with the fluctuations experienced by the Surrey Society, a pattern wholly typical of the newer societies. The national character of the Society is most clearly seen in its dealings with the Archaeological Institute, which in its title at least was claiming an interest and perhaps ultimately a role in Scottish archaeology. Contact between the two societies began soon after the foundation of the Institute, and a letter from Albert Way to W. B. D. D. Turnbull indicates the positive stance adopted by the Society:

> I am directed by the Central Committee of the Institute to request that you would take an early occasion of communicating their acknowledgement of sincere thanks for the important services and the encouraging demonstration of friendly feeling, on the part of the Society of Antiquaries of Scotland, which have been received at the recent meeting at York. The Central Committee would advert most gratefully to the kind liberality which has bestowed so valuable an addition to the curious exhibition at their museum at York, in the precious objects of Antiquity entrusted to their care, selected from the Collections of your Society and which they hope have been restored in perfect security. The Committee have also to express their warm thanks for the donation of the Transactions of the Antiquaries of Scotland, a most valuable accession to their Library, comprising so many memoirs and evidences of the highest interest, and utility in giving furtherance to their present endeavours. The Committee have to express, with no less hearty thanks their

acknowledgement of the honour which has been done to the Institute, and the encouragement which they have derived from the requisition communicated on the part of the Antiquaries of Scotland, inviting the Institute to hold their annual meeting in Northern Metropolis, on an early occasion. The Committee entertained the earnest hope that at no distant period they may be able to visit a city, where not only so rich a field of Archaeological interest is open to them, but where they have the gratifying assurance of so hearty a welcome, as is afforded by the invitation which they have had the gratification to receive. The opening of reciprocal intercourse between the Society of Antiquaries and the Archaeologists of North Britain, and the Institute must conduce in an important degree to the furtherance of the common object.[11]

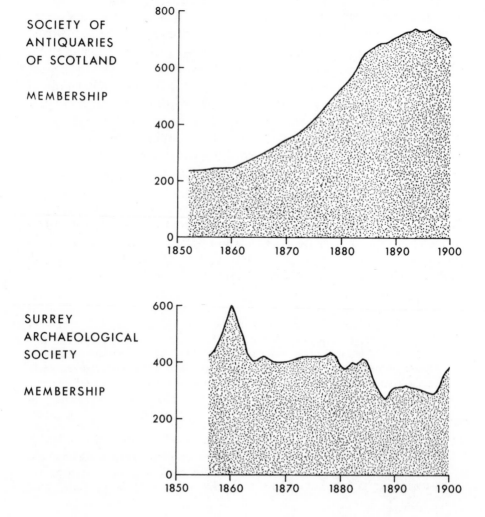

The invitation was not taken up for a further ten years, but when the Archaeological Institute finally visited Edinburgh,

> It was a source of peculiar gratification to the Fellows of this Society to welcome to our city, — so rich in objects of archaeological interest — the members of an Association devoted to kindred pursuits, and to many of whom the science of the past is deeply indebted to the extent of their researches and the accuracy of their inductions. We could not but hail their visit as tending to give a fresh impulse to archaeological studies, not only by the prestige of their presence, but still more by the large diffusion of information respecting the objects and materials of antiquarian research to which their meetings and exhibitions could not fail to give rise . . . It is gratifying to know that the result more than surpassed our expectations; and it is with no ordinary pleasure that we now look back on the period of agreeable and profitable intercourse which we then enjoyed with our brethren from the south. We have reason to believe that the gratification was mutual, — that not only were our visitors pleased with the attentions they received from Fellows of this Society, but that they rejoiced to find here so many who could meet them on equal terms in their favourite walk, and reciprocate the instruction and interest which they received.[12]

This description of the visit by one of the Vice-Presidents of the Society leaves no doubt that they received the Institute with no sense of inferiority, and that consequently any emphasis on the importance of the visitors served to underline the importance of their own society.

This awareness of new developments and changed times in the antiquarian world, reflected in invitations to such as the Archaeological Institute, did not lead to any significant change in the Society's procedures except in the field of publication. Taking as its model the volumes of *Archaeologia* published by the Society of Antiquaries of London, the Society had from an early stage in its history produced some volumes of *Transactions*, later named *Archaeologia Scotica*. Their appearance had, however, been very irregular, in marked contrast to the steady stream of *Archaeologia* produced by the London Antiquaries. Both serials were lavish productions intended to reflect the wide range of interests of the respective societies, and their format was firmly rooted in the topographical publications of the late eighteenth century. None of the newly emerging societies attempted to emulate the style of these volumes but all firmly announced their intention to publish a journal regularly. They were to contain reports on activities but, more important, articles and notes which represented the fruits of antiquarian labour in the society's area. Usually a modest octavo volume was produced, the format owing much to the growing periodical press. The use of this new size led to more efficient and rapid

J

production,[13] and if the older societies felt able to ignore most aspects of the new societies' activities, they did not adopt the same indifferent attitude in the case of publications. The new, small-style *Proceedings of the Society of Antiquaries of London* completed its first volume in 1849, and volume I of the *Proceedings of the Society of Antiquaries of Scotland* covered the three sessions 1851-1854. The London Antiquaries' production was rather a formal affair for the years 1843 to 1849, the first volume, and was originally produced to counter criticisms of the Society's management, but its introduction of wood-cuts in 1849 can only be interpreted as a response to the publication efforts of the younger societies.[14] The Scottish journal is best interpreted as an attempt to establish, in the face of the achievements of other societies, a more regular publication than had been possible with *Archaeologia Scotica*.

Of course, the value of such a journal to members residing at a distance from Edinburgh would have been largely nullified without an efficient means of distribution. This was provided by the recently reformed postal services: 'It is difficult,' wrote Disraeli in *Endymion* (1880), 'for us who live in an age of railroads, telegraphs, penny posts, and penny newspapers, to realise how limited in thought and feeling, as well as incident, was the life of an English family of retired habits and limited means only forty years ago' — remarks which applied with greater force to Scotland.[15] The penny post undoubtedly provided the most significant contribution to the postal system by bringing a previously expensive service into widespread use, but it was not by itself of considerable significance to archaeological societies, since the Post Office initially lacked the ability to deliver widely in rural areas. Seven hundred new posts were established, however, by 1850, and the general revision and improvement of country services, begun in 1851, was largely complete by 1858; by 1864, 94% of the letters were delivered to the houses to which they were addressed. Equally valuable was the introduction of a book post in 1848 with a reduction in rates from 1855.[16] It is interesting to note, however, that the Society did not at first consider that their responsibilities extended to paying the postage. A printed billet of 1853 reads:

> Members residing at a distance, who have not yet received their copies of the FIRST PART OF THE SOCIETY'S PROCEEDINGS, may have it forwarded by post, on sending 6 postage stamps to Mr. Wm M'CULLOCH, Assistant Librarian of the Society of Antiquaries of Scotland, 24 George Street, Edinburgh.[17]

A similar position was adopted by the London Antiquaries, but their

Scottish counterparts do not seem to have followed their example in having copies of their *Proceedings* printed on thin paper for posting to country members.[18]

These alterations in the accepted ways of presenting archaeological information, combined with the emergence of a considerable number of new journals, inevitably led to an increase in the available published material. Equally important was the expanded range of information now recorded in permanent form. Small excavations and chance discoveries, which would previously have lain unrecorded or at best been entrusted to a manuscript diary, began to appear in ever-increasing numbers in the pages of the county journals. The result was not only an explosion of information but also a change in the whole structure of archaeological publication, which became much less dependent upon the wealth of the author or patron or the whim of a publisher. Yet these quite fundamental changes were brought about by societies with wholly traditional aims which took little account of the implications of the new situation — 'an important object which this and Kindred Societies have in view is to supplement the older County Histories by a close attention to the details of parochial history'.[19] They were not, however, blinkered in their attitudes, for there was an early and general realisation of the benefits of the exchange of publications between societies. Daniel Wilson, giving an Anniversary Address in 1851 to the Society of Antiquaries of Scotland, congratulated the Society on the decision 'to resume the printing of our Proceedings in a modified form, which, while it will, as I trust, furnish a new source of energy to ourselves, will also restore us to a more active intercourse with Kindred Societies, both at home and on the continent'.[20]

In the same address Wilson noted that 'the long delay which has taken place in the printing of Transactions, has not been allowed to pass without repeated remonstrances from those who were ignorant of the conflicting claims on the very limited resources at our command'.[21] Principal among these claims was, of course, the cost of maintaining the Society's museum, and Wilson devoted much of his address to explaining the new arrangements which had been made for the maintenance and development of these collections:

> by a deed of conveyance prepared by the Lords of Her Majesty's Treasury, with the concurrence of the Honourable Board of Trustees for the encouragement of Arts and Manufactures, and now finally approved of, and adopted by, the Society, we have made over to the Crown, as public property, the whole collections of Antiquities, Coins, and Medals, MSS., Books, etc., formed during

the last 70 years, to be the nucleus of a National Archaeological Museum for Scotland. The Lords of Her Majesty's Treasury, in accepting this gift for the nation, agree, on their part to provide at all future times fit and proper accommodation for the preservation and exhibition of the collections for the public, in the galleries of the Royal Institution, or other public buildings in Edinburgh, as well as for the meetings of the Society, and reserve in the hands of the Society's Office-Bearers the curatorship of the entire collections. This arrangement has been completed after mature deliberation, as the one best calculated to secure the advancement of Archaeological science, to promote popular education, and to excite a national interest in the preservation of the monuments of early art and ancient civilisation; and we have the satisfaction of believing that, in making some personal sacrifice in the relinquishment of our proprietary interest in these valuable collections, we are thereby providing the best of all securities for their permanency and extension.[22]

Despite these protestations of 'sacrifice', the Society was enabled by this agreement to use its financial resources in other areas, particularly in the *Proceedings*, without relinquishing total control of it collections. The history of the Museum is reviewed elsewhere in this volume, but a few general remarks are necessary here to understand the central place it and its officers occupied in Scottish archaeology during the late Victorian period. Since the Society retained control of the management of the Museum and the two institutions consequently acted in concert, they represented a formative influence on Scottish archaeology. Perhaps surprisingly, this influence seems to have strengthened as the nineteenth century progressed. In 1851 Wilson felt that 'we cannot, with justice, consider the collections formed by the Society as in any sense fit to constitute a National Archaeological Museum. Valuable as they are, they are merely the fruits of private zeal, and of the persevering exertions of a small body of men, labouring, under many disadvantages, to accomplish, with extremely limited means, what is elsewhere regarded as the proper duty of the Government.'[23] Yet by 1892 an unstated author, probably Joseph Anderson, writing a description of the Museum, could say that it 'has now been opened to the public, in the spacious premises appropriated to it by the Board of Manufactures, consisting of the entire east wing of the National Portrait Gallery buildings. . . . The result of the great increase of space and new methods of arrangement is that the series of Scottish Antiquities is now seen to be a representative collection, national in character and unsurpassed in scientific interest by any national collection in Europe.'[24] We must, of course, take into account the fact that these commentators were both intimately involved in the Museum and had their own reasons for wishing to emphasise its deficiencies or qualities. Nevertheless, the essential accuracy of their statements is, I think, indisputable.

Yet the increase in quality and power of the National Museum during the nineteenth century took place against the background of an expanding number of local museums. The nineteenth century was indeed the period of the greatest expansion of public museums in Britain. Fewer than a dozen existed in 1800, but the number had grown to almost 60 by 1850, and between 1850 and 1914 nearly 300 were established, almost a hundred occupying new buildings.[25] In many cases the same building served to accommodate museum, art gallery and library, which reflected the concern felt in urban areas, where these new foundations were concentrated, to compensate for the bleak physical environment with an improved cultural one. The Museums Act of 1845 and the Public Libraries Act of 1850 marked the beginning of legislation designed to encourage their foundation, although in many cases the establishment of a museum involved the union of private philanthropy and public resources. Patrons like James M'Lean, a timber merchant in Greenock, or Thomas Smith in Stirling were often crucial in the translation of local initiative into a fully operating institution. Even so, the results were often far from speedy and the result in museums less than effective. In 1851 Adam Arbuthnot, a merchant in Peterhead, bequeathed his collection to the town. His will stated that the Trustees of his collection should be the Provost, Magistrates and Council and that 'in case any Act shall be passed by the Legislature for the vesting, management and maintenance of Museums of Works of Art, or others, in Burghs, then my said Museum and Cabinet of Coins shall be placed under the provision of such Act'. But George Black, visiting the Museum in 1887, found that 'few things of any Archaeological or Antiquarian value have been added since then [1851]'.[26]

The reasons behind the establishment of museums were very much concerned with raising the moral tone of the population at large, with a consequent benefit for the whole of society. They were intended to provide an opportunity for the working classes to obtain a better understanding of the trades and industries in which they were employed and to observe designs of the highest quality, since exposure to such information could only benefit trade and manufactures. To this very practical base could be added the less specific, but not unimportant, aim of bolstering the social order: 'where our people are systematically excluded from the sight and enjoyment of the proofs of our present refinement and progress in the arts, and never by the remotest chance see such testimonies of the national growth to greatness — of our progress from early times in art and science, or learn to be proud of our national history by its monuments — of its heroes by the memorials of them which art can alone provide, there is an element of decay,' wrote one commentator as part of his advocacy of provincial museums.[27] The architectural styles of the buildings which housed these museums, whether it was the Neo-classical Hunterian Museum in Glasgow or the Gothic edifice in Dundee, reflected less explicit but equally strongly-held attitudes. Both styles lent themselves to the construction of buildings with a monumental quality which suitably reflected civic pride and were fitting tributes to the philanthropy which was so often an integral part of their foundation. Similar factors lay behind the display systems adopted, for behind the expressed aim of ministering to the culturally impoverished was the implicit demonstration of national or local communal wealth. Museums were, one modern commentator remarked, 'the cultural counterpart of that other Victorian innovation, the department store'.[28] Like those stores, the emphasis was on variety and mass to such an extent that the primary communication was not involved with the object but with a positive statement about the society which had made such displays possible.

These attitudes meant that the academic role of these institutions was extremely ill-defined and certainly not easily reconciled with the primary aim, as stated in the 1845 Act, of providing 'for the Instruction and Amusement of the Inhabitants'. Anderson and Black in their survey of local museums in Scotland (1888) constantly complained of the lack of any systematic organisation in the arrangement of the collections, and their remarks were as pertinent to the museums run by local societies as those supported by the rates. The lack of any firm policy, which these criticisms indicated, combined with an emphasis on variety, perhaps explains why the National Museum was able to establish such a dominant holding of Scottish archaeological material and to do so moreover without coming into serious conflict with the local museums. 'If the National Museum were non-existent', wrote Joseph Anderson, 'and if all the contents of all the local Museums (so far as these contents are known to be Scottish) were brought together, they would fail to furnish the materials for a systematic Archaeology of Scotland, as we now know it. To take a striking instance. In the Museum at Forres, which is the nearest to the Culbin Sands, I found that extraordinarily rich locality represented by a dozen arrowheads; while the result of the systematic effort made by the Society of Antiquaries of Scotland to ascertain the capabilities of the Culbin Sands as an archaeological index, has been the accumulation in the National Museum of upwards of 15,000 specimens, chiefly of Flint and Stone Implements; while from another sandy district in the south of Scotland, which is scarcely represented in any local Museum, we have amassed about 10,000 specimens.'[29] This lack of concern with material from the area in which the museum was located is reflected in the attitudes of local antiquaries. Many of them chose to send the objects they most valued to the National Museum in Edinburgh where they could feel that their objects, if not displayed — and most of them were — could at least contribute in full to the developing knowledge of Scotland's past (I owe this point to Mr R. B. K. Stevenson). No analogous situation developed in the south, but in Scandinavia, an area with which the Society maintained particularly strong links, the National Museums played a similarly influential role in the development of archaeology which went far beyond the mere acquisition of objects.[30]

This review of the organisational basis for Scottish archaeology has shown that the adopted pattern differed in some respects from that which evolved in England. In turning now to consider some of the central issues in archaeology in the second half of the nineteenth century, we shall find a greater degree of coherence between the attitudes of Scottish workers and those of their counterparts in areas to the south. It has become customary in writings dealing with the history of archaeology to discuss it in terms of the views of the major figures of the time, with the implication that they were carrying all before them. While they were undoubtedly influential and are therefore worthy of great consideration, it would be a mistake to treat their views as representative of all archaeological opinion at the time. A single example will serve to make the point. In his preface to the first edition of the *Archaeology and prehistoric annals of Scotland*, Daniel Wilson wrote,

> It has fared otherwise with Archaeology. Rejected in its first appeal for a place among the sister sciences, its promoters felt themselves under no necessity to court a share in popular favour which they could readily command, and we have accordingly its annual conferences altogether apart from those of the associated sciences. Archaeology, however, has suffered from the isolation; while it cannot but be sooner or later felt to be an inconsistency at once anomalous and pregnant with evil, which recognises as a legitimate branch of British science, the study of the human species, by means both of physiological and philological investigation, but altogether excludes the equally direct evidence which Archaeology supplies. It

rests, however, with the archaeologist to assert for his own study its just place among the essential elements of scientific induction, and to show that it not only furnishes valuable auxiliary truth in aid of physiological and philological comparisons, but that it adds distinct psychological indices by no other means attainable, and yields the most trustworthy, if not the sole evidence in relation to extinct branches of the human family, the history of which possesses a peculiar national and personal interest for us.[31]

It is evident from this and other writings of Wilson that he firmly believed that archaeology should unite with other sciences, and indeed that archaeological evidence was of such value that archaeologists should not hesitate to involve themselves in matters which had hitherto been the province of other subjects. Yet Alexander, in delivering the Anniversary Address of 1856 to the Society of Antiquaries of Scotland, showed that Wilson's views were altogether too radical for some:

> I am not desirous that we should extend our enquiries beyond the department to which they have hitherto been for the most part confined. The use of the term 'Archaeology', which has become of late the favorite designation of our science, has, I think, betrayed some into a wider conception of what we aim at than entered into the minds of the founders and early members of the Society, or than is in my humble opinion, at all favourable to the success of our pursuits. . . . Hence, men may be true and zealous archaeologists, though they leave unexamined many objects belonging to the past, and confine themselves to such as lie within a certain well-defined sphere. That sphere I take to be that which is determined by the *usages* and *products* of those who have lived in the ancient time. What they themselves were, to what race they belong, or whence they migrated, or how they came to the place of their settled habitation, and by what deeds of battle or of enterprise they signalized their name, it is for other sciences, such as History and Ethnology, to declare. The province of the archaeologist lies within the region of their everyday life, as exist in a given locality; he has to ask how they lived, — in what way they used their ingenuity and labour to provide themselves with what might supply the necessities or minister to the luxuries of life, — what were the implements they used, the dwellings they erected, the garments they wore, the language they spoke, the food they used, the rites they followed, and the methods they employed generally to secure the objects for which all men with more or less of intelligence seek. This I take to be the sphere, as respects our own country, which properly belongs to us as Scottish antiquaries; and I cannot but believe that no small advantage will accrue for our exploring this sphere to the full, and keeping ourselves to it.[32]

These two quotations show quite divergent views about the aims which archaeologists should be adopting, but it would be a mistake to suppose that they represented the only opinions current at the time. Perhaps the most characteristic feature of British archaeology in the period after 1840 was the variety of positions which were championed to a greater or lesser extent. This is hardly to be wondered at when we consider the upheavals caused by the considerable number of people wishing to be active, at least to the extent of joining a society. In a sense the disquiet now came from within for, as the ridicule which had been heaped on antiquarianism now faded away, there emerged a strong desire that the subject should have redefined aims more befitting its new status. Further, it must be remembered that there was as yet no professional group, and no significant institutions, which could provide a lead in such matters. There were antiquaries whose reputation and work eventually made them influential, but in charting their emergence we should not forget that many of their views were of no significance in the long term, and that below them were a mass of workers with very little in the way of orthodoxy to guide their speculations.

Whatever differences existed with regard to the role of archaeology, all were agreed that the achieving of those aims required the adoption of new methods and approaches. When he was presented with the Grand Cross of the Order of Dannebrog, Thomsen chose as his motto 'things first, books later',[33] and in those few words he has effectively summarised the change in attitude. 'Nearly all antiquarian pursuits in this country have heretofore,' wrote Daniel Wilson, been based 'on classical learning', with the dire consequence that 'it has been accepted as an almost indisputable truth, that, with the exception of the mysteriously learned Druid priests, the Britons prior to the Roman period were mere painted savages'.[34] This dependence upon classical authors for insight into man's past was now to be firmly rejected in favour of inductive archaeology.[35] There was widespread support among antiquaries for the efficiency of an inductive approach, if by that phrase we understand a belief in the pattern of reasoning which enables one to pass from statements of particular pieces of information to general pronouncements which not only summarise the matter contained within the statements of information but also expand our understanding beyond that summary. The appeal of this new philosophical position was that its adoption brought archaeology into the framework of current scientific practice and the adoption of such procedures would, it was believed, lead to a comparable structure of laws similar to those achieved in the natural sciences. Simpson described Stuart's work on the sculptured stones of Scotland (Vol. 1, Aberdeen 1856) 'as a memorable example, and as a perfect Baconian model for analogous investigation on other corresponding topics — in the way of the full and careful accumulation of all ascertainable premises and data before venturing to dogmatize upon them'.[36] Induction, therefore, held out the glittering prospect to antiquarian workers of transcending the mere description of discoveries and cataloguing of facts to arrive at a broader and deeper understanding of prehistoric man. It gave a firm intellectual air to what was otherwise in danger of becoming an activity orientated towards collecting. The sterility of collecting with no greater prospect than the accumulation of yet larger assemblages of material was one that had worried antiquaries in the past.[37] The new philosophy dealt effectively with this problem, since it was now clear that the more information that was acquired, the greater was the potential for that knowledge other than a summary of the facts.

Few antiquaries, of course, were claiming that their own work or the work of others had carried the process of induction through to a conclusion. Indeed, Simpson offered stern warnings about the dangers inherent in attempting to do so:

> . . . all past experience has shown that it is useless, and generally even hurtful, to attempt to frame hypotheses upon one, or even upon a few specimens only. In archaeology, as in other sciences, we must have full and accurate premises before we can hope to make full and accurate deductions. It is needless and hopeless for us to expect clear, correct, and philosophic views of the character and of the date and age of such archaeological objects as I have enumerated, except by following the triple process of (1) assiduously collecting together as many instances as possible of each class of our antiquities; (2) carefully comparing these instances with each other, so as to ascertain all their resemblances and differences; and (3) contrasting them with similar remains in other cognate countries . . .

> The same remarks which I have just ventured to make, as to the proper mode of investigating the classes of our larger Archaeological subjects, hold equally true also of those other classes of antiquities of a lighter and more portable type, which we have collected in our Museums . . . It is only by collecting, combining,. and comparing all the individual instances of each antiquarian object of this kind — all ascertainable specimens, for example, of our Scotch stone celts and knives; all ascertainable specimens of our clay vessels; of our leaf-shaped swords; of our metallic armlets; of our grain-rubbers and stone-querns, etc etc; — and by tracing the history of similar objects in other allied countries, that we will read aright the tales which these relics — when once properly interrogated — are capable of telling us of the doings, the habits, and the thoughts of our distant predecessors.[38]

Yet the long-term nature of these goals and the difficulties in achieving them served only to emphasise the importance of the contribution of every worker, however minor. The situation was succinctly summarised by R. W. Cochran-Patrick in issuing the following plea to the Ayrshire and Galloway Association:

that more workers in the localities should come forward. As the object of the Association is simply to record facts, and provide materials for future generalisations, no profound or special archaeological knowledge is required. Accurate descriptions and truthful drawings of remains or relics are all that is necessary, and contributions of that kind will be of the greatest use both to the Society and to Archaeological Science.[39]

In this new atmosphere even casual finds of antiquities had a significance which demanded interest and concern. It is surely these views that lay behind the concerted attack on the operation of the law of Treasure Trove in the 1850s. Wilson claimed that 'its operation has constantly impeded researches into the evidences of primitive art, and in many cases has occasioned the destruction of very valuable relics'.[40] Rhind, who devoted a pamphlet to the subject, was even more outspoken in his remarks: 'practical inquirers have so frequently found that the species of terrorism, which it bears in the popular eye, has had a hand in dooming to secret destruction, or scarcely less fatal concealment, so many objects not more precious intrinsically than ethnographically, that a tendency has, perhaps naturally, sprung up to regard this law as the bugbear of Antiquarianism'.[41] Every object was important now, and certainly those that would be claimed as Treasure Trove.

This desire to adopt methods and approaches which could be regarded as truly scientific was reflected in attempts to weld alliances with subjects whose status was not in doubt, particularly geology and ethnology. Geology had a considerable reputation amongst the sciences during the nineteenth century, and achievements in this field were certainly influential in changing attitudes to the past. 'See, also,' wrote Alexander, 'how one of the most commanding and progressive sciences of modern times, I mean geology, seems almost to demand the researches of the archaeologist to complete that record of primeval man of which her readings among the earth's strata furnish the first traces. Geology has finished her lessons in this department when she has showed us at what stage in the world's progress man became a dweller on its surface.'[42] In this sense the alliance with geology was to be welcomed since it could only enhance the standing of archaeology in public esteem. Nevertheless it contributed little to archaeological method, although Simpson thought there were analogies between the two subjects,[43] and, except for the important question of man's first appearance on earth, it contributed little to the interpretation of archaeological finds. Ethnology was altogether more important in this respect and we have seen that the radical element in archaeology represented by men such as Wilson considered the fostering of this relationship to be of prime importance. The contribution of ethnology was to be twofold. The first involved the use of data from other areas of the world to provide comparisons for and insights about prehistoric material. This was not, of course, a particularly new theme, although its perceived relevance greatly increased its use, and the more explicit comparisons depended upon the newly appearing and better-documented studies of non-European man. Ethnology's second contribution was of much greater fundamental importance since it involved archaeology with racial theory and later social evolutionary theory. Racial theory, particularly that concerned with the history of man, was a subject of great concern to many more people than ethnologists and archaeologists in the middle of the nineteenth century.

It is not surprising, therefore, that before the mid-1860s concern with the integration of ethnology and archaeology was almost wholly centred on racial matters. At the time when Wilson began extolling the value of a link between the two subjects in the early 1850s, the standard ethnological orientation, exemplified in the attitudes of Prichard and Latham, can be essentially characterised as linguistic ethnology. The central belief of original human unity (monogenesis) was little doubted, and the role of ethnology was to demonstrate that unity by providing information on the time between the dispersal of man across the earth and the beginnings of historical material for each nation. Such documentation relied heavily upon diffusionist and historical explanation, particularly comparative linguistics, with a dependence on environmental factors to clarify the problem of contemporary variations. Yet even as these aims were being formulated they were being threatened by the emergence of a more strongly physical and anatomical approach to man, together with the resurgence of belief in polygenesis or a multiplicity of races of man. It was these latter developments that particularly appealed to Wilson and in which he saw the possibilities of a greater archaeological involvement. 'It is to be regretted,' he wrote, 'that this branch of physical archaeology has heretofore been so little esteemed in this country in comparison of the contributions afforded by philological researches to ethnology. It is a matter of great importance, to know whether the nomadic Celtae peopled for the first time the unoccupied waste and forests of Europe, or superseded elder aboriginal races. . . . Still greater is its value in relation to the other questions which demand a reply from the ethnologist, as to the origin of the human family from one or more stocks, and the migration from a common centre, or cradle-land, which, in so far as relates to the historic races, appear distinctly to coincide with the Mosaic history of the human race.'[44] These were important aims, some of the most central questions of the day, and if archaeology could have been seen to have contributed significantly to their resolution, then its position as a major science would have been assured. Wilson used the physical approach to demonstrate the kind of information that could be achieved. He measured 39 Scottish skulls, using procedures developed by Morton in America, to suggest that people with a dolichocephalic skull were succeeded by people with a brachycephalic skull and that these skull-forms were significant in racial terms. Rather interestingly, this conclusion was at variance with the findings of Nillson, whose work with that of Retzius had clearly been influential in directing Wilson to this line of enquiry.

Despite his pioneering efforts Wilson's work in this field was limited, but it did ensure that the Scottish material was not ignored. Others were keen to take on the research, and in 1850 John Thurnam announced that he was 'collecting information in reference to the crania from tumuli of different ages, with the view of producing, if possible, some conclusions as to the form of the skull, and other characteristics of the skeleton in the aboriginal and succeeding races who settled in the British Isles. . . . I shall feel indebted to any gentleman who may possess crania from barrows, the age of which can be authenticated by the associated remains, who will allow me the use of them, for the purpose of being measured and described.'[45] This concern with skeletal material and particularly the crania was something new in archaeological studies, since hitherto there had been a general reluctance to do anything other than re-inter any human remains found during the excavation of burial mounds. It cannot be explained simply as a product of the increased awareness of the relevance of ethnological methods for archaeology. Attempts to determine racial varieties in man were not new by the mid-nineteenth century. Blumenbach, whom Barnard Davies saw as the pioneer of such work through the analysis of skulls, had published his first important work in 1775 and his dedication of the third edition of *On the natural variety of mankind* (1795) to Sir Joseph Banks shows that his work was at least known in Britain.[46] There are, moreover, other references in the earlier British antiquarian literature which show that the reluctance to collect skulls can not be attributed to any ignorance of the work of craniologists.[47] The answer, I think, lies more with the activities of the resurrectionists, especially in the early nineteenth century. At that time the demands of a growing population for medical services led to expansion of the medical profession and particularly medical research. However, the failure to develop a satisfactory system for the provision of bodies for the teaching of anatomy led to most corpses supplied to anatomy schools being those of people recently deceased, buried and illegally disinterred. The difficulties for large medical schools like those in Glasgow and Edinburgh involved going as far afield as Ulster to obtain an adequate supply of corpses;[48] in 1832 it was estimated that British medical schools required 1100-1200 bodies per annum to meet their requirements and that the vast majority of these were provided illegally.[49] Although this illegal practice caused widespread public concern and disquiet, successive governments were reluctant to introduce legislation since anatomical experiments also aroused public indignation. The deteriorating situation led to a Select Committee being established in 1828 and its recommendations resulted in the Anatomy Act of 1832.[50] This certainly eradicated the activities of the resurrectionists, but public prejudice towards scientific research involving human bodies was only slowly reduced.[51] In these circumstances it seems reasonable to interpret the reluctance of the excavators of burial mounds to collect human remains as a desire to avoid association in people's minds with the resurrectionists rather than with a simple disinclination to interfere with the physical remains of the dead.[52]

These prejudices had clearly subsided by the time Wilson, Thurnam and others began seriously to promote the value of analysis of human skeletal material. Yet it did not achieve the importance which these workers anticipated in their early pronouncements, largely because it became embroiled in wider controversies which were largely peripheral to archaeological concerns. The first demonstrations of the potential of this method, exciting though they were, disguised the fact that ultimately this interpretation of British prehistory could not rest solely, or indeed largely, on data collected in Britain. There were, moreover, considerable problems in integrating this information with other archaeological material, a point which Thurnam alone seems to have appreciated. However, the principal reason for the failure of racial analysis to be established as an accepted archaeological method was its involvement in a controversy concerning monogenesis and polygenesis. Both had considerable histories by the middle of the nineteenth century and, although polygenist thought had acquired support in France and America, the alternative hypothesis had remained the orthodox Christian viewpoint and accepted British attitude. The re-emergence of this old controversy took the emphasis away from matters to which British archaeology could make any serious contribution. The adoption of polygenesis by Davis and Thurnam, who became the leading exponents of this method, meant that the relative importance of racial analysis was dependent upon the supplanting of monogenesis by polygenesis as the orthodox position. This failed to come about because, although polygenist thought continued after and indeed felt supported by the publication of Darwin's views,[53] the latter provided the essence of a new approach based on cultural evolution. The controversy provoked institutional upheavals within ethnology,[54] with the result that the importance of anatomical work in archaeology was minimised in favour of the new orthodoxy of cultural evolution.

The emergence of social evolutionary theory provided the dominant theme in anthropological thought during the last thirty-five years or so of the nineteenth century,[55] and precluded the continuing development of racial studies as part of the mainstream of anthropological work. There is no clear-cut division between the two approaches in archaeological writings. Huxley, for instance, who was clearly to be associated with social evolutionary ideas, was quite happy to contribute an analysis of the human remains to Samuel Laing's study of Caithness material[56] and even to be sympathetic to Thurnam's work, but there was no longer any sense that this methodology was central to archaeological activity. Nevertheless, Tylor put the prevailing point of view quite bluntly in *Primitive Culture:*

> These pages will be so crowded with evidence of such correspondence among mankind, that there is no need to dwell upon its details here, but it may be used at once to override a problem which would complicate the argument, namely the question of race. For the present purpose it appears both possible and desirable to eliminate considerations of hereditary varieties or races of man, and to treat mankind as homogeneous in nature, though placed in different grades of civilisation. The details of the enquiry will, I think, prove that stages of culture may be compared without taking into account how far tribes who use the same implement, follow the same custom, or believe the same myth, may differ in their bodily configuration and the colour of their skin and hair.[57]

The questions were now to be about diffusion or independent invention, and Stocking notes that the cultural evolutionists, in adopting the idea of plurality of origin in the notion of independent invention, turned the polygenist argument on its head by making such diversity into evidence of unity of psychic make-up, the very thing which the polygenists rejected.[58] Such aspects, however, should not lead us away from the essential point that race was no longer recognised as an issue of substance.

The essentials of the evolutionary approach and their particular relevance to archaeological material were best summarised by Lane-Fox in his description of the principles of classification which formed the basis for the arrangement of his own collections (1875). Further, he left no doubt as to the source of these ideas:

> What the palaeontologist does for zoology, the prehistorian does for anthropology. What the study of zoology does towards explaining the structures of extinct species, the study of existing savages does towards enabling us to realise the condition of primeval man. To continue the simile further, the propagation of new ideas may be said to correspond to the propagation of species. New ideas are produced by the correlation of previously existing ideas in the same manner that new individuals in a breed are produced by the union of previously existing individuals. And in the same manner that we find that the crossing of animals makes it extremely difficult to trace the channels of hereditary transmission of qualities in a breed, so the crossing of ideas in this manner makes it extremely difficult to trace the sequence of ideas, though we may be certain that sequence does exist as much in one case as the other.
>
> Progress is like a game of dominoes — like fits onto like. In neither case can we tell beforehand what will be the ultimate figure produced by the adhesions; all we know is that the fundamental rule of the game is *sequence*.[59]

These allusions to zoology emphasise the clear kinship of these formulations with Darwinian ideas in biology, although there is no simple parentage which can be inferred; Darwin, notes Burrow, 'was certainly not the father of evolutionary anthropology, but possibly he was its wealthy uncle'.[60] Indeed there were those, such as Bastian, who rejected Darwin but accepted cultural evolution.[61] This theory contains three elements of relevance to anthropology, although all were controversial. The first was that man was not outside nature but a part of it through sharing a clear relationship with animals. Secondly, Darwin's views appeared to support those aspects of racial theory which saw differences in terms of environmental factors acting over a long time span. Finally, there was the principle of natural selection which entered sociology and anthropology in the unfortunate 'survival of the fittest' viewpoint. Of course, behind Darwin was Lyell's uniformitarianism outlined in the *Principles of Geology*. Lyell's work assumed a continually operating law, the effects of which are still observable and from which could be inferred past processes. Further, his hypothesis necessitated an enormous time scale. The achievement of Lyell and Darwin was to show how the presently determinable laws of nature could indicate the causes of even the greatest changes, provided a sufficiently long time scale could be accepted. The final part of this scientific support system, as far as evolutionary anthropology was concerned, was provided by the acceptance of a high antiquity for man following Prestwich and Evans' visit to the Somme gravels.

Together with Pitt-Rivers, the principal archaeological advocates of the new theories were members of the anthropological establishment whose interest was strongly archaeological, Lubbock and Evans. In their works,[62] especially those of Evans, can be seen the beginnings of typological analysis based on evolutionary premises that found its greatest expression in Abercromby's work on Bronze Age pottery (1912).[63] For most archaeologists these typological studies were an altogether too sophisticated response to the new approach, which was reflected rather crudely by a resurgence of belief in progress, with the general implication that the 'ruder' an object was, the greater its antiquity. There can be no doubt that the racial debates earlier in the century had temporarily weakened the appeal of progress as a mechanism for chronological judgements, but it had remained a potent theme for general explanation in archaeology. Stuart, for instance, drew attention to the importance of the 'accumulations of materials for illustrating the progress of man in times antecedent to his knowledge of writing'.[64] There were considerable difficulties in relating a simple idea of progress to individual finds, but in general terms the evidence seemed to be there. Few would have disputed Tylor's claim that

> by comparing the various stages of civilisation among races known to history, with the aid of archaeological inference from the remains of the pre-historic tribes, it seems possible to judge in a rough way of an early general condition of man, which from our point of view is to be regarded as a primitive condition, whatever yet earlier state may in reality have lain behind it. This hypothetical primitive condition corresponds in a considerable degree to that of the modern savage tribes, who in spite of their difference and distance, have in common certain elements of civilisation, which seem remains of an early state of the human race at large.[65]

Further, the mutual dependence inherent in Tylor's hypothesis did not cause much heart-searching among anthropologists or archaeologists, or weaken its appeal for either group. It must have seemed to archaeologists late in the nineteenth century that the subject really had become part of the prestigious field of Science. Scientific modes and attitudes had become part of the fundamental philosophy, particularly the idea that the progress of a subject was to be measured in terms of accumulation, for knowledge once acquired remained immutable.[66] Certainly, it seemed a far cry from the topographical tradition that dominated archaeological thinking in the early decades of the century.

Yet that same sense of national pride which is so evident in the work of the topographers was still a powerful source of motivation for the newer 'scientific archaeologists'. Nowhere is this more clearly demonstrated than in the work of the doyen of Scottish archaeology at the end of the nineteenth century, Joseph Anderson. Just as Wilson had done in the middle of the century, Anderson reflects the trends and approaches of his time, moulded and applied to the Scottish material. Both men attempted the systematic arrangement of the evidence from Scotland and in so doing had occasion to make explicit statements about how they believed their aims could be best achieved. Superficially, of course, there are points of great similarity between the major works of Wilson and Anderson, particularly in their use of the Three Age system. What is important, however, is the differences between the two, since what was new and radical in Wilson's day, such as the use of the Three Age system, had become commonplace by the time Anderson wrote.

A survey of Anderson's archaeological work has recently been published,[67] and there is no need to repeat the information collected there. But it is, I think, worthwhile looking in some detail at his first Rhind Lecture, given on 14 October 1879, and published, as delivered, in the first volume of *Scotland in Early Christian Times*.[68] This is without doubt Anderson's most important statement of his philosophy and shows not only the impact which the trends we have been discussing had on Scottish archaeology but also in some respects points the way to developments which did not come to fruition until after Anderson's death.

There can be no doubting his fervent sense of national pride, displayed in remarks such as:

> We know that the history of Scotland is not the history of any other nation on earth, and that if her records were destroyed, it would matter nothing to us that all the records of all other nations were preserved. They could neither tell the story of our ancestors, nor restore the lost links in the development of our culture and civilisation.

Or even more passionately:

Is there any scientific, or other reason, which demands that our Archaeology should not begin at home? Can we possibly be more interested in the ancient history of other nations than in the ancient history of our own people? Are the sculptured stones of Nineveh really of more importance to us than the sculptured stones of Scotland? Can we possibly have an interest in the themes and legends of Egyptian or Assyrian sculptures which we cannot feel for the themes and legends carved on the monuments of our forefathers? It cannot be the fact that we have greater regard for other men's ancestors than for the memory of our own. I think, if we try to persuade ourselves of this, we shall fail, and if we deal closely with the question, we shall be obliged to confess that Scotland and its antiquities have claims to our attention and regard that are prior to all other lands, and all other antiquities.[69]

But we should not interpret these remarks as indicating a narrow-minded parochialism on Anderson's part. He had a clear sense of the way things should develop — 'when a number of limited areas have been exhaustively investigated, and the results placed on record, it may be possible to proceed a step farther, and to formulate general conclusions applicable to wide areas, such as Europe, or Eastern or Western Asia, or Africa or America, but at present no body of materials exists from which the archaeology of any one of these larger areas may be studied systematically'.[70] This was the essential justification for what he was attempting in his Rhind Lectures, and a mere glance at any of the works in his long list of publications will show how well informed he was about European procedures, attitudes and discoveries, particularly those in Scandinavia. The appeals to national feeling were not designed to promote any sense of insularity but rather were the means by which Anderson sought to ensure that Scottish antiquaries met their responsibilities to this wider goal.

The title of Anderson's lecture was 'the means of obtaining a scientific basis for the archaeology of Scotland', and there was no doubt in his mind that such a 'scientific basis' could be obtained. In view of the considerable emphasis placed upon archaeology becoming a science, the use of the term 'scientific archaeology' is in no way remarkable, nor is his emphasis on the importance of collecting facts. These were to be the 'exhaustive collection of materials' from which was to be extracted 'the story of human progress on Scottish soil'.[71] But they had to be properly collected, 'for it is obvious that if the observations by which materials for comparison and induction are accumulated have not been scientifically made, the conclusions drawn from them can have no scientific value, and that the first necessity in every scientific enquiry is accurate observation, exhaustive in its range, and recorded with the requisite precision and fulness of detail'.[72] Once all this information is assembled it is to be subjected to a 'natural method' which is 'nearly akin to the scientific method' and involves two basic questions about the object's function and the material of which it is made. Thus,

> by following this natural method, and interrogating each of the implements separately as to its purpose, we find no difficulty in getting out all the edged-tools and arranging them in separate heaps, consisting of different types of tool — such as axes, chisels, gouges, saws, knives, and so forth — or types of weapons such as arrow-heads, spear-heads, daggers, and so on. During this process of getting out the edged-tools and arranging them by their typical forms, a singular fact will have disclosed itself. In the first of our sorted heaps we shall have nothing but axes but we have axes in three materials — stone, bronze and iron. Every group has the same triple repetition of the tool in the same three materials. This, then, is the second problem — What is the meaning of the fabrication of the same tools in these three materials?

> The testimony of universal experience tells us that the less suitable and effective material is always supplanted in time by that which is more suitable and effective, after it has become generally procurable. The more unsuitable implement may maintain the struggle for existence for a longer or shorter period, according to circumstances; but when it comes to be a competition of materials, the law is, that the fittest shall survive, and the less fit dies out by a process of degradation of the type and purpose of the implement for which the material continues to be used.[73]

Here, indeed, is the social evolutionary legacy, and one would have to search very hard for a clearer explanation of how typology and function became so inextricably combined in the search for sequence. Anderson did not believe that archaeology could by itself determine actual dates without recourse to historical sources, but he attaches the same high importance to sequence that Pitt-Rivers did in his remarks quoted earlier. All of this is very much in keeping with the views of his time, but Anderson, cautious as he was, could partially perceive future developments. In particular, his emphasis on the importance of association, the geographical distribution of material, and the need to determine imports were all to become fruitful areas of study, some of them initially in the hands of other Scottish workers like Abercromby and Munro.

This survey has concentrated on broad trends in archaeology in the second half of the nineteenth century in order to show that it was very much a part of general archaeological development in Britain during that period. It was never wholly provincial in attitude and indeed at times, particularly at the end of the nineteenth century, it numbered among its practitioners archaeologists who will bear comparison with the best in Europe. In no small measure, the Society through its activities provided the environment in which archaeology of this quality could flourish. Certainly, some of the ideas seem less soundly based now than they did to people at the time, but no one who is seriously engaged in studies of Scottish archaeological material can avoid consulting the literature of this period, and the legacy must still be considered a significant one today.

NOTES

1. O. J. R. Howarth, *The British Association for the Advancement of Science: a retrospect, 1831-1921* (London 1922); A. D. Orange, 'The British Association . . ., the provincial background', *Sci. Stud.* i (1971), 315-29; A. D. Orange, 'The origins of the British Association . . .', *Brit. Jnl. Hist. Sci.* vi (1972-3), 152-76.

2. The only recent consideration of this affair is the wholly one-sided account in J. Evans, 'The Royal Archaeological Institute: a retrospect', *Archaeol. Jnl.* cvi (1949), 1-11, pp. 1-5.

3. Piggott, 'The Origins of the English County Archaeological Societies' (1974), in *Ruins in a Landscape* (Edinburgh 1976), 171-95.

4. F. J. Haverfield, *The Roman Occupation of Britain* (Oxford 1924), 81.

5. Quoted in J. M. Crook and M. H. Port, *The History of the King's Works* vi (London 1973), 641.

6. Society of Antiquaries of Scotland, Correspondence Books, 7 June 1844.

7. S. Piggott, *Ruins in a Landscape*, 191.

8. K. S. Inglis, 'Patterns of religious worship in 1851', *Jnl. Eccl. Hist.* xi (1960), 74-86.

9. J. Anderson and G. F. Black, 'Reports on Local Museums in Scotland, obtained through Dr R. H. Gunning's Jubilee gift to the Society', *P*[*roceedings of the*] *S*[*ociety of*] *A*[*ntiquaries of*] *S*[*cotland*] xxii (1887-8), 422.

10. S.A.S. Corr., 29 March 1844.

11. *Ibid.*, 5 August 1846.

12. W. L. Alexander, 'Anniversary Address', *PSAS* ii (1854-7), 300.

13. M. Plant, *The English Book Trade* (2 ed., London 1965), 269-419.

14. J. Evans, *A History of the Society of Antiquaries* (Oxford 1956), 237, 276.

15. See A. R. B. Haldane, *Three Centuries of Scottish Posts: an historical survey to 1836* (Edinburgh 1971), 248-73.

16. H. Robinson, *Britain's Post Office. A history of development from the beginnings to the present day* (London 1953), 163-5, 175, 194.

17. S.A.S. Corr., 1853.

18. J. Evans, *A History of the Society of Antiquaries* (1956), 305.

19. *Surrey Archaeol. Collections* vi (1874), vii.

20. D. Wilson, 'Anniversary Address', *PSAS* i (1851-4), 2-7.

21. *Ibid.*, 6.

22. *Ibid.*, 2-3.

23. *Ibid.*, 3.

24. [J. Anderson], 'Description of the National Museum of Antiquities', 1892. TS. in N.M.A.S. Library.

25. J. M. Crook, *The British Museum: a case-study in architectural politics* (Harmondsworth 1973); J. Jones, 'Museum and art gallery buildings in England, 1845-1914', pt i, *Mus. Jnl.* lxv (1966), 230.

26. J. Anderson and G. F. Black, 'Reports on local museums', *PSAS* xxii (1887-8), 364-5.

27. D. Murray, *Museums, their History and their Use* (3 vols., Glasgow 1904), 270; C. H. Wilson, 'On the formation of provincial museums and collections of works of art', *Trans. Archit. Inst. Scot.*, iv(1) (1854-5), 56.

28. M. Brawne, *The New Museum: architecture and display* (New York 1965), 8.

29. Anderson and Black, 'Reports', 421.

30. O. Klindt-Jensen, *A History of Scandinavian Archaeology* (London 1975), 49-96; C. A. Nordman, *Archaeology in Finland before 1920* (Helsinki 1968), 9.

31. D. Wilson, *The Archaeology and Prehistoric Annals of Scotland* (1 ed., Edinburgh and London 1851), xiii.

32. W. L. Alexander, 'Anniversary Address', *PSAS* ii (1854-7), 301-2.

33. Nordman, *Archaeology in Finland*, 9.

34. Wilson, *Archaeology and Prehistoric Annals* (1851), xiv.

35. J. Y. Simpson, *Archaeology: its past and future work* (Edinburgh 1861), 5, marginal note.

36. *Ibid.*, 37-8.

37. E.g. Sir R. C. Hoare, *The Ancient History of North Wiltshire* (London 1819), 93.

38. Simpson, *Archaeology*, 40-42.

39. *Archaeol. Hist. Coll. Ayr & Galloway*, vi (1889), xvii.

40. Wilson, *Archaeology and Prehistoric Annals* (1851), xix.

41. A. H. Rhind, *The Law of Treasure Trove: how can it be best adapted to accomplish useful results?* (Edinburgh and London, 1858), 5.

42. Alexander, 'Anniversary Address', *PSAS* ii (1854-7), 304.

43. Simpson, *Archaeology*, 44-5.

44. D. Wilson, 'Inquiry into the evidence of the existence of primitive races in Scotland prior to the Celtae', *Notices and Abstracts of Communications to the British Association* (1850), 142.

45. J. Thurnam, 'Observations on Danish tumuli, and on the importance of collecting crania in tumuli', *Archaeol. Jnl.* vii (1850), 35.

46. See T. Bendyshe (ed.), *The Anthropological Treatises of Johan Friedrich Blumenbach* (London 1865), 149-54.

47. E.g. Sir R. C. Hoare, 'An account of a stone barrow, in the parish of Wellow, at Stoney Littleton in the county of Somerset, which was opened and investigated in the month of May, 1816', *Archaeologia* xix (1821), 47.

48. A. McClelland, 'The resurrection men', *Ulster Folk Transport Museum Year Book* (1977-8), 15.

49. *Hansard*, 3 ser. ix (1831-32), 580.

50. J. B. Bailey, *The diary of a Resurrectionist . . . and a short history of the passing of the Anatomy Act* (London 1896), 89-119.

51. F. K. Donnelly, 'The destruction of the Sheffield School of Anatomy in 1835: a popular response to class legislation', *Trans. Hunter Archaeol. Soc.* x(3) (1975), 167-72.

52. Cf. F. Celoria, 'Burials and archaeology: a survey of attitudes to research', *Folklore* lxxvii (1966), 161-83.

53. G. W. Stocking, *Race, Culture and Evolution: essays in the history of anthropology* (New York 1968), 42-68.

54. G. W. Stocking, 'What's in a name? The origins of the Royal Anthropological Institute (1837-71)', *Man* n.s. vi (1971), 369-90.

55. I. L. Murphree, 'The evolutionary anthropologists . . . John Lubbock, Edward B. Tylor, and Lewis H. Morgan', *Proc. Amer. Philos. Soc.* cv (1961), 265-300; J. W. Burrow, *Evolution and Society. A study in Victorian social theory* (Cambridge 1966).

56. S. Laing, *Pre-historic Remains of Caithness* (London and Edinburgh 1866), 83-160.

57. E. B. Tylor, *Primitive Culture: researches into the development of mythology, philosophy, religion, language, art and custom* (London 1871), i.7.

58. Stocking, 'What's in a name?' (1971), 385-6.

59. A. Lane-Fox, 'On the principles of classification adopted in the arrangement of his anthropological collection, now exhibited in the Bethnal Green Museum', *Journ. Anthrop. Inst.* iv (1875), 308.

60. Burrow, *Evolution and Society*, 14.

61. R. H. Lowie, *The History of Ethnological Theory* (London 1937), 30-38.

62. J. Lubbock, *Prehistoric Times, as illustrated by ancient remains and the manners and customs of modern savages* (1 ed., London and Edinburgh, 1865); idem, *The Origin of Civilisation and the Primitive Condition of Man* (London 1870); J. Evans, *Coins of the Ancient Britons* (London 1864), 17-32; idem, *Ancient Stone Implements, Weapons and Ornaments of Great Britain* (1 and 2 eds., London 1872, 1897); idem, *Ancient Bronze Implements, Weapons and Ornaments of Great Britain* (London 1881).

63. J. Abercromby, *A Study of the Bronze Age Pottery of Great Britain and Ireland and its associated grave-goods* (2 vols., Oxford 1912).

64. J. Stuart, *Recent Progress of Archaeology: an address given at the opening meeting of the Glasgow Archaeological Society session 1865-6* (Glasgow 1866), 8.

65. Tylor, *Primitive Culture*, 21.

66. H. Dingle, 'The scientific outlook in 1851 and in 1951', *Brit. Jnl. Philos. Sci.* ii (1951-2), 98.

67. A. Graham, 'The archaeology of Joseph Anderson', *PSAS* cvii (1975-6), 279-98.

68. J. Anderson, *Scotland in Early Christian Times. The Rhind Lectures in Archaeology — 1879* (Edinburgh 1881), 1-28.

69. *Ibid.*, 9, 11-12.

70. *Ibid.*, 2, note 1.

71. *Ibid.*, 71.

72. *Ibid.*, 21.

73. *Ibid.*, 17-18.

The Museum, its Beginnings and its Development

Part II: the National Museum to 1954

R. B. K. Stevenson

We plead for the accumulation of antiquarian objects in our own and other public collections. The Museum has been gifted over by the Society of Antiquaries to the Government — it now belongs, not to us, but to Scotland — and we unhesitatingly call on every true-hearted Scotsman to contribute, whenever it is in his power, to the extension of this museum, as the best record and collection of the earliest archaeological and historical monuments of our native land.

Professor Sir J. Y. Simpson MD, January 1861*

The seven years of transition after the Conveyance of 1851, before the collections could be transferred, housed and financed by the Government, helped to disguise the contradictions and disadvantages inherent in the simple pragmatic solution that had been provided. The distinction between 'our Museum' and the Government's was blurred in practice; but in such a way that the troubles of being a step-child in a marriage of convenience were to be recurrent, and ultimately made necessary another legal status for it. The Society, effectively its Council, co-operating with the Secretary of the Board of Manufactures over plans for accommodation and staff, treated the Museum as a trust while the conditions for the transfer were unfulfilled. Once Government money was voted, and the Society began to exercise the 'charge and management' on the Board's behalf, everything went on much as before. The advantages, obvious at the start, were not only financial, though the very prospect of being freed of the expenses of accommodating the Museum and itself was enough to allow the invaluable

* For a general bibliographical note, see p. 210. As explained on p. 31 above, detailed references to sources, largely related to the Society's own minute-books and records, will be inserted in a copy in the Society's Library.

yearly *Proceedings* to be started, as we have seen. The Museum remained a *raison d'être* for the Society, as Lord Buchan had wished, adding some prestige by its new status; and it in turn benefited enormously from the regular publication and from the growing number of members throughout the country (250 Fellows in 1860), who formed as it were its body of Friends.

Settling in at The Mound, 1859-69

The curious fact that for thirty years from its reopening in November 1859 the Museum had two names in regular use, betrays two continuing points of view. In welcoming the signature of the Conveyance, Daniel Wilson had written that 'the establishment of a Museum of Historical Antiquities in the Scottish Capital, such as will supply to the scientific Archaeologist the elements of unwritten history, is an object that cannot be achieved by the most zealous private exertions', so that the collections formed by the Society were not yet 'fit to constitute a National Archaeological Museum'. Neither of these possible names, however, seems to have won support during the transition. From the reopening onwards, the official address was Museum of Antiquities, Royal Institution; but the Society's own address was shown on the monthly billets, beginning March 1860, as National Museum of the Antiquaries of Scotland. This version was expanded at the same time, in a circular to schoolmasters, by inserting 'the Society of', and the *Catalogue of Antiquities* published in 1863 had this fuller form on the title-page — without the prefix National. The title on the spine of this small book is CATALOGUE OF ANTIQUITIES — ANTIQUARIAN SOC. SCOTLAND, corresponding to what was probably the most frequent spoken form, Antiquarian Museum (used as a heading in the 1849 catalogue). The form National Museum of Antiquities, used in the Edinburgh *Courant* on the eve of the opening in 1859, came into regular offical use at the time of the move in 1890. One of the earlier occurrences, the heading of a newspaper advertisement for the post of Keeper in 1869, suffered the unfortunate misprint NATURAL.

In the world of cultural institutions in which the Museum had to find its position, much happened in Edinburgh between 1851 and 1859. The Act of Parliament in 1850 which provided for a National Gallery of old master pictures as well as for the modern pictures of the Royal Scottish Academy and its life class, all within buildings that were to be erected on The Mound, ensured that there would be space again in the Royal Institution for the Museum. It also made the expensive development of the National Gallery the centre of the Board's interests, instead of the School of Design. Though the only Government body in Scotland suitable to be entrusted with the Museum, the Board had no reason to be enthusiastic about it, even supposing that the friction of a few years before had left no mark, and they clearly stated that no extra charge on their funds should be incurred. The idea of letting the Antiquaries look after the antiquities while the Board in whom they were vested concentrated on art, was evidently welcome to both parties. It also left the Museum in a weak position, which was weakened further by the Treasury Minute of 25 February 1858 intimating the funding for 'the reception and exhibition (free) to the public of this rare collection' and for 'a proper staff of officers to manage and take charge of this Museum'; for it ruled that the Board would have to pay out of their own funds the £300 p.a. for running costs and whole-time staff. (The Society continued to have curators and a librarian among its own office-bearers.) The Board did not get their own way entirely over the Royal Academy either, as the Treasury made them responsible for the whole cost of maintenance of the new building, and insisted that the part-time salaried Curator of the National Gallery should be chosen from among the Academicians, thus recognising their special knowledge and their contribution of pictures.

Meantime pressure from Edinburgh, following the foundation in London of museums of industrial art and science because of the success of the Great Exhibition of 1851, resulted in the Industrial Museum of Scotland being established in 1855. It formed part of the Department of Science and Art (at that time under the Board of Trade). Its Director was appointed first Regius Professor of Technology in Edinburgh University, and the University gave to the Department its Natural History Museum, by then very important; to this a large part of the Royal Society's Museum, excluding geology, was added in 1859. After the Department had been transferred from Trade to Education, Parliament in 1858 voted money for a new building which would house both its Museums, combined in 1864 under the name of the Edinburgh Museum of Science and Art — now the Royal Scottish Museum.

As fostering art in industry had been one of the important functions of the Board of Manufactures and the original purpose of its School of Design, it was logical that in 1858 the School should be placed under the central control of the Department. The arrangements for the National Gallery and for the Museum were not disturbed, one reason presumably being that to collect and exhibit pictures and antiquities was not considered part of education in the same sense as the School and the other Museum, perhaps because connoisseurship rather than training was involved. Probably also it seemed natural to the Treasury for administration in Edinburgh to be like that in London, for the Industrial Museum within a Government Department and for the National Gallery under Trustees. The British Museum, under Trustees, included a Department of Antiquities (so called since 1833). As none of the Government's museums in London, other than the Gallery, was called National, and as the Industrial Museum in Edinburgh was in that sense no less national than the Museum of Antiquities — for which another possible name, 'Museum of National Antiquities', may have been thought unduly restrictive, considering its sizeable foreign element — the plain-jane name was probably not due to discrimination by the Board, but rather to adherence to precedents in what had become a complex situation. The Antiquaries' self-assertive alternatives were unfortunate but understandable.

It was not back to the series of small rooms at the sides of the Royal Institution, where the building was divided into two floors, that the Museum and library moved in 1859, though this was the intention in 1851. They were allotted the three lofty principal rooms along the centre, entered from the pillared portico on Princes Street and across the entrance hall; there the Board's porter took sticks and umbrellas at one penny each, and on some days sixpences for entry, and supervised the Museum's turnstile. The Royal Institution no longer used the building called after it, and by 1860 existed only nominally. The Board's School of Design remained on the East side with its Statue Gallery, upstairs above the Board's offices. The Royal Society, on the West, had a side door of its own. From the entrance hall one went straight into the Museum's first room, an octagon 29 feet each way and 18 feet up to the cornice. (The present long flight of steps leading up to pairs of large rooms the full width of the building, above smaller rooms partly below ground level, all date from the total interior reconstruction in 1909.) In line with the octagon there was an octagonal gallery of the same breadth but 62 feet long. This was followed by another octagon. Above the cornice a high coved ceiling rose to central rooflights from which there hung gas chandeliers, so that all of the wall-space was usable for exhibits as well as the 3,240 sq. feet of floorspace. After considerable argument the height of the wall-cases, modelled on those of the British Museum, was fixed at 10½ feet. They were entirely of wood rather than partly metal, as would have been preferred but for cost. Floor-cases were added over several years. The further octagon was fitted for the library with book-shelves and a gallery. It was also the hall where the Society normally met, though on special occasions the Royal Society allowed the use of its hall. The library was also the office, with stationery cupboards by the fireplace, and a safe into which trays of coins and other precious exhibits were moved at night. The general ventilation of the Museum and its hot-water heating was unsatisfactory and was examined by a member of the Council's museum sub-committee, Thomas Stevenson, R. L. S.'s father.

As Keeper, with a salary of £150 p.a. from January 1859, the Council appointed William Thomson M'Culloch, a former apprentice of David Laing's, who had become librarian of the Edinburgh Subscription Library, then in the same building in George Street as the Society, and so had been able to do occasional clerical work for it, with the office of assistant librarian in 1849. He helped in arranging and preparing articles in the Museum for exhibition, and in copying and making facsimiles, 'having always had a turn for mechanical contrivances'. After appointment he continued in his own time to be assistant secretary and librarian of the School of Arts, as well as to do some additional work for the Society, paid from its own funds. He sometimes gave popular lectures on Edinburgh, illustrated by photographs from old drawings and engravings 'exhibited by oxy-hydrogen light'. His thorough history of The Maiden was published posthumously in the *Proceedings* (1867-68). From May 1859 one Robert Paul, paid £50 p.a., was his assistant, with duties ranging from lighting fires and stoves, dusting and carpentry, to arranging objects. There was also a cleaner at £10; other expenses such as heating and lighting and taxes were estimated at £90.

A considerable committee was concerned with the arrangement, and with considering a report by the Keeper on the many objects of natural history and spurious antiquities not suitable for the purposes of the Society. (It was not minuted what these things were, nor what happened to them.) The committee included J. M. Mitchell, James Drummond, J. A. Smith, Joseph Robertson as librarian, and Cosmo Innes. Advice, which was largely followed, was sent by A. H. Rhind, recently elected an Honorary Fellow at the age of 24. The office of curator of coins was filled again, after George Sim WS joined the Society in 1860 and undertook the rearrangement of the Scottish and English coins.

Details of the arrangement are given in the catalogue published in 1863, after considerable rearrangement and completion of labelling. This was briefer in its entries than that of 1849, and unillustrated. Two thousand copies were printed, and another thousand in a revision about 1866. The plan which it records may be said to be in some ways more old-fashioned than that devised by Daniel Wilson. Instead of placing foremost their speciality the Scottish antiquities (which Wilson in 1851 had claimed to be much greater in extent and value than the native antiquities in the British Museum), they gave pride of place to Egypt, and to the classical, Indian, and other foreign exhibits, as in London though on a far smaller scale. The reason was partly the accident that the smaller room suitable for them had to come first, but principally the recent acceptance of A. H. Rhind's collection from his excavations at Thebes in Egypt, where he had gone from Caithness for the sake of his health. It numbered over 600 items of many kinds, ever-popular mummies as well as important papyri. Significantly, Rhind discussed the use of bronze and iron in Egypt and its 'relevance to general archaeology' in a paper read to the Society.

When it came to the large room — British Antiquities etc — the catalogue abandoned the attempt to separate Stone and Bronze Periods. As a principle that could be applied to Scotland it had met with considerable disagreement within the Society, and Wilson's great collection of the available information in his *Archaeology and Prehistoric Annals of Scotland* (1851) had not managed to make it clear. (His wish to be comprehensive and his use of comparisons led him to be discursive, and to include linguistic and historical evidence, and racial concepts, under the broad umbrella of archaeology.) So the hazardous word Celtic, previously applied to all the prehistoric material, had been dropped entirely, and Anglo-Saxon very nearly; only the Romans were left to link early antiquities with history. However the new arrangement was, very patchily, chronological clockwise round the room. Several useful innovations were made. There was a more detailed classification of objects by type, the foreign and ethnographical parallels being placed alongside the Scottish. With this went a tentative beginning to the Museum's individual system of class-letters and numbers, rather like modern car-registration numbers. Stone objects came first in the wall-cases, though it was thought that the battle-axes and hammers could scarcely have been bored for their handles except by iron. Flints occupied one of the floor-cases; very soon they included two

implements out of the Somme gravels from Joseph Prestwich, who with
John Evans had authenticated their geological age only a few months
before, the event that, with the publication of the *Origin of Species*,
made 1859 an *annus mirabilis* in human studies. A small section was
called 'Articles found in "Picts' Houses", Crannoges, Tumuli etc', note-
worthy as the start of identifying and exhibiting settlement sites — but
the intrusion of burials into domestic ruins and the presence of
domestic refuse in burial chambers, as well as the minute size of the
sample as yet examined, led inevitably to confusion. This was followed
by another new grouping, sepulchral remains — skulls, urns with
associated finds, iron objects from graves — which came before Bronze
Implements etc. The splendid collection of gold, silver and bronze
personal ornaments, prehistoric to Norse, was shown in the second
floor-case.

Sculptured stones formed a considerable group, for in addition to
originals the series of casts was growing, related to Stuart's corpus of
early *Sculptured Stones* of which volume II was still to be published
(1867); some were made by Henry Laing, cataloguer of Scottish seals.
J. Y. Simpson gave casts of Scottish early Christian inscriptions, and
various striking new discoveries were brought to public notice in the
same way; the tomb-shrine at St Andrews (early ninth century), the
Govan sarcophagus (c 1000), and the runic inscriptions in Maeshowe,
Orkney (eleventh century). This didactic use of copies was also normal
at South Kensington, but in contrast the British Museum was specifically opposed to casts. Next came medieval and later stone carving,
much of it from Edinburgh owing to Daniel Wilson's activities; the
casts of carvings from Trinity College featured in 1849 had, however,
all but one been removed.

With a wide range of Romano-British items from sites in England as
well as Scotland there was now a good series of Roman inscriptions
and some sculpture. The more adequate space becoming available had
induced Sir George Clerk of Penicuik to give three altars and statue-
bases, a relief of Brigantia and other carvings, collected in the early
eighteenth century by Sir John Clerk from the Walls of Hadrian and
Antoninus, and from Birrens in Dumfriesshire. The Advocates had
already passed on two altars from Newstead and Cramond.

The main range of medieval and later exhibits was grouped by
subject, subdivided more than before, though 'Jacobite relics' were no
longer a group. The small amount of costume started with the
academic gown worn by Alexander Henderson in mid-seventeenth

century and ended with Sir Walter Scott's volunteer helmet. The Maiden and several small cannon stood out on the floor. The floor-cases must have been quite large, for the third held finger-rings, brooches, watches, charms and so on, as well as over thirty seal-matrices, notably the beautiful twelfth century seal of Brechin Cathedral and the Privy Council's recent gift of the silver matrices of the Scottish Great Seal of George III (used for the Society's Charter), and the quarter-seal of William IV. The fourth floor-case had series of coins, Anglo-Saxon, Scottish and English, tradesmen's tokens, royal and miscellaneous historical medals. Weights and balances, and no less than 128 dies for striking the coins of Charles II received newly from the Exchequer, were in a wall-case. On the end wall to the right of the entrance a subdivided case exhibited weapons, ecclesiastical items including finds from bishops' graves in Orkney, Ross-shire and Glasgow, a cast of the skull of king Robert Bruce, and a domestic miscellany. The larger 'iron weapons' and armour, flags, wood carvings, 'horns and skulls of animals', portraits, paintings including seventeenth-century panels, and two copies of the National Covenant of 1638, were arranged round the walls, beginning above the stone axes. This room thus contained a remarkably wide-ranging, truly national and for its time comprehensive exhibition, in which ancient and recent past were not arbitrarily cut off from one another. For general information there were only the headings in the catalogue, but its preface claimed 'each Article in the Museum has a label, stating the place where, and date when found, also by whom presented' — an ambition that has persisted. It was all no doubt rather like the photographs of thirty years later (pl. 2-3), only less crowded.

The preface of the catalogue also carried a notice about 'Treasure Trove etc, appartaining to the Crown', dated January 1859:

> The Lords Commissioners of Her Majesty's Treasury having been pleased to authorise payment to finders of ancient coins, gold or silver ornaments, or other relics of antiquity in Scotland, of the actual value of the articles, on the same being delivered up for behoof of the Crown, I now give notice to all persons who shall hereafter make discoveries of any such articles, that on their delivering them, on behalf of the Crown, up to the Sheriffs of the respective counties in which the discoveries may take place, they will receive, through this department, rewards equal in amount to the full instrinsic value of the articles.
>
> John Henderson, Q. & L.T.R.

This was repeated in the Society's eleven-page letter, illustrated with woodcuts from the *Proceedings*, sent to the Schoolmasters of Scotland in 1860 — a distant predecessor of schools' broadcasts, probably inspired by Danish success in enlisting teachers' help in rescuing and recording national antiquities. Three thousand five hundred copies were printed. The Exchequer also circulated its notice, not only to Procurators Fiscal but to be put up in all post offices in Scotland. Evidently proposals discussed by a deputation from the Society with the Lord Advocate in 1847 had been fully accepted at last. Over the next twenty-five years in particular, this move to a positive and equitable use of the common law of Scotland, which differs widely from the narrower version which is the law of England, resulted in finds of many kinds being added to the national collections. As coins of base metal were an important part of Scotland's currency from much earlier than in England, it was fortunate that those, as well as the pots that contained hoards, could be included in 'treasure trove etc'. After 1858 the Museum was normally given first choice because of its new status; coins not selected were returned to the finders, as is still the case, and so increasingly reached collectors rather than the melting pot. One of the most important hoards known in Scotland came just in time for the re-opening, the treasure of Norse tenth-century silver ornaments and coins found in 1858 at Skaill in Orkney, mostly secured through the exertions of George Petrie, who persuaded 'the finders to rely on the recent enactment' on rewards.

The re-opening address was given on 23 December 1859 by Lord Neaves, of the Court of Session, to an invited audience of three hundred ladies and gentlemen, among them representatives of public bodies, in the hall of the Royal Society. They then moved to inspect the Museum and its library, where tea and coffee were served. It was much less grand than the opening of the National Gallery and Royal Scottish Academy with two military bands, but an enormous step forward not only from George Street but from the earlier circumstances at The Mound.

The most obvious result was the rapid increase in visitors. The attendances averaging under 20,000 in the late 1850s, and in the smaller rooms at The Mound in the early 1840s, became almost 80,000 in the first complete twelve months in 1860-61. They averaged nearly 88,000 for the next five years. The public opening days soon became Tuesday, Wednesday and Saturday 10.0 a.m. to 4.0 p.m. and Saturday evening 7.0 to 9.0. On Thursday and Friday, to match the National Gallery's copying days, admission cost sixpence, except for design students, members of the Antiquaries and friends introduced personally; as this was extra opening, and the money did not go to the Government, it was not held to violate the condition of free exhibition. (That, incidentally, though only one word in brackets in the Treasury Minute of 1858, was considered to be a sufficient impediment to change to require removal by Statutory Order following the Museums and Galleries Charges Act (1972), which was soon repealed.) Some 2% of visitors came on paying days, providing in 1861 £45 for purchases of books, coins and relics, and 10% on Saturdays — August attendances were much higher than other months except January, around 20% of the total in each case; on public holidays, New Year in particular, barriers had to be erected outside the front of the building to control the crowds. In George Street 1,330 visitors had been recorded in 1851 on New Year's Day, but in 1873 there were 11,271 to Museum and Statue Gallery. The cocoa-matting on the Museum floor had not been intended for such hard wear, and in 1864 was replaced by Kamptolicon (a predecessor of linoleum). During each November the Museum was shut for cleaning, rearrangement and other work; until 1864 this was also the only chance the Keeper had for a holiday.

A short annual report was sent to the Board for the Treasury from November 1860 onwards, and printed as part of the Society's annual general meeting in the *Proceedings* until 1907. It included the monthly attendance figures, number of items donated and purchased for the Museum and library, and mention of the principal donors and their gifts.

The late 1850s and 1860s saw the spade and pickaxe being accepted as, in J. Y. Simpson's words, 'indispensable aids to some forms of archaeology', 'quickened with the life and energy of the nineteenth century'. The results were not as spectacular as those in foreign lands, but they provided factual evidence, with relics that would in due course yield relative dates. They revealed the remarkable masonry as well as the later runes at Maeshowe, the full plan of the Callanish stones in Lewis, the early Christian cemetery at the Catstane near Edinburgh, and the grave of James III at Cambuskenneth Abbey, all without small finds for the Museum. More productively for it they uncovered the plans and contents of broch sites, not only in the counties of greatest concentration, Orkney, Caithness and Sutherland where work was stimulated by a £400 fund from Rhind's bequest, as reported in a series of papers in *Archaeologia Scotica* V.2 in 1874. Isolated brochs were cleared out near Stirling, near Dundee and in Berwickshire, and similar finds recovered from underground chambers in Forfarshire. The per-

L

plexing houses at Skara Brae in Orkney produced a quantity of stone and bone objects, many of which also seemed comparable. A major part of the finds from these widespread excavations came to be preserved in the Museum. Canon Greenwell's incursion into Argyll, however, lost Scotland the finest (neolithic) pot recovered from a chambered tomb, and finds from some of those in Caithness were lost entirely by the Anthropological Society of London. The uncertainty of local custody was underlined by the sale of Kirkwall Museum in 1862; its archaeological portion was fortunately rescued by an Orcadian landowner, and entrusted to the national collection.

Awareness of what was being done in Europe helped to direct enquiry. Samples of animal, bird, fish and molluscan remains, named by species as far as possible, figured prominently among the excavated material given to the Museum as listed in the reports. Bits of reindeer antler identified among broch fauna and stray finds in Scotland were discussed by J. A. Smith when a number of other objects were received in 1869 from Lartet and Christy's excavations in the Dordogne cave of l'âge du renne. He followed this with a series of papers on elk, cattle and other animals. A report on Dowalton loch in Galloway (1865) was accompanied by a paper by John Stuart on Scottish and Irish crannogs of Roman and later date, with comments from Dr Keller in Zürich, an Honorary Fellow, contrasting their construction with that of the Swiss lake dwellings.

Despite an instruction to Fiscals from the Exchequer in 1847 specifically on finds from railway construction sites — following the loss of a 4½ foot gold torc discovered near Edinburgh (fortunately represented by a replica) — only a few things were recovered officially and given in 1864: a cinerary urn from Banff, a spearhead from Hawick, and a silver-inlaid sword from Morayshire. Later a fine gold lunula (early bronze age) was also recovered from the Strathspey line, apparently from the spot where a grave was found in 1863 containing large gold ear-ornaments, one of which was accidentally rescued from a jeweller in Aberdeen. A few Roman finds from Castlecary fort on the Antonine Wall cut through in 1841, were given to the Museum by the proprietor ten years later. By then other Roman material had come from railway work at Newstead and part of an alabaster jar from Falkirk. The hoard of Pictish brooches and ornaments unearthed at Rogart in Sutherland in 1868 was dispersed, the two finest being bought by the Museum in 1888.

The Exchequer seems to have been more successful over coin hoards.

Two of them had the added value of dating associated gold, silver and jet ornaments — the still unparalleled group of coins of David I and Stephen, from Bute, and an Edwardian cache from Dumfriesshire. Starting with these and others in 1864, George Sim published hoard reports in the *Proceedings* at intervals for twenty-three years, and selected specimens for the Museum. Two bequests in the 1860s added considerably to the collection, Scottish coins and miscellaneous medals (and other valuables) from W. W. Hay Newton, and from an unknown John Lindsay (living in Perth not Cork) a large number of mainly English and foreign coins, many of them gold. Gifts of lead and white metal communion tokens began a quasi-numismatic collection, of rather limited appeal.

After 1,500 items had been added to the library from the Rhind bequest in 1863, additional shelves, and glazing of the old ones, were approved by the Treasury. Then the weight of exhibits given or promised in the next two years threatened excessive floor-loading. An eight-foot square relief of Assur-nasr-pal II from Layard's excavations at Nimrud, gifted by J. Y. Simpson, had to have support built from the foundations, but was never included in any printed catalogue. Four Roman altars from Birrens, formerly in the C. K. Sharpe collection, were given by Edinburgh University, and about the same time the only Roman milestone from Scotland, long kept in the College from Sir Robert Sibbald's lost seventeenth-century collection, came via the Museum of Science and Art. Two massive granite Pictish symbol stones from Aberdeenshire were bought, and the handsome 1597 pulpit from Parton in Kirkcudbrightshire was donated. Finally the Bell collection of over 1,400 antiquities, mainly Irish but Scottish-owned, was purchased by a special Government grant of £500, and needed further cases. Sanction was given in 1868 for a major reconstruction. The floor in all three rooms was lowered 32 inches 'to its original level' with additional supporting walls. A range of desk-cases was added below the tall wall-cases; the idea of adding a gallery had come to nothing. A hatch was made in the library floor for storage; previously some casts and old benches were kept under part of the Board's premises. Additional gas branches and wall-brackets were fitted. The replaced heating system was less satisfactory than ever.

After this upheaval M'Culloch rearranged the collections 'in an admirable manner' and he was to prepare a new edition of the catalogue, but he died in May 1869. His post was not pensionable, so members of the Society purchased an annuity for his widow and his sister.

Joseph Anderson and a scientific basis for archaeology in Scotland, 1869-91

It was clear that the new Keeper of the Museum ought to be much more than a skilled custodian of the fast-growing collections. The need was for the archaeological finds to be interpreted and organised for study, following the lead not only of Scandinavia and Switzerland but of England. There John Evans, Thurnam and Wollaston Franks were beginning period studies in classification, and since 1851 Franks had been developing in the British Museum a room of British and Medieval Antiquities into a Department (combined with European archaeology and world ethnography). The Council were supremely fortunate in being able to select, from the written applications, Joseph Anderson who, after seven years as teacher in Arbroath and Constantinople, had for eight years edited the *John o'Groats Journal* in Wick. Having excavated chambered cairns in Caithness for the Anthropological Society of London, he had been elected in 1866 a corresponding member of the Antiquaries. (The Society had become more sparing of this form of free membership, using it as a step towards honorary membership for men outside Scotland, and a recognition for particular local field-workers and donors to the Museum; the honorary grade of Lady Associate was instituted in 1869.) Anderson had submitted what Angus Graham in a recent study of his archaeological publications has characterised as clear and logical reports 'quoting English and Continental analogies with great facility'. He had also excavated several brochs for the Society's Rhind fund.

Anderson took post in August 1869. The salary which he accepted was still only £150 p.a. There was one assistant, recently replaced, at £60 plus £20 for cleaning duties. Both posts were unpensioned, unlike those of the Gallery's assistant and the Board's staff other than teachers; the question of what sort of examination should be undergone to obtain the necessary certification by the Civil Service Commission was resolved by the Treasury withdrawing the examination option from what it called the Society's Museum, without comment from the Council. In 1873 the Treasury was persuaded to improve (but out of the Board's funds) the 'very inadequate' salary of the Keeper, to £200. The Society had been supplementing it by up to £60, also making £10 grants for visits to the museums in Dublin and the Scandinavian capitals. The assistant's pay rose to £70; he worked for 47 hours a week and had three weeks' holiday.

When Anderson became also the Society's Assistant Secretary, a new post in 1877, the annual supplement became a firm honorarium. Sooner or later this also involved being editor of the *Proceedings*, which in 1879 changed into a stout annual bound volume, of some 400 pages or more. As the editorship was undertaken by holders of some more formal office it was rarely mentioned, but probably both David Laing and J. A. Smith, certainly active in 1876, continued so more or less until they died in 1878 and 1833. Because of some printing problem David Douglas, a publisher, was in 1874 made 'one of the joint editors'. His predecessor as Treasurer wrote in 1871 that £500 a year was being spent on publication and purchases.

As curator of coins George Sim arranged, in 1872 and subsequently, the transformation of the coin collection. He negotiated the purchase from the Faculty of Advocates of the collection they had bought in 1705 from James Sutherland. The offers accepted were £300 for the Roman, English, Anglo-Saxon and foreign coins and medals, and £500 for those relating to Scotland, among them some extreme rarities (all less £16 8s 0d for items acquired by gift), £33 12s 0d for various gold rings, seal matrices etc, and also £50 for the finely ornamented French cabinet which produced an important sequel in 1881.

To finance this expenditure three members of Council advanced £150 each, and the general fund the balance. Then duplicates were selected from the combined collections, of which that of the Antiquaries probably contributed the largest part, formed as it was from several private collections, treasure trove hoards (not all of which were ever regarded as reclaimable loans), and nearly a hundred years of isolated gifts from which the sale of duplicates had often been proposed. There were two auctions at Dowell's authorised by the Treasury — one in April 1873 of Scottish coins (77 gold, 347 silver, 381 base) with 47 English gold, realised £741; the other in June 1874 included some more gold, much more Scottish base metal, medals, 1150 English silver and nearly 4,000 Roman gold, silver and copper alloy, and came to £428, and this was paid into a separate account for the purchase of coins, medals and numismatic books. The catalogue of the first sale was by Edward Burns, whose offer to catalogue the Scottish collection was also accepted; but he was possibly not consulted over the selection by Sim and Carfrae, the other curator concerned, because coins were sold which he would, later on at least, not have considered to be duplicates, and many more which modern interest in base coinage and minutiae regrets. The solid foundations of that interest were laid during the next dozen years by Burns, using as the second major source for his *Coinage of Scotland* (published posthumously in 1887) the re-formed Antiquaries' collection, in addition to that of his patron Thomas Coats to whom his purchases at the sales of duplicates probably went. Sim, in editing the second part of Burns's work, acknowledged the help of Joseph Anderson without which it 'might never have been completed'.

Although a proposal in 1867 to move the library through the wall into one of the Royal Society's rooms had been found impracticable, pressure of new accessions (such as half a 45-foot dugout canoe from Kirkcudbrightshire) made extension of the Museum's exhibition into the library's octagon ever more desirable. So the idea was very seriously considered by all concerned in 1875, when the Royal's lease was coming up for renewal. The Antiquaries stated that the collections were now worth at least £150,000, and had been visited in the present premises by nearly one and a half million people. (The 1870-74 yearly average was 118,968 — the public were avid for museums: Science and Art recorded almost 456,000 in 1875). The Royal Society renewed an idea that the Museum should be moved into the Science and Art's buildings being constructed in Chambers Street, mooted in 1868 to a Commission on Science and Art (Ireland) by the Director, who thought it would be economical to absorb the Antiquarian Museum. The main argument against this was that 'to incorporate the National Collection in a section of general antiquities in another institution was calculated to destroy both its scientific value and its public utility, by depriving it of its distinctively national character'. Counsel's opinion was taken on the Societies' rights, and the matter left with the Royal a lasting impression that the Antiquaries had wished to have them turned out of the building. The Board's compromise, that the Antiquaries should have the use of the Royal's tea-room but for their meetings only, was declined as it would not free the octagon from the books.

Though the Keepership of the Museum was to be for many years the only professional archaeological post in Scotland, there was at the time of Anderson's appointment an ambitious scheme for a combined Government inspectorship of ancient monuments and lectureship in archaeology connected with the Antiquaries, to be held by John Stuart at the same rate as his £400 p.a. post in H. M. General Register House. (The regius professorship in connection with the other Museum was not mentioned, but was presumably in mind.) This was submitted to the Treasury over the signatures of office-bearers of the Society headed by the Duke of Buccleuch, supported by a dozen dukes, earls, peers and MPs, the Lord Provost of Edinburgh, Principals at St Andrews and Aberdeen, Hill Burton, Cosmo Innes and others. But it was effectively still-born and is not mentioned in the *Proceedings*.

Later the Society expressed approval, in 1872, of the general aims of Sir John Lubbock's long series of attempts to get his Ancient Monuments Protection Bill passed. In 1879 they objected strongly, however, in a letter to the Home Secretary signed by the Marquess of Lothian, to the British Museum Trustees' being made responsible for the whole country: moveable sculptured stones such as had been presented to the National Museum came within the scope of the Bill, and the Board of Manufactures would be the proper body for Scotland. In the end neither was made responsible under the rather emasculated Act of 1882, from which special Scottish provision was removed after most Scots MPs had gone home on the Friday when it was debated. Afterwards the Society was occasionally consulted, through the Board, by the inspector for Britain, General Pitt-Rivers.

It had been hoped that the scheme for a lecturer-cum-inspector might anticipate and improve upon the lectureship funded by A. H. Rhind's bequest to the Society, which was still inoperative because of a life-rent on the capital, over £5,000. Rhind had originally intended to found a professorship of archaeology and history in Edinburgh University, but stated in his will in 1862 that because of changes there, including the endowment of a chair of history, he had entrusted the Society with the project. The wide terms of reference for annual courses, open to the public, on archaeology, ethnology, or allied topics, are such that they have attracted many distinguished lecturers, more often than not on subjects relevant to the Museum. For many years the name of the lecturer and his subject followed the list of Council at the beginning of the *Proceedings*.

The first Rhind lecturer in 1876, appointed for three years unlike his successors, was Arthur Mitchell MD, inspector of lunatic asylums, a frequent contributor to the *Proceedings* and to the Museum, and one of the Society's Secretaries — the senior Secretary, John Stuart, had declined because of health and age. Published as *The Past in the Present* (1880), the lectures were a product of the great mid-Victorian debate on evolution and progress. Mitchell took examples of 'neo-archaic' objects, obsolescent and sometimes degenerate survivals from old methods and ways of life, such as the single-stilted plough, the hand-quern, the spindle and whorl and Hebridean pottery, illustrated by what he had collected, and often given to the Museum, or by

Hebridean houses drawn and surveyed by his friend Captain Thomas RN. He was interested in what happened when old and new ways met with users of equal intelligence, in how the rudely chipped stone implements of Shetland were not palaeolithic though older than the brochs, how the primitive was not necessarily ancient, and how one could understand the past by working back from the present. Unlike the great folk-museum movement launched contemporaneously by Hazelius in Sweden, from which country-life studies everywhere have grown, only sporadic collecting resulted from Mitchell's work. Here there were no picturesque survivals (Highland dress apart) to draw a wider public — or Mitchell himself — to take interest and pride in a whole way of life for its own sake; his lectures after the first year went on to propound a philosophy of civilisation.

In complete contrast the Rhind lectures from 1879 to 1882 by Joseph Anderson (in two two-year appointments) were a systematic and concise ordering of the facts of Scottish archaeology, traced backwards in time following Mitchell's precept. They were the result of ten years' study of the Museum's collections and their records (he had re-written the catalogue, published in 1876), of the few excavations he had been able to undertake as Keeper, notably the unusually complete examination of a bronze age cairn at Collessie in Fife, and of some travel and much reading. The first two volumes, *Scotland in Early Christian Times* (1881), dealt with architecture as well as moveables and sculpture, and were stimulated by the Irish material in John Bell's collection as well as by the newly acquired St Fillan's crozier from Canada and St Fillan's bell back from England. The second two, *Scotland in Pagan Times, The Iron Age* (1883) and *The Bronze and Stone Ages* (1886), started with Viking times and formed, as Gordon Childe noted fifty years later, a comprehensive and scientific view of Scottish prehistory such as then existed in no other country. Two of his papers in the *Proceedings* had been as it were preparatory studies: Notes on the evidence of spinning and weaving in the brochs (which followed a notable study by a medical student in 1871, helped by Anderson, Sir William Turner and others, of the physical and practical aspects of long-handled combs and ethnographical examples in the Museum, and elsewhere — the author and illustrator Millen Coughtrey emigrated and was lost to archaeology); and Notes on the relics of the Viking period of the Norsemen in Scotland (1874), which Anderson himself had preceded by editions of the Orkneyinga Saga and of Low's Tour of Orkney and Shetland. He had contributed an earlier paper to a series on brochs that was published in 1874 (*Archaeologia Scotica* V.1; V.2, pp. 285-364, appeared in 1880). He had also written a family history of the Oliphants. His understanding of artistic craftsmanship and of art history, and of the importance of plentiful good illustrations, had no doubt been fostered by James Drummond, curator of the National Gallery and long one of the Society's curators, whose fine coloured drawings of sixteenth to eighteenth-century Scottish weapons, powder-horns and accessories he edited and annotated for publication (by David Douglas) after Drummond's death in 1877. (Drummond bequeathed his own collection to the Society. His drawings of arms, and of West Highland sculptured monuments later published by the Society, were added by the generosity of over seventy Fellows, as were those of Old Edinburgh in a single gift. The influence of artists in the Council was continued after his death by Fettes Douglas, and by Noël Paton, for long one of the members from the Board.)

Anderson was, in the ground he covered in the lectures, much less ambitious than Wilson in the *Prehistoric Annals*, concentrating on archaeology in the narrower sense of the study of evidence from the material remains, from which a clearly structured view of the past could be formed, made up of ages and periods of indefinite length. The new evidence obtained in the thirty years since Wilson wrote, much of it from excavations, made it possible for Anderson to lay a far more thorough and secure foundation for future workers, both field-workers and users of the Museum's pre-eleventh-century collections. Because he saw no scientific way by which broad periods could be given a quasi-historical chronology, he considered attempts to do so to be un-archaeological guesses, even though he did not doubt that the same processes of change had gone on in prehistoric as in historic centuries. To achieve as clear a view as possible he did not try to bring in either Roman archaeology or fully historic times; he simply omitted some problematic subjects, such as cup-and-ring sculptures (already very fully treated by J. Y. Simpson and Romilly Allen in the *Proceedings*), or Skara Brae where the stone tools and the sophisticated furnished houses, which he described only in a footnote, doubtless seemed hopelessly contradictory, as they did for fifty years more. Having no Old Stone Age in Scotland, as is still the case, he could ignore the controversies on the antiquity of Man. He concentrated strongly on Scottish evidence, and except for Christian art used his knowledge of wider similarities mainly to recognise local peculiarities. These and the nature of the evidence, rooted in its own area, more than justified in his opinion the call to create and maintain Scotland's 'own school of investigation', with which he concluded this series of Rhind lectures. In stressing the scientific inductive method in archaeology, while avoiding technological and ethnographical theories of progress, he did not fail also to remind his audience of the individual human reality which the dusty evidence represents: 'in the varied phenomena of their burial customs, the preparation of the funeral pile, the fabrication of the finely ornamented urns, and the costly dedication of articles of use or adornment . . . we realise the intensity of their devotion to filial memories and family ties, to hereditary honour and ancestral tradition'.

From 1881 until 1893, when the Coin Cabinet Fund was exhausted, the average annual expenditure on purchases for the Museum (with separate funding for the library) was higher than during the following sixty years. This came about by the sale to a collector, believed to be French, of the Louis XV cabinet that had held the Sutherland collection, after offers unexpectedly received from two quarters had risen from £2,100 to £3,500, the Society's negotiators being Arthur Mitchell and Robert Carfrae. Treasury authorisation was necessary because the cabinet, bought without Government money in 1872, was national property by the terms of the 1851 Conveyance; and the Treasury rejected the Society's suggestion that the Faculty of Advocates should receive for their Library £1,000 of this windfall. (Amends were made when valuable books were gifted to the National Library in 1949.) It was agreed, however, that the Council should use the proceeds for the purchase for the Museum 'of objects, or collections of objects, illustrative of the unwritten history of Scotland'. Money not immediately required was to be invested in the names of the Secretary of the Board of Manufactures and of the Queen's Remembrancer. After the Secretary had challenged payment for Polynesian canoe paddles, the Treasury accepted that such ethnographical items, as well as European prehistoric and later objects, might be bought out of the Fund when suitable for the comparative collection. This was not then a local or outmoded eccentricity, for even forty years later on prehistory and ethnography were taught as one subject at Oxford, as T. D. Kendrick has recalled.

Up to 1881 purchases had mainly been acquired, as we have seen, as gifts from individual Fellows, or from the proceeds of the second sale of coin duplicates, or from pay-day fees. In 1877 payment of 500 dollars (£100) had been made on the Society's behalf to Alexander Dewar for St Fillan's crozier (p. 39), he himself having remitted 200 dollars of the agreed price, so becoming joint-donor. There are figures for 1879-80 when admissions came to £87 18s 6d, and the museum and library fund was credited with catalogue sales of £26 12s 6d; while purchases exceeded receipts by £28 11s 7d. (The strength of the library was being built up steadily over the years, with attention to foreign books.) The Society's total income, excluding the Rhind bequest, was £770, of which £375 had been spent on publication and £116 on working expenses. The general fund had £1,200 invested.

A purchase committee was appointed in 1881, to meet every Saturday and to consist of the curators, treasurer, librarian and secretaries with a quorum of three, to purchase objects under £100 and to recommend others; and the Keeper might spend up to £5 on his own. Despite the amount available and the average of over £300 spent during the twelve years, small sums predominated and quantity rather than quality. There were a few notable exceptions: the eighth-century Hunterston brooch, still the finest goldsmith work in the Museum, for which £500 was paid in 1891; the two rather later Rogart brooches (£200) and eleven of the Lewis chessmen (£105). These last were bought at auction for less than half the expected sum, and other prices for important pieces were also relatively low, such as the unique enamelled Romano-British patera from West Lothian for £15. On the other hand £1,200 was vainly sought from the Government in 1892 for the Arbuthnot Missal, which went elsewhere and came to belong to Paisley. A couple of hundred pounds all told was spent on coins, rather lower amounts on foreign prehistoric items, on ethnography and more recent foreign exhibits, on reproductions and casts, and on Scottish prehistoric metal objects, pottery and associated groups, notably the pottery etc from the chambered tomb at Unstan in Orkney (£45); small contributions from what was left of the Rhind Excavation Fund continued to acquire finds from other northern sites. When the Museum at Lerwick was sold up in 1882, £70 was spent on most or all of its exhibits. About £500 went on adding to the medieval and recent collections, particularly the latter — a pair of brass Highland pistols dated 1614 was however declined, while mainly ordinary weapons were acquired; but there was a fine targe for £56 14s 0d, and the finest silver-inlaid basket-hilt for a sword for £7 7s 0d. No provision was made against the possibility that the two medieval harps from Dalguise, deposited on loan in 1880, might be put up for sale.

It was perhaps unfortunate that collections of flint implements, small ornaments and so on, picked up from the coastal sands near Glenluce in Wigtownshire, and from Morayshire including the Culbin Sands, had been the subject of recent papers and donations. At any rate the existence of the purchase fund stimulated a constant trade from those areas which went on for decades; one man retired to Forres for the purpose, and spent seven years collecting at Culbin. Unassociated flint and stone implements from there and elsewhere in Scotland accounted for about one-third of the Cabinet Fund. The Assistant Keeper visited Culbin in 1890 and published a report of localities and finds, but otherwise as Callander noted in 1911 there was no scientific exploitation or control; the difficulty of so doing except on selected sites was shown in the 1950s by an unsuccessful expedition to Luce Bay from Edinburgh University. Already in 1883 it was a matter of pride to Anderson that 'there is no collection in Europe which at all approaches the Scottish collection of arrowheads and small-sized implements of flint', and no series of polished stone implements that he had seen, unless that of Denmark, exceeded that of Scotland in extent and variety. R. W. Cochran-Patrick reported to the Glasgow Archaeological Society in 1887 that the National Collection of objects of purely national interest comprised: implements and ornaments of stone 25,104, of bronze etc 1,394; sepulchral remains from graves etc 959, domestic remains from hut-circles, brochs, lake-dwellings etc 4,137; ecclesiastical, medieval [and recent] etc 7,107; miscellaneous (for use in comparing etc) [foreign ?] 7,192. By 1892 the printed catalogue summarises 25,000 stone items from Culbin alone, and over 8,000 from Glenluce; as yet little archaeological use has been found for them.

There seem to have been two main weaknesses in Anderson's conception of archaeology. One was this over-emphasis on the accumulation of artefacts, major basis for archaeological knowledge though that certainly was. The reason in his case was probably not the collector's instinct, but rather a reverence for the available evidence; and was thus linked to the second weakness — failure to realise how the science would develop through the further evidence associated with artefacts to be got by close observation and recording particularly in excavations, and by new techniques. The extensive article which he wrote on Archaeology, along with short articles on specific topics, for the *Chambers Encyclopaedia* published in 1895, is valuable as a summary of his mature views, and for showing that, though he went on to treat mostly of prehistoric times, he retained for archaeology an unlimited time-span, and for the Museum Buchan's aim of comparing the past with the present state of Scotland. Three separate extracts are particularly relevant to us:

> History deals with events and incidents as manifestations of human motive and action; archaeology deals with types and systems as expressions of human culture and civilisation. The archaeology of a historic period may be capable of illustrating and supplementing the records of contemporary historians by disclosing a multiplicity of unchronicled details relating to the common life of the people, of which we should otherwise be left in ignorance.

> The professed antiquary of the 18th century, bound by the tradition of scholarly research, did little in the way of original investigation; but he unconsciously laid the foundation of the science by his passion for collecting.

> The basis of all scientific knowledge of archaeology in every national area must be such a general collection of the remains of its human occupation as will be completely representative of all the various manifestations that have characterised the progress of its people towards the existing culture and civilisation. . . . As the scientific knowledge disclosed by the national collection [of monuments and relics of the progress and development of the national culture] must necessarily increase in precision and value according to the nearness of the approach of the collection to a thoroughly exhaustive representation, the science must be progressive in its results . . . When the several national collections have reached the stage of representative completeness, a new departure of the science in the direction first of comparative archaeology, and secondly of general archaeology, will become possible.

As Anderson finished his Rhind lectures an Ayrshire doctor, Robert Munro, who had been excavating three crannogs there, published his reports in a book, *Ancient Scottish Lake-Dwellings* (1882), and, Anderson commented, 'systematised the whole subject in a manner that leaves nothing to be desired'. The finds from his first excavation are preserved in Kilmarnock Museum, but those from the others, notably the post-Roman site at Buston, were given to the national collection, which already had among its comparative material several hundred items from the very different Swiss sites. Munro retired early from medical practice and became one of the Secretaries of the Society. He boldly turned to comparative archaeology, and in the remarkably wide-ranging *Lake Dwellings of Europe* (1890 — the Rhind lectures for 1888) founded the important tradition of international prehistoric archaeology in Edinburgh.

The Move to Queen Street, 1883-91

The complicated crisis which resulted in the Museum being moved into the building which still houses it in Queen Street took place in 1883 and 1884. It was initiated by the Board of Manufactures who wished more space, to begin with for the School of Art, as in 1844, and the Museum's needs took second place to the similar needs of others. By then it was the Council's view that the Museum's accommodation in the Royal Institution had been 'for years past quite unsuitable for the public exhibition of the collections', even if it might 'for some time serve its present purpose as a store-house'—there was only a small amount of true storage, in an unventilated inaccessible cellar. It was said that the 2,500 square feet of the Museum contained 50,000 objects, 20,300 (mainly very small) added in the previous three years. Large objects in the passage-ways rendered one side of the show-cases inaccessible to the public, boxes were packed under the desk-cases and classified objects were heaped on one another. The Council's priorities put increasing and preserving the collections ahead of exhibition, even with an annual average of 110,000 visitors over the past ten years; it is not surprising that this fell to 80,000 at the end of the eighties.

From the Antiquaries' minutes it might appear that the trouble began over security. The Council represented to the Board that the Museum was insufficiently protected from fire and burglary, in a building which had a score of open fires and two caretakers housed in the south end as the only overnight protection. The Board's Secretary replied that fire-extinguishers had been introduced as recommended by the city's fire-master, and asked for suggestions on protection from house-breaking. When the Council made none he wrote that the Board 'disclaim all responsibility for the safe custody of the collection of antiquities, which is entrusted to the exclusive charge and custody of the Society' (March 1883). This extraordinary statement was countered by a long letter signed by the Marquess of Lothian as President of the Society, and by the two Secretaries, one the recently appointed J. R. Findlay, proprietor of the *Scotsman*. When on police advice a night-watchman was appointed, the Treasury refused to pay the Board for him. The Society agreed in a conciliatory gesture to contribute one-third of his wage for the first six months, but the responsibility was still not fixed. By then even wider issues had overtaken the matter.

The School of Art, it will be remembered, while administered by the Board, came under the Department of Science and Art of which the Museum in Chambers Street was part, and which was within the Home Office's remit. The Board's minutes show that in January 1882 a letter to the Treasury from the Secretary of State of the Home Office had strongly advocated the move of the School to the Industrial Museum, 'on the ground that the room in the Royal Institution now occupied by the Art School could be used for giving increased accommodation to the Museum of Antiquities'. A new factor appeared in the autumn. When in 1879 Laing had bequeathed to the Society twenty-six historical portraits it was in the hope that, along with its earlier miscellaneous acquisitions, they would become the start of a national portrait collection. Following this idea but not bringing in the Society, an anonymous donor offered to give £10,000 to help finance a Scottish National Portrait Gallery, if the Board would found it and the Government would match his gift. Both these matters must then have been discussed unofficially, along with the Board's probable attitudes, such as fear that its control over the School might be lessened. At any rate in June 1883 the Treasury officially proposed that the School of Art should be moved — but alternatively asked, 'if the Board oppose a move by the School, would the Museum of Antiquities not be transferred [the idea already floated in 1868 and 1873]; and if so room might be found in the Royal Institution for the Scottish Historical Portrait Gallery which there is now a prospect of founding'. In July the Board's Committee on the School of Art rejected any move by it, giving no very strong reasons, and the alternative was put to the Antiquaries.

They replied that because of the 'apparent difficulty of attaining any more suitable arrangement and *in view of the other interests involved*' (my italics), they 'may feel themselves compelled to acquiesce in the proposal'. All the conditions mentioned in the Treasury Minute of 1851 must however remain in force, including the mutual relations between them and the Board. Four or five times the space occupied in the Royal Institution was needed. By October plans from the Office of Works of what was proposed in the front block of new (west) wing of the Museum of Science and Art were found totally unsatisfactory. Situated on the second and upper floors, the exhibition space was to be 6665 square feet, rather over two and a half times that on The Mound, but three and a half was needed without provision for the future, and windows instead of roof-lights seriously reduced wall-space. The library and meeting-hall was to be 941 square feet, compared with 738, but, having windows and not much more than half the height, it would not accommodate the collection as it stood, in wall-shelves with a gallery. Access was poor, there was no workroom, no accessible storage, and so on. 'The proposal, to store the priceless National Collection of Antiquities in two small upper floors of a building in which these floors probably represent about one-fiftieth part, would be in a national sense discreditable.' Though told that only minor changes would be possible, the Council ventured 'to suggest that if the whole west wing of the front block were separated from the other portions of the Industrial Museum building by solid party walls rising from the foundations through the roof, and provided with adequate entrances, it would not be difficult to make the internal arrangements such as would meet the requirements of the National Museum and of the Society'.

The Board then recommended to the Treasury 'favourable consideration of the Council's objections'; they also objected to having to pay for the removal of the Museum from their own funds; and they set up a Portrait Gallery Committee, including several Trustees who happened to be on the Antiquaries' Council, Fettes Douglas, Noël Paton and J. R. Findlay. The Treasury, having agreed to provide the matching £10,000, formally agreed to the scheme for founding the Portrait Gallery to be housed in the Royal Institution; and stated that it was not practical to consider removal costs until the Society had accepted the proposals without serious modification; if the Board persuaded them, there would be no difficulty over costs. In November, the Society strengthened its Council by adding Lord Rosebery to the vice-presidents Arthur Mitchell and the Earl of Stair, and by making R. W. Cochran-Patrick MP Secretary along with J. R. Findlay. The Board's representatives on the Council through all this were Noël Paton and Francis Abbott, Secretary of the Post Office in Scotland. The Queen's Remembrancer J. J. Reid was a councillor as an individual.

By February 1884 the Treasury admitted that the space offered the Museum was somewhat less than might naturally be desired. However, more would be unjust to the other Museum, and rejection of the offer would imperil the foundation of the new Gallery. The Council still objected, and protested at the failure of the Office of Works architect to appreciate information given him, and his partiality to the Museum of Industry. So the Board resolved that the Museum of Antiquities should be removed to the Industrial Museum, its representatives on the Council dissenting.

Three months elapsed before the Society finally declined to move. The day before its letter was sent, a conditional offer was made to the Board, passed on to the Treasury on 11th June:

> The Gentleman who formerly made a gift to the Board of Manufactures to aid in the establishment of a National Portrait Gallery for Scotland, has now very generously proposed to give the sum of £20,000 for the purpose of building or

acquiring premises for the accommodation both of the National Portrait Gallery and the Museum of Antiquities.

The offer is made with the desire to provide a separate building for the Portrait Gallery, and also under the impression that his former gift has indirectly had the effect of prejudicing the Society of Antiquaries as the custodian of the Museum of Antiquities, and with the desire that they should be provided with better accommodation than they are to obtain in the new wing of the Industrial Museum, Edinburgh.

The Board recommended the offer 'because of the advantages to the School of Art as well as to the Museum'. A central site had unexpectedly come on the market for £7,500 and the Board were prepared to use £2,500 of the capital they had earmarked for the School of Art. The Treasury approved, and agreed to provide the necessary £5,000.

In December the Board sent the preliminary plans of the building to the Council, which noted that 'the eastern wall of the central block divides the two collections from basement to roof . . . The only thing in common . . . is the central entrance from Queen Street'. A committee under the President, with Findlay as Secretary, received the idea with much satisfaction and approved generally the plans and elevations, followed by the Council. Some practical suggestions were made, such as that the front and back galleries should have their floors at the same level and that they should be joined by wide archways instead of small doorways, and that as the Board were unfortunately unable to cover the full extent of the ground, temporarily closed archways at the end should allow expansion. These improvements were made, the eastern extension being built before the building was finished, so allowing for a Council room separate from the library cum meeting hall, for workrooms in a mezzanine, and for strong rooms. The proposed coin room opening out of one of these never materialised; it was made the chief officer's room.

From 1885 the Board, instead of dealing directly with the Treasury, came under the new Scottish Office and Secretary for Scotland. Before long Lord Lothian, the Society's President, was holding that office, and Findlay as the Society's Secretary was writing to him officially about improving the finances of the Museum for the time it would enter its new premises. The value of the Museum and Library, he stated, could not be less than £200,000, yet 'it may be safely asserted that no other national Museum in this or any other country has ever been acquired on such easy terms by the nation; or has received such scant support from national funds'. For not only were the new building and its

M

contents a free gift to the country, but even the cost of providing for the Museum in the Royal Institution (£4,410) and salaries and other costs at £410 p.a. had been provided out of the Board's own Scottish funds — not out of Imperial Funds like those in London and Dublin. This was fully set out in an enclosed article from the *Scotsman* (12.3.87), which also dealt with the history of the National Gallery, treated only somewhat better. (The theme was repeated in the newspaper in April 1890 and February 1906.)

A salary of £400-£500 was asked for the Keeper (unpensioned), compared with the £300-£500 (pensioned) of the Keeper of Natural History in Chambers Street, and the £500 starting point of an Assistant Keeper in the two British Museums. For the Assistant Keeper £250 was suggested. An annual purchase grant of £500 was also requested, making a total budget of £1,700. Even with friends in office (and the Scottish Office confirmation was signed by R. W. Cochran-Patrick), approval in 1891 was only for £860, the Treasury adding £450 to the Board's enforced commitment. This allowed for just three attendants, with army pensions, for four rooms, so the Society had to pay for the man in the library, who also acted as clerk. The new Assistant Keeper, George F. Black, was to act as relief attendant and be paid £100; he had for some years been 'extra man' paid by the Society, and was appointed by the Board in 1891 on the Council's nomination, confirmed by the Secretary for Scotland in accordance with a new procedure. Anderson was to get £400. There was no purchase grant, but the possibility of special grants was confirmed.

Consultations with the city's chief constable resulted in the magistrates providing two policemen, one at a time, for night duty in the building, with a tell-tale clock for rounds. (Police watchmen, paid for by the Board, were not finally withdrawn till the Second World War.) The Council demurred at having stanchions on all the ground floor windows, preferring a telephone to the police and fire brigade. As the question of responsibility remained unsettled, the Society consulted their law agents about insuring the collections vested in the Board, and were advised it might be prudent to do so. They decided, however, to insure only the library, and curved and plate glass case tops; the Board repaid for these at last.

Suspension of work on the Museum's half of the building for some eighteen months, causing extra costs and difficulties with the contractors, and a question in Parliament, was mainly due to a dispute between the Board and the Treasury. When the sums gifted by the anonymous donor (increased by £12,000 for the extensions at either end) were all exceeded by the rising costs, the Board were prepared to pay from their own funds for the finishing work on the Portrait Gallery, but not for the Museum's half. This they, and the Society, considered to be the Treasury's responsibility, as undertaken in 1851 though then forced on the Board to implement, and as implicit in the proposed move to Chambers Street. The Treasury in February 1888 accepted furniture and moveable fittings, but refused to meet painting, heating, lighting, fire appliances, hydraulic lift and motor. The Society prepared a memorandum of protest detailing the terms of the Conveyance and the Treasury Minutes, to brief T. R. Buchanan, MP for Edinburgh, and circulated it in July to all Scottish MPs.

The Board offered to advance £528 to allow some work on the two sides to be continued as one operation, but the Lord Advocate advised the Secretary for Scotland that they could not use their own funds for the Museum building even as a loan, as their powers were limited to the improvement of education in the fine arts. (This would have made all their expenditure on the Museum *ultra vires,* and three years later the Scottish Office pointed out that decorative and ornamental arts, and taste and design in manufactures, were also specified in their Act, so the Museum was covered.) When the Advocate's advice was fresh, however, the Secretary of the Board, accompanied by Cochran-Patrick, discussed the matter in July 1888 in London with the Chancellor of the Exchequer, without progress. Scottish pressure, and a £500 contribution by the Board 'towards removing misunderstanding', led the Treasury to compromise in March and insert in the Estimates £1,550 for structural fittings (£150 less than it had originally refused, and now not allowing for electric light or a lift, or apparently any lighting at all in the exhibition galleries); the Office of Works would get £1,700 for furniture with a further £1,500 in 1890-91. Removal costs of £700 were also allowed. The building, like those at The Mound, was to be owned and maintained by the Board, who dropped their attempt to have the maintenance of the interior of the Museum accepted by the Treasury. For a while they did pursue efforts to stop paying the £410 'contribution' to salaries and running costs of the Museum, even it was said to the length of threatening to close it.

The Treasury finance to restart work on the Museum came in time to allow a good face to be put on things by Lord Lothian when as Secretary for Scotland he took the chair and opened the Portrait Gallery on 15 July 1889. The Board's Chairman, Lord Justice-General

Inglis, paid tribute to Lord Buchan, his correspondence with Lord Hailes already in 1778, and to Carlyle and David Laing, and noted that the present Donor had not proposed that the Society should undertake the Portrait Gallery because it would require the influence and means of the Board, who possessed apartments most suitable for the purpose. Unfortunately they were occupied by the Museum; when a solution could not be found, the Donor had undertaken to house both. Owing to rising estimates this had now cost him £50,000, without any statues, which it was hoped others would give. (He later added another £10,000 'for decoration'.)

The Donor was then revealed as J. R. Findlay. He gave his own account of the foundation, and in conclusion referred to the fight against the proposal 'to shunt the Society and its collections to a pendicle of the Museum of Science and Art'; and he described the association of Museum and Portrait Gallery in one building as peculiarly felicitous, because the two collections would be mutually illustrative.

While the rearrangement of the collections was being planned for the new building, the Society, like several other bodies, benefited from a gift, soon increased to an endowment, by R. H. Gunning MD, in honour of the Queen's Jubilee in 1887. In this case it was specifically for travel, in order to study or research in other archaeological museums or collections. In the first year Anderson visited fourteen museums in Scotland and Black eighteen. Their report published in the *Proceedings* comprises catalogues of those collections, which for many are the best record of what was in them; the conclusion was that 'if all the collections of the local museums were brought together they would fail to produce the materials for a systematic archaeology of Scotland'. In 1889 Anderson broadened his background still further by going to Mainz, Paris and on to north Italy, and published summaries of what he saw in sixteen museums in Switzerland and twelve in Italy.

As a source of additions to the Museum, Treasure Trove and its practical problems were being considered. In a printed memorandum for the Council in May 1890, the Secretaries listed what had been received from the Exchequer since 1808, quoted in full previous circulars issued by the Remembrancer, and summarised the procedures in Ireland and Scandinavia. They discussed defects, difficulties and uncertainties that prevented the National Museum's benefiting fully from the law of Scotland. They pointed out that the intervention of the police and Fiscals associated the system with 'the popular odium attached to the criminal department', as Anderson wrote in a companion article in the *Scotsman*. They proposed that the Museum should be given a regular grant, and authority to receive finds and administer payments, as the Royal Irish Academy did (and the British Museum subsequently), while the Crown's claim could still be enforced if finds were withheld or misappropriated. In practice a sort of compromise took place, the Museum being allowed to purchase most finds offered it. This was reinforced by an opinion of the Crown law-officers in 1907, that the Crown's right to all finds was not prejudiced by not being exercised, in particular by failure to claim what was of small value.

Before leaving The Mound, the Society issued in 1890 the final part of *Archaeologia Scotica* (V.3). There were only two papers, on the Duns of the Outer Hebrides and on King's College, Aberdeen, besides a donation list of 79 pages, filling the gap from 1830 to 1851, when lists began in the *Proceedings*.

The rooms in the Royal Institution were emptied from November 1890. The arrangement in the new building can be rather generally deduced from the information about location given in the catalogue compiled by Anderson and Black, published by the Society in 1892 — splendid value, nearly 400 pages and 650 woodcuts, 5,000 copies in paper covers at one shilling (cost price £216), boards and larger paper 500 at half-a-crown. The classification is very detailed for the prehistoric collections, and for comparable stone and bone artefacts from elsewhere, keeping together finds from important sites. Yet some of the headings (each with a two-letter prefix to the number) which applied to recent Scotland embraced a great variety of objects, such as MP 'Tools, Implements and Miscellaneous'. Most of the ethnographical and foreign collections, coins, medals, and unexhibited manuscripts got little or no mention. Things collected from countries other than Scotland were all exhibited in the large roof-lit room on the second floor, with a few exceptions — medals, seals and armour.

On the first floor, allotted to prehistoric times, no periods or ages were explicit, and everything was 'in the shop window'; there were no drawers or cupboards. Cases in the southern half of the gallery started with the contents of chambered tombs followed by bronze objects typologically arranged, bronze cauldrons with iron hoards, Celtic bells and crannog finds; classified flints were at either end and in the window recesses. In the other half there were similarly the various types of pottery and associated objects from graves, the great collection of surface finds from the Culbin Sands at one end, with Early Celtic metalwork adjacent, and finds from domestic sites in the windows. At the other end were large cases of stone axes and more flints, but also prehistoric goldwork and post-Roman ornaments and through the archway foreign gold (all for easy removal each night), Viking grave-finds and early church croziers; in the rest of the extension were the excavated finds from brochs and caves, and stone urns.

The historical gallery was (and to a considerable extent has remained for ninety years) basically divided into domestic things in the southern part, and in the larger northern part a sequence of topics — sculptured stones and casts from early Christian to medieval West Highland, 150 items, within the box-like western end, below banners high on the walls; next to these the ecclesiastical collections, followed by accoutrements and weapons, many of them up on the walls, while in the window cases were charms, seals, watches etc. Coins and medals were set out immediately at the entrance of the gallery. The Roman finds from Scotland were at the far end of the north side, probably with the antlers and ox skulls above them. In the low room at the extreme east end were dug-out canoes, cup-and-ring boulders, The Maiden and other instruments of punishment, and more weapons.

The opening in Queen Street by the Marquess of Lothian took the form of a Conversazione on 14 August 1891, to which representatives of learned societies and public institutions in the city were invited. They met on the ground floor of the Portrait Gallery which, because not yet required for pictures for quite some years, was let to the Royal Scottish Geographical Society. Its lecture hall in the southern half was regularly used by the Antiquaries, who had arranged that the Royal Archaeological Institute of Great Britain should be holding its summer meeting there, and should join them for the opening. A further historical attraction that summer was an important Heraldic Exhibition mounted in the upper part of the Gallery.

The building, with its highly decorated Italianate Gothic exterior of red sandstone, to be completed with many statues, was so far the most discordant intrusion into the New Town of Edinburgh. The architect, Rowand Anderson, had worked in a variety of styles and was doubtless selected and influenced, as well as financed, by J. R. Findlay. Even more startling to Scottish taste, one would have thought, were the large parts of the interior where polished rich red brick walls combined curiously with the sculptured and ashlar architectural features. They dominated the entrance hall and main staircases for over fifty years, and also the whole ground floor of the Museum, which there opened out of the Portrait Gallery. The connecting doorway had carved on it the Society's shield of Arms with its royal tressure (not coloured till almost ninety years later), and the name that was at last agreed, if only tacitly, National Museum of Antiquities of Scotland.

The ground floor exhibition hall is well designed for floor space (about 4,350 square feet), particularly lofty except at the extension, 20 feet to the ceiling, and lit by large pointed-arch windows so that space for attaching exhibits to the walls is reduced and mostly high up. Faced with this difference from the Institution's roof-lit rooms, Joseph Anderson was heard to say at the Conversazione, as related long afterwards by A. O. Curle, that 'the Gothic style of architecture is unsuited to a Museum'. When Rowand Anderson countered, 'But I have made it suited', the reply was, 'Well, you should at least have turned the windows upside down'. Unfortunately there are no photographs to show how the newly arranged halls actually looked. Up each main half, separated by wide arches, there were 12-feet long cases, some flat, some upright, at first varied by shorter cases at right angles to them. Neither these nor the smaller cases in the window-recesses yet held drawers or cupboards. The first floor is similar, with more but narrower windows, and only two feet lower, while the extension goes to the full height. The architect wanted the walls painted green, but the Council preferred red. The cases were longer, nearly 15 feet, set parallel to one another like platoons on parade, a column of ten on the north side and seven on the south; later, as downstairs too, additional long cases had to be inserted till they were only three feet apart. Some of the original shallow wall-cases set at the ends of the halls, with narrow desk-cases projecting from them, still survive *in situ*. Upstairs the high roof-lit 'comparative gallery' had a floor area of 2,000 square feet, and the adjacent library 1,500 surrounded by a cat-walk gallery. Attics were available for the boxed manuscripts. The 2,000 square feet cellar was probably just a dump, for there were no fitments for storage.

Emphasis on Research, 1891-1913

The new, much more spacious displays, and the conjunction of the Portrait Gallery, did not compensate for what had probably not been anticipated, the disadvantage of going 250 yards northwards from Princes Street. The new attendance figures, counted inevitably at the joint front door, were for the first fourteen months at less than half the rate of the previous full year's 83,597. By next year at 23,500 they were less than a quarter of the average before exhibition conditions at the old Museum had become so bad. The figures for the rest of the decade were lower still, and by 1906 fell below 15,000. In contrast the old Statue Gallery still at The Mound, on its own, had 40,000 visitors in 1902. In 1908 entrance fees in Queen Street were abolished by special permission of the Treasury, 'owing to the out of the way position' of the Portrait Gallery building.

Situation alone could not cause the attendances to continue declining for so long, not could the stamp-album form of display, a general fashion for much longer. To provide as a matter of fairness the same amount of space in the building for each institution was to build-in a handicap to the Museum, and to underrate the differences in scope and potential between collecting the portraits of four or five centuries, and material illustrating a people's life over millennia, even neglecting those same centuries. As seen in 1911 by a Glasgow businessman writing in the *Glasgow Herald* (C. E. Whitelaw, 11 November) — an article on the arrangement of an ideal National Historical Museum based on his experience in organising the remarkable Palace of History at the Scottish Exhibition in Glasgow earlier that year — the Museum of National Antiquities in Edinburgh lacked certain essentials. For there

> a magnificent collection of material is quite paralysed through being housed in an ill-adapted building, only allowing half the space necessary for the adequate display of the objects, and in the matter of funds having only a miserable pittance, quite inadequate to its needs, and a scandal to this country. It has however the best brains at its call.

The brains of the Society, with the two curatorial members of staff, were maintaining and applying the momentum of archaeological thought, increasing the size of the collections and their importance to specialists. They were also sharing the new knowledge with the 700 members and the wider public through the meetings, the *Proceedings*, Rhind lectures, newspaper reports and other publications. The interest generated continued to draw in accessions much more comprehensively relevant to the Museum's field than the research, so that exhibition inescapably became less satisfactory than ever, until radical change was possible.

It was a period when categories of antiquities were being investigated in detail and catalogued, with final or preliminary publications in the *Proceedings*, using, illuminating or adding to the Museum's collections. G. F. Black, the Assistant Keeper, wrote up Scottish charms and amulets in 1893, and there were similarly extensive papers unconnected with the Museum, for example on the archery medals of St Andrews and Aberdeen, and on Scottish medieval tomb effigies. A calendar of the Scottish charters 'in the possession of the Society' was published in 1907.

Directly relevant to the Museum, though going far beyond it and forming one of the Society's major enterprises, was the corpus of the *Early Christian Monuments of Scotland* before the twelfth century, much more accurate and complete than Stuart's work of a previous generation. It was carried out by J. Romilly Allen CE with the co-operation of many members of the Society and others. The Council in 1890 awarded him the Gunning Fellowship for two years at £100, and later for five more, to finance his travel, photography (particularly in 1894), and innumerable drawings. The publication was based art-historically on Joseph Anderson's early Rhind lectures, and incorporated as its introduction Anderson's lectures of 1892. Allen was himself a Rhind lecturer, on Christian symbolism in 1885, and extended the original scope of the *corpus* by adding in his exhaustive study of the formal patterns and their distribution, as well as of the Pictish symbols. He wished to have casts of four of the finest Ross-shire stones made, but the Council did not see their way to this; the South Kensington Museum, however, did the one at Nigg. After publication in 1903 the total expenditure was reckoned at £2,240, of which only £730 was recouped from early sales (at four guineas, but two for Fellows and three for subscribers), and £780 from the Society's general fund. This indispensable work had the effect by its very thoroughness, as had Burns's *Coinage,* of inhibiting further constructive study of its subject for more than a generation.

Estimates for an illustrated catalogue of the Scottish coins in the Museum were obtained in 1895. The draft was prepared by A. B. Richardson, curator since 1888 and donor of a 1575 £20 piece of James VI. Few additions had been made since the Exchequer in 1882 had given generous selections from a remarkable series of hoards, found in the previous five years and studied by Burns and Sim — notably Alexander III to David II silver from Montrave, Robert III groats from Fortrose and gold of James III from New Cumnock; selections from two fourteenth-fifteenth-century hoards came in 1893. From 1897 to the publication of the catalogue in 1901 an active, but far from ideal, policy was pursued to make its range more complete in conformity with Burns's *Coinage.* At the same time as making purchases, authority was obtained to dispose of 'duplicates and specimens unconnected with Scottish numismatics'. Duplicates from mints in Britain, and continental sterlings, were sold at Sotheby's in January 1899 ('the property of the Society of Antiquaries of Scotland'), among them many of the coins selected in 1882 which one fears may have been die varieties, such as Burns had not always specified, though well aware of them. In August 1900 there were sold anonymously there the many hundreds of Greek and foreign coins and medals, including the Ruthven collection accepted in 1884 and also foreign coins from Scottish hoards, that were thus part of our currency if not our numismatics. Fortunately those from early archaeological contexts such as Viking bullion hoards were excluded. Burns's English selection from the Montrave hoard was kept intact. From the proceeds of the sales over 270 Scottish coins were bought from the Pollexfen collection in 1900 and inserted into the catalogue as an appendix. The handsomely bound volume cost 'within £300' for 250 copies, and was sold at 21s, at a loss even apart from the numerous complimentary copies.

A more economical scholarly Museum publication was printed in the *Proceedings* in 1899, a catalogue of the objects in the Egyptian collection by Margaret Murray, Lady Associate 1900-63.

After Black resigned in 1896 for better prospects in the United States, fortunately to continue working and writing on Scotland, F. R. Coles succeeded him temporarily, then after a year with a higher salary (£140), raised in 1905 to £200. He had been a corresponding member, publishing surveys of forts and stone circles in Galloway since 1890. Reports illustrated by his plans and sketches of stone circles in northeast and central Scotland, surveyed on the Gunning Fellowship (at a much lower rate than Romilly Allen's) were for eleven years a feature of the *Proceedings*, to which he also contributed notes on burial finds, until in 1912 he too left for financial reasons.

A wide range of archaeological investigations was always recorded in the volumes. Most important for the Museum was the systematic and sustained series of excavations financed through the Society that began in 1890. Credit for much of this was due to David Christison, Secretary with Robert Munro and like him a doctor of medicine; Joseph Anderson's part was chiefly editing the sometimes very stout volumes of *Proceedings* and writing the find-reports, which brought him to subjects new to him, Roman material and the entirely novel mesolithic from caves at Oban. For recording, a set of six-inch maps was issued to the Society by the Ordnance Survey, once there was house-room for it.

Christison started off with some unproductive examination of forts in Argyll (helped by a colleague whose excavation was illustrated by the first half-tone blocks in the *Proceedings* in 1891), within a series of field studies of forts in various areas which led up to his pioneer book on *Early Fortifications in Scotland* (1898, the Rhind lectures of 1894). Roman Archaeology then took over. The Glasgow Archaeological Society had begun in 1892 making a series of soundings in sites along the Antonine Wall (proposals for acquiring stretches of the Wall for preservation were put to the Antiquaries in 1894) and a leading Glasgow Fellow, James Macdonald, was making studies of the Roman roads in southern Scotland. In 1895 he as well as Christison, J. H. Cunningham (then the Antiquaries' Treasurer) and John Barbour in Dumfries undertook the supervision of a very successful excavation at Birrens, from where the Museum had long had altars and other finds. The suggestion came from the Dumfries and Galloway Antiquarian Society, and much of the work was done by Barbour. A clerk of works provided continuous on-site control.

Once fired, the Antiquaries carried on. Full use was made of the professional skills of architects, Barbour and Thomas Ross (joint author of 'MacGibbon and Ross'), of Cunningham who was a civil engineer, and later of the surveyor Mungo Buchanan. Professor F. J. Haverfield of Oxford was close adviser and financial helper. They chose next the even more heavily fortified Ardoch in Perthshire, where digging continued for twelve months with the same clerk of works, and Cunningham himself in charge. The traces of the timber buildings were discovered and planned. They then returned to Dumfriesshire to the forts at Birrenswark, where Barbour had under him Alexander Mackie who was in course of becoming the Antiquaries' permanent clerk of works, in the field for most of the year; he and a friend had been discovered excavating in their spare time the iron age fort at Abernethy in Perthshire, with its elaborately timber-laced rampart. There followed Lyne, Camelon, and the fortress at Inchtuthil (where a native palisade-trench was identified for the first time), then on the Wall, Castlecary, and Rough Castle in 1902-03. For most of these Christison was the named author of the promptly published reports. That of Inchtuthil was by John Abercromby (incorporating one by Ross). He had substantially assisted the financing there and at Castlecary; a subscription list was opened for Rough Castle. Guidance came from the work of German archaeologists on their *Limes,* and a wide range of foreign archaeological literature was being bought and exchanged for the library.

Meantime T. H. Bryce, professor of anatomy in Glasgow, was being assisted from what was left of the Rhind excavation fund, with new capital from Carfrae and Primrose bequests, to investigate chambered tombs in Arran and Bute. Not only were his finds valuable for the Museum, but he published a notable study, later often forgotten, of the context of Scottish neolithic pottery, showing its resemblances to the pottery of the Scandinavian megalithic tombs, and its closer affinities to that of western France and Spain (1902).

He may have been influenced by Abercromby, who in a paper in 1902 to the British Association and more fully in the *Proceedings* in 1904, made a preliminary survey of British beakers — 20% of them, including some Scottish, in the British Museum, 19% in the National Museum from Scotland alone. This developed into his classic *Bronze Age Pottery of Great Britain and Ireland* (1912) which also dealt with the associated objects and the European background. Stuart Piggott has described it as a new approach to archaeological evidence, essentially that still in use, and has commented that the view taken from Scotland in those days was more international than that from southern England, with Arthur Evans as an exception there.

Christison returned to his study of forts in Argyll, and in 1902 Abercromby offered up to £200 a year for excavations on 'British' sites. So Bryce continued on chambered cairns, and Abercromby himself, now joint Secretary, explored and recorded in detail hut-circles with 'earth-houses' (of the Iron Age) in Aberdeenshire. Christison went to Mid-Argyll with Alexander Mackie in 1904, and investigated four forts. The main one was Dunadd, a stronghold of the early Scots, where they recovered for the Museum objects of many kinds from that little-known period. At the excavation committee for the next year Abercromby was planning to excavate the comparable site at Dundurn in Perthshire, and Christison was apparently omitted, but divergencies soon widened. Abercromby in March wrote resigning from the Council and discontinuing his financial support, because of the Society's system of excavation. The Council accepted his decision non-committally with much regret. At the next election Christison resigned his Secretaryship after seventeen years; archaeologically he had failed disastrously at Dunadd, where he had not obtained any information on the nature of the occupation of the different parts of the site, by not having recorded the relationship of the finds with each other and with the recognisable walls, not to speak of the less tangible evidence of perished structures. Abercromby did not stop publishing in the *Proceedings*, and returned as President in 1913. It appears, however, that his bequest to the University of Edinburgh, formulated in 1916, to found the chair of Archaeology that carries his name, was a result of the quarrel. Robert Munro, who had long wished that there should be regular university instruction in archaeology, founded the Munro Lectureship in Anthropology and Prehistoric Archaeology in Edinburgh in 1910.

Just before Abercromby withdrew his support from the Society's excavations, work at Newstead under James Curle began early in 1905, for which a public appeal for funds was then made from time to time, raising ultimately £1,850. Curle was a lawyer in Melrose nearby, who had excavated two brochs in Selkirkshire in 1891 and as a result had started to study Samian pottery. His campaigns at Newstead, continuous through the year, lasted into 1910, with Thomas Ross surveying and Mackie as clerk of works. Of them Ian Richmond forty years later wrote that 'Dr Curle's excavations, which were far in advance of contemporary practice, disentangled a detailed plan of much of the fort and its surroundings', but that the stratigraphy of the five phases that he had distinguished was much looser than could be determined by modern methods; in addition they had 'produced a collection of relics so notable that they have never ceased to excite wonder'. After an interim series of Rhind lectures in 1908, Curle's published report, *A Roman Frontier Post and its People* (1911), was no less admirable, except for some omissions presumably due to its extreme promptness. A close study of the parallel evidence on the Continent with the help of foreign scholars (five of whom were made Honorary Fellows), and the good fortune of pit-deposits separated by a period of abandonment, made the work a lasting contribution to the chronology of Roman military equipment and pottery. Finely produced by James Maclehose, this monograph cost the Society £500 in addition to copies gifted by it or bought for later sale, and £300 contributed to the actual excavations from the funds. In the same year the first edition of George Macdonald's *The Roman Wall in Scotland* was published by the Oxford University Press.

Besides genuine relics from excavations, the Museum received and kept for permanent reference some others quite different. Excavations near Dumbarton at a small hill-fort and two crannog-like structures in the Clyde, undertaken locally between 1896 and 1901, gave rise to great controversy in newspapers and periodicals on account of the many unheard of things found, decorated geometrically and with faces, slate spearheads, shale figurines, miniature cup-and-ring stones.

Andrew Lang led the defenders and Robert Munro wrote *Archaeology and False Antiquities* (1905) because the conflicting opinions caused 'the very existence of such a thing as scientific archaeology to be doubted'. The best account is in French (de Pradenne 1932). A discussion in the Society in 1900 was, quite exceptionally, published. In it Joseph Anderson said, 'I prefer to suspend my judgment—merely placing the suspected objects (as they place themselves) in the list of things that must wait for further evidence, because they contradict present experience'. In the spirit of simply allowing everyone to see and judge things for themselves that was characteristic of the Museum, the 'Clyde forgeries', and some genuine objects found with them, were exhibited uncatalogued but without warning of suspicion, until withdrawn to store in 1939. On the same principle, possibly, various bronze axes acquired in the 1880s which should have roused suspicions, were bought and catalogued without comment. On the other hand a massive carving of a Roman cavalryman, found at Camelon in circumstances that seemed to show it was of some age, and published in 1902 after being claimed as 'treasure trove', was relegated to the cellar unnumbered. Another puzzle, a set of bagpipes dated MCCCCIX, published in 1880 and bequeathed to the Museum in 1911, was often doubted before satisfactory proof of falsity was published in 1974.

Turning now away from research, we can see that while relations with the Board and the Treasury lost most of their tensions once the Museum was rehoused, further important principles were not settled without difficulty. The provision from 1895 of an annual purchase grant, that might accumulate in the Society's hands, 'for ordinary small articles of interest', was an advance, though at £200 it was considerably less than the £500 asked for, and promised only for five years at a time. It also had to meet the cost of treasure trove rewards, previously paid from the Exchequer's own vote. The condition that the Remembrancer should sit on the Council, provided he was or became a Fellow, like the Board's two representatives, strengthened the long-standing co-operation.

The very large and unique medieval Glenlyon brooch was auctioned in London in May 1897. A painful argument on the morning of the sale between Robert Carfrae, elderly chairman of the Antiquaries' purchase committee and C. H. Read, who had succeeded Franks as Keeper at the British Museum, resulted in the two Museums making final bids against one another, and the loss of the brooch to Scotland at £220. The British Museum was at that time in dispute over the extraordinary gold hoard recently found at Broighter in Ireland, and bought privately by the Trustees. Under pressure from Irish MPs, and simultaneously the Scottish Office, A. J. Balfour as First Lord of the Treasury set up a strong Parliamentary committee to enquire into the case of the 'Celtic ornaments found in Ireland', and to consider and suggest regulations for avoiding undue competition between museums supported out of public funds in Scotland and Ireland on the one hand, and the British Museum on the other, 'for the acquisition of objects of antiquarian or historic interest, and for ensuring that . . . the museum situated in the country [peculiarly] interested should be afforded . . . [priority]'. They were also to consider whether legal obstacles to the British Museum's parting with objects once acquired should be relaxed. The evidence and recommendations were printed in full with, in appendices, the Society's internal report of 1890 on the operation of the law of Treasure Trove (House of Commons 1899, 179). A code of conduct on competition was suggested, which for Scotland has been followed ever since, but relaxation of the British Museum's restrictions, even as between the national museums, was only tentatively supported by a majority. The Crown had to sue the British Museum's Trustees in 1903 for illegal possession of treasure trove, to return it to Ireland; but this remedy was not possible for the brooch. Read was evidently unrepentant over either case, for he resigned from the Society in 1904 after unsuccessfully laying claim to the bronze age armlet found at Melfort in Argyll, Crown property in Scotland, on the grounds that it had been bought by his predecessor. The British Museum Trustees on the other hand had quickly presented in compensation excellent facsimiles not only of the Glenlyon brooch but also of the Lochbuie brooch, the larger brother of the Brooch of Lorne.

The Treasury went back on the spirit if not the letter of its earlier statements on special grants in 1904, when the medieval harps on loan were withdrawn for auction. The £1,000 requested was provided only by advancing four years' ordinary grant. So the 'Queen Mary' harp at £892 10s absorbed four and a half years' money despite further argument centred on the library and periodicals. The Lamont harp was bought by W. Moir Bryce, and in time bequeathed to the national collection. Before the grant commenced again, two eighth-century silver brooches, long known, were offered for sale, to be bought for £250 by a loan on most generous terms from C. E. Whitelaw. The only income for purchases then was from the two paying days each week (soon afterwards abolished), which came under £20 a year as it was divided between the Museum and the Portrait Gallery.

Since Black had reported in the *Proceedings* in 1893 on the Scottish antiquities in the museums in London and in the Royal Scottish Museum, the latter had acquired the Noël Paton collection. Following a request from the Director in 1906 for the Egyptian and Assyrian objects to be placed on loan in Chambers Street, there were discussions in which the Society tried to have the respective spheres of the two museums more clearly defined. Schemes for purchase or exchange, particularly concerning the Scottish items in the Noël Paton collection estimated as worth £1,000, were put forward unsuccessfully, but Dr Dobbie left open the possibility of purchasing the Egyptian collection. A. O. Curle as Secretary replied for the Society, regretting that the Royal Scottish would not effect an exchange, but hoping that the bringing in touch with each other of the two Institutions might tend to their mutual advantage.

The Board of Manufactures was replaced in 1906 by a new and much smaller Board of Trustees for the National Galleries of Scotland, with no further responsibility for the art schools. This followed a long enquiry by a committee appointed in 1902 by the Secretary for Scotland, Lord Balfour of Burleigh (Cmd 1812-3, 1903). Much ancient history had been reviewed, often rather one-sidedly, with the usual confusion — the Museum (without the National) being described throughout as belonging to the Society, and even the staff similarly. Three recommendations were made regarding the Museum: that the Society should nominate one member to the new Board (it was however constituted without nominated members), that the purchase grant should be made permanent, and that an additional £200 should be paid to the staff. The two changes were accepted by the Treasury promptly, the Keeper's salary being raised to £500 p.a., the same as the new whole-time post of Director of the National Gallery, but without pension. The Assistant Keeper and to a small amount the attendants were given rises, but the Society was still left for several years to pay the fourth attendant, in the library, who also acted as clerk. (The Society paid too for recataloguing, but binding could be paid from the purchase grant.) The relationship between the Museum and the new Board was exactly the same as before, except that the buildings were transferred to the Office of Works. To it a request for electric instead of gas lighting in the Society's meeting room was soon sent. Efforts to have a lift installed were unsuccessful.

The retirement of Joseph Anderson was put off as long as possible, because his post was not pensionable. A deputation discussed the matter with the Secretary for Scotland, but a Treasury letter in autumn 1912 explained that even if it had been prepared to make a change at the time the Board was reconstituted in 1906, Anderson had then already been five years over the maximum retiring age for a civil servant; however a gratuity would be granted if he now left. The size of this when paid (£412 5s 3d), as well as discussion whether the post would in future be pensionable, may explain why pressure from the Scottish Office was necessary before he gave four weeks' notice that he would retire at the end of March 1913. He was aged 81, but in addition to making him an Honorary Fellow and collecting £600 for him from co-workers and friends, the Society retained his services as editor at £50 p.a. until he died in September 1916. Besides his LL D from Edinburgh (1882), he was an honorary member of the Royal Society of Northern Antiquaries in Copenhagen, of the Society of Antiquaries of Stockholm, and of the Royal Irish Academy, also Professor of Antiquities of the Royal Scottish Academy.

Meantime the vacancy for Assistant Keeper had been filled, after fourteen months, in summer 1912 by the appointment of A. J. H. Edwards, who had been five years a technician (preparer) in the natural history department of the Royal Scottish Museum. The salary was £150-£200, to start with unpensioned.

Modernisation and contraction, 1913-45

Most of the protagonists for the next thirty years were now on the stage. Sir Herbert Maxwell was in the last of his thirteen years as President, during which, it is stated in the *Proceedings*, the 'National Museum of Scotland' would have been in a much worse position that it was, but for his efforts to obtain fairer treatment from the Government. Under him the principal Secretaries were A. O. Curle, BA WS, brother of James Curle and since 1908 Secretary and archaeologist of the new Royal Commission on the Ancient and Historical Monuments of Scotland, and Robert Scott-Moncrieff WS. The Curators were James Curle and J. Graham Callander, shortly to be archaeologist to the Commission, with George Macdonald as curator of coins since 1903. Their offices were not only indications of their interest in the Museum; like the Secretaryship they did not rotate at regular intervals and so could be held for even thirty years. James Richardson, who in 1914 became first Inspector of Ancient Monuments for Scotland (then a part-time post), had recently joined the Society, and Angus Graham, later Secretary of the Society (1938-66), was about to do so.

A committee of Council, including Macdonald and Callander, quickly recommended that A. O. Curle should become Director of the Museum, after the Council had decided that the post should be pensionable with a more adequate salary, and still combined with the assistant secretaryship in view of the Society's responsibilities. The appointment was made in May 1913 by the Secretary for Scotland in terms of the National Galleries of Scotland Act 1906, and the Treasury agreed that it should be pensionable (on issue of a Civil Service Commission certificate) and regarded as whole-time notwithstanding the commitment to the Society; the salary was however to remain at £500 as 'ample for the post'.

It was the need to conserve James Curle's Roman finds of leather, wood and metal, particularly iron, and his instigation, that led to Edwards's selection because of his museum experience and knowledge of chemistry. So the Gunning Fellowship was used to send him in the middle of 1913 to Berlin to learn archaeological conservation under Professor Rathgen and Dr Regling, after which some elementary equipment was obtained through the Office of Works. Soon a preparer too was employed temporarily, and Edwards was 'established'. This was a pioneer development in British museums.

The congestion, to which new cases for Newstead had added, gave urgency to a scheme for fire-proofing under new wooden flooring. It may be assumed that A. O. Curle was particularly active in the committee appointed in December 1912 to consider the temporary removal of the collections and cases into the Portrait Gallery's premises, and subsequent changes — the extensive provision of drawers in the window bays was proposed, lighting for the cellar, and long loans such as of models of Edinburgh buildings to the city's museum; a stock-taking desired by the Committee of Public Accounts was envisaged for when the Museum would be closed to the public. Though provided for in the Board's Estimates for 1913-14, the closure and move (in five weeks, leaving the top floor meantime) did not take place till spring 1914, perhaps to allow the new Director to investigate the state of the Museum and its deficiencies and uncatalogued categories, on which he reported. The cellar in particular needed to be fitted up as proper store-rooms; Edwards long afterwards recalled finding a table there, collapsed under a great weight of things.

In lesser details of administration as well as in personnel a more modern Museum was taking shape. As the Board had at last secured permission to pay for the library attendant, the Council decided to use the savings to employ a clerk for the Society. So the Minutes from July 13 were typewritten, from October by Miss E. M. Dennison who did not retire till 1944. She also typed the Director's correspondence and did other work for the Museum, at the Society's expense, as was the telephone then installed. A system of catalogue-index cards was begun. Some money was saved by making the Assistant Secretary's honorarium only £10. A proposal made in 1912 after a meeting with the secretary of the Edinburgh School Board, that short descriptive accounts of different sections of the Museum might be printed for school visits, does not seem to have been followed up. Nor was the opening on Sunday afternoons as proposed by the new Director, even though opposition to it within the Society was unsuccessful on a vote. One change made was that the Council, rather than the Secretaries, made the report on the year to the Society. This included a summary of accessions to the Museum and other matters relating to it, such as had come to replace in the *Proceedings* the Council's formal report to the Board; attendance figures were dropped from 1907. The format and binding of the *Proceedings* were improved in 1915, but the arrangement of the contents was not altered, with the full donations lists set out monthly until consolidated in 1939, when modifications were begun for more economical and handier volumes.

More important, in May 1914 the Society recommenced its own excavations. In connection with his work for the Royal Commission, and with a contribution from the Society, A. O. Curle had excavated at the vitrified fort of Mote of Mark in Kirkcudbrightshire in 1913, obtaining for the Museum a remarkable collection of moulds for dark age ornaments. Though it was also hoped to explore the fort at Mumrills on the Antonine Wall, a campaign was begun under Curle, with support from Abercromby, within the recently recognised ramparts on Traprain Law near Haddington. The complexity of the structural remains found, and even more the quantity and variety of relics both native and Roman, opened a new dimension in the archaeology of Scottish native sites. The proprietor, the Rt. Hon. A. J. Balfour, promised all the finds to the Museum. Work had to be suspended after a second season in 1915, but particularly well illustrated reports were promptly published in the *Proceedings*. Another landmark, in the volume for 1918, was the first listing of Roman coins found in Scotland, by Macdonald, who also kept up his series of accounts of coin hoards from other periods.

With the major changes started, and the Museum already closed, the onset of war prolonged and intensified the beginning of modernisation. Edwards and some of the attendants left at once for the Forces. Curle remained to place valuable exhibits in the cellar, and later to dismantle the library (and replace it in 1917) and the comparative gallery, as under-floor fire-proofing continued; unwanted pottery from Newstead was, according to oral tradition, mixed in with the concrete. Re-flooring was delayed and ultimately took place in 1919, using soft instead of hard wood-blocks, for economy. For several years to the end of 1919 the empty galleries were used by the Timber Supply Department of the Board of Trade. The Society's meetings until December 1918 were held in the Royal Society's rooms, which by coincidence had been transferred to 24 George Street. The Museum's purchase grant ceased for the duration, but savings allowed purchases for the library to continue to within a few months of its recommencement in 1919; the few purchases of objects had included a gold lunula and torc once in Adam Sim's collection, at a Red Cross sale.

In 1916 A. O. Curle was appointed Director of the Royal Scottish Museum in the Scottish Education Department. Because the Museums were closed he continued to be responsible for Queen Street, and to work part-time there. His successor, on the same terms (which now included editing the *Proceedings*), was Graham Callander, aged 46. He was proposed by the Council in March 1919 but not appointed till September, after they and the Board had considered an application from Donald A. Mackenzie, brother of the Secretary of the Commission. Callander had left the Commission for war-work but had continued to be Secretary of the Society, in succession to A. O. Curle, and to contribute papers on prehistoric material in each volume of the *Proceedings*. Edwards returned in 1919 and succeeded in getting a salary rise, of £50. The new post of preparer was filled by William Darroch, for some years on a temporary basis. A camera was soon provided for him, and a lantern and screen (on hire) for the Society's evening meetings. Curle joined Macdonald and his brother as a Curator, and remained the Society's representative on the Ancient Monuments Board.

In May 1919 the Duke of Atholl, as chairman of the Committee planning the Scottish National War Memorial in Edinburgh Castle, wrote about the Scottish Historical Museum that was part of the scheme. He proposed that the Society should approve the transfer of the collection in their charge to suitable buildings to be provided for it in the Castle. The Council declined to recommend this to the Board, while agreeing that more accommodation would permit the existing collection to be properly displayed and allow for future expansion. There were obviously many difficulties but the only ones minuted were the disadvantage of moving the library to the Castle and the need to hold the meetings elsewhere (the Castle being still garrisoned). The Memorial committee founded instead the Scottish United Services Museum which, transferred to the Government in 1948, has needed all the accommodation yet available in the Castle.

The excavations at Traprain Law were begun again in 1919, and continued seasonally until 1923. At the very beginning they uncovered the largest quantity and variety of cut-up pieces of late Roman silver plate known from a single hoard. Probably because all the finds were promised to the Museum, the Crown made no claim of treasure trove. A Treasury grant of £1,000 paid for annealing and cleaning by Brook and Son, jewellers in Edinburgh, who were allowed to make replicas, on which royalties were paid to the Society. Publication of A. O. Curle's fine monograph, *The Treasure of Traprain* (MacLehose and Jackson, Glasgow 1922, 3 guineas), was arranged by the Society. Two hundred copies for presentation to libraries and institutions around the world were bought at the members' subscription rate (2 guineas) by John Bruce, who had financed the 'Clyde forgeries' excavations, and who was a generous supporter of the Society's excavations and purchases for the Museum. A general appeal in 1921 for the Traprain excavations raised nearly £400. In addition £100 grants over several years were given by the Carnegie Trust. The excavations ceased when instead a rescue excavation similarly financed was begun at the Roman fort of Mumrills, which lasted four and a half years; meantime a series of non-Roman occupation sites and cairns was examined in Galloway, Lewis and Caithness by the Assistant Keeper on the Gunning Fellowship. Archaeology had not yet formulated the questions which excavations at large hill-forts such as Traprain should try to answer, and the publication in the *Proceedings* in annual reports was probably not seen as unsatisfactory, however short on conclusions. Indeed as it set out the finds, covering five centuries at least, in broadly stratified 'levels', it was a considerable advance, and accessioned in the Museum the material was readily accessible for further study.

Because the Museum remained closed, a temporary exhibition of the Treasure in Chambers Street lasted over two years. Co-operation began while Curle was still Honorary Director in 1919, when a considerable bequest of almost entirely English china and silver from James Cowan-Smith was accepted after agreement to lend what was not Scottish to the Royal Scottish Museum. The idea of relieving pressure by lending Egyptian and other foreign material was considered, but as neither side yet favoured large-scale transfer, little but 134 Greek pots and figures and Roman lamps was placed on long loan in 1921, followed by seven hundred or so ethnographical specimens in 1924. A collection of military uniforms was lent to the United Services Museum in 1930, a few years after being accepted.

Various outstanding accessions came to the Museum before it was reopened. The great Pictish monument from Hilton in Ross-shire was given by Macleod of Cadboll after remonstrations against its initial acceptance by the British Museum; the Thomas Coats of Ferguslie collection of Scottish coins, the type-collection of Burns's *Coinage*, was gifted by the Coats family on condition that it remained in the Museum in all time coming as a separate entity accessible to students. Gifts to the prehistoric archive were on a lesser scale, among them a rare middle bronze age hoard from Glentrool in Galloway, Erskine Beveridge's iron age finds from North Uist, and Lady John Scott's varied collection from Berwickshire.

Despite a request in 1920 for the purchase grant to be raised to £600 it remained at £200, except for an increase of £20 from 1936 to cover freight, travelling etc, until stopped again in 1940. (The Board averted a threatened stop in 1932.) Out of this came purchases for the library, now important because of the many periodicals received in exchange for the *Proceedings*, particularly from abroad; it was stated in 1920 to contain 15,042 volumes and 1,004 pamphlets. Binding ceased to come out of the grant; after the Society had contributed to arrears in 1929, this was undertaken by the Stationery Office as for other government libraries.

Good use was being made of the grant for buying museum objects. The fantastic pre-Roman Torrs chamfrain (really a pony-hat it seems), long at Abbotsford, was bought at auction in 1921 for £305, the medieval Guthrie bell-shrine privately for £250, and the gold signet of Joan Beaufort, James I's queen, for £100. Through treasure trove came twelfth-century ornamental spoons and gold fillets from Iona, and late medieval coins from Perth, but the opportunity of more than a partial selection of coin varieties was not taken. When the Mary Queen of Scots jewels and fan from Penicuik were sold in 1923, the Council lacking funds left it to Dr Walter Seton, and Sir Bruce Seton, one of the

Fellows, to raise subscriptions from the King and Queen and many others, helped by a guarantee from the Marquess of Bute much larger than the auction price of £420. A policy of trying to purchase old finds, such as the Culbin armlet, or secure them on loan if not as gifts, was being actively supported by James S. Richardson. He began shortly afterwards in 1925 his forty-five years of constant association with the Museum, first as a Curator (on A. O. Curle's moving to Librarian) and then as a Trustee; the recorded flow of small gifts from him of 'bygones' and good craftsmanship was but one aspect of his encouragement of the more varied as well as the aesthetic sides of the collections, beyond the prehistoric accumulation to which he also regularly contributed gleanings. For a while in the 1920s the Council welcomed donations of eighteenth and nineteenth-century domestic silver, 'poorly represented in this Museum', before a restrictive policy change concentrated on spoons.

The Museum was reopened in January 1923, by the Chairman of the Board deputising for the Earl of Balfour, indisposed. In July it was visited, along with other parts of the Galleries, by the King and Queen. One main change was that the Roman collection, with the new treasure in a specially secure metal case, had been moved upstairs to the north-west end of the first floor. On both floors large numbers of glass-topped drawers set under cases in the window-bays had, along with cupboards in the basement, allowed a great thinning of what was on open display. To continue this process, the gradual replacement of the floor cases by ones with storage underneath was to be a major programme over the years. The comparative gallery, closed until 1927, was the first completed, by 1938. The chance that part of the basement became the workshop of one of the Office of Works carpenters gave the Museum an advantage in calling on his services for fitments inside the cases.

By the early 1930s the thousands of exhibits were rearranged, as well as maintained, largely by Edwards, who had visited museums in six countries abroad. Mounted on unbleached linen, with labels and individual numbers (in place of large adhesive figures) in Darroch's clear, if necessarily minute, script, they gave the whole Museum a clean and cared-for look, despite the density of display and the long cases no more than three feet apart. A much larger proportion of the collections was intentionally kept visible than was already fashionable. Particularly in the prehistoric gallery, this was partly due to the concept of keeping the range of archaeological evidence for anyone to study unhindered; but equally, since the National Museum drew discoveries from the many diverse parts of the country, it was thought right that the visitors from each part should always be able to see typical things from their own area. The need in this for a geographical location index of the first floor was voluntarily supplied from the mid-1930s by one of the attendants, W. J. Ross, and widely appreciated. The exemplary maintenance of the polished floors and case-glass was part of the attendants' routine.

Much of Callander's time was spent in writing for the *Proceedings* and editing it, with an editorial committee consisting of Macdonald, A. O. Curle and W. K. Dickson of the Advocates', later National, Library. Among the papers he contributed in the 1920s were several of the main descriptive discussions of categories of Scottish material, much of it in the Museum, which as Graham has noted were a feature of the *Proceedings* at this time — those on the Museum's first collection of mesolithic flints, on neolithic pottery, bronze age hoards, and medieval brooches; perhaps rightly the fewness of comparisons outside Scotland has been criticised as a turning away from the days of Munro and Abercromby, but introversion was not really characteristic of the period when J. H. Craw demonstrated a connection between gold lunulae and jet necklaces, and James Curle inventoried Roman stray finds. It was not of course only Scottish prehistory that was placed more fully in an international context by V. Gordon Childe, appointed in 1927 first Abercromby professor in Edinburgh. At the beginning he was not wholly welcomed, but elected to the Society's Council in 1930 and a Foreign Secretary from 1932, he was increasingly involved with the Museum's affairs, as well as using the collections and library for research and teaching.

Behind the scenes there were serious tensions. In 1925 Callander submitted a memorandum on the salaries and status of the staff, claiming that the Museum had been downgraded in 1921 and that it should be regarded as equivalent to a department in the Royal Scottish Museum (of which there were three). At the same time Edwards requested that it should be made clear that he was the second officer, and so equivalent to the Keeper in the National Galleries (the curator of the Portrait Gallery). Comparabilities are vexed matters even when there are standardised grades and pay, which did not then exist for the goverment museums service, but pay-scales do reflect, and condition, attitudes affecting the whole institution. A considerable harmonisation of scales in the London institutions took place in 1913, and in 1919 the Royal

Scottish caught up to the extent that its Keepers and Assistant Keepers stopped where their London equivalents began. Under the National Galleries' Board in Edinburgh the picture and museum sides had in 1920 been equivalent to one another in pay, but in 1921 the Director of the Galleries had risen to £800-£900, well above the Keepers in the Royal Scottish, while the National Museum's Director had been put by the Treasury at £600, just above the latters' minimum, instead of at their maximum £700 as agreed by the Board and Council; the Galleries' second post received an Assistant Keeper's salary but the Museum's at £250-£350 went no higher than an Assistant (Asst. Keeper II), against the wishes of the Council. There was 'considerable discussion' in 1925 in the Council, but a committee under George Macdonald, in consultation with the Board's Chairman after the National Galleries' Whitley Council had taken the matter up, declined to press it. When after further correspondence, including a representation from the Association of Professional Civil Servants, the Board in 1929 agreed to ask the Treasury to bring salaries into line with those in the Royal Scottish Museum, the Council 'disassociated themselves from the independent action of the officers of the Museum', and the Scottish Office supported the Treasury's refusal. Whatever the Council's reasons, and influence with the Scottish Office, the existence of the distinguished Curators may have seemed to the Treasury to reduce the responsibilities of the staff, and to make the Museum less than fully public.

Following the appointment in 1927 of a Royal Commission to enquire into and report on the National Museums and Galleries in London and Edinburgh, the constitutional peculiarity of the Society's role was certainly so handled and placed on record, that the seventy years' intermittent but persistent efforts to secure for the Museum and its staff financial treatment comparable to that of other national museums were set back for another twenty-five years. Among the eleven commissioners the only domiciled Scot was Sir George Macdonald, now in his seventh year as Secretary of the Scottish Education Department. He was at that period the most usual chairman of the Society's Council, but was absent when an invitation to give evidence to the new Commission was considered together with a draft submission. Both representatives of the Board were present, one its chairman, Sir John Findlay, son of J. R., on the Council since 1907. 'After considerable discussion certain emendations were decided on', and the text left to the Secretaries and the chairman James Curle to complete. The long memorandum as printed by the Commission is almost all factual, setting out the Museum's history, constitution, relation with other institutions, staffing, congested lay-out, facilities, benefit from excavations etc. It specifies as anomalies in the constitution that the attendants were under the management of the Board, and that the Board were represented on the Council but not the Council on the Board. Then, after noting that in 1851 there was no Secretary for Scotland and the Board had then a much more considerable variety of public duties, it asserts:

> Except for the fact that the Museum is installed in the same building as the National Portrait Gallery and that accounting may be simplified through the cleaning, and to some extent the appointment of attendants being under one body, there does not appear to be any strong reason why the entire charge of the Museum of Antiquities should not be entrusted to the Society of Antiquaries acting directly under the Secretary of State for Scotland . . . The time must come, and that at no distant date, when the Museum must be housed elsewhere in a larger building; in that event any reason which may exist for the retention of control by the Board of Trustees will disappear.

(It may be wrong to speculate whether two drafting hands can be identified according to whether the term Museum of Antiquities is used, as always by the Commission (occassionally adding Scottish) or National Museum of Antiquities (alternatively National Museum) as in most of the memoranda, and in the Commission's final index.)

When James Curle as curator gave evidence to the Commission in London in 1928, along with Findlay and Callander, he was first asked to sum up the advantages of control of the Museum by the Society of Antiquaries, which he reported had now over 1,000 members. Callander spoke only about cases and attendance figures. Much of the questioning was done by Macdonald, whose final question to the Chairman of the Board was, 'When the happy time comes when there will be provided another Museum for the Society of Antiquaries, do you think that the dual control should continue?' 'No, I do not think that the Board would have any particular interest in continuing that control. I think they recognise that in the Council of the Society of Antiquaries you have as good a body for the management of the Museum as you could have.' Earlier answers made it clear that those concerned misunderstood their history. They believed that the Queen Street building would naturally 'revert' to the Portrait Gallery, with perhaps £5,000 credited towards the new building as representing what J. R. Findlay had spent on adding the Museum to the building he had always intended for the Portrait Gallery. It was supposed that the other claimant for space in the Royal Institution had been not the portraits but the Royal Scottish Academy (which did not move there till 1912), and the donor's long and very active concern for the Museum was apparently forgotten. Far from the opportunity being taken to press the Government to honour the responsibilities undertaken in 1851, even the possibility that the Society might provide a fresh printed catalogue 'without expense to the Treasury', and its payments for typewriting the Museum's correspondence and registers, were accepted as natural. Nor did any of the very experienced Commissioners question whether Parliament would readily hand over what was legally an integral part of the National Galleries, to a Council which was almost entirely self-perpetuating.

In their Final Report (1929 Cmd 3401) they said:

> The time is not far distant when the Museum of Antiquities will require a separate building if it is to play the part it ought to play as an educational institution, specially designed to stimulate Scottish archaeological studies and the teaching of history . . . If a separate site and building could be provided for the Museum of Antiquities a solution of the problems indicated above affecting the National Gallery, the National Portrait Gallery and the Museum itself, would have been found . . . To bring the plan to immediate fruition may not seem easy in present financial circumstances, but its speedy realisation would be assured if the tradition of private munificence so conspicuous in the history of the English and Scottish Institutions is maintained.

When that happened the control of the Museum should be placed 'formally and absolutely under the Society of Antiquaries'.

In addition to recounting measures already begun to help congestion, they took up a point made by A. O. Curle, when as Director of the Royal Scottish Museum he noted textiles and furniture as areas of overlap between the two Museums, and expressed his personal view that furniture should be concentrated in Chambers Street; the Commission advised that the council should be careful

> not to aggravate the congestion by purchasing or accepting objects which are suitable for exhibition in an Art Museum, even though, if more space were available they might rightly be regarded as falling within the scope of the Museum of Antiquities. Any danger of their being lost to the nation could be got over by finding them temporary lodgement in the Royal Scottish Museum.

A Standing Commission was appointed in 1931 to advise on the development of the National Institutions and related questions, and to stimulate and direct the generosity of benefactors. It included several of the original members, with Macdonald, now retired, chosen by the Scottish Institutions. In their first Report in 1933, still in the shadow of the world financial crisis, they wrote that while the Royal Commission had been impressed with the need for a Gallery of Modern Art in Edinburgh, and still more by the difficulties hampering the Galleries and Museum, other solutions than the provision of a new building for the Museum of Antiquities had since been proposed, and the first step must be to reach a clear decision on what was ultimately desirable; the Galleries' interests were once more tangling the Museum's case. In their second Report in 1938 they briefly reiterated that undoubtedly the need for a new building for the existing Museum of Antiquities was very great, while the absence of a Gallery of Modern Art was a serious deficiency: 'both projects may naturally be expected to appeal more particularly to Scottish benefactors'. However, following a recent extension of the Royal Scottish Museum, they also recommended a lecture hall there, with no question of waiting for benefactors for it, any more than in the past.

A necessary preliminary to a new building was to consider where it should be. In December 1930 the Council wrote to the Office of Works and to the Lord Provost's committee on town planning, suggesting that a site at or near Brown Square (alongside the Royal Scottish Museum) might be suitable.

Throughout the 1930s a series of transfers on 'permanent loan' was organised in order to reduce congestion in the Museum, and make the staff's task more realistic. From 1934 to 1937 there were lent 'by the Society of Antiquaries of Scotland' to the National Library the Haxton collection of 124 bibles, a few other books, notably the first folio Shakespeare, and nearly 350 manuscript items, one of them the Drummond of Hawthornden volumes; and to HM General Register House nearly 750 charters and documents. (Quite a number of parchments and other manuscripts were kept on view, and cleaned by the Stationery Office.) Following 550 English trade tokens in 1929, almost 1,000 items of the Egyptian collection and 280 South American and Mexican went similarly to the Royal Scottish Museum in 1939. This freed the comparative gallery for other use, once the remaining ethnology and the Danish, Swiss and most other non-Scottish archaeological exhibits had been stored away. It was easy to reach, along with the library, by the lift at last installed in 1930, with a new door into the Portrait Gallery.

Within its own specific field, the Museum continued to grow. Two collections which notably strengthened representation of the seventeenth to nineteenth centuries, promised as bequests, came first on loan

— the Clanranald family and Jacobite relics, with the 'Red' and 'Black' manuscript books (1931), were never to be removed on loan; and a large part of C. E. Whitelaw's Scottish weapons, accessories etc (1929) with a similar condition, another part going to Glasgow. All 1,925 Roman coins found at Falkirk, and claimed as treasure trove, were kept. When the Monymusk Reliquary, a Celtic house-shaped shrine of about AD 700, which probably once held relics of St Columba carried at Bannockburn, was auctioned in 1933, the National Art-Collections Fund bought it for £2,500 after the Society itself had raised £1,222. Three exhibits from the Empire Exhibition in Glasgow in 1938 were also bought for in all £1,200, and presented by the Fund — a two-handed West Highland sword, and medieval and Renaissance carved oak panels respectively from Montrose and Killochan in Ayrshire; some members of the Council considered that the panels should rather go to the Royal Scottish Museum, but gaining the support of Sir John Stirling-Maxwell, J. S. Richardson successfully opposed this. In 1939, however, it was decided to make no offer for Renaissance panels from Dundee carved with biblical scenes. Next month the Scottish Secretary of the National Art-Collections Fund, Edward Meldrum, undeterred by a *non possumus* from Edinburgh, secured for £440 an enamelled armorial pendant of Mary Queen of Scots, by persuading the Duke of Hamilton to add in what he bid to get it for Holyroodhouse, and later getting more than half the remainder from the Museum.

In an important break with precedent, fine prehistoric, Pictish and later metalwork and stone and bone carvings were lent to an exhibition in 1939, that of Scottish Art at the Royal Academy in London.

Excavations were the main source of archaeological accessions. The Society, while continuing to make contributions out of comparatively small bequest funds, soon left the initiative to others. There was, however, first an attempt to recover more information about Dunadd under J. H. Craw, who after retiring from farming became one of the Secretaries in 1929. He found that Christison's 'turning over' had been too thorough, and moved to the broch at Aikerness in Orkney, acquired for the Society by a Canadian benefactor, T. B. Macaulay. The Office of Works took over the site before Craw died in 1933, and continued the excavation, under Richardson's general supervision as Inspector.

The Ancient Monuments branch of the Office of Works was becoming a major factor in Scottish excavations. Previously archaeological relics had been to some extent collected during the tidying up of monuments in guardianship, but this material was rarely published or made accessible. Exceptionally the finds from a drain at Crossraguel abbey were published by Macdonald in 1920 because of the remarkable coins, and reached the Museum in 1939 as part of a tentative start by a disposal committee, while finds from Urquhart castle, though never published except for two brooches, were deposited on loan in 1924 by the Seafield Trustees. After protests from Orkney at the way Skara Brae was being treated just as an architectural problem, Childe was asked to observe the digging, rather than excavate, but he published reports in the *Proceedings*, followed by a book in 1931, and many finds were placed in the Museum on loan. (Childe was still uncertain that they really belonged to the Stone Age rather than to extremely retarded aborigines. Callander's paper on why they must be immediately pre-broch in date is an instructive example of a well-argued case flawed by using unreliable associations, and underestimating ancient people.) A. O. Curle, invited in 1931 to uncover the buildings at Jarlshof in Shetland, where he discovered two thousand years of settlements and the first Viking houses known in Britain, was able to take full charge and publish interim reports, as he had done for Traprain, and his finds were stored in the Museum. Excavators of lesser standing, chosen in the belief that 'what is known as archaeological excavation may be supervised by any interested antiquary', were generally more restricted; Macdonald in a presidential address to the Society in 1935 protested at 'official secrecy'. Inadequate organisation and manpower, compounded by the outbreak of the Second War, frustrated the plan to publish monographs, pending which the finds and information remained inaccessible. Metal objects, however, came to the Museum to be treated, and with other selected finds were in some cases given to it by the landowners.

Several unofficial series of excavations were in progress. Childe investigated a variety of sites as part of his university teaching programme, with donation of the finds to the Museum and prompt publication in the *Proceedings*. (Papers by his students began to appear there, notably one on bronze age beakers in 1934. More importantly his *Prehistory of Scotland* (1935) reshaped its subject in the light of all the work since Anderson at home and abroad.) The Glasgow Archaeological Society was investigating Roman sites in the West, placing its finds in the Hunterian Museum. Walter G. Grant, distiller and landowner in Orkney, uncovered a complex broch-site and various neolithic chambered tombs in the Island of Rousay, which Callander wrote up for the *Proceedings* after co-operating in the supervision. Grant invited Childe in 1938 to take over his excavation at Rinyo which had turned out to be another Skara Brae and provided new evidence for an early date, still accepted with 'extreme reserve'. Grant gave the relics from his sites to the National Museum, generally fairly promptly. So did the landowners of sites which Lindsay Scott, a civil servant in London, excavated in Skye and North Uist and published in the *Proceedings*, principally chambered cairns.

Instead of a fairly simple world of antiquarian bodies having little to do with each other, even when local ones had personal links to the Council, the Society and Museum now had to respond to the growth of a network of organisations. Edwards and Robert Kerr, who was a keeper in the Royal Scottish Museum, after he became curator of coins in 1933, began to attend the Museums Association conferences as delegates of the Society; Edwards as well as Childe represented it at the international Conference of Prehistoric and Protohistoric Sciences in Oslo in 1936. There was also representation on the Conference of Archaeological Societies, organised by the Society of Antiquaries of London. In 1938 the Society joined the new Scottish Federation of Museums and Art Galleries, devoted to changing the depressing state of affairs reported by the Royal Burghs in their evidence to the Royal Commission in 1927, and only confirmed by Callander and Edwards when they toured the Scottish local museums in 1932.

In this situation, small improvements in the staff's salaries served to emphasise the anomalies of their position within the national museums, not evident to the outside world. When the Board's initiative got for Edwards in 1931 the same scale as that of the Galleries' second post, the Treasury gave Callander a maximum £700, which Royal Scottish Museum Assistant Keepers had had since 1921. The Council were split on whether to accept. Childe and W. Douglas Simpson supported Callander's memorandum of protest, but Macdonald argued strongly in favour, mentioning that the Council had been satisfied with the figure in 1921, when the Treasury had refused it. While accepting his advice, the Council doubled the Director's honorarium as Assistant Secretary, to £120. Later general increases did not alter relativities. Recognition came to Callander in other ways, by his LLD from Aberdeen in 1932 and by his appointment as member of the Royal Commission on Ancient Monuments in 1938.

Callander died suddenly in March 1938, seven months before retirement. The Council recommended Edwards's promotion; as his health was not good, they agreed Childe should edit the *Proceedings*. They then crushed the idea of a small increase in the Director's salary (standing at 20% lower than that of the Galleries' Director, which at its top was £1,058, like those of Keepers at the Royal Scottish, and Deputy Keepers at the British Museum). However, they asked that the prospective assistant should be a graduate and styled Keeper, apparently to ensure for him the full salary scale of an Assistant Keeper II elsewhere, on the upper part of which Edwards had been, like the Keeper in the Galleries. All this was agreed to by the Board and the Treasury. After advertisement and interviews conducted by the Civil Service Commission, the Secretary of State appointed, in preference to Rainbird Clarke among others, an Edinburgh graduate R. B. K. Stevenson, aged 25 with a London diploma in prehistoric archaeology and a year's varied experience of excavation. He took post in December. The Museum also got a typist of its own that year.

On the approach of war the basement was reinforced, and shortly before the Museum was closed, on 1st September 1939, the transfer of exhibits to comparative safety there was begun. The display cases, some filled with boxes from store, and sculptured stones protected by sandbags, had to stay in the galleries, which for that reason were never successfully requisitioned for war-time offices. Edwards and Darroch continued to work on the collections and the trickle of accessions; later on substantial additions came through Kerr to the communion token collection. Stevenson, transferred early in 1940 into the Department of Health for Scotland, gained experience of administration for two years before being called up into the army. After the first winter the Society's meetings were resumed, in the afternoon. The library remained open.

Sir George Macdonald died in 1940 after nearly seven years as President of the Society. His successor on the Standing Commission, Lord Normand the Lord Justice-General, joined the Society and became very concerned with the future of the Museum. By the summer of 1943 post-war planning of all kinds could be taken seriously. After consulting with him then, Richardson, Edwards, and other members of Council replied to a questionnaire from the advisory committee on Edinburgh's city development. As possible localities for the new museum building, they named the vicinity of Holyrood (favoured by Richardson) and of Bristo (Brown Square as previously suggested), also Bruntisfield House. Soon afterwards information was sought from the secretary of the University Court about its extension scheme which might affect Bristo. To a question about a site for a folk-museum, the

Tower of Liberton was mentioned by way of an example; this was a subject which the Council had decided was premature in 1931, when raised after the Commission had supported the idea of one for England. In another area of planning, there was the new Council for British Archaeology; Lindsay Scott was asked to represent the Society, which through Childe took the lead early in 1944 in starting the regional group for Scotland.

In the difficult period that followed Edwards's death in July 1944, Macdonald's successor as President of the Society was widely influential, being Sir John Stirling-Maxwell KT, among other things Chairman of the Ancient Monuments Board and a Trustee of the Galleries. Richardson, as a Curator, briefly stood in until Childe could be appointed by the Secretary of State as Honorary Director, which he accepted for one session, with the status of a temporary civil servant from 1 September. The Council then had before it three proposals: that they should nominate A. D. Lacaille of the Wellcome Medical Museum, a Glaswegian and contributor to the *Proceedings*, or V. E. Nash-Williams of the National Museum of Wales, or recommend the promotion of the Keeper, despite his short experience of museum work and if he could be released soon from the army in Italy. The Board, while preferring public advertisement, decided not to support any permanent appointment for the present. Discussion continued, involving the Secretary of State, Tom Johnston, and his successor Arthur Woodburn, with Childe stressing his time-limit in order to secure the return of the Keeper, which the Scottish Office was working on, or failing that the appointment of Nash-Williams. In the event Childe continued (with limited responsibility) past the end of 1945, and during the last months Ian Finlay of the Royal Scottish Museum was lent half-time.

Meanwhile the ground floor of the Museum was reopened on 21 March 1945 by Lord Normand, whose address, printed in the *Proceedings*, ended with the hope that many Scotsmen would come to appreciate the great value of the National Collection, and resolve that it be displayed in a more suitable and commodious building. Childe and Richardson, with Darroch the Technical Assistant, had set out an exhibition, 'From the Stone Age to the '45', to tell the story of the development of culture in Scotland and commemorate the Jacobite bicentenary. The Annual Report described how 'cases were set back to back so as to allow space for viewing the contents; the choicest sculptured stones were made visible for the first time by consigning the remainder to the stairs or cellars; . . . and The Maiden was set up on a

P

scaffold where it could be seen'. The exhibits, few but typical, included some lent, or specially acquired to be attractive, such as the suit of an eighteenth-century Earl of Rothes. They were accompanied by large distribution maps, photographs, plans and explanatory labels, supplemented by a six-page guide sold for threepence. When the war in Europe ended, the finest pieces were put back on show, and in the autumn the first floor was reinstated, with the help of a trainee Technical Assistant J. A. Brown (whose fine drawings soon began to appear in the *Proceedings*). In the first seven months the exhibition had 32,000 visitors, with the Portrait Gallery still closed but Sunday afternoon opening at last introduced.

Preparing for a new deal, 1946-54

The senior post was finally filled from October 1946 by Robert Stevenson promoted to Keeper (in-charge), thus returning to Anderson's title as appropriate to a one-department institution, and more in line with the salary which was still that of an Assistant Keeper I. He had been released in January, and was *de facto* in charge next month. As the Council had decided in May 1945 to fill separately their vacant post of Assistant Secretary (and Editor) — later choosing H. M. Paton, due to retire from the Register House — they had ended the eighty-year-old partial subservience to the Society, which must long have prejudiced the Treasury, and the inferiority at the council-table which Edwards had also much disliked. After a year as Librarian, the Keeper was made a member of the Council *ex officio* by a change in the Society's laws in 1947.

It was agreed that the collections from recent centuries ought to be more systematically looked after and developed, and that a historian rather than another prehistorian should be found, perhaps from among the many ex-servicemen graduating in 1947. Civil service procedures were slow, so Stuart Maxwell, the Edinburgh graduate selected as a regular Assistant Keeper (II), did not start work till October of that year. The following month the Keeper as a civil servant opened direct contact with the Scottish Home Department (such as became normal later), on account of a Treasury review of salaries in museums which had resulted in his falling below the level of an Assistant Keeper I.

The correct channel for such matters was through the Galleries' Board, but it was not flowing smoothly. Following a reconstitution in 1947, when Sir John Stirling-Maxwell had stood down, neither of the representatives appointed by the Board of the Council was there legally, not being a Fellow although several other Trustees were. (The King's and Lord Treasurer's Remembancer had for the same reason dropped out in 1941.) Further, a paper circulated to the new members of the Board had embodied the bad history recorded in the Royal Commission's report in 1929, to the effect that they had no real concern with the Museum and its contents, apart from staff and salaries — which were not helped by the anomaly that the Director of the Galleries had naturally always attended their meetings but never the Director of the Museum. The Antiquaries with their President, the Earl of Haddington (1945-50), hoped that adjustments could be made. The Board came to the conclusion that the constitution was no longer workable, but meantime Alexander Maitland joined the Society and, with Lady Watson, attended Council meetings. After considering the Keeper's salary, the Board in 1948 recommended that it should be at the rate of a Keeper in the Royal Scottish Museum; they also agreed that there should be a second Assistant Keeper and a second permanent post of Technical Assistant after Darroch retired, as well as a librarian for three years to reclassify and catalogue the library; and appointments were made to the latter two posts.

The Third Report of the Standing Commission on Museums and Galleries, published next year, discussed the Gallery of Modern Art proposals more fully than the accommodation 'essential' for the Museum, on which the Society was noted as consulting the Planning Authority. It expressed the view however, that the extent of the site required was bound up with the possibility of a Scottish Folk Museum, for which the Society was also looking for a site ('a matter of urgency', as material was disappearing fast). It agreed with the Galleries' Trustees that the problems should be reviewed as a whole. In June 1949 a sub-committee of the Commission visited Edinburgh for this purpose, and the Chairman Lord Harlech discussed their findings with the Prime Minister C. R. Attlee and later with the Secretary of State Hector McNeil: these included emphasis on 'the need for the Museum to have a building to itself' and a recommendation that without waiting for this it 'should be given definite status as a National Institution with a Board of Trustees appointed *ad hoc* on which the Society of Antiquaries should be strongly represented' (Fourth Report, 1954).

This cutting of the Gordian Knot might have been welcomed by the Council if it had been discussed with them before being proposed, and if it had not come when the Treasury had shown that it considered the

Museum to be less than a Department in the Royal Scottish Museum: in September 1949 it turned down the Board's recommendation on the Keeper's salary (which had been supported by the Commission), in favour of grading as an Assistant Keeper I with £100 allowance (the same as departmental deputies in the Victoria and Albert Museum). Moreover the new Secretary of State Arthur Woodburn, in informing Lord Haddington in November of the Commission's proposals, put forward for discussion two further courses which might be interim or permanent — to transfer the responsibilities of the Galleries' Trustees to the Secretary of State while leaving management with the Society, or to transfer the responsibilities and also have the Museum administered along with the Royal Scottish Museum, leaving the Society to act in an advisory capacity. The Council much preferred management by a Board of Trustees to being taken over by a Government department, and suggested to the Galleries' Board that the appointment of a Trustee able to advise them on the Museum would be sufficient. Refusal by the Board to discuss these matters with the Council reinforced the fear that any major change geared to the then extremely unpropitious circumstances would harm rather than help the Museum's future. (Other straws in the wind were that the Board had declined to support a request for increased purchase grant for which Colonel Gomme-Duncan MP had got an encouraging reply from the Secretary of State, and that the Commission seemed to favour a Research Assistant instead of the proposed second Assistant Keeper.)

In September 1950 the Secretary of State dropped the departmental alternatives, and in accepting the Commission's recommendations for a new Board he asked what further points the Society wished him to consider. To obtain support for the Council's view of the Museum's underestimated worth and potentiality, the reply requested that a committee should be set up to enquire into the scope and status of the Museum, for example a representative of the Civil Service with a member of the Standing Commission and an archaeological specialist, possibly Dr Kendrick, Director of the British Museum. As a result the Philip Committee was appointed in April 1951 (p. 207).

While these fundamental administrative matters were being debated, no less attention was being paid to the collections. The broad aim was to make the future Museum more educationally useful by having good representative collections of all periods to move into the new building when it came. This embraced both helping to make the material itself and the results of archaeological research more widely known, and fostering the study of the ordinary (as well as the exceptional) things of modern historical times in what might be called an archaeological way. A basic task was to build up into significant series the accumulated curate's eggs of whatever had been made or used in Scotland — within practical limitations, such as avoiding the specialities of other institutions and (for the time being) the products of industrial technology.

The most urgent task was to make the best of what the Commission's Third Report called 'the present cramped quarters, where the Museum's primary purpose of preservation and research is well nigh irreconcilable with it secondary object of popular education'. The oppressive red brick walls of the ground floor were painted cream in 1948, and the display there was completely rearranged, with bays formed by placing cases back to back to enclose and separate Highland weapons, cannon and relics of Stuart, Jacobite and Hanoverian causes, from the ecclesiastical and the burghal exhibits. There were also some changes in lay-out and density in the prehistoric gallery upstairs. Next year brighter fluorescent tubes replaced the gallery lights. *A Short Guide to Scottish Antiquities* was published, a succinct cultural history covering most kinds of things shown rather than a case to case guide (first edition 1949, 33 pp. text, 6 pp. ill., price 1s). Because there was a little more room to move about and see in, the Museum could be used by the city's new Schools' Museum Officer, T. A. Davis; children taught by him in the galleries (later on, if not then, with stack-away chairs), or less often by their own teachers, numbered over 5,000 in the year from November 1950. On the top floor one-third of the former comparative gallery was kept for temporary exhibitions, the rest being closed off for storing the exhibits thinned out from downstairs. This was not sufficient or suitable for the growing costume collection, which could only be shown a very little at a time, and the reference collection of weapons augmented in 1948 by some 150 items from the Colville collection, on indefinite loan from the Scottish United Services Museum (still the only major transfer of any kind *into* the National Museum).

To make way for these the library stacks in the attic rooms had to be reduced. As the 1,500 books and pamphlets selected for removal had come by presentation or exchange, the Council considered that the spirit of the original donation required them to be transferred to Government-owned and independent institutions alike free of charge except for transport costs. Any residue might be sold to buy books (in the event £77 worth). Of the 940 items so transferred in 1949, nearly

400 went to the Scottish universities. As many went to the National Library, 48 of them pre-1600, making over 500 for it with the 1934 loan then given outright — the manuscripts continuing on loan. (A further disposal, mainly of duplicates and offprints, was not effected until 1955.) Then under a Disposal of Surplus Material Order (1951) the non-European comparative collection was reduced to about 500 items by giving to the Royal Scottish Museum some 2,000, plus the more valuable 1,300 lent before the war, as well as 160 Greek and Roman objects, three-quarters of them previously on loan. After advice from the British Museum 700 foreign classical antiquities were auctioned in London (1954, £460). Nearly 700 flint implements were given to the British Museum (Natural History). Finally 90 skeletal items from Scotland, mostly crania, were in 1954 placed on loan in Edinburgh University's Anatomy Museum.

Small temporary exhibitions began in December 1948 with archaeological air-photographs from Kodak by J. K. S. St Joseph, followed by Scottish and comparative foreign objects in the Museum — ancient and modern, air-photographs of castles and religious houses, ladies' dresses, and in 1951 costume accessories followed by spinning and weaving. This last was devised by a post-graduate archaeology student, Audrey Henshall, and resulted in a full catalogue in the *Proceedings* of most of the Museum's pre-1700 fabrics. The first idea for an exhibition of some of the finest objects in the collections as part of the Festival of Britain (1951) was to have it at The Mound, away from the Museum's inevitable clutter, and, though this was not possible, Glasgow Art Gallery and Museum mounted it strikingly and colourfully in the vast central hall at Kelvingrove. Many of the 191 exhibits were shown properly for the first time (*Scotland's Ancient Treasures*, 32 pp., 8 pls. two in colour). A few 'treasures', notably the Hunterston Brooch, had instead to be submerged in the official 'Living Traditions' exhibition in Edinburgh. Another successful co-operative enterprise, with and in the Portrait Gallery in 1952 during the sixth Edinburgh Festival and supported by the Arts Council, was a largely loan exhibition, 'Eighteenth Century Costume', arranged and catalogued by the Assistant Keepers of each side.

Short outward loans to exhibitions became not infrequent. They comprised some clocks and watches to Kelvingrove in 1949, four pieces of the Traprain Treasure to Colchester in 1950, local objects to historical exhibitions in 1951 (Musselburgh, Galashiels and Dumfries), the recently found Anglo-Saxon hoard from Iona to the Hunterian

Museum in Glasgow (1952), and the main archaeological finds from Lewis shown for a few days in Stornoway in 1953.

The Museum's curatorial staff tried to visit and keep in touch with museums all over Scotland, and to visit museums abroad, aided by the Gunning Fellowship. The Society too, over a few years, showed the flag by holding a joint meeting with local societies, beginning with Glasgow and Perth. The Regional Group, to which by 1949 eighteen societies and six museums belonged, stimulated joint enterprises; the Assistant Keeper for several years helped to organise its excursion, while the Keeper contributed a bibliography to its annual report, and a Scottish book-list for teachers for the parent Council of British Archaeology, and also spoke at the Group's first Summer School in 1952 devoted to the Problem of the Picts. Lecturing to societies far outside the Museum was an increasing commitment.

The improved display, publicity through exhibitions and acquisitions, and wider involvements coincided indeed with a general increase in public interest in archaeology and the arts. The attendance figures for the building, which had averaged 46,000 for much of the 1930s, rose in the early 1950s to over 70,000 and jumped to over 100,000 in 1953.

Along with those activities went the development of the collections. The number of donors soon returned to the annual fifty or so, as before the war. Encouragement of post-medieval donations, to which fewer than half had been contributing, led to considerable increases in donors, at first to eighty or so from 1950. Much of the early increase was for the costume collection. Two exceptional gifts in 1952 were the c. ninth-century carved wooden box found long before in Orkney, from A. Henderson Bishop who gave most of his collection to the Hunterian Museum, and Colonel le Rossignol's bequest of Stuart jewellery. Excavated collections received included pre-war finds, already published (Midhowe Broch, Orkney) or just then reported on in the *Proceedings* (neolithic North Uist and Bothwell Castle medieval pottery). After Childe moved to London in 1946, Stuart Piggott, his successor as professor and soon in the Society, began a series of research excavations in southern Scotland mainly on neolithic and early bronze age sites; the most remarkable was that at Cairnpapple in West Lothian. Mrs Piggott did the same for the Iron Age, particularly in Roxburghshire, of which the Royal Commission were preparing an Inventory to a new higher standard. C. S. T. Calder's discovery and almost single-handed investigation of a late neolithic culture in Shetland started at Stanydale in 1949. The Society contributed to the work at these and other sites from which the finds are preserved in the Museum. Several of the directors took part in a joint Scottish universities scheme for giving students some experience of excavation, which developed into more formal training on Roman sites under Miss A. S. Robertson of the Hunterian Museum — the Scottish Field School in Archaeology, instituted in 1947; the Society's representative on its committee was the Keeper of the National Museum. The Ministry of Works excavations at Jarlshof were completed under J. R. C. Hamilton, but the Society was unable to share in the publication, discussed in 1953. Shortage of finance had recently threatened the *Proceedings* themselves, until the Society's subscription rate was doubled after more than a century, to two guineas in 1952.

High quality, or scarce and collectable, things from recent centuries had most often to be bought. The purchase grant was restored at last from 1947-48 but, though double the old amount, could not at £440 go far to buy books for the library and treasures for the nation, even when price rises had not begun to accelerate sharply. (The library needed to be kept abreast of developments in European archaeology and in the study and context of the modern collections.) So the council decided to supplement the Government grant with a Special Purchase Fund to be launched at a suitable opportunity. This came with the purchase in 1948 of Charles I's coronation ampulla of gold, withdrawn from auction on the Society's offer of £1,000. For this, after £200 from the National Art-Collections Fund, the Council used up the money, by then £900, long earmarked for updating the 1892 printed catalogue — no longer a practicable or desirable proposition, nor replaceable by subject catalogues while the staff was so small. The public appeal brought a contribution from the Queen consort, £1,000 from the Pilgrim Trust, and over £1,000 more from other well-wishers. The Fund next year bought 135 historical and nineteenth-century prize medals for £780 from the R. W. Cochran-Patrick collection, including a gold medal of James VI on his marriage (£440), but failed over Charles II's coronation gold medal of 1650. Ordinary purchases of other medals, and of coins and tokens, were regularly being made; there were also losses through theft in 1948-9, due to inadequate supervision of an apparently trustworthy visitor, most of which were recovered. All the upwards of 300 Anglo-Saxon coins from Iona were acquired through Treasure Trove. The clothing and other finds from a bog-burial at Gunnister in Shetland also came from the Crown. Outstanding targes, basket-hilted swords and accessories, in all twenty-five items, from the Milne-Davidson sale were acquired in 1952 for £880, from R. I. Cochrane's bequest to the Society's Fund and from the National Art-Collections Fund. The Galloway Mazer (1569) — a most important purchase for itself, for its effect on the responsibility for buying Scottish domestic silver (as the Royal Scottish Museum had declined to bid for it because of other priorities), and because of the £7,500 additional Government grant toward the final price of £11,500 — was unsuccessfully bid for in March 1954; but was later secured on the recommendation of the Export of Works of Art Committee, and with £1,000 or over from each of the Pilgrim Trust and the two other generous Funds.

When in 1948 the Council learned that Miss I. F. Grant wished to give up her Highland Folk Museum at Kingussie, they began negotiations with her, hoping to form a Trust with various public bodies to re-establish it on a more suitable site. This proved unacceptable to her, as did a proposal for cataloguing her collection, financed by the Pilgrim Trust through the Society. Miss Grant was, however, the Rhind lecturer for 1950, speaking on 'Periods of Highland Civilisation'.

The Secretary of State's departmental committee (p. 202), consisting of Sheriff J. R. Philip, Sir Thomas D. Kendrick, Director of the British Museum, and P. J. Rose, a former Assistant Under-Secretary for Scotland, were appointed 'To enquire into the scope and functions of the National Museum of Antiquities of Scotland and its relations with other institutions and to make recommendations for its administration in the light of the conclusions reached on these matters'. After considering evidence received from twenty-eight organisations and individuals, they met in the Museum on 18-22 September 1951 to hear oral evidence, and visited museums in Edinburgh, having seen national museums in London and Wales. The evidence was not published, but in 28 pages the Report covered in some detail the Museum's history, existing situation, future government and development, its relations with other museums, services required by various categories of user, and staffing and designation (Cmd 8604 1952). The chief recommendations were that the Museum, with any projected (but physically separate) Folk Museum, should come under a new Board of twenty-one members (without local authority *ex officio* representatives but otherwise on lines suggested by the Society following the 1925 precedent of the National Library); and that a central site should be obtained at the earliest opportunity for the new Museum building, which the Secretary of State had accepted as a Government responsibility in principle shortly before he appointed them (House of Commons, 9 March 1951). However, as this new building 'would probably not be available for use in less than twenty years', additional accommodation with a larger staff should be provided in the interim; and during this the Museum should undertake the preservation of material suitable for a folk-museum, though to a much more limited degree than was later accepted by the Trustees' policy of a comprehensive balance of all periods. In the discussion on the designation National Museum of Antiquities, 'which has the advantage of covering both archaeology and prehistory on the one hand, and also history on the other', their impression that the 'exhibits are mainly archaeological and prehistoric' was even then a misleading description of the iceberg, if one went by bulk and interest to the public rather than mere numbers of small items. For the name and other matters the Committee reasonably recommended no change.

The Philip Committee's recommendations were accepted by the Government, and a Bill to effect the constitutional change was published in November 1953. The more favourable climate which the Committee stimulated can be traced in other ways. Though the third curatorial post was graded only at Research Assistant (II) level — filled in February 1952 by Miss A. S. Henshall to specialise in the prehistoric collection (and act as librarian) — the Keeper's post was from April 1953 at last graded as equivalent to those in the Royal Scottish Museum with a scale rising to £1,435, and the skills in conservation, illustration and so on of J. A. Brown in charge of the laboratory, with two assistants, were recognised by regrading to Research Assistant I like his opposite numbers; Stuart Maxwell had been given normal promotion from Assistant Keeper II to I in 1951. The purchase grant, which shared with other museums a 25% increase in 1953, was to be trebled for the new Board, to £1,500. Of greatest practical importance were premises at 18 Shandwick Place, the westward prolongation of Princes Street, made available in the autumn of 1953, into which the laboratory and much of the growing stored collections were moved, and where there was a hall and other space to be adapted for public display.

The Scottish Home Department had also, with the help of Sheriff Philip, searched on its own for a site for the new building in the area recommended and had identified as very suitable, and perhaps the only one likely to be available without planning complications, Brown Square at the south-west corner of Chambers Street, which as we have seen the Society had tried to earmark with the local authority in 1930 and again later. Confirmation or otherwise of these interim and permanent sites was referred to the new Board, the latter specifically by the Secretary of State's initial letter to the Chairman.

The National Museum of Antiquities of Scotland Act 1954 transferred to its new Board the powers and duties relating to the Museum previously vested in the Board of Trustees of the National Galleries and in the Society of Antiquaries. It thus relieved the Society of the charge and management but did not alter its other relations with the Museum, such as the mutual arrangements represented by the library and the housing of the Society, undertaken by the Treasury in return for the gift of collections. The Trustees who were to assume responsibility on 1 April 1954 were appointed in several ways: by the Secretary of State, the Chairman Lord Normand and eleven others intended to represent a wide range of public interests — two of them, as laid down in the Act, to represent archaeological interests, respectively in the West of Scotland (R. C. Reid) and the Scottish Regional Group of the Council for British Archaeology (R. L. Hunter); by the Society of Antiquaries of Scotland, its President *ex officio* (Sir William Calder) and four others (J. S. Richardson, I. A. Richmond, Miss A. S. Robertson, W. Douglas Simpson); and one each by the Senatus of the four universities (R. G. Cant, J. D. Mackie, R. D. Lockhart, and K. H. Jackson), and *ex officio* the Professor of Archaeology in Edinburgh University (S. Piggott).

Epilogue, 1954-80

The subsequent twenty-six years of the double-century have been as eventful as any of the earlier stages of the Museum's history, and they have been chronicled in the published annual reports of the Trustees to the Secretary of State for Scotland, laid before Parliament. Both the achievements and the failures require a more dispassionate review than is yet possible from within the Society, far less the Museum. The exhibited collections are confined to the same space as was criticised in 1911, although what is not visible has since then grown many times in real amount and in educational, not to speak of commercial, value. Staff numbers have grown to several times those of 1954, but are still considerably short of those employed in other museums with comparable tasks.

BIBLIOGRAPHICAL NOTE

These notes summarise the sources used for both parts of the chapters on the origins and development of the Museum, detailed references for which will be available in a marked copy in the library of the Museum and Society.

Manuscript materials include the Society's minute books, complete from 1780, with printed circulars, miscellaneous correspondence, etc., all in the library of the Museum and Society. In the Scottish Record Office, some of the records of the Board of Manufactures have been consulted, and some minutes of the Board of Trustees of the National Galleries of Scotland. Not much in the Museum's files antedates 1938, with the exception of accession registers and the 'coin cabinet fund' ledger. Dr S. A. Shapin's unpublished thesis (University of Pennsylvania 1971), 'The Royal Society of Edinburgh to 1820: a study of the social context of Hanoverian science', and Dr Marinell Ash's draft of her chapter in this volume, have been stimulating, as well as pointers to information.

Published sources that deal retrospectively with the Society and Museum comprise the two parts of W. Smellie, *Account of the Institution and Progress of the Society of the Antiquaries of Scotland* (Edinburgh 1782, 1784), and the later accounts in *Archaeologia Scotica* iii (3: 1784-1830) (1831), with lists of members, donations, communications, and (pp. xxiv-xxviii) Skene's address of 1826, incorporated in the 'Account' by S. Hibbert and D. Laing, 1831; and *Arch. Scot.* v (1: 1831-60 and earlier) (1890), with biographical notices (1874) appended to Laing's 'Anniversary Address' of 1861, supplemented by lists of members and communications in iv (3) (1857) and of donations 1830-51 in v (3) (1890); in the *Proceedings* (from i (1) in 1852, publication dates sometimes irregular), occasional anniversary and other addresses delivered by Wilson in 1851, Murray 1822, Cosmo Innes 1857, Neaves 1859, Simpson 1861, Laing 1868, various speakers 1874, Mitchell 1901 (on work of the Society since 1851), Guthrie 1913, Macdonald 1936, Normand 1945; also in *Proceedings*, annual and special reports to members and to the Board, notably in 1881 (coin cabinet affair and interpretation of the conveyance), 1892 (re-opening), 1899 (Glenlyon brooch affair), purchase grants, excavations, obituaries, and papers, e.g. those on the early history of the Society (Boog Watson, xlv 1911), on the Minor Society (Macdonald, liii 1919), on publications (Graham, cii 1969-70, cvi 1974-5), and on Joseph Anderson (Graham, cvii 1975-6).

Catalogues of the Museum: general, published principally in 1849, 1863, 1876 and 1892; of coins, Scottish (1901), Anglo-Saxon, with a history of the collection (1966). *Short Guides,* 1926 (revised 1935); 1949, revisions to 1962. On the Clyde Forgeries, see A. Vayson de Pradenne, *Les fraudes en archéologie préhistorique* (Paris 1932). Mons Meg, 1828-9, D. Caldwell, ed., *Scottish Weapons and Fortifications* (Edinburgh 1981).

The Departmental Committee's Report on the National Museum of Antiquities (Cmd 8604, 1952) published the 1851 Conveyance, which was also printed, along with the Treasury Minutes of 1851 and 1858 concerning the Museum, in the Society's memorandum for MPs in 1888 (on finishing the building). Parliamentary Commission on Science and Art (Ireland) 1869, xxiv (Evidence in Edinburgh). The evidence and report of the Departmental Enquiry on the Board of Manufactures are Cmd 1812-13, 1903; Royal Commission on National Museums and Galleries, evidence and reports in a series of parts (Cmd 3192, 1928, Cmd 3401, 1929, etc.); Standing Commission on Museums and Galleries, reports published 1933, 1938, 1948, 1954.

Treasure Trove, see preface to 1863 *Catalogue;* printed memorandum by Society's Council, 1890 (listing accessions 1808-82), published in House of Commons Report 179 (1899) (see p. 170 above); A. H. Rhind in his *British Archaeology, its Progress and Demands* (Edinburgh 1859).

Biographies, additional to the *Dictionary of National Biography:* R. Kerr, *Memoirs of William Smellie* (2 vols., Edinburgh 1811); John Stuart, *Memoir of Alexander Henry Rhind* (Edinburgh 1864); M. C. Hibbert Ware, *Life and Correspondence of S. H. Ware* (Manchester 1882); for A. Seton, see D. Selling, *K. Vitterhets Akad. Hist. o. Ant. Handlingar* lix.3 (Stockholm 1945).

Published histories of other institutions: J. Evans, *A History of the Society of Antiquaries* (Oxford 1956). Royal Society of Edinburgh: foundation, see S. A. Shapin, *Brit. Jnl. Hist. Science* vii (1974), 1-41; history to 1862, Introduction to *General Index of Transactions* (Edinburgh 1890). British Museum and British Antiquities: A. H. Rhind, *British Archaeology* (1859) (see above); A. W. Franks, *Proc. Soc. Ant. Lond.* iii (1856); Select Committee on the British Museum, Report and Evidence, 1860, xvi. National Gallery of Scotland: Colin Thompson, *Pictures for Scotland* (Edinburgh 1972). Royal Scottish Museum: D. A. Allan, *The Royal Scottish Museum* (Edinburgh 1954). Royal Scottish Academy: Esmé Gordon, *The Royal Scottish Academy 1826-1976* (Edinburgh 1976), with details of Royal Institution building. Portrait Gallery: J. M. Gray, *The Scottish National Portrait Gallery, The Building and its Contents* (Edinburgh 1891). Also S. Piggott and M. Robertson, *Three Centuries of Scottish Archaeology* (Edinburgh University Library exhibition 1977); David Murray, *Museums, their History and their Use* (3 vols., Glasgow 1904); G. E. Daniel, *A Hundred Years of Archaeology* (London 1950); O. Klindt-Jensen, *A History of Scandinavian Archaeology* (London 1975).

In Piam Veterum Memoriam

Angus Graham

In 1935 I was suddenly plummeted down, as if by parachute, into the
Secretaryship of the Ancient Monuments Commission of Scotland, a
position close to the centre of contemporary Scottish archaeology. It
was a drastic change from my immediately previous job, which had
been concerned with large-scale forestry in Canada; but on recovering
my breath I came to see a great deal, and at very close quarters, of the
methods and personalities of the principal actors. Being now invited to
write something for the Society's bicentenary volume, I have tried to
marshal some memories of my early experiences, both as the Commission's secretary and as one of the honorary secretaries of the Society
itself, thereby bringing down the scope of this collection of studies to
within living memory. I hope that, as what I have to write is concerned
with men, and not with the winds of antiquarian doctrine, they may
not appear — to quote, I think, Poo-Bah — as 'a bald and un-
convincing narrative'.

Scottish archaeology, at the time when I first came into it, was
largely dominated by three outstanding figures — one of their enemies,
indeed, was heard to say that it was owned by them in fee simple.
These three were Sir George Macdonald and James Curle, the
Romanists, and the latter's brother Alexander, enormously distinguished for work with the Commission and the Society, as Director
of the Royal Scottish Museum, and numberless projects in the field.
Underground opposition, possessing little actual power but vocally
bitter, was fomented by John Graham Callander, Director of the
National Museum of Antiquities, while trouble would also be expected
from time to time from James Richardson, the Office of Works
Inspector of Ancient Monuments. At the same time, archaeology of a
totally different kind was growing up in Edinburgh University, intro-

duced there by Gordon Childe, appointed a few years earlier to the Abercromby Chair of Prehistory. Childe's eminence in the discipline was of course far above question, but he held no place in the Establishment's counsels on account no doubt of its fear of the winds of change, coupled with dislike for his Marxist politics and peculiar quirks of temperament. Episodes of antiquarian life in this uneasy period and later will be the more readily understood if read in this kind of context.

The first of the shades to rise in the steam of the seer's cauldron cannot be other than that of Sir George Macdonald. In 1935, as President, he held absolute power in the Society, and he had been appointed Chairman of the Ancient Monuments Commission a year before I arrived. He stood at the head of every conceivable tree, scholastic, antiquarian and official, and seemed able to come and go very much as he pleased among the seats of power. He once advised me that, in order to get anything done, one should go either to the man at the very top, who was able to bring about an earthquake, or else to whatever little dog's-body actually drafted the orders and could slip things through unobtrusively, but on no account to get involved with the middle ranks who specialised in delaying tactics. His K.C.B. approach could sometimes hold up matters of major policy — for example, in the matter of staff salaries he was apt to think that anyone who had started right at the bottom of a ladder was *ipso facto* a groundling, and ought to be content if he had mounted a modest number of rungs without looking for further advancement. But in combating official penny-wisdom in routine affairs he would put up a vicious fight, and with the greater chance of success as he was known to go easy on sensitive issues. He took enormous trouble to train me in Civil Service ways, and it was astonishing to see his stored experience in action — as he wrote, say, a longish and precise memorandum, straight off in longhand, without pause or correction. His writings were in fact models, as of a past master of English. At the same time he was well aware of the use that could sometimes be made of a vernacular expression to sharpen a point. 'It was like a witches' kitchen', he said to me once, after listening to a German broadcast of one of Hitler's rallies; or 'Ye may howk till ye hear the De'il hoastin', but ye'll no' find it', adapting the opinion of an early coal-prospector to discredit a project for Roman excavations in Fife.

In some quarters, however, he was feared and deeply hated, as his way with the inefficient had gained him a reputation for ruthlessness.

In particular, he had found the Commission in a state which fell far short of his standards, and had begun to sweep it out with a new and urgent broom. Much of the trouble had originated with my predecessor, Dr W. Mackay Mackenzie, a dedicated scholar, deeply learned in Scottish medieval history, of whom Vivian Galbraith, when Professor of History in Edinburgh, once said, 'That old man's erudition flabbergasts me'. But his learning seems to have left him high and dry when it came to the running of even a small department. He seemed to have seen no need to help or advise the Commissioners in formulating general policy; and he held that the reports of the outdoor staff should be printed more or less as they stood, without editorial polishing or shaking together — a strange doctrine for one whose first duty it was to produce learned publications. I gather that Sir George did chivvy him in a merciless way; at any rate his health broke down and he duly retired. I knew nothing of all this at the time, of course, but Sir George's enemies bubbled over with defamatory gossip, and in the office one could sometimes detect the faint burnt-powdery smell that hangs about after an explosion. I began to understand why an old Edinburgh friend had enquired anxiously how I was getting on; 'I was afraid for you,' he said, 'when I heard you were going to be under that man.' But I was able to assure him that I had fallen squarely on my feet and was finding Sir George a wise and helpful chief. Nor have I ever had reason to change this opinion. On the other hand I certainly admit that he might have been a dangerous enemy, and the painter Maurice Greiffenhagen evidently saw the same point — or why should a more or less neutral observer have remarked, after viewing his portrait, 'How cruel the hands look'? All this was typical of the way in which the antiquaries waged the war that I mentioned at the beginning of this paper.

It is interesting now to recall that R. G. Collingwood, who knew and admired Sir George, once expressed the opinion that strife among learned men was a sure sign of vigorous forward movement in whatever discipline was concerned.

In addition to the tightening of screws in administrative matters, Sir George would sometimes plan a bizarre *coup,* and one of these, which failed, remains in my memory. It concerned the building in Queen Street that housed, and still houses, the National Museum of Antiquities. This building, which was opened in 1891, was much too small and was also quite unsuited to the purposes of a modern museum. Many requests had been made for its reconstruction or improvement, though so far without result; but when, at last, the Treasury showed some signs of a readiness to produce funds, Sir George caused the Society, which in those days managed the Museum, to reject the Government's offer, having, as it seemed, a more ambitious plan of his own. The possible content of this plan possesses no basis of fact; but the retailers of malicious gossip pointed to a certain very generous distiller of whisky, who had lately been giving large sums to archaeological projects, and alleged that he was to put up a round million pounds to pay for a brand-new Museum of unparalleled splendour while Sir George would obtain him a peerage as a *quid pro quo*. If so, however, Jeannie, in the words of the folk-song, 'keepit her bawbee', the proposed victim preferring a million pounds in the hand to a peerage in the bush. The Museum thus fell between two stools, and remained as we see it today.

Outstanding scholar as he was, Sir George plunged head-over-heels into the improvement of the Commission's Inventories. One of these, covering Orkney and Shetland, was well advanced at the time when I came on the scene; another, on the City of Edinburgh, was also in hand; and an ill-considered start had been made on the counties of Roxburgh, Peebles and Selkirk in the pathetic belief that these could be combined in a single convenient volume. In the event, they took up five volumes, the last of which only appeared more than thirty years later. This was the kind of approach that particularly annoyed Sir George — 'an unmethodical man', he stigmatised my unhappy predecessor. He read and amended all the typescript of Orkney and Shetland, and wrote an introduction to replace two drafts of mine, both rejected. I remember the air of defeat with which he once complained that he could think of no other way but mine of treating a certain point. This propensity I could sometimes turn to my own advantage, when any of the Commissioners — at least three of whom were taking part in the fieldwork — supplied an article for the Inventory in some quite unsuitable form; for while it is unpleasant to criticise one's colleagues for jargon and split infinitives, to do so with one's bosses is naturally awkward as well. To Sir George, however, such a *contretemps* was meat and drink, as his friends would cheerfully recognise. 'Don't I even get a mark for handwriting?' asked Alexander Curle, as he watched Sir George furiously blue-pencilling his manuscript as they crouched behind a dyke to shelter from the Shetland wind. But with enemies it was another matter. 'That man would rewrite *The Scotsman*,' one of them fumed; while another burst out with 'A dominie, and the son of a dominie!' This latter jibe happened to be factually correct, as his father had been Rector of Ayr Academy and he himself, after ten years in the Department of Greek at Glasgow University, had joined the Scottish Education Department and had finished his career as its head.*

He never let up, almost to the day of his death. When illness finally caught up with him, he used to call me to his house to discuss affairs in his bedroom; and it was only at the last, and in face of a peculiarly tricky problem, that he surrendered and told me to work up something in the office. Ian Richmond said, as we came out from his funeral service, 'The last of the great men.'

Of Alexander Curle I can write with pleasure and confidence, as he was a valued personal friend of long standing. I had first made his acquaintance as a very young man, when, having begun to take an interest in ancient monuments, I had wandered into the National Museum of Antiquities, of which he was then Director, to ask some amateurish questions. He received me in the kindest way, advised me what to read, and encouraged me to try my hand at some small excavation, perhaps a cairn which had been rifled by seekers for treasure. 'We've had enough of old 'Christison,' he said, 'going round the forts and measuring them up with his umbrella. We must have more excavation.' It must, of course, be recognised that excavation, as he saw it in those days, was largely a matter of securing a body of relics as examples of typology and dating; and studies of this kind he was admirably fitted to carry out, as he possessed what may be called a museum mind, trained and sharpened in an earlier phase of his career by contact with Joseph Anderson. Even his garden reflected this point of view, the greenhouse in particular containing whole battalions of small and inconspicuous plants, quite uninteresting to the layman, all lined up and ticketed like a case of fine flint arrowheads. He considered himself to have been lucky in his finds of significant objects, but in fact he had developed a considerable flair for detecting the best places to explore on an ancient site; patches of nettles, in particular, he recommended to the beginner's notice, as likely to indicate middens. His luckiest find of all was the great Roman treasure on Traprain Law — he was leaving the site one evening after the diggers had knocked off,

* A detailed account of his achievements was published in *Proc. Soc. Ant. Scot.*, 74 (1939-40), 123 ff.

when a gleam of silver exposed in the loose soil of a half-dug cavity just happened to catch his eye.

Although I was out of archaeology for more than ten years, while living in Canada, we always maintained a correspondence and I saw him from time to time during holiday visits to Scotland. It was he who advised me of the vacancy on the Commission's staff when my predecessor retired; and after I had taken up duty I consistently valued his advice, as he had himself served as the secretary when the Commission was first appointed, in 1908, and consequently he knew all the ropes.

The fact of his appointment to that post, and at that date, calls for a comment here, as it marked a significant step in the progress of Scottish archaeology. Their Letters Patent instructed the Commissioners to make an inventory of the ancient monuments of Scotland of earlier date than 1707, leaving them free to go about their task in whatever manner they chose. This licence fortunately covered the appointment of a secretary, and here the Commissioners showed a pioneering spirit. Today it would seem natural to appoint some kind of archaeologist to an archaeological post, but this simple view did not necessarily apply in 1908—nor, for that matter, was the post necessarily regarded as being an archaeological one. The ordinary method of supplying a Commission with a secretary was to second a Civil Servant temporarily from a large Department, and this plan admittedly possesses several virtues; it ensures, for example, that the Commission's business is conducted in a regular manner, it gives a good man an opportunity to show his paces, and if the man is less than good it gives his Department a welcome relief from his presence. But these Commissioners boldly struck out on a new line, and appointed an outdoor man in the person of Curle. They emphasised the outdoor approach in one of their early minutes, which ruled that the secretary must 'visit each county in turn, with the object of personally inspecting each monument so as to satisfy [them] as to its true character and condition'. Their first survey, which was of Berwickshire, immediately showed what this could mean, as Curle, who was a tall and powerful man of splendid physique, succeeded in recording, single-handed, in a whirlwind campaign of three months, a total of over two hundred and fifty monuments, of which seventy were new discoveries. There used to be preserved in the office a small-scale Ordnance Survey map on which he had marked his daily bicycle-journeys, with lines of red-ink dots. Again, a passage in the Commissioners' Third Report, which accompanied the Caithness Inventory, records that the secretary 'conducted the survey of the county of Caithness (whereof the greater part is desolate moorland, involving prolonged physical exertion) with indefatigable zeal'. It could have added, with truth, that on occasion he had even walked native stalkers to a standstill. Perfectly in character was the fact that, at the age of seventy-nine, he climbed Rubers Law to show me some Roman stonework, re-used in a dyke at a spot known only to himself.

At the time when we resumed effective personal contact he had lately retired from the Royal Scottish Museum, to the Directorship of which he had moved after only a few years at the National Museum of Antiquities. With his public career behind him, he now figured as a kind of unofficial arbiter of archaeological ideas, of subjects connected with the common life and manners of old Scottish society, and of questions of art and connoisseurship.* By the end of his life he had contributed to the Society, as author or co-author, no fewer than forty-eight papers, on subjects ranging from the excavation of major archaeological sites to his collections of brass candlesticks. For me personally his support possessed particular value in the years following Sir George Macdonald's death, when the latter's successor in the Society's Presidency and in the Chairmanship of the Ancient Monuments Commission, Sir John Stirling-Maxwell, was cut down by a crippling stroke and I, as secretary of both bodies, found myself left in a considerably exposed position. Again, when the Commission was working, after the war, on the inventory of the county of Roxburgh, his inbred Borderer's knowledge of the country people's ways, combined with his affable approach, could sometimes produce useful information on local matters.

Much more detail would expand this sketch to an unacceptable length, but I cannot forbear to record his narrow escape, in company with Sir George and Lady Macdonald, from a dramatic death at the beginning of the Second World War. On the afternoon of the sixteenth of October 1939, the Macdonalds set out to have tea with him at his house in Barnton Avenue. Leaving their taxi at the gate, they were walking up the garden path, with its bed of the newly-introduced meconopsis poppies alongside, when there came a sudden roar overhead and the path received a hearty burst of machine-gun fire. 'Disgraceful,' said Lady Macdonald, 'there ought to be a law against it' —

---

* A detailed account of his work and of his personal circumstances and tastes was published in *Proc. Soc. Ant. Scot.*, 88 (1954-6), 234 ff.

she thought it was the R.A.F. out for an afternoon's exercise, but in fact it was the Luftwaffe's raid on the Forth Bridge.

The remaining member of the Society's ruling triumvirate was James Curle, Alexander's elder brother and, like him, an Ancient Monuments Commissioner. I treat him here after Alexander for the reason that I knew him less well, and also saw less of him in the course of the Society's and the Commission's affairs, as he lived in Melrose, and only came to Edinburgh for meetings. His fame as a Romanist, based on his work at Newstead, is outside the scope of this memorial; and I remember him chiefly as a kind and cheerful host at Priorwood, when I happened to be stationed at Hawick during the First World War, and later at Harmony, a smaller Georgian house. Of the latter he remarked, when cooks and housekeepers vanished into the munitions factories in 1940, 'I shall be alone in the kitchen with a tin-opener.' In official business his advice was invariably wise and moderate; and I remember him saying to me once, *à propos* of the Commission's staffing, 'You must get some more education into this thing.'

Emeritus Professor T. H. Bryce had lately retired from the Chair of Anatomy at Glasgow when I joined the staff of the Ancient Monuments Commission, and he was then the leading authority on chambered tombs in all their aspects. His calibre may be judged by the facts that he was a Fellow of the Royal Society, and that Childe, in the preface to his *Prehistory of Scotland*, classes his work in prehistory with that of Geikie, Munro and Abercromby as having 'exercised a guiding influence all over the world'. His Fellowship of the Society dated from 1902, and he served from time to time as Council member and Vice-President; but my own contacts with him were brought about less by the Society's affairs than by those of the Commission, on which he had sat since its formation in 1908. When I took up duty as secretary, the survey of Orkney and Shetland was well under way, fresh work was being done on the great Orkney cairns, already known and recorded, and completely new types of cairn were coming to light in Shetland, particularly the so-called 'heel-shaped' type discovered by the Commission's investigator C. S. T. Calder. His expert opinion on these structures was thus urgently needed, and he responded by supplying a sheaf of reports for the prospective Shetland Inventory, composed on the strength of a vigorous campaign in the field. It seems a shame to have to admit that his reports on these monuments tended to excessive length, and also contained some passages of strangely poor English; they almost blunted Sir George Macdonald's blue pencil, but he took it all in good part. He was, in fact, a friendly and charming old man. Alexander Curle once described him as a 'ladies' pet'. He lived alone, as a widower, in a large house in Peebles, where I often went to visit him on a Sunday afternoon. He must have been an artist *manqué*, as I remember vividly a set of water-colour diagrams, larger than life, of the internal apparatus of a rabbit.

_ THE   URRN _

Sir George Macdonald and Dr Graham Callander at a Council meeting, circa 1930; drawn by James S. Richardson.

A figure which bulked large on my horizon in the 1930s was that of John Graham Callander, Director of the Museum and an Ancient Monuments Commissioner. I knew him well, but now find it hard to write of him without falling into caricature, while at the same time producing a picture credible to the present generation. This difficulty is due to his having possessed some odd personal traits. His background was a farm in Aberdeenshire which incorporated a small distillery, the produce of which was said never to have reached the market, being all required for consumption on the spot by the large family and its retainers. It is known that, in consequence, a certain retainer once lost his arm in the turnip-cutter. The place lay on the very margin of human habitation, with nothing beyond it but moorland, moss and quarries; and it amused Callander to describe himself as a 'yokel', and to tease intellectuals by speaking and acting in character. This attitude he combined with a rooted dislike of change, largely because he was still held fast by the spell of Joseph Anderson, who had dominated Scottish archaeology, greatly to its advantage, from 1864 until well into the twentieth century, and tended to take little interest in matters outside the Master's scope. For example, I once asked him the probable date of some object, and got told that 'Anderson said that there were no dates in prehistory, only periods'; or again, when I told him that I was finding large numbers of cultivation terraces which had not been reported previously, he replied, 'Aye, too daamned many'. It was not that he had any specific axe to grind in the matter of lynchets — he just recoiled from the idea of opening a new and tiresome window.

Another of Callander's foibles was a general dislike of anything English. For example, he utterly eschewed the Society of Antiquaries of London. In this he was probably influenced partly by what we now know as Scottish nationalism, partly by the impatience of the 'yokel' with external scholarship, and partly by the conservative's fear of such fresh ideas and methods as younger archaeologists from England might be thought likely to introduce. Childe, of course, ensconced close by in the University, was typically 'new' in this sense, and, however thoroughly Callander may have disliked Sir George Macdonald and the Curles, he certainly followed their example in cold-shouldering Childe. He was bitterly hostile to Childe's book *The Prehistory of Scotland*, which was published in 1935; and I well remember how, when he found in it a passage which said that five examples of some type of object existed, he exclaimed, in furious protest, 'It's daamnable — there's siven!' On the other hand, in spite of his skill with pottery and stone implements, the 'yokel' who ignored scholarship and took no interest in the standards of high-flying Edinburgh society was not at all cordially accepted by his Establishment colleagues.

'But he's such a nice chap,' I once said to a pillar of conventional propriety; 'I don't think he is at all' came the slightly offended reply. However, his friends were fond of him, and after his death we missed his subversive impact on the strait-laced Edinburgh circle.

Gordon Childe's achievement as Abercromby Professor of Pre-historic Archaeology has, I believe, been criticised on the grounds that no active group, devoted to archaeological studies on up-to-date lines, grew up either in his Department or on its intellectual margin. As to whether this criticism is valid or not in strictly academic terms, I can naturally form no opinion, never having been one of his students; but I aver that personally, in the course of long association with Childe in archaeological fieldwork and reporting, I found him a most stimulating teacher and generous in dispensing rich stores of knowledge, to the enormous advantage of a pupil not greatly disturbed by his occasional fits of temperament. That the temperament existed cannot, of course, be denied, and it can well be explained by what is known of his early history. For instance, at some stage in the second decade of his life he spent two years in bed, with infantile paralysis; and on recovering from this found that he had lost half of one of his lungs from tuberculosis, never diagnosed until the long rest in bed had actually cured it. Hints have likewise been heard about incompatibility with older members of his family, while further emotional disturbance might well have been caused by his notable ugliness of face.

In view of the coolness that obtained between Childe and my chiefs in the Edinburgh archaeological establishment, at which I have done more than hint in earlier parts of this paper, it is not surprising that my offical contacts with him in the earliest years of my service should have been only of the slightest. I knew him, naturally, in the ordinary social course, and found him most friendly and agreeable, but although he was one of the Society's 'Secretaries for Foreign Correspondence', I do not remember him attending meetings of the Council, nor was he, at that time, an Ancient Monuments Commissioner. It was, in fact, the question of his appointment as a Commissioner that first brought him urgently to my official notice.

Callander, as I have said, died in 1938, and Sir George arranged that the vacancy so created should be filled by R. W. Fairlie, the leading authority on Scottish mediaeval buildings, as our projected work in the old city of Edinburgh called for the best architectural advice obtainable. However, the news of this appointment elicited a furious letter to Sir George from Childe, demanding his own appointment in violent terms. I now forget the actual wording of the letter, but do recall that another of the Commissioners, a doctor, murmured the word 'paranoia'. Sir George, though deeply incensed, replied in a soothingly courteous Whitehall tone, assuring Childe that he would have been *hors concours* under normal circumstances, but pointing to the Commission's need of an architect-member. In this way the lightning was deflected, and Childe quietly appointed to the next vacancy.

Whether as a result of this antic or on general grounds, Sir George's personal view of Childe was jaundiced. For example, when security rules were being tightened up just before the beginning of the war, some archaeological matter came into notice which had a security aspect, but which I thought ought to be notified both to Childe and to O. G. S. Crawford, then Archaeology Officer to the Ordnance Survey. I duly consulted Sir George, who agreed to informing Crawford but not Childe. 'But if Crawford, why not Childe?' I asked; 'they're both Communists.' 'Yes,' he replied, 'but Crawford's not an ass.'

It was during the war that I really discovered Childe. By 1943 the situation had changed materially — two of his chief opponents, Sir George and Callander, were both dead; Alexander Curle had come round to his side, won over by a candid apology for some absurd insult, and Childe himself was safely installed as a Commissioner. By this time a new problem had come up, that of protecting ancient monuments from damage by troops in training — for which purpose large areas of land had been earmarked in the Highlands and in other scantily populated regions. It was the antics of some Polish artillery that first brought the matter to notice, when it cheerfully shelled an important chambered cairn conspicuously set on a hill-top. Protests by Society or Commission, and well-meaning general orders by Scottish Command, seemed unlikely to have much effect, so it was decided to forestall damage by a quick survey of all unrecorded monuments in the areas in question. Childe volunteered to conduct the survey himself, and I was detailed to drive him about in my car and to act as his assistant and secretary. We were thus brought into close practical partnership over periods of weeks at a time.

My recollection of the man as I saw him in the course of those tours remains extremely vivid, and relates in the main to two aspects of his character. In the first, and less important, place was the unstable temperament which showed itself from time to time. Wartime conditions in the north were apt to give occasion for such outbreaks, as the whole country north of Inverness was named as a security area and the police were consequently more in evidence there than elsewhere. Again, as the local economy was geared to sheep-farms, deer-forests and grouse-moors, the doings of lairds and the rights of property in general may have bulked unusually large. To Childe, of course, as an emotionally dedicated Communist, lairds and the police were *bêtes-noires*, with suspicion of most forms of authority thrown in for good measure. I remember very well how once, when we were based at Dingwall, he got the idea that his mail was being secretly opened, and spent a whole day in the train travelling to Kingussie and back in order to post a certain letter outside the security zone. And then there was the dreadful day when we walked into the path of a grouse-drive, and were vigorously rebuked by the head keeper whose careful arrangements we had nullified. It was the laird, however, rather than the keeper who was deemed the villain here, for practising upper-class sports and for forcing a supposedly proletarian servant into capitalist ways through fear of losing his job.

It was from the second group of characteristics, however, that Childe's true value came out, and here I record with gratitude the example that he set to all followers of the archaeological discipline and the lessons that I believe I was personally able to learn. First, perhaps, came an unremitting pertinacity in the face of material obstacles — he would work for long hours in the open, undiscouraged by weather or bad going, and ignoring some physical handicaps which seemed to have persisted from his early infantile paralysis. Nor would he relax at the end of quite a gruelling day — I once saw him come in, tired out, at about half-past five, and proceed to write up his day's notes on the strength of four glasses of milk laced with rum. A bad draughtsman, content with a schoolchild's ruler and compasses and dipping an ordinary pen into the hotel's inkpot, he would yet produce simple plans which at least illustrated his points. In the field he could call on a powerful visual memory and vast practical experience, with the result that I found myself receiving, as it were, a course of personal tuition in stone circles, earthworks and forts. And behind all the points of detail there lay the influence of a logical scheme, which widened the whole of the prehistoric horizon.

Finally, in assessing the full debt that the Society owes to Childe, I recall how he came to the rescue in 1944, when Arthur Edwards's sudden death left the Museum without a director and the *Proceedings* without an editor. He generously assumed responsibility for care of the Museum until a regular appointment could be made at the end of the war.

One of his *obiter dicta*: 'Typology is the last refuge of a second-rate mind.'

So far I have written of Fellows who have enhanced the Society's fame by their work as archaeologists and scholars, but must end with a note on one who gave equal service in the field of practical affairs. This was Sir John Stirling-Maxwell, who became a Fellow in 1892 and was our President from 1940 to 1945. Even the most cursory record of Sir John's career gives a picture of one who excelled in public spirit and was devoted to the common welfare. Material evidence of this spirit can be found in his stained glass in Glasgow Cathedral, in his provision for the handing-over of Pollok to the citizens of Glasgow, and in experiments in the afforestation of high-lying peaty moorland which he made on his estate at Corrour long before such matters began to be considered by the State. Knighthood of the Thistle and honorary degrees from three Scottish universities are pledges of his public standing; and further, at one time or another, he served as a Member of Parliament; as Chairman of public bodies — the Forestry Commission, the Ancient Monuments and Fine Arts Commissions of Scotland, and the Scottish Ancient Monuments Boards — and also as a Trustee of the National Galleries of Scotland and as President of this Society. The scope of his unofficial interests is likewise shown by his honorary connection with the chief bodies concerned with art and architecture, and by an admirable book on an architectural subject, *The Shrines and Homes of Scotland.*

It is, however, his service to the Society as President that calls for record here. The Presidency falling vacant on the death in 1940 of Sir George Macdonald, Sir John was elected in his place at that year's anniversary meeting. The result was welcomed by everyone, as he was a man who radiated charm and warm personal interest in colleagues and subordinates. This was particularly true in my own case, as I had known him for many years, since the days when I had been employed by the Forestry Commission, and I greatly valued his friendship. It was typical of his kindly approach that, after the first meeting of the Commission at which I functioned as Secretary, he made a small joke about a book which I had just had published, and asked whether my hero was real or whether I had invented him.

At the time of his election he was abroad, and known to be visiting South Africa. Hopes were gaily expressed that he would get home without being torpedoed, and would take up his functions shortly. After his return, however, a certain vagueness seemed to attach to news of him; then it began to be rumoured that he was seriously ill, and in the end we were told that he had had a devastating stroke and was wholly incapacitated for business. This disaster affected not only the

Society but also the Ancient Monuments Commission, of which he had been appointed Chairman — again replacing Sir George. The war was now hotting up, and it seemed that nothing could be done, so both bodies had to put up with administrative makeshifts and wait to see what would happen. Then came the surprising news that Sir John had partially recovered, and would be able to conduct the next meeting of the Society's Council; in due course he came over from Pollok in the hands of a nurse, and presided at the meeting slumped helplessly in a skew-wise posture in a wheeled chair. Only his right hand would move, permitting him to sign letters and minutes.

That meeting set the general form of our subsequent procedure, and to it he persistently stuck throughout the five years of his Presidency, overcoming, in a devotion to duty fired by the urgencies of war-time, disabilities which would certainly have crushed anyone less totally committed. Moreover, handicapped or not, he carried his Presidency through with perfect success, his prestige being such that even the highest authorities found it impossible to ignore him.

It is therefore proper for the Society, in celebrating the memory of great figures of the past, to think not only of its scholars and archaeologists but also of one who cared for its practical interests with such outstanding fidelity and courage.

Two Centuries of Scottish Numismatics

Ian Stewart

Two centuries ago the newly founded Society of Antiquaries of Scotland chose a nobleman as its (absentee) president and an archivist as its resident secretary. Each was, amongst other things, a numismatist, and each represented an important strain in the history of the subject. The President, James, 3rd Earl of Bute, Prime Minister in 1762-3, was the foremost Scottish coin collector of his time. The Secretary was James Cummyng, Keeper of the Lyon Records, and author of a paper on Scottish coins of the fifteenth century published in the Society's first volume of *Archaeologia Scotica*. Ever since their day the pursuit of Scottish numismatics has continued to fall chiefly to amateur collectors, or to curators with other primary responsibilities, like the distinguished Keeper of the National Museum who was President of the Society when this volume was launched.

By Scottish numismatics in this essay I mean the study of Scottish coins and coinage, and more widely of the currency of Scotland during the same period, from the twelfth to the seventeenth century. In another context the term might quite properly be taken to cover coins of earlier periods (notably the Roman and Saxon) found in Scotland, and of more recent times, since the currency of Scotland became part of that of the United Kingdom, although sometimes with characteristics of its own as in the token and countermarked issues of the end of the eighteenth and beginning of the nineteenth centuries. But each of these other series belongs in a different framework with a specialism of its own, and on the whole there is little interplay between them and Scottish numismatics of the sort considered in the following pages.

There has never been a professional post in Scottish numismatics, and very few in medieval numismatics at all except in museums. Philip Grierson, one of the outstanding medieval numismatists of modern

227

times, held a personal chair at Cambridge, but there are now no full-time teaching posts in the historical faculties of our English or Scottish Universities. Two of the three great English Museum cabinets, the British Museum, the Ashmolean and the Fitzwilliam, have medieval coin specialists on their staff; but the attention paid by them to the Scottish series tends to be occasional and incidental, the result of personal inclination, such as Dr Michael Metcalf's interest in northern hoards, or of new finds with Scottish coins, like those of David I from Prestwich on which Miss Marion Archibald has been working in the British Museum. With neither University posts nor a flow of students, the academic continuity of British numismatics has inevitably been at times precarious, while for Scottish it has often been non-existent.

In practice the study of Scottish coins has tended to flourish when there have been active collectors of the series, and to have faded when there have not. The golden age of Scottish numismatics was undoubtedly the period from the 1850s to the 1880s. From the 1830s many coin-hoards had been discovered in the course of new building and the construction of the railways. John Lindsay's *View of the Coinage of Scotland* (1845) provided collectors with a convenient work of reference, and the interest that it stimulated led to the publication of supplements in 1859 and 1868 containing details of the many new varieties which it enabled collectors to identify. This vigorous phase of activity culminated in the appearance of two outstanding works of detailed scholarship that still provide the basic material for the subject a century later, R. W. Cochran-Patrick's *Records of the Coinage of Scotland* (1876) and Edward Burns's *The Coinage of Scotland* (1887).

The only other period of sustained work has been the last 25 years, coinciding with a great expansion of interest in coin-collecting generally, and in the case of Scotland assisted by the availability for the first time of a modern handbook, *The Scottish Coinage* (1955). Prior to the mid-nineteenth century and during the first half of the twentieth, Scottish coins were not widely collected and their study received only occasional attention. Of course many collectors, even at active periods, take only a superficial interest in their coins, but competition to acquire rare and interesting items seems to encourage them to look more closely at the material, and so to acquire a degree of technical knowledge from which it is only a short step to academic study. Conversely, a collection too easily acquired and a scarcity of fellow enthusiasts with whom to exchange ideas are not conducive to detailed work, and although some, like H. J. and C. H. Dakers in the 1930s, have overcome such drawbacks, more stimulating conditions might have encouraged them to put down on paper more of their knowledge for the benefit of others.

If there is one principal cause of this cultivation of numismatics by amateurs, and of its neglect by professional scholars, it must be the nature of the material. Coins are in many ways unlike most other forms of evidence available to the historian. Physically their affinities lie more with the world of archaeology than with the library or archive. Being more pervasive, continuous and durable than other classes of medieval artefact, they are generally much more abundant. Furthermore, this great mass of evidence is not concentrated in a limited number of public institutions, like most of the historical material, documentary and otherwise, with which students are concerned, but it is widely scattered so that collation of the material in any series is itself a difficult and lengthy task. This situation is the inevitable consequence of the attractions which coins hold for collectors. They are small, portable and usually of precious metal; they are varied and plentiful; and their designs are often of historical and artistic interest. As such they are almost ideally designed for the tastes of antiquaries and collectors, while in recent years they have also come to be regarded as a medium for investment. Before proceeding further, we therefore need to look at the nature of the material, its extent and its disposition, and this involves consideration of the role of the coin market as well as the parts played by museums and private collectors.

Scottish coins were first struck in 1136, when David I captured Henry I's mint at Carlisle. At this time, and until the middle of the fourteenth century, the basic coin in the British Isles was the penny, or sterling. In the 1140s the coinage of David and his son Earl Henry was little more than one among the many issues of rival factions in the Stephen Civil War, but when peace was restored a royal issuer and an independent territory enabled this one of them alone to survive. The emergent coinage of Scotland then became more isolated from England for the rest of the twelfth century, although two recoinages show that William the Lion recognised the convenience of having a currency that was interchangeable with the English. Scottish coins earlier than 1195 are rare: they probably number no more than 600 or 700 in all, more than half of them being of the crescent coinage of the 1170s and 1180s. The voided cross issues which followed, the Short Cross series of 1195-1250, and the Long Cross of 1250-c1280, are much more plentiful, partly because of the increase in minting which went with the great economic expansion of the thirteenth century and a favourable balance of payments, partly because of the recovery of several large hoards; and the same is true of the Single Cross coinage of Alexander III (1280s). At a guess, there might be some 6,000 Scottish sterlings from the thirteenth century extant today. Of these the least plentiful are those from the Short Cross period, since although some large hoards of the first half of the century have been found in England, such as Eccles (1864) with 96 Scottish sterlings, and Colchester (1902) with 168, Scottish coinage was not yet extensive enough to have formed more than a tiny part of the English currency. In contrast, Scottish Long Cross sterlings are relatively common as a result of the discovery in 1908 of the huge Brussels hoard, with over 2,000 Scottish in a total of above 80,000 sterlings from the British Isles, and of the 1969 Colchester hoard with 490 out of 13,000. The Single Cross sterlings of Alexander III are even more plentiful because of their regular occurrence in hoards buried during the Wars of Independence in the north of England and the Scottish lowlands. The 1969 find at Middridge, Co. Durham, with some 280 Scots out of a total of 3,072, is one of the most important recent discoveries in a series which includes Bootham (1953), Loch Doon (1966), Renfrew (1963) and many others over the years.

Later medieval coinage is characterised by the use of coins of higher face value, either of gold or of larger size in silver (groats). It was also a period in which all western coinages were debased in weight or fineness, though in differing degrees, and this caused a divergence of standards in the fragmentated currency of Europe. The Scots quickly fell below the very high standard maintained by the English, and their coins are thus much less well represented in hoards from England than they had been during the Sterling period. Scottish medieval gold does not seem to have been struck on more than a limited scale except in the 1390s and 1420s-1450s. Groats are more plentiful, although between the 1460s and 1520s an increasing proportion of the available silver was allocated to debased coins (billon) of lower value. Gold coins of the later middle ages can perhaps be counted only in hundreds, but silver and billon must run into a few thousand each. Similar totals, though probably with more billon, survive from the reigns of James V to James VI, a period only half as long. The sixteenth century saw a great expansion in European coinage, assisted by new sources of gold and silver from Africa and the Americas. It was also an age of rapid inflation in many countries, including Scotland, where successive coinages followed each other with increasing rapidity as the century progressed. Gold was still very limited until the 1590s, but issues of silver were erratic, with substantial amounts coined in the 1550s, 1570s and 1590s, alternating with huge issues of small change in billon from the 1540s. Although several thousand coins of Mary and James VI exist, most of them are billon; before the 1590s little of the silver was coined into smaller denominations, so that the total number of silver coins was relatively low.

Scottish coinage of the seventeenth century is no less plentiful than that of the sixteenth, although it is very different in kind. One of the consequences of the Union of Crowns in 1603 was the harmonisation of the coinage of Scotland with that of England. As the century progressed, they began to diverge again until permanent unification finally came about with the Union of 1707, following which the Edinburgh Mint spent the last two active years of its existence recoining the old Scots money. Except in the earliest years of the century gold coinage was again sparse, and disappeared altogether after Charles I except briefly when a consignment of gold dust was sent to the mint by the Darien Company in 1701. In Charles I's reign minting machinery was introduced by the French expert, Nicolas Briot; at first only the copper coins were struck by machine, but from 1637 the whole coinage was made mechanically, although initially on an experimental basis. Although much of the silver seems to have been in the form of foreign dollars, they were not for the most part reminted in Scottish coins of equivalent size but into those of lower denomination, which were issued on a considerable scale under Charles I and are common today. Copper coins of a token nature replaced billon, and very large quantities of these were struck, particularly in the middle of the century. Because of this emphasis on the lower values, Scottish coins of the seventeenth century are probably more numerous today than those of earlier periods, although it is impossible to assess at all accurately how many turners and bawbees have survived.

It is equally difficult to estimate the total number of extant Scottish coins, but it could be of the order of 25-30,000 specimens, with the bulk of them belonging to the petty currency of the sixteenth and seventeenth centuries, which is of relatively little historical interest. From the middle ages, for which numismatic evidence is so much more useful to the historian, Scottish coins are unfortunately much rarer. The numbers of several series would undoubtedly have been considerably greater if until the middle of the nineteenth century and beyond it had not been customary to melt down many of the silver coins of commoner types from newly discovered hoards unless they were in particularly good condition. Some of the victims of this destruction would certainly have been acceptable to collectors in times of stronger demand and less discrimination, but the loss to study of so many specimens, particularly of the sterling period, which would now be regarded as legible, is painful to contemplate. The only really abundant medieval series are those of which substantial hoards have been found since 1900, notably the sterlings of the second half of the thirteenth century and the billon coins of James IV, although sterlings of the earlier thirteenth century and groats from 1358 to the 1460s have survived in sufficient numbers to enable a detailed picture of the coinage to be drawn.

All Scottish gold coins are rare — the country was not rich and they were never minted on a large enough scale to be otherwise. But, despite their rarity, we probably possess a fairly complete series of them because of the high survival rate of coins in precious metals. The best way to judge whether such is the case is to compare the contents of newly discovered hoards with known material. If, as with the gold crowns of James II from Fishpool, the sterlings from the Aegean, or the coins of David II from Aberdour, they are all or mostly from recorded dies, then it is likely that most of the varieties are already known. But to the extent that unrecorded items continue to appear, as among the billon pence of James III from the 1956 Glenluce and 1959 Rhoneston hoards, then we must admit to gaps in our knowledge so long as the process continues. Sometimes a hoard shows our previous knowledge to have been not so much incomplete as insignificant, in the way that the early coinage of David I was revealed by the 1972 Prestwich find to have been of an extent and variety that were quite unexpected. Beside such dramatic additions, there is a continuous accretion of less spectacular material from new finds which is gradually enlarging the body of available evidence and narrowing or eliminating the remaining lacunae. In time we may hope, almost perhaps expect, to attain something approaching a complete representation of the products of the mints of Scotland from 1136 to 1709. While new documents do appear and fresh sites are excavated, few branches of written history or archaeology can compete with such prospects, and in this respect numismatists are uniquely fortunate. New hoards from Scotland, or from elsewhere containing Scottish coins, are currently being discovered at a rate of more than one a year. Since treasure-hunting with metal detectors became a popular pastime in the 1970s the pace of discovery has quickened, but if the English experience is repeated, the chances of obtaining accurate reports of find-spots, context and total contents have correspondingly diminished.

Today the first pick from new finds goes to the National Museum of Antiquities in Scotland and to the British Museum in England. The Treasure Trove provisions are limited to gold and silver in England but in Scotland cover coins of any metal and so avoid dispute about billon and copper. The holdings of the two national collections and various other public collections probably amount to over ten thousand Scottish coins in all. Much the most important of them, and the only one to contain a systematic and comprehensive series, is the National Museum of Antiquities. With over six thousand specimens, it is one of the two largest collections of Scottish coins in existence today, and is particularly rich in the later period, from the fifteenth to the seventeenth centuries. It is based on three main cabinets, those of the Faculty of Advocates, the Society of Antiquaries, and Coats of Ferguslie, but significant additions have been made in the last fifty years from Treasure Trove and by purchases at the sales of great private collections such as Cochran-Patrick and Lockett. Other public collections in Scotland with notable material are the Hunterian Museum, Glasgow, which has Hunter's select series intact with some later additions, the Royal Scottish Museum, with a small but representative selection of high quality, and various regional bodies ranging from Aberdeen University and the City of Perth, each of which has a large part of the residue of a major medieval hoard (the 1886 find of sterlings from Aberdeen, and the 1920 Perth find of fifteenth-century coins), to the smaller museums which often contain items from local hoards and finds.

If Scottish coins in the main public collections are highly unrepresentative of the total material in their proportions, because of the process of selection, at the same time they are abnormally rich in varieties, particularly of gold and silver, especially when material from large hoards has been available. Conversely, the commoner, less glamorous and more uniform series, like groats of Robert II or the small silver of Charles I, have been relatively neglected. For these reasons and others, the coverage of the British Museum collection is rather patchy. Little attempt appears to have been made in modern times to compile a systematic series, and it therefore consists of a good, small general base, made up of the Museum's original holdings with some later gifts and bequests, to which have been added very important accessions from Treasure Trove. The hoard material is naturally strongest for periods when Scottish coins circulated extensively in England. These include the mid-twelfth century (Prestwich and Outchester hoards), the sterling period (with Short Cross sterlings from Eccles and Colchester 1902, Long Cross from Colchester 1969, and Edwardian from many sources, especially Dover) and the earlier seventeenth century (from hoards lost during the Civil War), but there are also important items at random from other periods, for example Robert III billon pence from Skipton and Attenborough. The opposite is the case for several series which are little found in England, such as the Crescent sterlings of William the Lion or the light silver and billon issues from the end of the Middle Ages.

There is a small, balanced collection in the Fitzwilliam Museum, Cambridge with some individual items of note, and a splendid cabinet of gold coins at Oxford presented to the Ashmolean Museum by the late Alderman Horace Hird, a Bradford industrialist. It is also well to remember that continental museums may contain significant find material, such as a unique penny of David I in Stockholm and Short Cross sterlings from the Ribe hoards in Copenhagen, in addition to specimens collected for one reason or another, like the fine Scottish gold in the Bibliothèque Nationale, Paris, which includes good coins of Mary, who was briefly Queen of France.

The number of Scottish coins in private hands probably equals if not exceeds that in museums, though its extent is difficult to measure since in the nature of things its disposition is continually changing between different collectors and the coin market. One collection has been put together on a scale comparable to that of the National Museum of Antiquities but with greater emphasis on the period up to the fourteenth century, for the purpose of compiling as complete a record as possible of all dies used and the combinations in which they are found. There are also a fair number of smaller private collections, some of them built up by students, others by collectors with varying degrees and angles of interest. Unlike public collections, private ones are of course fluid, individually as well as collectively. Their owners often replace one coin by another, either to have a better specimen, or to make their cabinet more representative. But most movement naturally takes place when whole collections are dispersed. Sometimes collectors have 'abandoned the pursuit', as nineteenth century sale catalogues quaintly note — a more recent example is that of Dr A. N. Brushfield, who gradually disposed of his other series, including a respectable sale of Scottish (1940), in order to concentrate on British Colonial in which he specialised. Others, because of high market prices (T. Mackenzie, 1831-1916), financial needs (H. A. Parsons, d. 1952) or failing health (R. Carlyon-Britton, d. 1960) have sold up only to collect again with greater vigour when circumstances changed. But disposal has usually taken place fairly soon after a collector's death, although their families have on occasions held on for generations (the Sharp, Bridgewater, Bute and Cochran-Patrick collections are examples).

Collections are sometimes sold *en bloc* to a dealer, or even to another collector (like A. B. Richardson's to J. G. Murdoch), but the more important ones have generally been dispersed at auctions and so, since the rise in prices of recent years, have many lesser ones as well. Whereas collections are usually broken up suddenly, they are often gathered together gradually over many years. Dealers therefore play an important part in handling the material, both in the disposal of whole collections and the formation of new. At times of neglect by collectors, when the supply of coins exceeds demand, significant proportions of those available may remain in the stocks of dealers. When Matthew Young's stock of coins was sold in 1839-41 after his death, it included hundreds of Scottish coins with many rare and interesting ones among them; and for ten years after the last War, before collecting interest revived in the 1950s, the market held extensive stocks from the dispersed collections of the previous generation. At other times, as in the present or a century ago, demand is so keen that good material is quickly bought up, collectors buying direct from auctions or soon afterwards from dealers' trays.

One of the consequences of an active market and strong collector interest is that the literature of numismatics differs considerably from that of most branches of historical study. Since the basic material of the subject consists chiefly of the coins themselves, any publication which includes illustrations or descriptions of individual specimens may be of use. Since collections are rarely catalogued during the lifetime of their owners, sale catalogues prepared for the purpose of their disposal by auction are a primary source for the student, and the best of them — Cochran-Patrick, Bute and Lockett are among the most often used — constitute works of reference in their own right. Even commercial lists issued periodically by dealers are of value if items for sale are well illustrated, and some of them, like Spink's *Numismatic Circular* (cited as *Num. Circ.*) and Seaby's *Coin and Medal Bulletin* (SCMB), also contain a section of articles and notes of general interest. Because of this, and of the popularity of other collectors' magazines, it is unusually easy for an aspiring numismatist to get into print, and the very uneven quality of numismatic writing reflects this. However, even the least scholarly articles often contain observations or photographs which should not be overlooked, while serious work of a scholarly standard, like Col. Murray's explanation of the Stirling bawbees of Mary, may appear in a trade publication. In recent years more important papers on Scottish numismatics have tended to appear in the *Numismatic Chronicle* (*NC*) and the *British Numismatic Journal* (*BNJ*), published respectively by the Royal and British Numismatic Societies, although the *Proceedings* of the Society of Antiquaries of Scotland (*PSAS*) still attracts contributions from time to time on Scottish coins or coins found in Scotland.

Although most of the history of Scottish numismatics belongs to the last two hundred years, it did not have a sudden beginning, and we need to look briefly at its origins. During the sixteenth century, the antiquarian interest of the Renaissance in the ancient world gradually extended to medieval and contemporary culture. With the spread of literacy, more legible Roman lettering replaced Gothic on the coinage and attention was paid to the designs and inscriptions of contemporary coins for various purposes. George Buchanan remarked on the significance of the titles on the earliest silver coins of 1565, which showed Henry's name as king, before that of Mary, and under his tutorship James VI grew up to take a close personal interest in his coinage. Modern coins and medals soon began to figure alongside antiquities in the cabinets of collectors and, whereas almost all medieval coins extant today derive from hoards, some of the best preserved from the sixteenth century and more from the seventeenth were undoubtedly taken from circulation or put aside at the time of issue and have been preserved casually or in collections ever since. Many of the items in the cabinet of the Earls of Bridgewater, dispersed at auction in 1972 but originating in the 1640s, come into this category, which explains the exceptional richness of the collection in great rarities of the period. Apart from non-numismatic contexts, such as the money lists of merchants and exchange dealers, which often contain important information (a gold coin with the name of John Duke of Albany as Regent for James V is known only from a rubbing in a French tariff book of the 1520s), the earliest illustrations of Scottish coins that I have found are, strangely enough, in Spelman's *Life of Alfred* (1678), in which some confused engravings of pennies and groats of Alexander III to Robert II have been added to one of the plates of Anglo-Saxon coins 'ne nimium vacaret haec tabula'.

By the end of the seventeenth century more serious efforts were being made to build collections and study their contents. William Nicolson's *Scottish Historical Library*, published in 1702, contained a chapter on coinage for which he acknowledged help from two of the leading collectors of the series, John Sharp (1645-1714) and James Sutherland (d. 1718). Sharp, who was Archbishop of York from 1691 until his death, had some two hundred Scottish coins amongst a large general collection on which he based his *Observations* on the coinages of the British Isles. These were not published until 1785, but had been available privately to others like Nicolson who were interested in the subject. Sutherland was Professor of Botany at Edinburgh University and sold his fine general collection of coins, including a rich Scottish series, to the Faculty of Advocates in 1705. In the same year, James Anderson received a grant from the Scottish Parliament to undertake publication of ancient Scottish charters. Eventually published in 1739 as *Selectus Diplomatum et Numismatum Scotiae Thesaurus*, with an introduction by Thomas Ruddiman, this work included a section on the coinage which, with sixteen plates of coins and medals, constitutes the earliest illustrated account of the series.

The eighteenth century, particularly the later part of it, witnessed a broad advance in antiquarian studies. Coin collecting became more popular and this led to the appearance of professional dealers, one of whom, Thomas Snelling, published a series of well-illustrated studies on British and other coinages of interest to his customers. His brief but competent *View of the Silver Coin and Coinage of Scotland* was published posthumously in 1774, accompanied by plates of gold and billon for which the text had not been written. In 1773 an unreliable English translation of Ruddiman's preface to Anderson was printed, but growing need for a work of reference on Scottish coins was not met until Adam de Cardonnel published his *Numismata Scotiae* in 1786. Cardonnel remarked that Anderson's book was now 'seldom to be met with' beside being very expensive for anyone who wanted it 'merely for the coins alone'; while even Snelling was 'remarkably scarce'.[1] Although unflattering about both Snelling's plates and his descriptions, Cardonnel used his material extensively. But his work did achieve a step forward, and not only in being the first to contain descriptions and illustrations of coins in all metals, since he added an appendix containing extensive extracts from Acts of Parliament relating to the coinage and so began the process of detailed reconciliation between documents and coins which was to be substantially completed by Burns a hundred years later. Cardonnel also recorded the discovery in 1780 of a hoard at Dyke, Moray(shire), consisting of sterlings of the crescent type which he was able to attribute for the first time to William the Lion.

Although now superseded for most purposes, eighteenth-century numismatic works should not be neglected today, and not only for their own elegance and interest as early books with charming though often rather quaint engravings. Cardonnel's first plate contains drawings of a selection of the crescent sterlings from Dyke accurate enough to indicate the composition of the hoard. Sometimes important but untraced coins are illustrated, like the 60s piece of William II (1699) figured by Anderson (who seems unlikely to have invented it, in a work so close in date) or the James IV gold half-unicorn with I in the centre of the reverse (S. fig. 299), which was figured by Snelling but escaped the notice of subsequent writers on Scottish coinage, as it lay in the Bute collection for nearly two centuries. Many of the other specimens illustrated in these early books can be identified today, and this may provide useful information about pedigree or provenance. They are also of value in establishing the current attributions of the time, so that references to coins of a particular type or reign in other contexts can be interpreted. The greatest area of confusion was in the coinages of the five Jameses, which have engaged the attention of many students from Cummyng in the 1780s to Mrs Murray in the 1970s, and even now are not yet finally resolved at every point. The early period also provided a number of problems such as the division between issues of Alexander II and III and the identification and attribution of the earliest coinages of the Scottish kings. Anderson and Snelling had attributed an Alexander short cross sterling to Alexander I and Snelling, while aware of the existence of coins of David I, Malcolm IV and William the Lion of the annulet, cross fleury and crescent types, had consigned them to the early kings of Man where a find of them had been made. Correct attributions did not, however, always prevail upon the popular imagination. Snelling and Cardonnel had both recognised that groats were first struck by David II, but this did not prevent coins of Robert II being associated with the illustrious Bruce. One writer early in the nineteenth century, for instance, interpreted the reverse inscription of a groat of Robert II, *D(omi)n(u)s P(ro)tector M(eu)s & Lib(er)ator M(eu)s* as *Dominus Protector Meis Ibat Turmis*, words that must 'unequivocally allude to providential deliverance from imminent danger . . . demonstrably applicable to Robert Bruce alone', and saw the piece as 'probably one of a number of medals struck to commemorate the battle of Bannockburn'.[2]

The growth of industrial towns led to the discovery of more hoards of this period, but unfortunately, while they were regarded as a welcome source of material for collections, their archaeological value was usually ignored. In many cases we can only guess at the existence of eighteenth-century and earlier finds which might have provided valuable evidence for the content of the currency. Archbishop Sharp's small collection, for example, includes a group of twelve sterlings of William the Lion, mostly of Hue Walter but lacking his latest varieties, most or all of which probably derived from a single hoard of some size that would have been of the greatest interest for the dating and sequence of this series. He also had four of the very rare halfgroats of James III and IV out of only six silver coins in all of the two reigns, undoubtedly drawn from a crucial but unrecorded find. Coins from new finds made their way not only onto the collectors' market but also directly or indirectly into the new institutional collections of Britain which often date from the late eighteenth century. One of these originated with the magnificent personal cabinet of William Hunter (d. 1783), the distinguished anatomist, which forms the basis of the collection in Glasgow University's Hunterian Museum. A different course was followed by the newly constituted Society of Antiquaries in Edinburgh (1780) which received 109 specimens from Hunter himself in 1781, but otherwise tended to rely on small gifts from fellows and occasional purchases until the Treasure Trove arrangements were altered in the Society's favour in 1808. A list of the Society's collection of Scottish coins in 1820 noted 187 different varieties and more than twice as many 'duplicates'.

The French Revolution and the Napoleonic Wars appear to have interrupted the intellectual recreation of such as in the eighteenth century had had the leisure and resources to collect and study coins. Meanwhile the Industrial Revolution in Britain began to create a new industrial and mercantile class whose leaders were in turn to move into fields that had previously been the preserve of the nobility and gentry, or of those in the Church or the professions, like Sharp and Nicolson, Sutherland and Hunter. Although the early nineteenth century was not a period of great numismatic activity, there was a gradual re-awakening of interest which culminated in a new period of broad advance in the 1830s and

1840s throughout Europe. Occasional attempts had been made previously to produce numismatic periodicals, but the new phase saw the founding of societies and journals in England, France, Germany, Belgium and elsewhere, many of which are still flourishing today, and the publication of major works of synthesis on medieval coinage, amongst which Joachim Lelewel's *Numismatique du Moyen Age* (1835) and Felicien de Saulcy's works on the coinages of the Byzantine Empire (1836) and of the Crusades (1847) were outstanding. Lindsay's series of *Views*, which covered the coinages of the Parthians, the Anglo-Saxon kingdoms and Ireland as well as Scotland, can be seen as part of this movement. Interest in the Scottish series was now developing fast, and not only among the traditional kind of collector in Scotland, such as William Ferguson, an Edinburgh lawyer, or lairds like W. W. Hay Newton of Newton Hall, Haddington. J. D. Cuff (1781-1853), who lived at Clapham and was an official in the Bank of England, and J. W. Martin (d. 1859), a founder member of the Numismatic Society in London (1836) and a Kentish vicar, exemplify English collectors who included a significant Scottish element in their cabinets of British coins. James Wingate of Linnhouse, Hamilton (1828-77), a marine insurance broker in Glasgow, and Thomas Coats of Ferguslie, Renfrewshire (1809-83), of the Paisley cotton family, who specialised in Scottish coins and formed two of the best collections of their time, both represented the new commercial prosperity of Clydeside.

During the first half of the nineteenth century, the supply of Scottish coins exceeded the demand. However, the existence of copies of a Hue Walter sterling of William the Lion and a gold noble of David II, based on two of the very few Scottish medieval coins engraved on the plates of John Pinkerton's *Essay on Medals* (3rd ed. 1808), perhaps points to a shortage of earlier sterlings as well as the obvious rarities of the series. In 1868, when interest in the subject was such as to encourage Wingate to publish an illustrated record of his splendid collection, he saw the Hay Newton sale of 1861 as a turning point, remarking that Scottish coins had previously been 'little sought after, but at the dispersion of that small but select cabinet, the prices realised were greatly in excess of the market rates of previous years'.[3] Writing to Cochran-Patrick in 1874, Burns commented that he believed 'Scotch coins to be far rarer than is generally supposed'; many of the rarer items that had been occurring in sales were now seldom seen, some having gone to museums and the rest being spread amongst an increasing number of collectors. Competition between them raised the price of some items at this time, like the rarer mints of Alexander III, to levels not again reached until the 1950s.

One of the most valuable parts of Lindsay's book was an Appendix listing all the finds made in Scotland that he could trace, amounting to about eighty in all, mostly from the previous seventy-five years. Although the information is often sketchy, it is still of value today not only for the overall picture that it provides, but also because it sometimes enables unprovenanced groups of coins to be associated with a recorded discovery. Thus a group of seven crescent sterlings of Roxburgh and a York Short Cross penny of Henry II acquired in the 1960s by a London dealer from a northern source coincide exactly (allowing for the revised attribution of English Short Cross coins since Lindsay's day) with the record of a small find made at Baddinsgill in Peeblesshire in the summer of 1834.[4] The first scientific hoard report from Scotland was the work of J. H. Pollexfen, an English clergyman with a specialist interest in Scottish coins, who published an admirable paper on the small but important find of David I sterlings on the Isle of Bute (1864) — still the only hoard of the period recorded from Scotland. Unfortunately his example was not always followed, although Burns published a scholarly account of the Robert III groats from Fortrose Churchyard (1880) and in his book made extensive use of hoard evidence, especially that of the great find of sterlings and early groats from Montrave (1877).

While the archaeological aspects of coin-finds thus began to be recognised, Lindsay's work also illustrates the more systematic description of types and varieties that was characteristic of European numismatic work in the middle of the nineteenth century, and it made a further step forward in collating the documents and bringing them to bear on the arrangement and dating of issues. These developments paved the way for the emergence of numismatics as a modern science with its own methods and disciplines in the later part of the century. That this step was achieved earlier and more successfully in Scotland than almost anywhere else in Europe was due to the good fortune that brought together two scholars of such outstanding ability as Burns and Cochran-Patrick. Robert Cochran-Patrick of Woodside (1842-97) was an Ayrshire landowner of remarkable energy: Member of Parliament for North Ayrshire (1880-5), Permanent Under-Secretary for Scotland (1887-92), an ardent collector, and author of three works on Scottish mining, coinage and medals that still hold the field today. He was a close friend of Edward Burns (1823-86), a man of antiquarian interests, whose deafness prevented him from following a career in the church or business as he had planned, and so led him to devote the later years of his life to numismatics. In 1875 he went to Ferguslie to catalogue the Coats collection, and in the following year he made a selection from it to exhibit at the meeting of the British Association in Glasgow. The two volumes of Cochran-Patrick's *Records*, which also appeared in 1876, provided Burns most opportunely with the written evidence for the history of Scottish coinage that he needed over the next ten years to accompany his detailed work on the coins themselves.

Cochran-Patrick's work is much more than a collection of extracts from nearly 800 Acts of Parliament and Privy Council, Mint and Exchange Accounts and so on, which touched upon his subject, although that in itself was a major contribution, since two-thirds of them had not previously been published. It contains in addition a long introduction devoted to various general themes that has served as a starting point for most subsequent study. Among the most useful of its sections are those on the published works on Scottish numismatics from the early eighteenth century up to the author's own time; on the organisation of the mints, especially in the sixteenth and seventeenth centuries; on their sources of bullion and methods of assaying and coining; and on the weights, values and fineness of the coins. There is also a substantial chronological survey of the records themselves that incorporates many advances in the process of identifying the coins to which each refers and — an important innovation — a set of photographic plates to illustrate them. Photography first came into use for numismatic books in the 1870s and quickly established itself as a new tool of enormous importance to the future of the subject. The photographs were usually taken from plaster casts which, being of consistent colour and matt surface, enabled coins varying in appearance to be reproduced in an even tone. By using photographs and casts it now became possible for comparison to be made of a much greater number of specimens than could ever have been brought together physically for study.

Before the late nineteenth century it had often been thought that if two coins were found to be from the same pair of dies they must be modern forgeries, but scholars were now able to establish that two or more specimens often survive from individual dies and that each obverse or reverse was not always combined with the same pair. The implications of this discovery were fundamental to the analysis and arrangement of any series of coins and revolutionised the whole subject. It was brilliantly exploited by a Swiss collector of Greek coins, Friedrich Imhoof-Blumer (1838-1920), from the 1880s; but it was not applied systematically to medieval coinage until the twentieth century, except by Edward Burns. (Sir John Evans was one of the few numismatists of the time capable of achieving comparable progress in the study of English coins, but most of his energies were devoted to archaeology on a much wider scale.) It is no exaggeration to say that with the publication of Burns's great work in 1887 the study of Scottish coinage had reached a more advanced stage than that of any other state in Europe, and it would be proper to regard him as the pioneer of medieval numismatics as a modern science. Burns first developed his technique of die study in 1875 on the sterlings of David I, which are so poorly struck that several duplicates are often needed to complete a reading. This exercise therefore necessitated the collation of specimens from many private collections, as well as those of the British Museum and the Society of Antiquaries, and from it Burns developed his plan to apply the same treatment to the whole Scottish series, using the Ferguslie cabinet as the nucleus. This plan was triumphantly fulfilled in the three volumes of *The Coinage of Scotland*.

The book contains illustrations of over a thousand coins and detailed descriptions of many more. Burns recorded the weights of individual specimens, noting their relevance to the arrangement of several series, like the successive issues of David II; he also recognised that fineness could throw light on problems of attribution and chronology — he even commissioned the destructive analysis of a thistle and mullet groat in order to determine how base the issue was. Indeed, only in the second half of the twentieth century have numismatists begun to take the use of metrological evidence much beyond the stage reached by Burns. He was one of the first numismatists to appreciate the value of hoards in indicating the relative date of types and varieties, and he made further progress in the interpretation of the documentary evidence. But his greatest achievement was probably to recognise the implications of the fact that both the dies used in medieval coinage and the punches from which the dies were made were often replaced by others with slightly differing features. Since die replacement did not occur simultaneously, he found that some coins were struck from an obverse of one issue or variety and the reverse of another. Such coins, now known technically as mules, assisted in establishing the sequence within a series, often with a high degree of accuracy as in the case of the Edinburgh groats of Robert III. The observation of individual dies and their relationships, and the progressive wear or damage they exhibited from extended use, also revealed aspects of the anatomy of the coinage, one of the most important of which concerned the combination of certain obverse dies with reverses carrying names of different mints. Attention to letter forms and other minutiae of design and ornamentation then showed that the dies themselves could be arranged in approximate sequence of manufacture by noting the deterioration of individual punches and their gradual replacement by others. By such means an entirely new technique was evolved for the analysis of medieval coinage and the Scottish series, ideally suited to such treatment because of its manageable size, was the first to benefit from it. During the twentieth century it has been applied to English, Irish and some other European coinages, but even today there are major continental series which are amenable to such treatment but have not yet received it.

Burns died while his book was in the press, and its publication brought to an end a generation of intense and fruitful study. While some classic works of scholarship serve as a foundation on which further advances are quickly built, others perversely seem to bring progress to a halt. That *The Coinage of Scotland* proved to be one of the latter kind may have been due in part to the natural cycle of academic fashion, after a period of so much attention, but it certainly reflected also the comprehensive nature of a work so far ahead of its time. In 1901 Adam Richardson, the Society's honorary curator of the coins in the National Museum, published a catalogue of its Scottish collection, a single, well illustrated volume, easy to use and of convenient size; but out of an original edition of only 250 copies some dozens remained unsold over half a century later. Richardson's catalogue was arranged faithfully according to Burns, but few others seem to have been willing or able to acquaint themselves with the classification on which it was based. As a result progress in Scottish numismatics actually went into reverse for a number of years, and some of the ground which had been gained in the second half of the nineteenth century was lost in the first half of the twentieth.

The process was begun by H. A. Grueber, Assistant Keeper in the Department of Coins and Medals at the British Museum, in his *Handbook of the Coinage of Great Britain and Ireland* published in 1899. Influenced perhaps by the primitive state of English numismatics, to which the new Scottish methods had yet to be applied, Grueber appears to have felt free to make capricious adjustment to the Burns arrangement on subjective grounds, without understanding that the detailed framework constructed by Burns was a coherent whole and not amenable to such selective amendment. Justifying this approach with the lofty comment 'In our order we have not followed the view of any one writer; but have adopted such a classification as the coins themselves would appear to warrant', he transferred from James III to James IV, without explanation, both the heavy portrait groats (Group VI) and one of the issues of gold riders (even noting in the latter case that riders found no mention in the documents of the later reign) and to James V the thistle and mullet groats (Group II) because 'the omission of the outer legend on the reverse is against an early attribution'.[5] Unfortunately Grueber's reattributions of these two types of portrait groat appeared to be supported by the absence of both of them from the Perth find of 1920. That Sir George Macdonald, a distinguished classical numismatist, was called upon to publish this important hoard reflected the absence of anyone in Scotland at the time who specialised in the later medieval period. He also recorded some large Edwardian hoards as well as other significant finds of fifteenth century coins, the hoard of groats from Whitburn (many of the coins from which ought to have gone to the National Museum but went to the British Museum instead) and the site finds of copper pennies and farthings of similar date from the drains of Crossraguel, which led him to speculate that these coinages might have been struck at the abbey itself.

During the early decades of the twentieth century English coinage was gradually subjected to scientific analysis of the kind that Burns had provided for Scotland, although many more students were needed for a series so much larger. Among the most successful of these were G. C. Brooke, L. A. Lawrence and the brothers J. Shirley Fox and H. B. Earle Fox. Brooke's *British Museum Catalogue* of Norman coins and Lawrence's and the Foxes' studies on the coinages of Henry II to Edward III greatly advanced understanding of their series and have only in recent years required amendment and extension. Brooke's *Catalogue* gave detailed treatment of the coinages of the Scottish border and northern counties which are relevant to the origins of Scottish coinage under David I and Prince Henry. Lawrence's papers on Short and Long Cross coins, which drew on newly discovered material from the 1902 Colchester and the 1908 Brussels hoards, supplied a scientific classification and a more refined chronology for the long series of English sterlings, to which the Scottish sterling coinages from William the Lion to Alexander III are related. The same was done for the Single Cross coinages of 1279 to 1344 by the Fox monograph. This was particularly notable for its correlation of the coins with the documents, although the problems of arrangement in this difficult series had previously been largely resolved by Burns himself in a brilliant digression on the English coins from the Montrave hoard. Thus, although Scottish coins themselves tended to be neglected during these years, progress in knowledge of the English coinages with which they ran parallel laid the foundations for a more detailed chronology of both series to be obtained from future hoards.

Along with this academic interest in English medieval coinage went a revival of collecting, although as with Scottish numismatics in the nineteenth century it is not entirely clear which of the two did more to stimulate the other. More detailed classification, however, undoubtedly led to more comprehensive series in the cabinets of collectors. Established firms of dealers like A. H. Baldwin & Sons, W. S. Lincoln, Spink & Son and from 1926 B. A. Seaby sought out varieties more diligently for their customers, and a number of general collections of high quality were formed. Some of their owners, like Lawrence, H. A. Parsons and F. A. Walters, wrote extensively about the series they collected. Of the many other active collectors of the time, much the most prominent were Lord Grantley and R. C. Lockett, who both collected on the grand scale over the broad range of ancient and medieval European coinage. Like many who collected more modestly, Grantley and Lockett devoted a due part of their attention to the Scottish coinage. Some respectable series of Scottish coins were compiled as a result, but very few collectors specialised in the series, and only H. J. and Captain C. H. Dakers, father and son, wrote much about them.

While the demand for Scottish coins remained relatively subdued in the absence of specialists, the supply was increased by sales and hoards. Towards the end of the nineteenth century pressure on the market had been eased by the dispersal of some of the major private collections and by three sales by the Society of Antiquaries. In 1872 the Society had acquired the Sutherland cabinet from the Faculty of Advocates, and decided in 1873-4 to sell almost 1,700 of the so-called duplicates that resulted in order to defray the cost of purchase. Since 1858, when the Society's museum was given to the government and so became an official national collection, the Treasure Trove regulations had begun to work more positively in its favour, and some weeding out may have seemed justified on this occasion and further in 1899, when Richardson undertook a reorganisation of the collection for the purpose of preparing his *Catalogue*. This shows that, although the museum possessed at the time a very thorough and well balanced collection of the main varieties, a great number of coins must have been dispersed in the sales that would now be regarded as valuable for the comparison of minor varieties and individual dies. These losses were partly offset when Sir Thomas Glen-Coats of Ferguslie presented his father's Scottish collection to the museum in 1921, with the provision that it should be kept intact as constituting the type-series constructed by Burns (the remainder of the Coats collection was given to the Hunterian Museum at the same time). Meanwhile new finds were continuing to add to the stock of material. Most important was the Brussels hoard of 1908 which multiplied by several times the number of specimens known of the Long Cross coinage of Alexander III. A. H. F. Baldwin, who purchased the British portion of this hoard *in toto* for his firm, produced a manuscript catalogue of the Scottish section. This fresh body of material enabled Baldwin to work out a new and more satisfactory classification of the coinage than Burns had been able to do on inadequate evidence, but there was so little general interest in the series that for some years, until the imminent dispersal of the Lockett collection led to its publication in 1956, the only printed version of the new arrangement was to be found in the sale catalogue of the Drabble collection. Although Lockett acquired over 300 of the Brussels Scottish from Baldwin, and other customers like Drabble and Dakers had good representative series, over 1,600 remained in stock as late as 1970. Among many Edwardian hoards, that from Boyton, Wilts. (1935) was admirably published by D. F. Allen, but Scottish coins in medieval hoards tended to receive less attention because of the difficulty of recording them by a classification as detailed as that in Burns, and much important evidence was probably thereby lost.

The new impetus in English numismatics during the first quarter of the twentieth century began to wane in the second. The coin market was not helped by the economic problems of the 1930s, by the ensuing war or by the austerity of its aftermath. The premature death of G. C. Brooke, and the loss of promising students like Captain Dakers and Lieutenant W. S. Marshall on active service, constrained the progress of British numismatics. Of the few whose involvement spanned the war years, mention should be made of Derek Allen, Christopher Blunt and James Davidson. The last of these was one of the very few pre-war Scottish specialists, and the other two have both made an enormous contribution to British numismatics generally. Dr Davidson improved the fine collection made by his father and brought to completion the detailed work on groats of David II begun by H. J. Dakers. In addition to reports on the hoards that came Allen's way during his spell as an Assistant Keeper at the British Museum in the 1930s, some of his other work was of direct relevance to the Scottish series — on the origins of the Carlisle mint (discussed in connection with the coinage of Henry II in his *British Museum Catalogue*), on Irish forgeries of David II and Robert II groats, and on Thomas Simon's work for the Scottish Mint under Charles II. Mr Blunt's earliest work was a definitive study of the coins of Berwick under Edward I, II and III, which is essential for understanding the Scottish issues of a mint that alternated between the two sides during the Wars of Independence.

Many of the best general collections with Scottish coins were sold between the 1930s and the 1950s — Walters (1932), Drabble (1939 and 1943), Grantley (1943-4), Lingford (1951), Parsons (1954) and, last and greatest, Lockett (1957 and 1960). Also dispersed were two of the great old collections, Cochran-Patrick (1936) and Bute (1951), and that of the Dakers (1946), formed between the wars. In the 1940s and 1950s coin collecting was still a relatively unusual occupation and the coin market, without the great generalists of the past, was not very active. Interest in Scottish coins was very slight and much of the material remained in the stock of dealers. During the 1950s a major revival in medieval numismatics took place, centred on the British Numismatic Society and its *Journal*. Coverage of English coinage from the twelfth to the sixteenth century was by the 1960s at last brought up to the standard reached for Scottish more than seventy years before.

Just as a new generation of student-collectors was emerging, increasing affluence and anxieties about inflation began to turn investors towards works of art and antiquities, amongst which the attraction of coins was obvious. The effect on prices was dramatic. The fabulous Lockett sales, at which prices for ordinary coins in prime condition were often two or three times those previously prevailing, revealed a growing demand for choice specimens as well as rarities, and the trend has continued ever since. Even the recession of 1974-6 caused only a temporary pause. Comparable coins today often fetch prices twenty or thirty times higher than in the Lockett sales. Relatively few good series of Scottish coins have been through the saleroom since — the most important were the ancient Bridgewater collection (1972) and the post-Lockett collections of H. Hird (1974), mostly in gold, and Mr Sheldon P. Fay, specialising in the reign of Mary (1976). The last of these, sold anonymously as the Dundee Collection in Los Angeles, illustrates both the new internationalism of the coin market and the reluctance of many owners to display their resources in an age of confiscatory taxation.

The huge increase in prices, as demand has outstripped supply, has had other effects. Before the war only the larger and more notable collections were normally sold at auction; smaller ones, odd groups of coins and even some of the better collections (like that of T. Bearman, d. 1922, whose Scottish coins were bought by Baldwins and formed the original nucleus of Lockett's collection) were generally sold privately. This pattern continued for a while after the war — Seaby handled the three British medieval collections of Raymond Carlyon-Britton, containing some important Scottish, which were sold in 1940, 1949 and 1959, and Spink bought the good Scottish collections of H. J. Marr and N. J. Asherson, a solicitor and a surgeon, in the 1960s. But vendors have since the 1960s turned increasingly to the saleroom in the hope of obtaining more competitive prices on a market almost perpetually short of good coins. Even hoard material, returned to finders under the Treasure Trove arrangements, now often goes to auction, as have many coins from the Prestwich, Colchester, Middridge and other hoards in the last few years. High prices have also flushed out many smaller collections and parcels of coins which their owners had not previously regarded as of much value, and most mixed sales with British coins now contain a few Scottish from various sources which are apt to include rare and unrecorded varieties that have not been on the market in recent years. Growth of collector interest in the series led to the publication in 1972 of the first dealer's catalogue, P. F. Purvey's well illustrated *Coins and Tokens of Scotland* in Seaby's series of Standard Catalogues, which provides convenient references to individual types and varieties for most purposes. But many of the prices given in it have soon been left behind by subsequent increases, partly encouraged perhaps by use of the catalogue itself.

As coins have gradually been dispersed into more and smaller collections, some of them overseas, it has become more difficult to consult the full range of available material, but this problem has to some extent been mitigated by great advances in coin photography, including the use of Polaroid cameras, by means of which serviceable pictures can be made very quickly and cheaply. Up to Lockett the plates of all major sale catalogues were still made by photographing plaster casts, but although this process produced excellent illustrations it proved too time-consuming and expensive for the more hectic market conditions of recent years. Most catalogues, like dealers' lists and many books and articles, are therefore now illustrated by direct photographs, often of high quality. Photography is also now much more extensively used for purposes of record. All the English and Scottish coins in the Lockett collection were photographed before dispersal and the plates are invaluable for reference and research. The contents of new hoards are now regularly recorded in this way, which will be of enormous value to future students.

As in the nineteenth century, a period of great collecting activity has been accompanied by significant progress in the study of Scottish coinage. By 1950 the standard work on the subject was more than sixty years old and its massive contents had been increasingly ignored by collectors, dealers and others except for the occasional purpose of looking up individual coins. It therefore seemed opportune to develop my working notes on the series, with an introductory text and illustrations, into a form suitable for publication as *The Scottish Coinage* (1955). That nothing of the kind existed on the subject is evidence of the measure of neglect that it had suffered for so long. The book was based on Burns, with a few slight rearrangements and the addition of some material that had come to light subsequently. Though it did seek to reverse the slippage caused by Grueber, it did not therefore pretend to advance the subject materially so much as to provide a summary of the state of knowledge at the time. As such it performed much the same kind of function for its time as Lindsay's *View* had done just over a century before, in providing a starting point for future enquiry, and in the same way it was followed by a supplement (1966) after a few years of renewed interest in the subject. Again very few students have been involved. One difference between the current phase and that from Lindsay to Burns is that recent work on Scottish coinage has been carried out in parallel with a broad advance in detailed research on English and Irish coinage. There has therefore for the first time been a team of students working in consultation on the coins of the British Isles who could pool their resources in studying new finds and obtaining the maximum information from them. This is especially important for the sterling period where scholars like Miss Archibald, Mr J. D. Brand, Mr C. J. Wood and Mr P. Woodhead have greatly advanced our detailed knowledge of English pennies of the thirteenth and early fourteenth centuries.

Greater attention to hoard evidence has been one of the most significant features of post-war numismatics, especially in England. For the medieval period the foundations were laid by J. D. A. Thompson's *Inventory* (1956), an indispensable classic for all its inaccuracies of detail. Other notable contributions to this line of study have been made by Professor Dolley, whose lists of hoards from the Viking age to the fourteenth century should not be overlooked because of the unlikely contexts in which they have been published; by Dr Metcalf, who has specialised in Scottish and northern hoards, and has lately produced a list of some 260 medieval finds from Scotland; and by Dr I. D. Brown who with Professor Dolley has compiled a bibliography of hoards buried after 1500. Certain groups of hoards have also formed the subject of special studies by M. Yvon (Short Cross sterlings from France), Messrs Seaby and Stewart (fourteenth century groat hoards) and Messrs Stevenson and Porteous (seventeenth century). Such work has obvious relevance to the study of the currency as well as of the coinage, and has proved of growing interest to economic historians. A Symposium held at Oxford in 1977 on Coinage in Medieval Scotland heard papers from Messrs Mayhew, Metcalf and Stewart based largely on the hoard evidence, with particular reference to the sterling period, while others by Dr Challis, Professor Nicholson and Mrs Murray, dealing with the later Middle Ages and the sixteenth century, drew more on documentary and more general historical evidence. Since the 1960s academic conferences of this kind and international congresses have been held more frequently. It is a development which, if not overdone, can be of considerable benefit to scholars, particularly those in more isolated fields like numismatics, by facilitating the exchange of ideas between related disciplines and communication between those from different countries and backgrounds.

The economic implications of coinage are thus now receiving more attention. Commercial considerations were of course a major influence on the location of mints. Carlisle, the cradle of Scottish coinage, had a mint to convert silver from the Cumbrian mines; Roxburgh's status as the principal, indeed sometimes the only mint, of William the Lion and Alexander II must have been due in part to its annual fair; and its replacement by Berwick from 1250 probably reflects the growing importance of the major wool port in the north-east of Britain. But such factors were not the only ones which determined the choice of mint towns. A royal residence (Kinghorn for Alexander III), a new palace (Linlithgow for James I), the centre of government (Perth for

Robert III), internal emergencies and civil war (Dumbarton under Robert III, Aberdeen for James III and Stirling for Mary of Guise), a siege (Roxburgh in 1460) and other such instances can be shown to have played their part. This whole topic, and its relevance to the arrangement and chronology of the coinage, has recently been reviewed in a monograph on *Scottish Mints* (1971), which supplements and in part replaces the relevant passages in the text of *The Scottish Coinage*, especially for the earlier centuries.

Some of the other general themes of Scottish coinage are now beginning to receive more systematic attention. Of much historical interest are the designs and inscriptions on the coinage. James III was responsible, surely personally, for the earliest Renaissance portrait coin in northern Europe, and one which from its relationship to the king's head on the Trinity altarpiece poses unresolved questions for the art-historian; the coinage of James VI shows a more concerted use of numismatic propaganda (foreshadowing its widespread adoption in the Thirty Years War) than any since the Roman Empire; and the imitation of foreign types — English groats, French crowns, Flemish riders, etc. — in Scotland and of Scottish types overseas illustrates the cultural and dynastic as well as the economic dimensions of Scotland's relations abroad. These aspects have already been discussed in print but many others await consideration. The personal names of moneyers, like Baldwin at Perth and Cnut at Aberdeen under David I; comparative features on seals and coins, like the saltire and annulet that occur on both the great seals and the silver groats of James I and II; heraldic details, like the modified tressure in the royal arms on gold unicorns, in accordance with the Act of 1471; the Reformation motto *Iustus Fide Vivit* on the coinage of catholic Mary — these are a few examples of the evidence that qualifies coins as historical documents in their own right but which in many cases awaits recognition, let alone interpretation.

In a limited but undeniable way coins are also of value to the historian as records of administrative activity. For example, a highly organised recoinage, like that of 1250, can hardly have been the work of a disorganised government, however little other evidence there may be for the efficiency of the administration at that time. Again in the fifteenth century, a more detailed picture of the coinage, say between 1424 and 1484, can probably be constructed than of any other relatively continuous function of government during that poorly documented period. As well as the general evidence of variations in output, quality of production, choice of metals, weights, designs and so on, which build up a view of the organisation behind the coinage, it is sometimes possible to deduce more specific information about events otherwise unknown or unreliably recorded. Thus the coins show that obverse dies used at Roxburgh in 1460 were subsequently used at Perth and Edinburgh in that order, suggesting an unrecorded visit by the travelling mint, and so perhaps also by the court, to Perth after the death of James II. Die-links between mints also hint at a brief association of Dundee (a known mint only on this one occasion) with Perth and Edinburgh towards the end of the reign of Robert II, perhaps c. 1385 when the English are said to have sacked all three towns, although the mention of Dundee in this context by Froissart has not been regarded by historians as very credible. An undocumented and very rough issue of groats of the later 1480s (S. fig. 124) could be a product of the final struggle of James III with the nobles, when the King's mint went to Aberdeen — but it certainly demonstrates the great gulf of technical competence between professional moneyers and the non-specialist metal workers who were sometimes called upon to produce coin dies. Seen as products of applied technology, medieval coins are not without their interest. Even Baldwin the Lorimer, despite his reputation in other forms of metalwork, made a pretty amateur job of his dies. With the advent of mass production at European mints in the thirteenth and fourteenth centuries a kind of international guild of moneyers, many of them from Italy, France and the Low Countries, came into being. There is a marked contrast between their work, evident in the brief issues of Robert Bruce and the 1358 recoinage, for example, and that of the local die-sinkers who were presumably responsible for most of the coins of John Balliol and the early pennies of David II. No one has yet attempted systematically to trace the international movement of moneyers by the coincidence of details of ornament and epigraphy in different places; but the clues are clearly there, like the occurrence of mullets indented with flowers, which apparently occur in only two cases, almost simultaneously, at Edinburgh in 1358 and Luxembourg in 1358-9.

Before such wider aspects of the coinage can be properly considered, it is necessary to determine its structure and chronology as accurately as possible. This is one of the main justifications for the record of minutest detail that occupies so much of the attention of numismatists but may seem pointless to the uninitiated. Much progress has been made in this respect in recent years as the techniques evolved by Burns have been developed and applied with increasing refinement to a

growing volume of material in the various series. Because there are
virtually no documentary references before 1358, the numismatic
evidence is of most historical importance for the sterling period, and
much work has been directed here in the last few years. The structure
and dating of the sterling coinages have become more apparent as a
result of die-analysis based on many more specimens than were seen by
Burns. Except for the Single Cross coinage of Alexander III, all the
Scottish sterling series have been, or are in the process of being, studied
on the basis of individual dies. This long and difficult task is still far
from complete, but some of the conclusions which are emerging have
been summarised in chapters III to V of *Scottish Mints.* Examples of
the more detailed work which underlies them can be found in papers on
the Long Cross coins from the Brussels and Colchester hoards, while an
overall estimate of the volume of early Scottish coinage has been made
by combining the evidence of dies with the proportions of Scottish to
English coins found in hoards. Reconsideration of the hoard evidence
has also been helpful in establishing a more exact chronology: for
example, the recognition of an interval between the burial dates of the
Short Cross hoards from Eccles (1230) and Colchester (c. 1237)
suggests that coins in the name of Alexander II may have started earlier
than was thought before.

Die-study of the silver and gold coinages of the later Middle Ages is
also under way, and promises to be of particular value in providing
chronological indicators for the long and superficially uniform coinage
of Robert II. The credit for this work is due to Mrs Murray, who has
also made important progress with the complex issues of the later fifteenth century, most notably with her rearrangement of the gold
unicorns. Technical numismatics are less useful for coinages of the sixteenth and seventeenth centuries, when the issues were often shorter,
much written evidence is available, and many of the coins bore dates,
but Colonel Murray has shown that there is much of value to learn. His
most substantial achievement has been to produce a satisfactory
arrangement of the difficult coinages of Charles I, where Burns seems
to have left his text in need of revision at his death. Although die-study
scarcely seems to have been attempted in the English milled series,
analysis of the Scottish copper coinages of 1691-7 proved unexpectedly
illuminating.

An essay of this kind could be annotated almost without limit. It has
seemed to me more useful to confine the references in the text to a few

specific points and quotations but to append a comprehensive bibliography in which most of the works referred to in the text can be identified without difficulty. Except for special reasons, I have not included minor items which have in effect been entirely superseded by later publications. Nor have I attempted to list all or indeed many of the vast number of notices and reports of hoards from Scotland, or from elsewhere containing Scottish coins, since references can be found in the cited works of Thompson, Metcalf, Dolley and others. Thesaurologists should have an easier task in future since the publication of an annual list of *Coin Hoards* (Royal Numismatic Society, 1975-), in which summary notes of new finds are recorded as well as new information on old ones. When I have included papers on individual hoards it has generally been because they contain illustrations, descriptions or discussion of Scottish coins or illustrate aspects of the currency concerning them. So far as possible I have divided the works into three chronological sections covering the sterling, groat and post-medieval periods. The first of these contains items relating to the Anglo-Scottish coinages of the Stephen Civil War and the last a number of works which treat the Edinburgh issues of 1707-9 as part of the English coinage. The general sections include respectively the main works of reference in modern use; the principal earlier works; a group of miscellaneous items including hoard lists and papers which relate to more than one of the three periods; and the most useful sale catalogues of the major private collections. Further information about earlier works can be found in Cochran-Patrick's introduction (pp. ii-xi), and there is a general bibliography of numismatic books published before 1800 by J. Lipsius, *Bibliotheca Numaria* (Leipzig, 1801), which has recently been reprinted (London, 1977), including a supplement of works up to 1866 by J. Leitzmann (Weissensee, 1867).

A good introduction to the history of the subject is E. Clain-Stefanelli's *Numismatics, An Ancient Science* (New York, 1965), but for its technical progress to the nineteenth century reference must be made to the introductions to the great works of synthesis on ancient and medieval coinage, E. Babelon's *Traité de monnaies grecques et romaines* (vol. 1, Paris, 1901) and A. Engel and R. Serrure's *Traité de Numismatique Du Moyen Age* (vol. 1, Paris, 1891). P. Grierson is the author of the best general bibliography, *Bibliographie Numismatique* (2nd ed., Brussels, 1979), as well as an admirable short modern survey of the whole subject, *Numismatics* (Oxford, 1975). He has also written more specifically on medieval numismatic method (*Later Medieval*

Numismatics, London, 1979, reprinting earlier papers). But the earliest and still one of the best expositions of the applied techniques of medieval numismatics that has ever been written is *The Coinage of Scotland* by Edward Burns. Having myself been fortunate enough to learn the subject first by this means, I would like to express a profound debt to those who have helped me on from there, in particular Christopher Blunt and Philip Grierson. I am also most grateful to the many who have assisted me directly or indirectly in the preparation of this paper, but to none more than Colonel and Mrs Murray who over many years have made the pursuit of Scottish numismatics so much more agreeable for me and, I hope, more fruitful.

NOTES

1. A. de Cardonnel, *Numismata Scotiae* (Edinburgh, 1786), 1.
2. *B.N.J.*, xxxiii.100.
3. J. Wingate, *Illustrations of the Coinage of Scotland* (Glasgow, 1868), 143.
4. J. Lindsay, *View of the Coinage of Scotland* (Cork, 1845), 268.
5. H. A. Grueber, *Handbook of the Coins of Great Britain and Ireland in the British Museum* (London, 1899), l, 183.

BIBLIOGRAPHY OF SCOTTISH NUMISMATICS

Modern Works of Reference

Burns, E., *The Coinage of Scotland,* 3 vols., Edinburgh, 1887.

Cochran-Patrick, R. W., *Records of the Coinage of Scotland,* 2 vols., Edinburgh, 1876.

——, *Catalogue of the Medals of Scotland,* Edinburgh, 1884.

Grueber, H. A., *Handbook of the Coins of Great Britain and Ireland in the British Museum,* London, 1899, reprinted with revisions (Scottish by I. Stewart), London, 1970.

Metcalf, D. M. (ed.), *Coinage in Medieval Scotland (1100-1600). British Archaeological Reports* no. 45 (1977) (cited as *CIMS*).

Purvey, P. F., *Coins and Tokens of Scotland* (Seaby's *Standard Catalogue*), London, 1972.

Richardson, A. B., *Catalogue of the Scottish Coins in the National Museum of Antiquities Edinburgh*, Edinburgh , 1901.

Stewart, I., *The Scottish Coinage,* 2nd ed. with *Supplement* (London, 1967); reviewed by J. E. L. Murray in *BNJ* XXXVII, pp. 201-2.

——, 'Scottish Mints', *Mints, Dies and Currency,* ed. R. A. G. Carson 1971, pp. 165-289.

Thompson, J. D. A., *Inventory of British Coin Hoards, A.D. 600-1500,* London, 1956.

Early Works

Anderson, J., *Selectus Diplomatum et Numismatum Scotiae Thesaurus*, Edinburgh, 1739, with Latin text by T. Ruddiman (q.v.).

Burns, E., *Catalogue of a series of Coins and Medals Illustrative of Scottish Numismatics and History*, Glasgow, 1876.

Cardonnel, A. de, *Numismata Scotiae*, Edinburgh, 1786.

Cummyng, J., 'A Disquisition into the Proper Arrangement of the Silver Coins Applicable to the First Four James's Kings of Scotland', *Transactions of the Society of Antiquaries of Scotland (Archaeologia Scotica)* I, 1792, pp. 199-205.

Folkes, M., *Tables of the English Silver and Gold Coins*, 1745, 2nd ed. 1763 (Scottish post-Union coins are included in this, the first comprehensive book on English coins).

Jamieson, J., 'Remarks on the Antiquity of the Earliest Scottish Coins now extant', *Trans. of the Royal Society of Literature*, ii, 1834, pp. 304-21 (first attribution of coins to David I).

Lindsay, J., *View of the Coinage of Scotland*, Cork, 1845; with supplements, 1859 and 1868.

Nicolson, W., *Scottish Historical Library*, London, 1702.

[Pembroke, Earl of], *Numismata Antiqua, in tres partes divisa. Collegit olim et aeri incidi vivens curavit Thomas Pembrochiae et Montis Gomerici Comes*, 1746 (includes one plate of Scottish gold and six of silver). The collection was sold by Sotheby, 31 July 1848.

Pinkerton, J., *Essay on Medals*, London, 3 editions, 1784, 1789 and 1808.

Robertson, J. D., *Handbook to the Coinage of Scotland*, London, 1878 (of little original value, but proposed correct sequence of James V groats which Burns did not).

[Ruddiman, T.], *An Introduction to Mr James Anderson's Diplomata Scotiae*, Edinburgh, 1773, reprinted 1783 (English translation of Ruddiman's preface by R. Robertson).

Sharp, J., *Observations on the Coinage of England etc.* printed as *Bibliotheca Topographica Britannica*, XXXV, 1785, including a section 'Observations on the Scots Money', pp. 52-66 (written before 1699).

Snelling, T., *View of the Silver Coin and Coinage of Scotland*, with plates of gold and billon, London, 1774.

Spelman, J., *Aelfredi Magni . . . Vita*, Oxford, 1678 (earliest illustrations of Scottish coins).

Thoresby, R., *Ducatus Leodiensis*, London, 1715.

——, *Diary and Correspondence*, London, 1830.

Wingate, J., *Illustrations of the Coinage of Scotland*, Glasgow, 1868.

Wise, F., *Nummorum Antiquorum Scriniis Bodleianis Reconditorum Catalogus*, Oxford, 1750 (Plate XXII, p. 293, contains Scottish coins reproduced from Anderson).

General and Miscellaneous

Cochran-Patrick, R. W., Four Notices of 'Unpublished Varieties of Scottish Coins', *NC* 1871, pp. 283-7; 1872, pp. 235-41; 1875, pp. 157-66; 1886, pp. 38-40.

Dakers, C. H., 'Die Interchanges Between Scottish Mints', *PSAS* LXX (1935-6), pp. 202-8.

——, 'Notes on Scottish Coins: (1) The REX SCOTTORUM Pennies of David II; (2) Edinburgh Light Groats of Robert III; (3) Some James II Groats of the Third Variety of the Fleur-de-lis Groats; (4) Gilbert Kirkwood's Mark on a Gold Coin of James V', *PSAS* LXXII (1937-8), p. 122.

Dakers, H. J., 'Initial Letters in the Field on Scottish Coins', *BNJ* XXI (1931-3), pp. 67-72.

Davidson, J., 'Coin Finds in Dumfriesshire and Galloway', *TDGNHAS*, vol. XXVI, pp. 100-13.

Davidson, J., 'Some Notes on Scottish Coins', *BNJ* XXIII (1938-40), pp. 159-61 (Hue Walter; Robert III Perth pence; 1553 testoon).

Dolley, R. H. M., 'Irish Hoards with Thirteenth- and Fourteenth-Century Scottish Coins', *SCMB*, Jan. 1970, pp. 4-10.

Finlay, W., 'Coins in Museums — National Museum of Antiquities of Scotland', *Coins and Medals*, May 1966, pp. 294-6.

Kerr, R., and Stevenson, R. B. K., 'Coin Hoards in Scotland, 1955', *PSAS* LXXXIX (1955-6), pp. 107-17.

Metcalf, D. M., 'Some Finds of Medieval Coins from Scotland and the North of England', *BNJ* XXX (1960-1), pp. 88-123.

——, 'The evidence of Scottish coin hoards for monetary history, 1100-1600', *CIMS*, pp. 1-59.

Murray, J. E. L., 'The organisation and work of the Scottish mint, 1358-1603', *CIMS*, pp. 155-69.

Rigold, S. E., 'The evidence of site-finds and stray losses for the currency of medieval Scotland', *CIMS*, pp. 61-4.

Seaby, W. A., 'Medieval Coin Hoards in North-East Ireland', *NC* 1955, pp. 161-71.

Stevenson, R. B. K., 'Scottish Coin Notes', *PSAS* XCI (1957-8), pp. 195-9 (NMA acquisitions from Lockett collection; 16th-century finds, recent growth of NMA collection).

——, 'On Coins Purchased for the Museum' (NMA; especially early Alexander III portraits), *PSAS* XCIII (1959-60), pp. 245-6; and XCIV (1960-1), pp. 325-6 (NMA acquisitions from Lockett II).

——, 'Treasure Trove in Scotland', *Cunobelin*, 1969, pp. 26-8.

Stewart, I., 'Some Unpublished Scottish Coins', 'Unpublished Scottish Coins: II' and 'III', *NC* 1955, pp. 11-20; 1956, pp. 303-12; and 1958, pp. 1-7.

——, 'Two Scottish Coins of New Demonination', *NC* 1960, pp. 195-9.

——, 'Some Scottish Ceremonial Coins' (I, The Amiens Medallion of James III; II, The Maundy Groat of 1512; III, The Piedfort Angel of James IV; IV, A Scottish Touchpiece of 1633), *PSAS* XCVII (1964-6), pp. 254-75.

——, 'Scotland', *A Survey of Numismatic Research 1966-71, and 1972-1977*, International Numismatic Congress, New York, 1973, II, pp. 190-2, and Berne, 1979, pp. 283-4.

——, 'Imitation in the Later Middle Ages: the Evidence of Scottish Coin Types Abroad', *Grierson Festschrift* (forthcoming).

Williams, J., 'Coin Finds and Hoards from Dumfriesshire and Galloway', *NC* LXXVIII (1970), pp. 288-9, 331-3, 388-9, 442-4 and 491-3.

Sterling Period

Allen, D. F., 'The Boyton Find of Coins of Edward I and II', *NC* 1936, pp. 115-55 (with 94 Scottish).

———, 'Treasure Trove, 1933-9 . . . 2. Hornchurch, Essex, 1938', *BNJ* XXIII (1938-40), pp. 274-9 (21 Alexander III in hoard of c. 1260).

Andrew, W. J., 'A Remarkable Hoard of Silver Pennies and Halfpennies of the Reign of Stephen found at Sheldon, Derbyshire, in 1867', *BNJ* VII (1910), pp. 27-90.

Askew, G., 'The Mint of Bamburgh Castle', *NC* 1940, pp. 51-6 (coins of Prince Henry as Earl of Northumberland).

Barlow, E., and Robertson, A., 'The Dun Lagaidh hoard of Short Cross Sterlings', *Glasgow Archaeological Journal*, 3 (1974), pp. 78-81.

Blunt, C. E., Jones, F. Elmore, and Robinson, P. H., 'On Some Hoards of the Time of Stephen', *BNJ* XXXVII (1968), pp. 35-42 (London Bridge, p. 41).

Brooke, G. C., *Catalogue of English Coins in the British Museum, Norman Kings*, 2 vols., London, 1916.

Carson, R. A. G., 'The Clifton (Lancashire) Find of Short Cross Pennies', *NC* 1947, pp. 80-2 (3 of Hue Walter in early Henry III hoard).

Dakers, H. J., 'The Kinghorn Mint of Alexander III', *PSAS* LXXI (1936-7), p. 411.

———, 'The First Issue of David II', *BNJ* XXIII (1938-40), p. 51.

Dolley, R. H. M., 'The Irish Mints of Edward I in the Light of the Coin-Hoards from Ireland and Great Britain', *Proc. Royal Irish Academy*, Section C, vol. 66, no. 3 (Jan. 1968), pp. 235-97 (with list and discussion of hoards).

Dolley, M., and O'Sullivan, W., 'The Chronology of the First Anglo-Irish Coinage', *North Munster Studies: Essays in Commemoration of Monsignor Michael Moloney*, ed. E. Rynne (Limerick, 1967), pp. 437-78 (includes hoard list of Short Cross period).

Dolley, R. H. M., and Seaby, W. A., *SCBI, Ulster Museum, Belfast, Part 1: Anglo-Irish Coins, John-Edward III*, London, 1968 (hoards listed on pp. xlviii-lv).

Dolley, R. H. M., and Stewart, B. H. I. H., 'The 1953 Bootham Treasure Trove', *BNJ* XXVII (1955), pp. 281-93 (Caution: remarks at pp. 284-5 on Alexandrian sterlings should be ignored).

Grueber, H. A., 'A Find of Silver Coins at Colchester', *NC* 1903, pp. 111-76 (greatest Short Cross hoard).

Lawrence, L. A., and Brooke, G. C., 'The Steppingley Find of English Coins', *NC* 1914, pp. 60-76 (late Long Cross hoard with 13 Alexander III, mostly late).

Mack, R. P., 'Stephen and the Anarchy, 1135-1154', *BNJ* XXXV (1966), pp. 38-112.

Mayhew, N. J., 'The Aberdeen Upperkirkgate hoard of 1886', *BNJ* XLIV (1974), pp. 33-50 (great Edwardian hoard).

———, 'Money in Twelfth Century Cumberland', *SCMB* Aug. 1980, pp. 254-5.

———, 'Money in Scotland in the thirteenth century', *CIMS*, pp. 85-102.

Metcalf, D. M., 'The quality of Scottish sterling silver, 1136-1280', *CIMS*, pp. 73-84.

North, J. J., 'The Broughton Hoard', *BNJ* XXXV, pp. 120-7 (Edwardian hoard from Hampshire, with 33 Alexandrian Sterlings listed by I. Stewart).

Pollexfen, J. H., 'On a Hoard of Gold Ornaments and Silver Coins found in Bute', *NC* 1865, pp. 57-72; also *PSAS* V (1865), pp. 372-84.

Seaman, R. J., 'A Re-examination of Some Hoards Containing Coins of Stephen', *BNJ* XLVIII (1978), pp. 58-72 (concerned with English coinage but has important implications for dating the Prestwich hoard and for the chronology of David I's coinage).

Scott, W. W., 'The Use of Money in Scotland, 1124-1230', *Scottish Historical Review*, October 1979.

Shirley-Fox, J. S., 'An Unpublished Halfpenny of John Baliol', *BNJ* XXII (1934-7), p. 191, but see also *BNJ* XIV (1917), p. 226, where R. Carlyon-Britton published the first St Andrews halfpenny.

Stewart, I., 'An Uncertain Mint of David I', *BNJ* XXIX (1958-9), pp. 293-6 (Carlisle).

——, 'A Twelfth Century Scottish Sterling from Annandale', *TDGNHAS*, vol. 49, 1972, pp. 116-17 (Cross fleury, group II).

——, 'An Eighteenth Century Manx Find of Early Scottish Sterlings', *BNJ* XXXIII (1964), pp. 48-56.

——, 'Some German Coins overstruck with Sterling Types', Berghaus Festschrift (forthcoming) (crescent sterling of Roxburgh overstruck on denar of Duisburg).

——, 'The Burial Date of the Eccles Hoard', *NC* (forthcoming) (discusses Short Cross Chronology).

——, 'Double Moneyers' Names on Early Scottish Pennies', *BNJ* XXVII (1952-4), pp. 276-80.

——, 'A Hoard of English Short Cross Coins from the Aegean', *Coin Hoards*, V (1979).

——, 'The Burial Date of the Eccles Hoard', *NC* 1980, pp. 194-7 (with comments on the chronology of the Short Cross coins of William I and Alexander II).

——, 'The Long Voided Cross Sterlings of Alexander III Illustrated by Burns', *BNJ* XXXIX (1970), pp. 67-77.

——, 'The Scottish Element' in the 1969 Colchester hoard, *BNJ* XLIV (1974), pp. 65-72.

——, 'The Brussels Hoard: Mr Baldwin's Arrangement of the Scottish Coins', *BNJ* XXIX (1958-9), pp. 91-7.

——, 'Some Edwardian Hoards from Scotland', *NC* 1973, pp. 134-43.

——, (Scottish coins in) R. H. M. Dolley, 'The Dover Hoard', *BNJ* XXVIII (1955-7), pp. 160-2.

——, 'The Volume of Early Scottish Coinage', *CIMS*, pp. 65-72.

Walters, F. A., 'A Coin of Prince Henry of Scotland as Earl of Carlisle, in the Reign of Stephen', *BNJ* XII (1916), pp. 31-7.

Woodhead, P., and Stewart, I., 'The Renfrew Treasure Trove, 1963' (Alexander III to Robert I), *BNJ* XXXV (1966), pp. 128-47.

Woodhead, P., Stewart I., and Tatler, G., 'The Loch Doon Treasure Trove, 1966', *BNJ* XXXVIII (1969), pp. 31-49 (46 Scottish in Edwardian hoard from 1330s).

Vaux, W. S. W., 'Some Notes on the Eccles Find of Silver Coins', *NC* 1865, pp. 219-54 (major Short Cross hoard).

Yvon, J., 'Esterlins à la Croix Courte dans les trésors français de la fin du XIIe et de la première moitié du XIIIe siècle', *BNJ* XXXIX (1970), pp. 24-60.

Later Middle Ages

Allen, D. F., 'An Irish Find of Forged Scottish Coins', *BNJ* XXVI (1949-51), pp. 90-91 (Pettigo hoard, 14th century).

Archibald, M. M., 'Fishpool, Blidworth (Notts.), 1966 Hoard: Interim Report', *NC* 1967, pp. 133-46 (includes James II gold).

——, 'The Attenborough, Notts., 1966 Hoard', *BNJ* XXXVIII (1969), pp. 50-83 (includes Robert III pence and halfpence).

Burnett, C. J., 'The Act of 1471 and its effect on the Royal Arms of Scotland', *PSAS* CV (1970-71), pp. 312-15 (cites unicorns).

Burns, E., 'Descriptive Notice of the Coins in the Fortrose Hoard, with Notes on the Corresponding Gold Coinage of Scotland', *PSAS* XIV (1879-80), pp. 186-219 (Robert III groats; with note of discovery by W. S. Geddie and J. R. Findlay, pp. 182-6).

Dakers, C. H., 'Two Unpublished Groats of James I', *PSAS* LXXI (1936-7), p. 90.

Dakers, H. J., 'TRACIA for GRACIA on Groats of James I', *PSAS* LXXI (1936-7), p. 413.

Davidson, J., 'Distinguishing Marks on the Later Issues of David II', *BNJ* XXVI (1949-51), pp. 155-63.

Gallagher, C., 'Neglected documentary evidence for the currency of Fourteenth Century Scottish Coins in N.E. Ireland', *BNJ* XXXVI (1967), pp. 93-5.

Gilbert, J. M., 'The usual money of Scotland and exchange rates against foreign coin', *CIMS*, pp. 131-53.

Jenkins, G. K., 'The Skipton Treasure Trove', *NC* 1947, pp. 253-7 (Robert III pennies).

Macdonald, Sir G., 'The Mint of Crosraguel Abbey', *NC* 1919, pp. 269-311.

——, 'A Hoard of Coins Found at Perth', *NC* 1921, pp. 294-316 (great hoard ending with James IV).

——, 'A Hoard of Coins found in Linlithgowshire', *PSAS* LVI (1921-2), pp. 321-4 (Whitburn; Groats of James II-III).

Mackenzie, T., 'Notice of a Collection of Groats of Robert III of Scotland', *NC* 1884, pp. 189-200.

Murray, J. E. L., 'Hoards in Scotland under James IV', *Num. Circ.* June 1969, p. 199.

——, 'The Early Unicorns and the Heavy Groats of James III and James IV', *BNJ* XL (1971), pp. 62-96.

——, 'The black money of James III', *CIMS*, pp. 115-30.

Murray, J. E. L., and Cowell, M. R., 'Some Placks and Base Groats of James III', *Metallurgy in Numismatics* I (1980), ed. D. M. Metcalf and W. A. Oddy, pp. 180-83.

Murray, J. E. L., and Stewart, B. H. I. H., 'Unpublished Scottish Coins, V: Light Groats and Base Groats of James III', *NC* 1970, pp. 163-86.

Nicholson, R., 'Scottish monetary problems in the fourteenth and fifteenth centuries', *CIMS*, pp. 103-14.

Seaby, W. A., and Stewart, B. H. I. H., 'A Fourteenth Century Hoard of Scottish Groats from Balleny Townland, Co. Down', *BNJ* XXXIII (1964), pp. 94-106 (with a list of hoards containing fourteenth-century Scottish groats).

Sim, G., 'Notes of Coins Recently Discovered in Scotland, Unicorns of James III and IV, Half Unicorns of James IV, Ecus of James V, etc.', *PSAS* VIII (1868-70), pp. 286-9 (Dunblane hoard).

Smart, V. J., 'More Light on the Balgonie Find — the Perthshire Evidence', *BNJ* (forthcoming) (Robert III).

Stevenson, R. B. K., '"Crossraguel Pennies" — Re-attribution to Bishop Kennedy', *PSAS* LXXXIV (1949-50), pp. 109-12.

Stewart, I., 'A foreign copy of a halfgroat of David II of Scotland', *BNJ* XXXV (1966), p. 195.

——, 'The Dipple and Balgony Finds of Fourteenth Century Scottish Coins', *BNJ* XL (1971), pp. 57-61.

——, 'The Attribution of the Thistle-Head and Mullet Groats', *BNJ* XXVII (1952-4), pp. 66-72.

——, 'The Identity of "The New Plakkis Last Cunyeit" Withdrawn in 1485', *BNJ* XXVIII (1955-7), pp. 317-29.

——, 'The Glenluce Hoard, 1956', *BNJ* XXIX (1959), pp. 362-81 and *Medieval Archaeology*, III (1959), pp. 259-79.

——, 'The Glenluce and Rhoneston Hoards of Fifteenth Century Coins', *PSAS* XCIII (1959-60), pp. 238-44.

——, 'The Heavy Silver Coinage of James III and IV', *BNJ* XXVII (1952-4), pp. 182-94.

Stewart, B. H. I. H., and Murray, J. E. L., 'Unpublished Scottish Coins, IV. Early James III', *NC* 1967, pp. 147-61.

Stewart, B. H. I. H., and Stevenson, R. B. K., 'The Rhoneston Hoard, 1961', *BNJ* XXXIV (1965), pp. 109-17.

Sixteenth and Seventeenth Centuries

Allen, D. F., 'Warrants and Sketches of Thomas Simon', *BNJ* XXIII (1938-40), pp. 439-48.

Armet, H., 'Sir John Falconer of Balmakellie, Master of the Scottish Mint', *The Scottish Genealogist* XIV, i (April 1967), pp. 1-9.

Bordeaux, P., *Les Jetons et les Épreuves de Monnaies Frappés à Paris de 1553 à 1561 pour Marie Stuart*, pp. 1-46.

Brown, I. D., and Dolley, M., *A Bibliography of Coin Hoards of Great Britain and Ireland, 1500-1967*, London, 1971; Brown, I. D., 'First Addendum to the Bibliography of Coin Hoards of Great Britain and Ireland, 1500-1967', *Num. Circ.* LXXXI (1973), pp. 147-51.

Challis, C. E., 'Debasement: the Scottish experience in the fifteenth and sixteenth centuries', *CIMS*, pp. 171-96.

Cochran-Patrick, R. W., 'Note on Some Mint Accounts of the Coinage of Scotland after the Accession of James VI', *NC* 1879, pp. 66-73.

Cope, G. M., and Rayner, P. A., *The Standard Catalogue of English Milled Coinage in Silver Copper and Bronze 1662-1972*, London, 1975.

Dodd, R. E., 'The Scottish Milled Coinage', *Num. Circ.* 1979, pp. 58-60, 118-20, 180-82, and 235-6 (cf. comments by J. K. R. Murray on p. 247, D. J. Rampling on pp. 389-90 and Dodd in reply on p. 453).

Farquhar, H., 'Patterns and Medals Bearing the Legend IACOBUS III or IACOBUS VIII', *BNJ* III (1906), p. 229.

Franks, A. W., 'Notice of Permissions given at Paris to John Acheson to make dies with the portrait of Mary Queen of Scots, 21st October, 1553, and to Nicolas Emery to make a die for Jettons, with the arms, etc., of the Queen of Scots, from a register preserved at Paris', *PSAS* IX (1873), pp. 506-7.

Grierson, P., 'The Eagle Crown: a Gold Coin of the Minority of James V of Scotland', *BNJ* XXVIII (1955-7), pp. 656-8.

Hoblyn, R. A., 'Milled Scottish Coins: 1637-1709', *NC* 1879, pp. 108-37.

———, 'The Edinburgh Coinage of Queen Anne: 1707-1709', *NC* 1879, pp. 138-41.

Hocking, W. J., 'Notes on a Collection of Coining Instruments in the National Museum of Antiquities of Scotland', *PSAS* XLIX (1914-5), pp. 308-32.

Mikolajczyk, A., 'Scottish Copper Coins of the Seventeenth Century found in Poland and the neighbouring Soviet Republics', *NC* 1974, pp. 148-57.

Murray, A. (ed.), *Accounts of the Treasurer of Scotland,* vol. xiii (1578-80) (comments on coinage and countermarking on pp. xxii-iv).

Murray, J. E. L., 'The First Gold Coinage of Mary Queen of Scots', *BNJ* XLIX (1979), pp. 82-6.

Murray, J. K. R., 'The Stirling Bawbees of Mary, Queen of Scots', *Num. Circ.* Dec. 1966, p. 306 and *ibid.* Sept. 1968, p. 265.

———, 'The Scottish Coinage of 1553', *BNJ* XXXVII (1968), pp. 98-109.

———, 'The Scottish Gold Coinage of 1555-8', *NC* 1979, pp. 155-64.

———, 'The Scottish Coinage of 1560-61', *Num. Circ.* April 1967, pp. 95-6.

———, 'Two Re-Used Scottish Dies' (Mary), *Num. Circ.* April 1966, p. 94.

———, 'A Further Note on the Forty-Shilling Piece of James VI of Scotland', *NC* 1968, pp. 161-7.

———, 'The Gold Forty-Shilling Piece of James VI of Scotland', *BNJ* XXXVIII (1969), pp. 193-4.

———, 'The Billon Coinages of James VI of Scotland', *NC* 1972, pp. 177-82.

———, 'Some Notes on the Small Silver Money of James I and VI', *NC* 1968, pp. 169-72.

———, 'The Scottish Gold and Silver Coinages of Charles I', *BNJ* XXXIX (1970), pp. 111-44.

———, 'The Scottish Silver Coinage of Charles II', *BNJ* XXXVIII (1969), pp. 113-25.

Murray, J. K. R., and Murray, J. E. L., 'Notes on the Vicit Leo Testoons of Mary Queen of Scots', *BNJ* L (1980).

Murray, J. K. R., and Stewart, B. H. I. H., 'The Scottish Copper Coinages, 1642-1697', *BNJ* XLI (1972), pp. 105-35; 'A Postscript', *BNJ* (forthcoming).

Parsons, H. A., 'Unpublished and Doubted Milled Scottish Coins, A.D. 1663-1709', *BNJ* XIX (1927-8), pp. 145-56.

Paton, E. R., 'An Interesting Variety of James V Unicorn', *Num. Circ.* XLV, 1937, col. 430.

———, 'An Unpublished Scottish Gold Coin' (Late James V crown), *PSAS* LXXI (1936-7), p. 92.

Rayner, P. A., *The Designers and Engravers of the English Milled Coinage, 1662-1953,* London, 1954.

Ruding, R., *Annals of the Coinage of Great Britain,* London, 3rd ed., 1840 (for post-Union coinage).

Ryabtsevich, V. N., 'Scottish coins of the first half of the 17th century in coin hoards found in Bylelorussia and neighbouring areas', *Numizmatika i Epigrafica* (Moscow) IV, pp. 251-61 (Text in Russian).

Seaby, W. A., 'A Small Hoard of Mary Queen of Scots Coins from Co. Antrim', *Ulster*

Journal of Archaeology vol. 35, 1972, pp. 45-7 (six testoons).

Stevenson, D., 'The Covenanters and the Scottish Mint, 1639-1641', *BNJ* XLI (1972), pp. 95-104.

Stevenson, R. B. K., 'The "Stirling" Turners of Charles I, 1632-9', *BNJ* XXIX (1958-9), pp. 128-51.

——, 'A Mint Account 1632-3', *Scot. Hist. Rev.* vol. XLVII, no. 2 (Oct. 1968), pp. 199-202.

Stevenson, R. B. K., and Porteous, J., 'Two Scottish Seventeenth Century Coin Hoards', *BNJ* XLI (1972), pp. 136-46 (with table of other hoards).

Stewart, I., 'The Maundy of King James IV', *The Stewarts*, XI, pp. 138-41.

——, 'Coinage and Propaganda: an Interpretation of the Coin Types of James VI', *From the Stone Age to the Forty-Five* (Stevenson Festschrift) (forthcoming).

Thompson, J. D. A., 'Two Ships from Sixteenth-century Coins', *Mariner's Mirror* vol. 39, no. 1 (Feb. 1953), pp. 57-8.

Truckell, A. E., 'Foreign Coins in a 16th Century Scottish Town', *Num. Circ.* 1971, p. 16.

Woolf, N., 'The Sovereign Remedy: Touch-Pieces and the King's Evil', *BNJ* XLIX (1979), pp. 99-121.

Auction Sale Catalogues of Principal Collections

(Note: unless otherwise stated, all collections were sold in London, by Sotheby before and by Glendining after 1937.)

Addison, R., 3-8 Dec. 1855 (good general sale, with over 400 Scottish; many from Pembroke and Thomas).

Antiquaries, Society of, 'Advocates Duplicates', Edinburgh, Dowell, 22 April 1873 and 5-6 June 1874; 16-18 Jan. 1900 (mostly early, with 28 gold of James I-II).

Bridgewater House (formed by Earls of Bridgewater in 17th and 18th centuries and including many 16th and 17th century varieties), Sotheby, 15-16 June 1972.

Brushfield, A. N., 28 March 1940 (unique halfgroat of James IV, lot 50).

Burns, E., 17-18 Dec. 1869 (catalogued by vendor).

Bute, Marquess of, Sotheby, 11 June 1951 (important 18-19th-century collection).

Carfrae, R., 8 July 1901 (select series).

Christmas, Rev. H., 1 Feb. 1864 (poor catalogue of a good collection without gold).

Cochran-Patrick, R. W., 30-31 March 1936 (major 19th-century collection; a few miscellaneous and duplicates were sold later, Sotheby, 9 Dec. 1957, lots 126-155; the medals were sold by Sotheby on 8 Nov. 1949).

Cuff, J. D., 8 June-4 July 1854 (part of lavish British collection).

Dakers, H. J. (and Capt. C. H., joint collection), 8-9 Oct. 1946 (important specialist series, inadequately catalogued).

Drabble, G. C., 4-6 July 1939 and 13-14 Dec. 1943 (good British general collection, with extensive series from Brussels hoard).

Duncan, Mrs M. (Aberdeen), 5 July 1972 (sold anonymously; lots 254-332).

(Fay, S. P.), 'Dundee Collection', Los Angeles, Spink with Bowers and Ruddy Inc., 19 Feb. 1976 (strong in coins of Mary).

Ferguson, W., 14-15 July 1851 (extensive series of collector who advised Lindsay).

Ford, J. K., 12-18 June 1884 (strong Scottish section, known to Burns).

Grantley, Lord, part V, 18 May 1944 (Scottish part of great universal collection); there were some Scottish in his earlier sale of gold coins, part I, 29 Nov. 1943.

Hay Newton, W. W., 18 March 1861 (many of his coins had gone to NMA).

Hird, H., Glendining and Spink, 6 March 1974 (sold anonymously; personal Scottish gold collection of Ashmolean benefactor).

Larsen, L. V. (of Coshocton, Ohio), 1 Nov. 1972 (English collection, with illustrations of good Edinburgh series of Anne).

Lindsay, J., 14 Aug. 1867 (over 600 coins in all metals; strong in groats of David II-James III).

Lingford, H. M., part I, 24-6 Oct. 1950 (major collection of crown-sized coins, with a few Scottish); part II, 20-21 June 1951 (excellent, specialist series of James VI and I).

Lockett, R. C., part I, 18-19 June and part II, 26 Oct. 1960 (major 20th-century collection); numbered parts V and XI of whole sale.

Mackenzie, Sheriff T., Chapman, Edinburgh, 14 March 1883 (well catalogued by Burns) and Sotheby, 21-2 February 1921 (extensive series of variable quality, poorly catalogued).

Mann, A., 29 Oct. 1917 (good general collection).

Marshall, Lieut. W. S., 29 April 1946 (several from Drabble and Grantley).

Marsham, Hon. R., 19-26 Nov. 1888 (good Scottish section).

Martin, Rev. J. W., 23 May 1859 (discriminating collector of means; had David noble).

Murdoch, J. G., 11-13 May 1903 (rich series, much drawn from A. B. Richardson and S. Addington) and 14-16 Dec. 1904.

Napier, D. S., 30 May 1956 (included unique halfpenny of James III, in lot 218).

Oman, Sir Charles, Christie, 31 Oct. 1972 (general British collection of distinguished historian and son, C. C. Oman).

Parsons, H. A., 28 Oct.-1 Nov. 1929 (James VI-Anne only) and 11-13 May 1954 (important British general collection, with strong Scots silver).

Pegg, H., Spink & Son Ltd, no. 11, 8-9 Oct. 1980 (interesting Scottish within good general British collection; lot 697 James II Edinburgh penny, class D).

Pollexfen, Rev. J. H., 26-28 June 1900 (important student's series; many now in Royal Scottish Museum, especially Mary gold).

Roth, B., part II, 14-17 Oct. 1918 (Scottish section includes many from Carfrae and Murdoch).

Ryan, V. J. E., part I, 28-30 June 1950 (English and Scottish gold); part II, 22-24 Jan. 1952 (silver).

Sinkler, W. (Philadelphia), 24-25 Feb. 1960 (good small selection of Scots).

Walters, F. A., 24-27 Oct. 1932 (lot 628, David II Edinburgh halfpenny probably genuine and unique).

Wills, R. D., 6-8 Dec. 1938 (gold only, investment collection).

Wingate, J., 29 Nov.-1 Dec. 1875 (superb series published in Wingate's *Illustrations*).

The Arms of the Society of Antiquaries of Scotland

Charles J. Burnett

On 13 February 1781 the following resolution was passed at a meeting of the Society: 'Moved by the Earl of Buchan, and agreed to, that the Secretary do construct an armorial Bearing for the Society; when he produced a Painting of one, with a Blazon, or description thereof in writing, which was approved of'. In asking the Secretary, James Cummyng, to produce a coat of Arms, the members were aware that Cummyng was also Lyon Clerk Depute at the Court of the Lord Lyon. At that time Lyon Court had more officials than today. Apart from the Lord Lyon and Lyon Clerk, there was a Lyon Depute, a Lyon Clerk Depute, six Heralds and six Pursuivants; the Deputes actually carried out the bulk of Lyon Court work, and the Lord Lyon and Lyon Clerk held sinecures, Lyon appearing only on ceremonial occasions.

The sequence of events concerning the granting of Arms to the Society is worth recording because it gives an insight into the rather casual manner in which Scottish heraldry was administered during the late eighteenth and early nineteenth centuries.

The Arms which Cummyng devised, lacking any evidence to the contrary, must have been what the Society now uses, i.e. 'Azure, a saltire Argent between an imperial crown in chief and a thistle in base Proper, all within a double tressure flory counter flory Or'. As Lyon Clerk Depute, Cummyng should have been familiar with Arms previously granted in Scotland to national institutions. There were four grants of Arms he might have looked at as models:

(a) The Company of Linen Manufacturers in Scotland. Arms granted 1694, viz: Azure a saltire Argent and in a chief of the second a cross of St George Gules.

Fig. 1. Medal design by Andrew Bell which appeared on the title page of Smellie's *Account of the Institution & Progress of the Society of Antiquaries of Scotland,* published Edinburgh 1782.

Fig. 2. Detail from the reverse of the medal showing the Arms devised by James Cummyng.

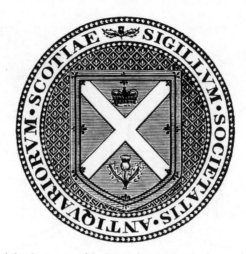

Fig. 3. Version of the Society seal bearing the Arms which was first used on the title page of *Archaeologia Scotica,* Volume One, published in 1831. It is likely that the size and style of this seal was based on the seal used by the Society of Antiquaries of London on the title page of *Archaeologia.*

(b) The Company of Scotland Trading to Africa and the Indies. Arms granted 1696, viz: Azure a saltire Argent between in chief a sailing ship, flagged of Scotland, in base a Peruvian sheep, flanked dexter by a camel and sinister by an elephant, all proper, the first two of these loaded and the last bearing a turret of the second.

(c) The Colony of Caledonia. Arms granted 1698, viz: Azure on a saltire Argent between a ship under sail flagged of Scotland in chief proper, a Peruvian sheep in base, a camel on the dexter and an elephant on the sinister both proper, the first two of these loaded and the last bearing a turret Argent, an escutcheon Gules charged with a thistle head crowned Or.

(d) The Bank of Scotland. Arms in use 1701, recorded 1849, viz: Azure a saltire Argent between four besants.

In each case the saltire or St Andrew's cross forms the main charge with appropriate minor charges to differentiate the Arms. Cummyng followed this precedent and used the saltire as the basis for the Society's Arms. When he considered appropriate lesser charges to differentiate the saltire, his choice of a thistle, the other well-used national symbol, is understandable. However, the other two charges, a crown and the double tressure flory counter-flory are much more significant, particularly the latter.

The double tressure has always been associated with the Scottish royal Arms; its use in heraldry has been restricted to the Scottish royal house or to those Scottish families with a close royal connection. The double tressure has also been granted as an augmentation, indicating royal favour or gratitude for services to the royal house. This has always been considered the reason why Aberdeen and Perth are the only Scottish burghs with double tressures in their Arms. For Cummyng, an official of Lyon Court, to suggest the inclusion of the double tressure meant that he was hoping the Society would have a close connection with the reigning royal house. The use of the crown, an additional royal symbol, would reinforce this hope.

The office bearers of the Society were anxious to obtain a royal charter of incorporation. This had been discussed by members at a very early stage, and suggested drafts were considered. A letter from Cummyng to Buchan the following month, dated 19 March 1781, is revealing: 'Two things seem to be necessary or desirable in [the Charter]. The one that the Society be designed Royal the other that where power is given as usual to have and use a Seal, that the blazoning or description of the Arms should be particularly mentioned and this which is accounted a very great favour, though of nominal value only, is termed in herauldic language a special concession in contradistinction to a general concession of Arms. The motto is not yet chosen.'

This shows that Cummyng at least hoped the charter would make the incorporation the Royal Society of Antiquaries of Scotland — hence his choice of royal charges for the Arms — and it also shows his disregard of Scottish heraldic law. One of the unfortunate aspects of heraldry through the ages has been the tendency of those engaged in its administration to wrap up the science in mumbo-jumbo to increase their own learned status. Cummyng is guilty of this in his letter; knowing that the Earl of Buchan was no heraldic scholar, he quotes a meaningless phrase. Under Scottish law the Lord Lyon, albeit in the name of the Sovereign, is the only person authorised to grant Arms. To incorporate the grant of Arms in the royal charter was irregular and a deliberate attempt to bypass the Lord Lyon. In 1781 the Lord Lyon was John Hooke Campbell of Bangeston, who did not concern himself with the day-to-day running of Lyon Court. Nevertheless Cummyng and Buchan, on behalf of the Society, should have petitioned the Lord Lyon for Arms, but it is most unlikely that the double tressure would have been granted. By seeking Arms through the royal charter, Cummyng showed himself conscious of this, and with the best of intentions was anxious to have royal status shown heraldically. The letter also reveals that it was Cummyng's intention to have a motto as part of the Arms, though nothing came of this.

On 3 April 1781 a draft charter was presented to members of the Society, and though no copy is extant it presumably contained the blazon of Arms devised by Cummyng. The Society now regarded the Arms as being as good as granted because in May 1782 William Smellie published his *Account of the Institution and Progress of the Society of Antiquaries of Scotland.* The title page contained an engraving by Artist Associate Andrew Bell of a suggested medal design featuring the profile of the Earl of Buchan on the obverse, and on the reverse a unicorn couchant, set in the Meadows with the skyline of Edinburgh behind, holding an oval shield bearing the suggested coat of Arms. (The Lord Lyon would have been within his rights to confiscate all copies of Smellie's book.)

The problems associated with obtaining the royal charter are dealt with more fully elsewhere in this volume. Suffice it to say that Buchan and Cummyng signed a petition on 21 May 1782 requesting the charter, and no mention of Arms was made. Almost a year later the royal warrant authorising the charter passed the Privy Seal on 29 March 1783, and this contained the blazon of Arms suggested by the Secretary. Unfortunately no authority was given for the word 'Royal' to appear as part of the title, presumably to the disappointment of Cummyng. Ignorance of Scottish heraldic law is again evident, as the various officials should have consulted the Lord Lyon for an opinion on the procedure.

One month later the royal charter was sealed in Edinburgh, on 6 May 1783, and thereafter the Society used the Arms on its official seal. In gratitude for his efforts, members voted that Lord Buchan should be presented with a medal bearing his likeness. The suggestion could scarcely have surprised Buchan, as Bell had produced the design during the previous year. The following year Buchan intimated that he had sat for Tassie in London so that a portrait could be modelled, but the medal was never struck, due to lack of finance.

From 1783 until 1827, the irregularly obtained Arms of the Society were borne on the seal. The earlier connection between the Society and Lyon Court was re-established when Edward Drummond Hay became

Secretary. At that time Drummond Hay was also Lyon Clerk, and the Society's minutes show him using his double role to correct the anomalous heraldic position of the Society.

In August 1827, Drummond Hay had been instructed to arrange for a diploma of membership to be engraved, which was to be sold to members for 5/-. The diploma was to be stamped with the Society seal as proof of its authenticity. In checking the seal the new Secretary noticed that the wording did not correspond with the royal charter. The seal was inscribed 'Antiquariorum Scoticorum Societat[is] Sigillum' instead of 'Scotiae', and on looking through Lyon Court records Drummond Hay realised 'that neither were the Armorial Ensigns given therein Matriculated, *as occurring to the Statues of the Realm,* in the office of the Lord Lyon King of Arms'.

In his minute of the Council meeting of 27 November 1827, Mr Drummond Hay stated that he

> had therefore, in his capacity of Clerk to the Lyon Court, entered a Matriculation of the Common Seal of this Society, under its proper title, namely that of The Society of the Antiquaries of Scotland, upon the Public Register of Arms on the 17th of the present month without waiting for further authority than that of the Royal Deed; And having reported thereupon to the Lord Lyon, and communicated with his colleagues in his Lordship's Office with regard to the same, he had now the pleasure to state that no fees are demanded and the writing clerk had also declined to receive any payment for extending the matriculation upon the Record.

Although the Secretary realised that the Arms were unofficial until matriculated in the Public Register of All Arms and Bearings in Scotland, he was as guilty as Cummyng in regarding the charter as sufficient authority. The correct procedure would have been for Drummond Hay to seek an interlocutor from the Lord Lyon, at that time Thomas Robert, Earl of Kinnoull, or from one of his Deputes, which would have been the true authority for matriculating the Arms. Drummond Hay overstepped his duties as a Lyon Court official, and again the Lord Lyon had been omitted from the procedure. The heraldic laws of Scotland were drawn up, outlining who could grant Arms and by what method, to give individuals and incorporations the best possible protection in law. If some other body had used the Arms of the Society between 1783 and 1827, the Society would have been powerless to seek redress in court. As far as the Lord Lyon was concerned, Arms had never been granted.

However, as soon as the following matriculation had been entered, as it was in volume I of the Public Register of All Arms and Bearings in

U

Scotland, folio 481, the Society at last became the legal owner of Armorial Ensigns:

> To the Society of the Antiquaries of Scotland instituted at Edinburgh in the year One thousand seven hundred and eighty and incorporated by Royal Charter on the twenty ninth day of March One thousand seven hundred and eighty three are given under authority of the same the following Ensigns Armorial for the purpose of a Common Seal viz: Azure the Cross of Saint Andrew argent between an imperial crown in chief and a thistle in base both proper all within the royal tressure Or.
>
> Matriculated this 17th day of November 1827.
>
> Edward Drummond Hay Lyon Clerk

By obtaining Arms in this manner the Society never received Letters Patent from the office of the Lord Lyon illuminated with the Arms. It also explains why the premier antiquarian society of Scotland does not possess a crest, motto or supporters to the Arms-heraldic, additaments which would no doubt have been granted if the Society had petitioned the Lord Lyon at the outset.

Once the Arms had been matriculated, the Council decided on 28 January 1828 to avoid confusion by destroying the seal formerly used by the Society. This small seal, engraved by Artist Associate David Deuchar, carried the incorrect title of the Society, and was responsible for motivating Drummond Hay into making the Arms of the Society legal.

REFERENCES

Society of Antiquaries of Scotland, Minute Books, 1780-84, and 1805-27.

Communications to the Society, I, 1780-84.

Sir J. Balfour Paul, *An Ordinary of Scottish Arms* (Edinburgh, 1893).

Sir Francis J. Grant, *Court of the Lord Lyon* (Edinburgh, Scottish Record Society, 1945).

Appendix I

The Society's charter, read to a meeting of the Society of Antiquaries of Scotland, 6 May 1783, translated from the Latin.

GEORGE, by the Grace of God, King of Great Britain, France, and Ireland, Defender of the Faith, to all true men to whom our present letters shall come, Greeting: Forasmuch as We taking into consideration that a humble petition has been presented to us in the name of the members of the Society of Antiquaries in Scotland, narrating that in the year one thousand seven hundred and eighty a number of noblemen and gentlemen in that part of Our kingdom of Great Britain called Scotland formed themselves into a Society to investigate both antiquities and natural and civil history in general, with the intention that the talents of mankind should be cultivated and that the study of natural and useful sciences should be promoted, and that the outcome of their endeavours had far exceeded their highest expectations; that many people, distinguished in their station or in letters, not only in our kingdom of Great Britain but in other realms, had by learned lucubrations and valuable donations contributed to the prosperity of the Society; that besides donations of relics of antiquity and natural curiosities, various noblemen and gentlemen had contributed money so that the Society might be able to carry out its laudable purposes; that the petitioners had bought a house in the City of Edinburgh so that they might keep in it their books, manuscripts and other objects; but that without being made a body incorporate at law, permanent possession of that house and of the other effects they at present possess or which they may later acquire could not be legally constituted; therefore the petitioners pray humbly that it may please Us graciously to grant Our letters patent under the seal specified below, constituting and erecting the present members of the said Society, and all who may subsequently be added as members, into one body politic and corporate or legal incorporation, by the title and name of Society of Antiquaries of Scotland, and that as such and through such title and name it may have perpetuity and succession and that it may have legal capacity in each and every of our Courts of Law to petition, to enter into actions as pursuer, defender or respondent, to enter into contracts, in judgement to be called as a party, to be cited as defender or respondent, with all and sundry other necessary provisions: And We, considering the laudable intentions of the petitioners and being desirous of promoting so useful an institution, have therefore erected, created and incorporated inasmuch as We by Our royal prerogative and special favour, on Our own behalf and on behalf of Our royal successors, by these present letters patent, do erect, create, and incorporate, on account of the purposes set out in the memorial of the petition, all and individually the present members of the said Society, and all who may be later added as members of the same, into one body corporate and politic, by the title and name of Society of Antiquaries of Scotland, instituted in the year one thousand seven hundred and eighty, of which Society We declare Ourself and Our royal successors to be Patrons: By which name and title it will have perpetual succession; further it will have and use a common seal, for which we give the privilege of bearing as insignia of gentility, on a field azure a cross of Saint Andrew argent, in chief an imperial crown and in base a thistle proper, all within a royal tressure or: And they and their successors under that same title and name shall have legal capacity to petition, to enter into contracts, to receive, acquire, hold and enjoy forever, for themselves and their successors, relics of antiquity, specimens of natural or artificial curiosities, books, manuscripts, goods, objects, and any other effects whatsoever, such as they own or may hereafter acquire, and to acquire by purchase and enjoy lands, tenements and other heritage not exceeding a value of one thousand pounds sterling, and to advance a sum or sums of money to any person or persons, and on such security as they shall consider suitable; and the said Society will order itself and its course of actions and its business in accordance with the statutes, ordinances, rules and byelaws made or to be made by it, with the power from day to day as need arises of changing and revoking the same and making new ordinances in their place as they shall judge suitable and convenient, provided that they are just, good and equitable, and so long as they are in no particular contrary to the laws of this kingdom. In witness whereof We have ordered to be appended to these presents Our Seal, appointed in terms of the Treaty of Union to be kept and used in Scotland instead and in place of the Great Seal of the same. At Our Court of St. James's, on the twenty-ninth day of March, in the year of Our Lord one thousand seven hundred and eighty three, and in the twenty-third year of Our reign.

As the signature superscribed by the hand of Our Sacred Lord the King. [*Endorsed:*] Written to the Seal, and registered, the 5th day of May 1783.

Thomas Miller, Subs. *Gratis.*

Sealed at Edinburgh the 6th day of May one thousand seven hundred and eighty three years.

John Wauchope, Dep. £80 Scots *Gratis.*

Because of the competitive circumstances surrounding the petitions of the Society of Antiquaries and of the considerably more distinguished proposers of the Royal Society,[1] and because the two charters were granted on the same day, the similarities and differences between them must be significant. As they differ very considerably, except for the phrases granting chartered status and the formal sentences at the beginning and end, it is evident that different draftsmen were involved; and the presumption that each party supplied its own draft is supported by the reference in the petition thirty years earlier by the London Antiquaries for their charter, to 'the Draft here unto annexed'.[2] So Lord Buchan's own interests and ambitions may be read into the charter and its more remarkable features.

The absence of the honorific 'Royal' from Buchan's petition served to sustain the analogy with the corresponding London society which both the Antiquaries and the new Royal were consciously pursuing.[3] The grant of patronage to the Antiquaries did not follow precedent, however, in so far as it extended beyond that of the King to his successors. The Royal Society of Edinburgh was granted the title 'Royal' without specific reference, except in the preamble, to patronage; in its revised charter of 1811 the King declared himself founder and patron, but without binding his successors, and patronage is sought formally from each successive monarch. Both bodies originally wished to diverge from the precedents to be called 'of Scotland' (*Account* 1784), but on this the Royal's promoters had second thoughts. No device was laid down for the London Antiquaries' seal, but that which they began using in 1770 probably influenced the Edinburgh proposal for armorial bearings (see p. 266). The charter of the Royal Society of

Edinburgh, rather surprisingly, did not mention a common seal.

While Buchan rather vaguely but all-embracingly took as the Society's subject-matter 'antiquities and natural and civil history in general', the Royal Society listed 'the Sciences of Mathematics, Physics, Chemistry, Medicine and Natural History, indeed moreover those concerned with Archaeology [sic], Philology and Literature' (see p. 47).

The members are referred to as 'Socii' in both charters. The London Antiquaries' petition referred to existing members, while their charter, which was in English, used for the chartered body the term 'Fellows', derived from the Royal Society's usage, which so translated 'Sodalis' from its seventeenth-century charter.[4] The Scottish Antiquaries, in minutes and publications, used only the term 'Member' (ordinary, honorary and corresponding) until the 1820s; the letters F.S.S.A. appear in the minutes in 1823, to be replaced by F.S.A.Scot. in March 1828. But William Smellie's biographer placed F.A.S. and F.R.S. after the name on the title page in 1811, F.A.S. being the form then used in London.

The Royal Society of Edinburgh was granted, as an incorporation, property and other legal rights, and it subscribed to the building of what is now the Old College. But its initial charter specified, because of the reasons that led to its formation, that the acquisitions would be placed in the University's Museum or the Advocates' Library. These restrictive provisions were removed by the charter of 1811 (see p. 58).

R.B.K.S.

NOTES

1. These included the Duke of Buccleuch, the Lord President of the Court of Session, the Lord Justice-Clerk, the Lord Chief Baron of the Exchequer, the Lord Provost of Edinburgh, and the Principal of the University.

2. Joan Evans, *The Society of Antiquaries* (Oxford 1956), 104.

3. In 1751 the London Antiquaries were anxious not to offend or to appear to rival the Royal Society (see Evans, *op. cit.*, 104ff), and as at that time no other *society* had Royal in its title, the omission of 'Royal' from their petition and charter is readily explained (though not commented on by Dr Evans). By 1783 Edinburgh had, for example, the Royal Medical Society (1778).

4. Evans, *op. cit.*, 105n.

Appendix II

Presidents of the Society of Antiquaries of Scotland

(Initial years of membership — *Honorary — are given in brackets.)

Founder and First Vice-President (1780-92), David Steuart Erskine, 11th Earl of Buchan.

1780-92 (1780)	John Stuart, 3rd Earl of Bute
1792-1813 (*1781)	James Graham, 4th Duke of Montrose
1813-19 (*1781)	Lawrence Dundas, Baron Dundas (later 1st Earl of Zetland)
1819-23 (1815)	Francis Gray, 14th Lord Gray
1823-41 (1823)	Thomas Bruce, 7th Earl of Elgin and Kincardine
1841-44 (1841)	James Bruce, 8th Earl of Elgin and Kincardine
1844-62 (1844)	John Campbell, 2nd Marquess of Breadalbane
1862-72 (1845)	Walter Francis Montagu-Douglas-Scott, 5th Duke of Buccleuch and Queensberry
1872-76 (1867)	George Granville William Sutherland-Leveson-Gower, 3rd Duke of Sutherland
1876-1900 (1870)	Schomberg Henry Kerr, 9th Marquess of Lothian
1900-1913 (1884)	Sir Herbert Eustace Maxwell of Monreith, 7th Bart.
1913-18 (1879)	John Abercromby, LLD (later 7th Baron Abercromby)
1918-23 (1888)	Thomas David Gibson-Carmichael, 1st Baron Carmichael
1923-33 (1917)	John George Murray, 8th Duke of Atholl
1933-40 (1900)	Sir George Macdonald, KCB LLD DLitt FBA
1940-45 (1892)	Sir John Stirling-Maxwell of Pollok, 10th Bart.
1945-50 (1945)	George Baillie-Hamilton, 12th Earl of Haddington
1950-55 (1930)	Professor Sir William Moir Calder, LLD FBA
1955-60 (1952)	James Latham McDiarmid Clyde, the Rt Hon Lord Clyde

1960-65 (1927)	James Frederick Gordon Thomson, the Hon Lord Migdale
1965-67 (1961)	Major-General James Scott-Elliott, CB CBE DSO
1967-72 (1938)	Professor Stuart Piggott, CBE DLitt FBA
1972-75 (1938)	Kenneth Arthur Steer, CBE PhD
1975-78 (1939)	Robert Barron Kerr Stevenson, CBE
1978- (1964)	Ronald Gordon Cant, DLitt

Keepers and Directors of the National Museum of Antiquities

(Initial years of Society membership — *Corresponding — and references to biographical notices are given in brackets.)

1859-69 ——	William Thomson McCulloch (*PSAS* vii.535-6)
1869-1913 (*1866)	Joseph Anderson, LLD HonMRIA HRSA (*Hon* FSA Scot 1913) (*PSAS* xlvii.334-40; li.5-6; cvii.279-98)
1913-19 (1893)	Alexander Ormiston Curle, WS (*PSAS* li.5; lxxxviii.234-6)
1919-38 (1898)	John Graham Callander, LLD (*PSAS* liv.11; lxxii.232-3)
1938-44 (1921)	Arthur James Howie Edwards (*PSAS* lxxviii.150-1, 148)
1944-45 (1927)	Professor Vere Gordon Childe, DLitt DSc FBA (*PSAS* xc.256-9) (Honorary)
1946-78 (1939)	Robert Barron Kerr Stevenson, CBE
1978- (1958)	Alexander Fenton

Index